PLATINUM garden

Created by Maki Fujita

Volume 5

TOKYOPOP®

HAMBURG // LONDON // LOS ANGELES // TOKYO

Platinum Garden Volume 5
Created by Maki Fujita

Translation - Mini Eda
English Adaptation - Sarah Dyer
Retouch and Lettering - Star Print Brokers
Production Artist - Bowen Park
Cover Designer - Anne Marie Horne

Editor - Hope Donovan
Digital Imaging Manager - Chris Buford
Pre-Production Supervisor - Erika Terriquez
Production Manager - Elisabeth Brizzi
Managing Editor - Vy Nguyen
Creative Director - Anne Marie Horne
Editor-in-Chief - Rob Tokar
Publisher - Mike Kiley
President and C.O.O. - John Parker
C.E.O. and Chief Creative Officer - Stuart Levy

A **TOKYOPOP** Manga

TOKYOPOP Inc.
5900 Wilshire Blvd. Suite 2000
Los Angeles, CA 90036

E-mail: info@TOKYOPOP.com
Come visit us online at www.TOKYOPOP.com

ISBN: 978-1-59816-365-0

First TOKYOPOP printing: October 2007
10 9 8 7 6 5 4 3 2 1
Printed in the USA

PLATINUM *garden*

Created by Maki Fujita

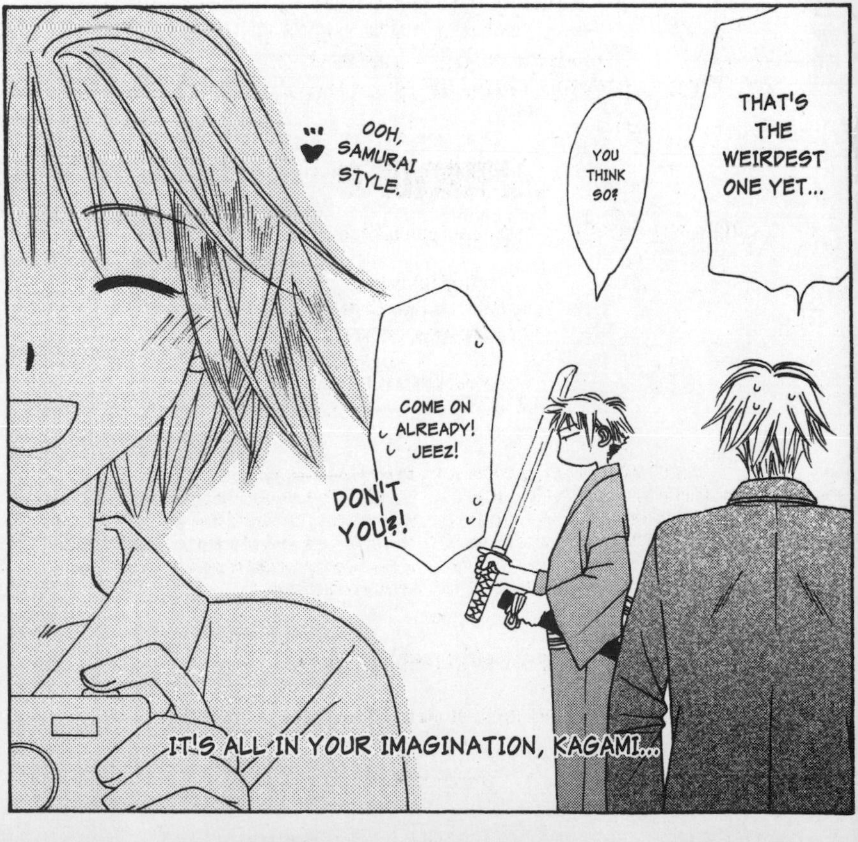
THAT'S THE WEIRDEST ONE YET...
YOU THINK SO?
OOH, SAMURAI STYLE.
COME ON ALREADY! JEEZ!
DON'T YOU?!
IT'S ALL IN YOUR IMAGINATION, KAGAMI...

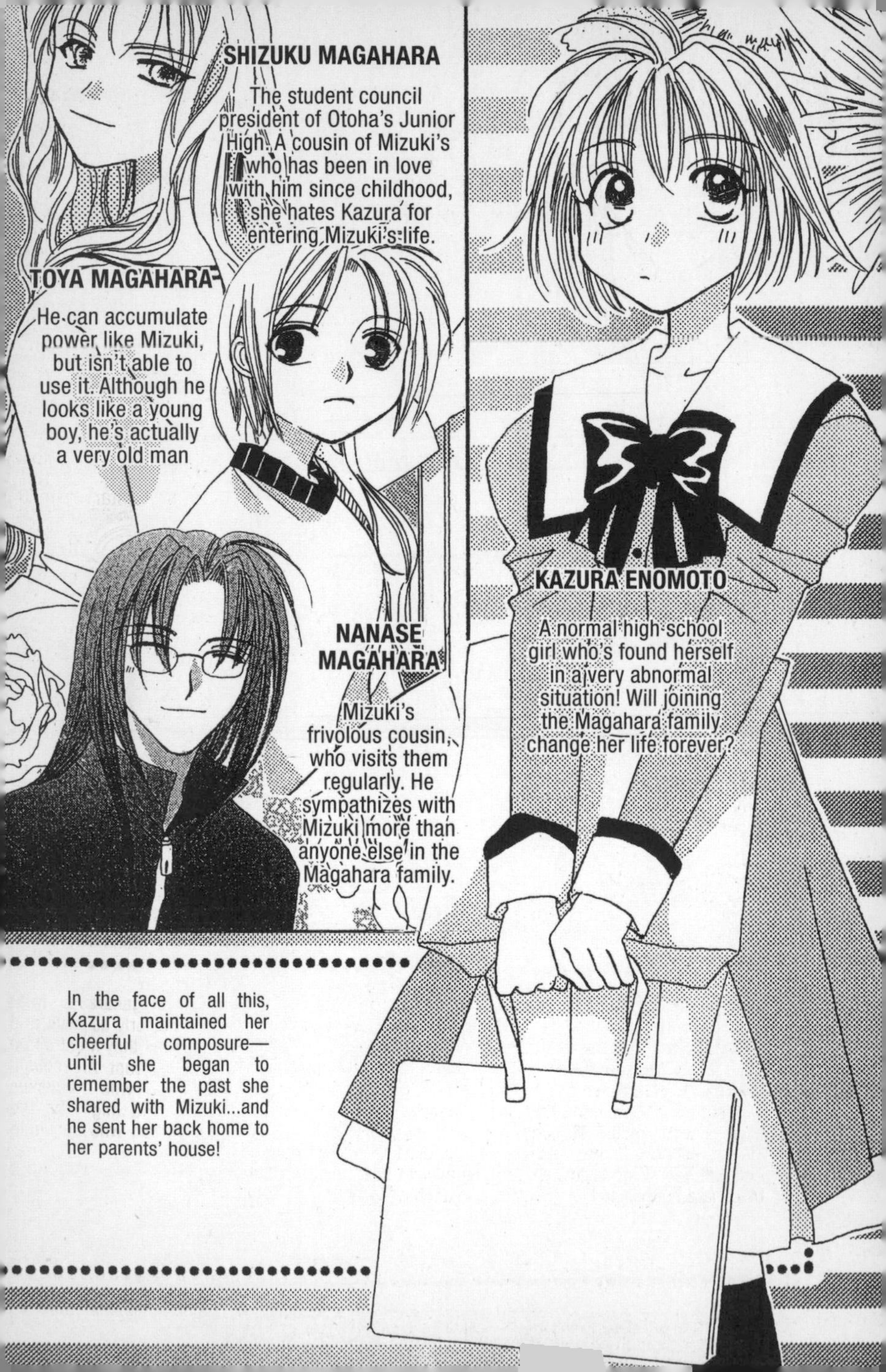
KAZURA ENOMOTO
A normal high-school girl who's found herself in a very abnormal situation! Will joining the Magahara family change her life forever?
SHIZUKU MAGAHARA
The student council president of Otoha's Junior High. A cousin of Mizuki's who has been in love with him since childhood, she hates Kazura for entering Mizuki's life.
TOYA MAGAHARA
He can accumulate power like Mizuki, but isn't able to use it. Although he looks like a young boy, he's actually a very old man
NANASE MAGAHARA
Mizuki's frivolous cousin, who visits them regularly. He sympathizes with Mizuki more than anyone else in the Magahara family.

In the face of all this, Kazura maintained her cheerful composure—until she began to remember the past she shared with Mizuki...and he sent her back home to her parents' house!

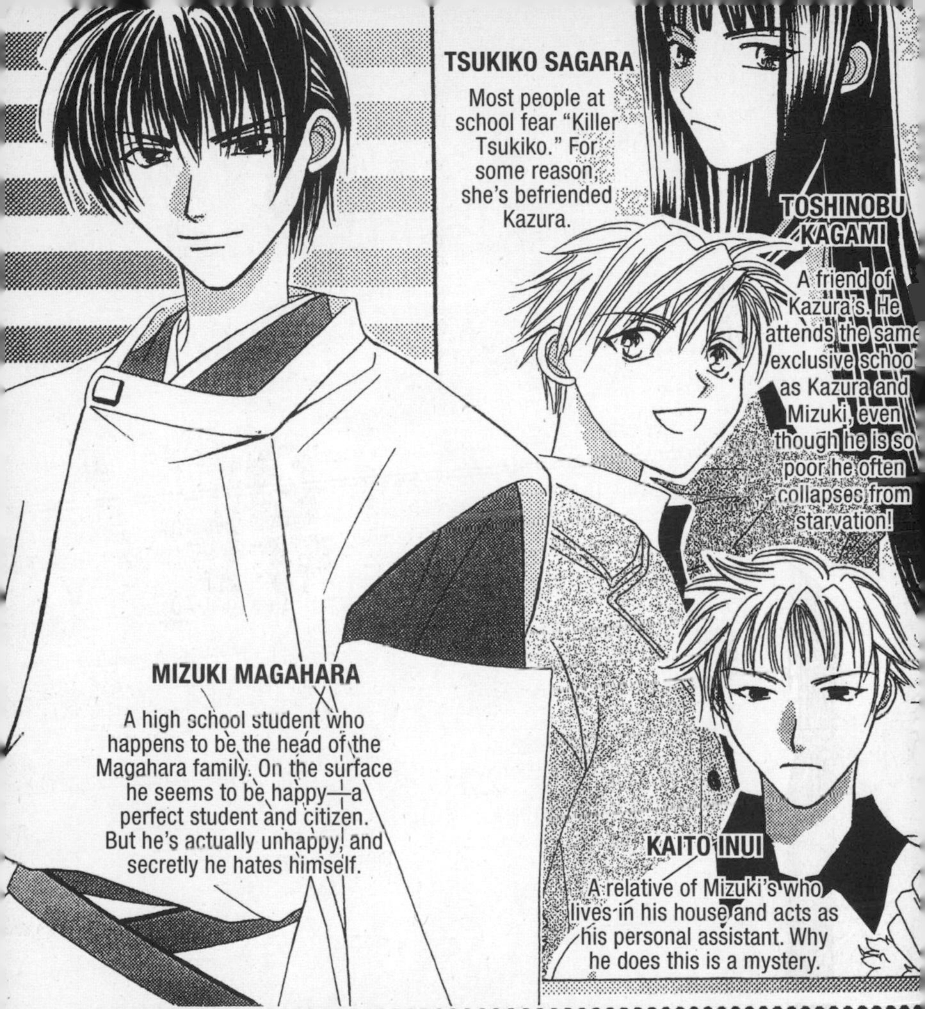
TSUKIKO SAGARA
Most people at school fear "Killer Tsukiko." For some reason, she's befriended Kazura.
TOSHINOBU KAGAMI
A friend of Kazura's. He attends the same exclusive school as Kazura and Mizuki, even though he is so poor he often collapses from starvation!
MIZUKI MAGAHARA
A high school student who happens to be the head of the Magahara family. On the surface he seems to be happy—a perfect student and citizen. But he's actually unhappy, and secretly he hates himself.
KAITO INUI
A relative of Mizuki's who lives in his house and acts as his personal assistant. Why he does this is a mystery.

Kazura Enomoto is a cheerful high school girl who's lived a relatively normal life...until now. When her grandfather died recently, he mentioned her in his will, and said "I promised I would leave you to **Mizuki Magahara.** Please carry out my wishes." And off she went to live in the Magahara household.

After living in the house for a while, Kazura discovered that Mizuki has a strange power—he can temporarily revive the dead! He supports the entire Magahara family by performing "soul returns" for hire, even though the family considers him "impure" and treats him horribly.

The Magaharas treat Kazura poorly as well, and she thinks they must all be awful—except his cousin **Nanase,** who believes that Kazura might be the only person who can help Mizuki.

OUR STORY SO FAR

PLATINUM garden

Volume:5

CONTENTS

KAZURA

Take17

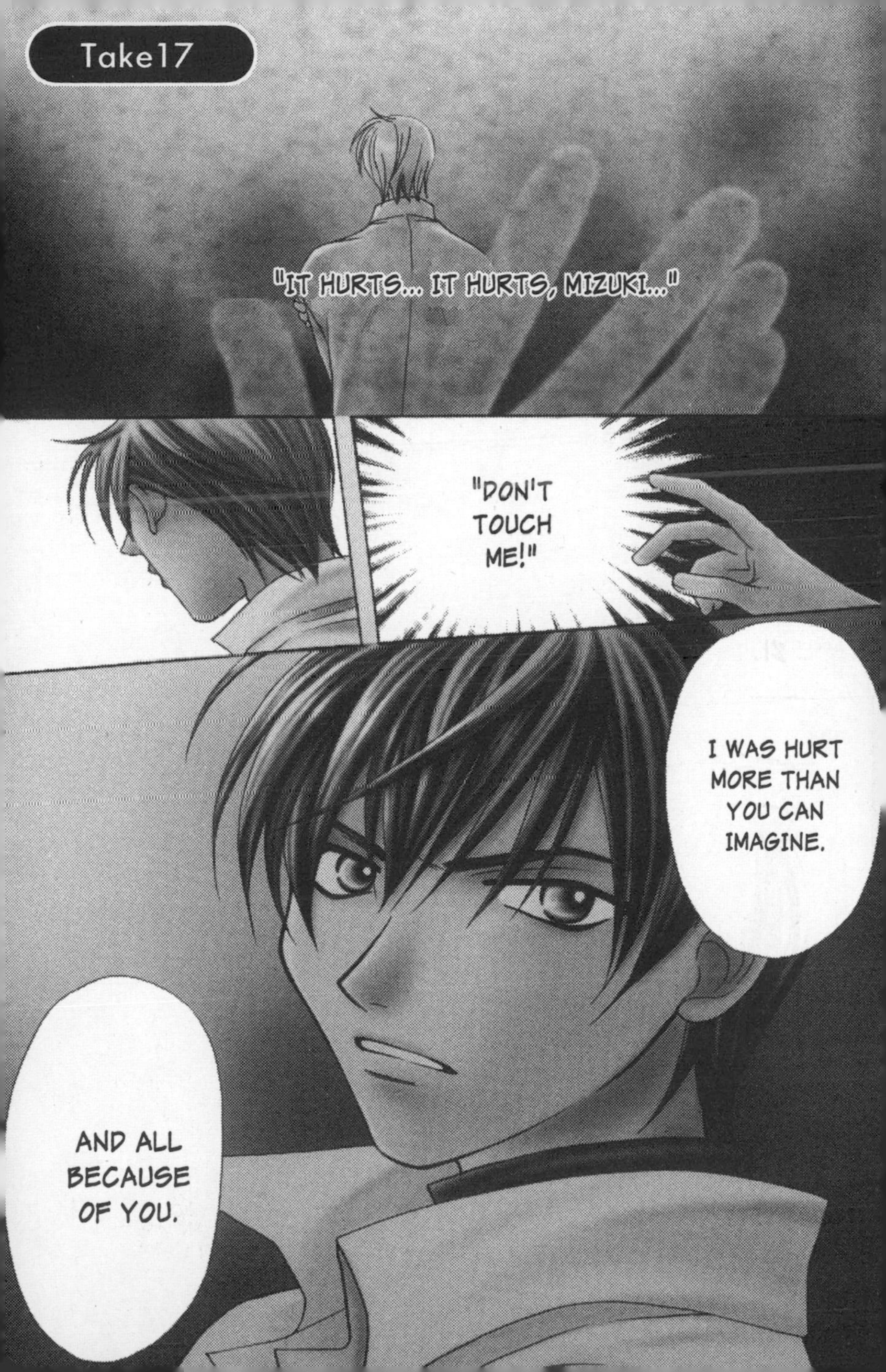
"IT HURTS... IT HURTS, MIZUKI..."
"DON'T TOUCH ME!"
I WAS HURT MORE THAN YOU CAN IMAGINE.
AND ALL BECAUSE OF YOU.

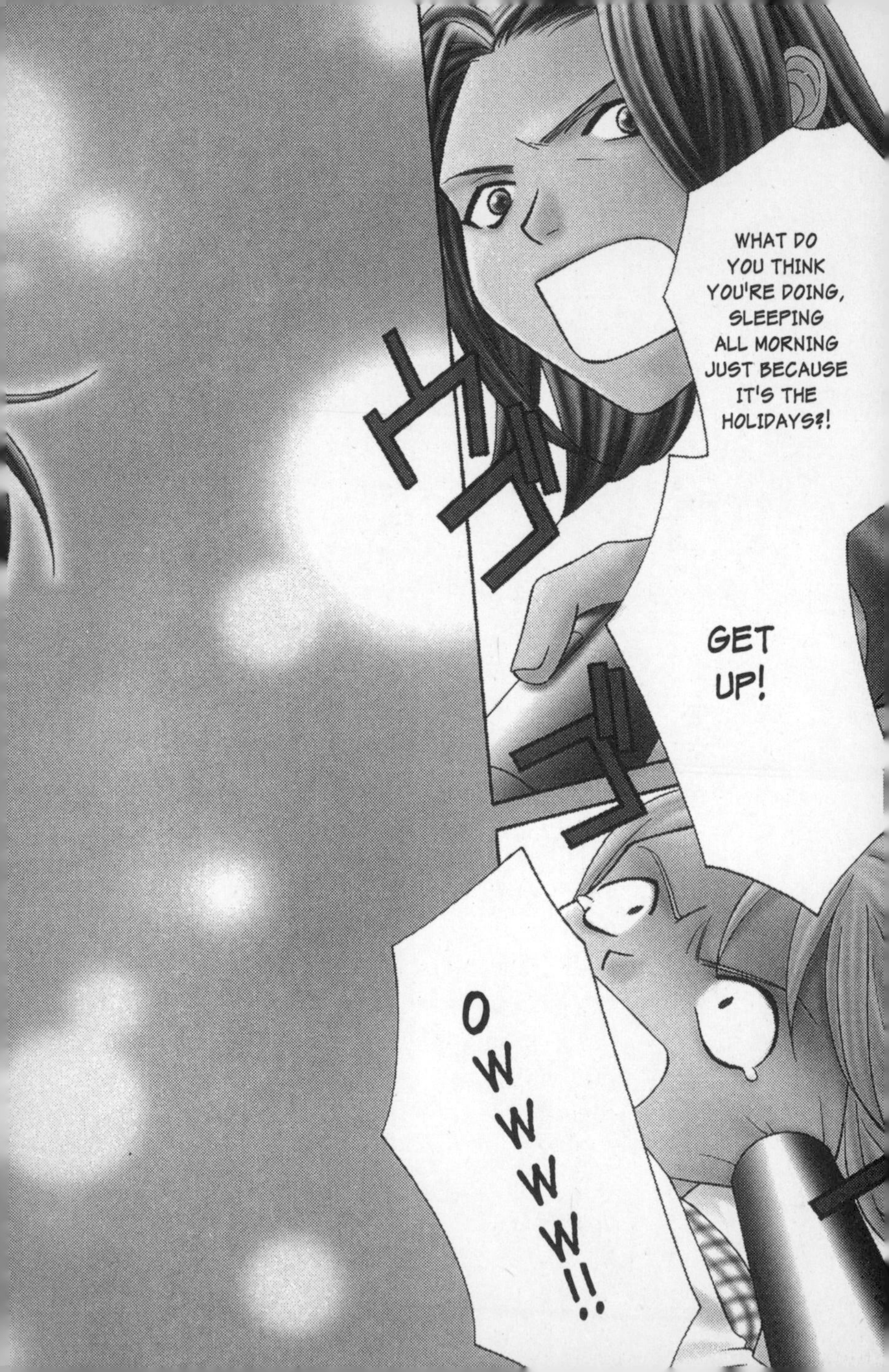
WHAT DO YOU THINK YOU'RE DOING, SLEEPING ALL MORNING JUST BECAUSE IT'S THE HOLIDAYS?!
GET UP!
OWWWW!!

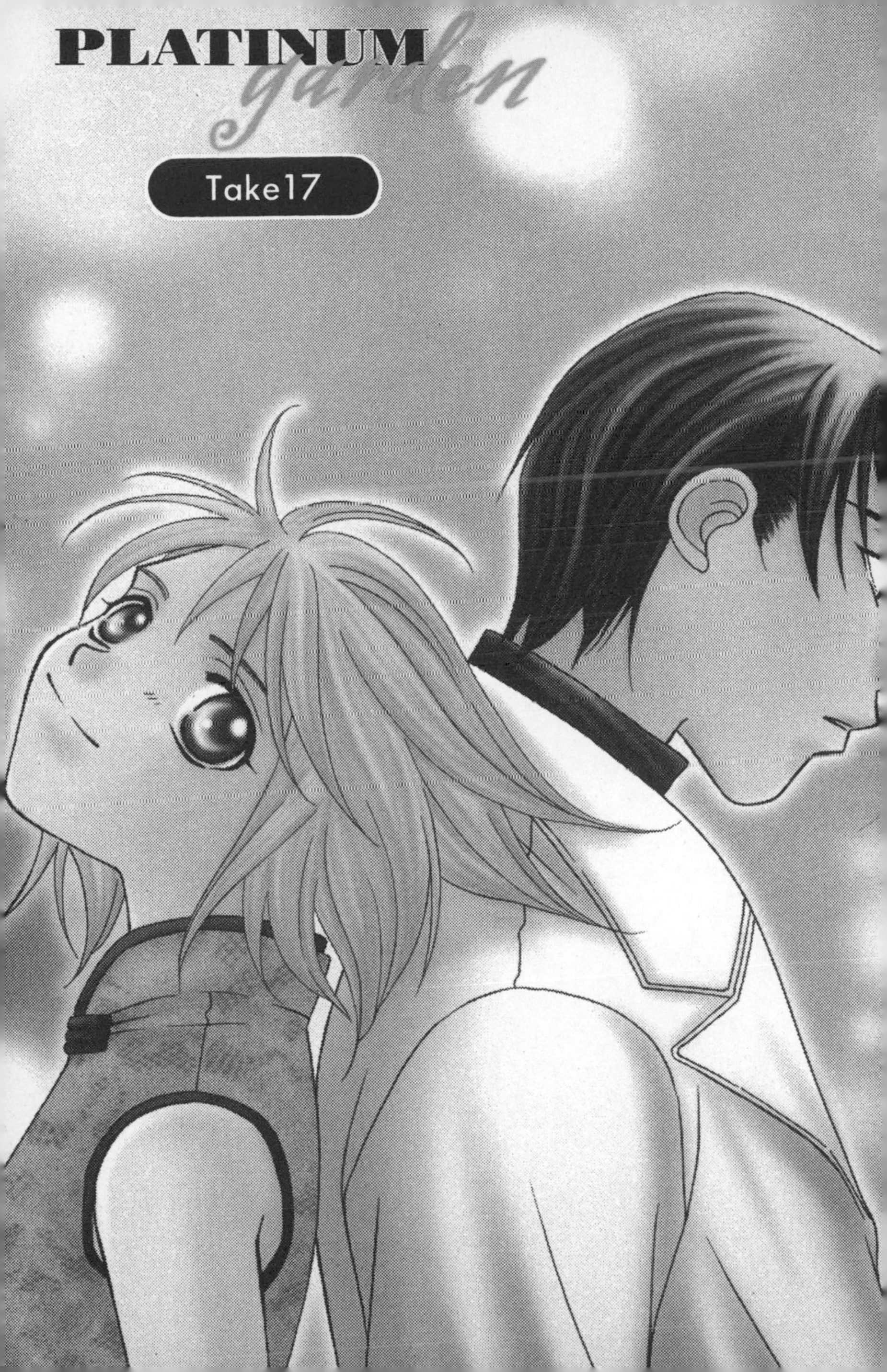
PLATINUM garden
Take17

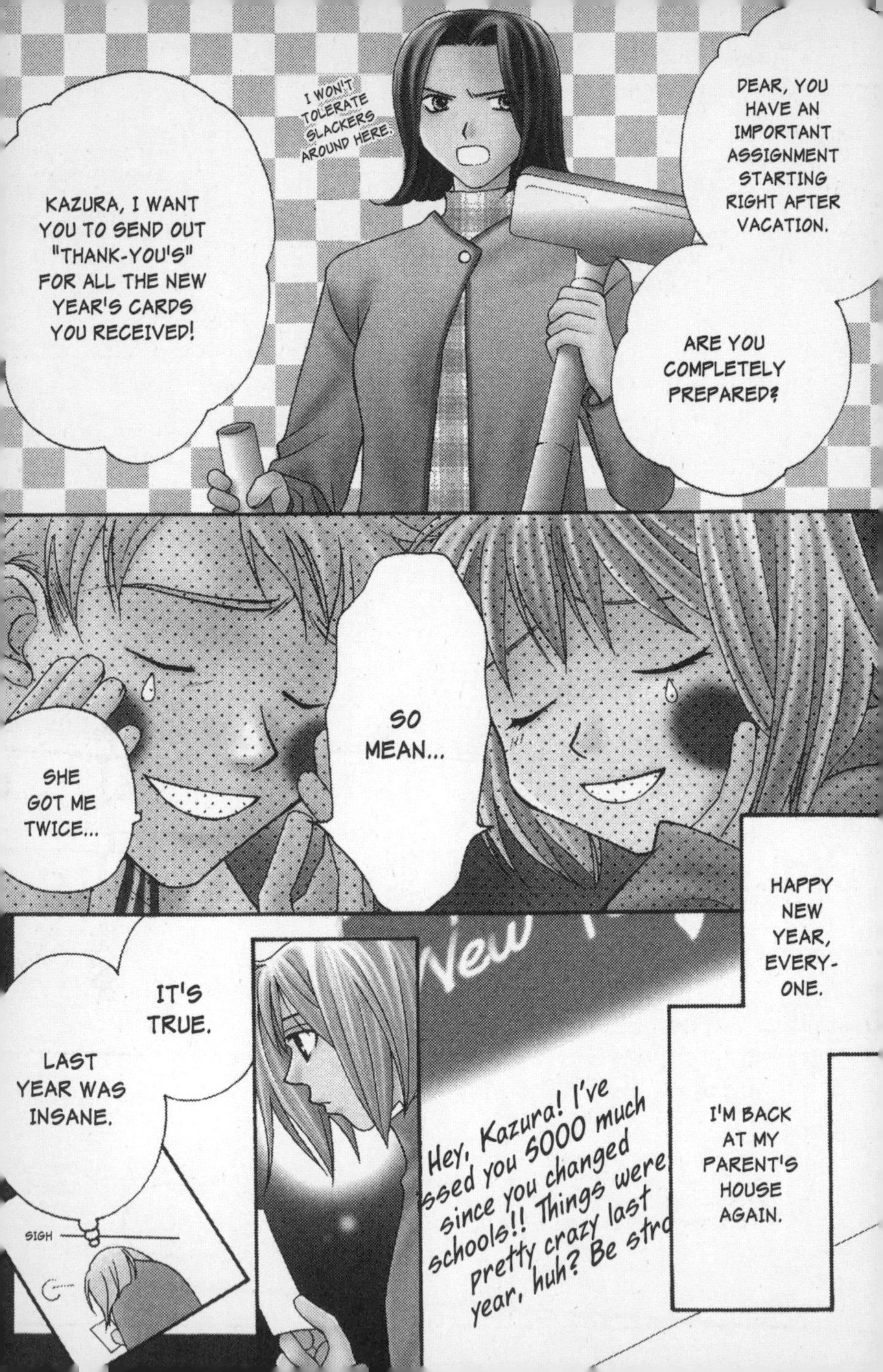
DEAR, YOU HAVE AN IMPORTANT ASSIGNMENT STARTING RIGHT AFTER VACATION.
ARE YOU COMPLETELY PREPARED?
I WON'T TOLERATE SLACKERS AROUND HERE.
KAZURA, I WANT YOU TO SEND OUT "THANK-YOU'S" FOR ALL THE NEW YEAR'S CARDS YOU RECEIVED!
SO MEAN...
SHE GOT ME TWICE...
HAPPY NEW YEAR, EVERY-ONE.
I'M BACK AT MY PARENT'S HOUSE AGAIN.
New
Hey, Kazura! I've ssed you SOOO much since you changed schools!! Things were pretty crazy last year, huh? Be stro
IT'S TRUE.
LAST YEAR WAS INSANE.
SIGH

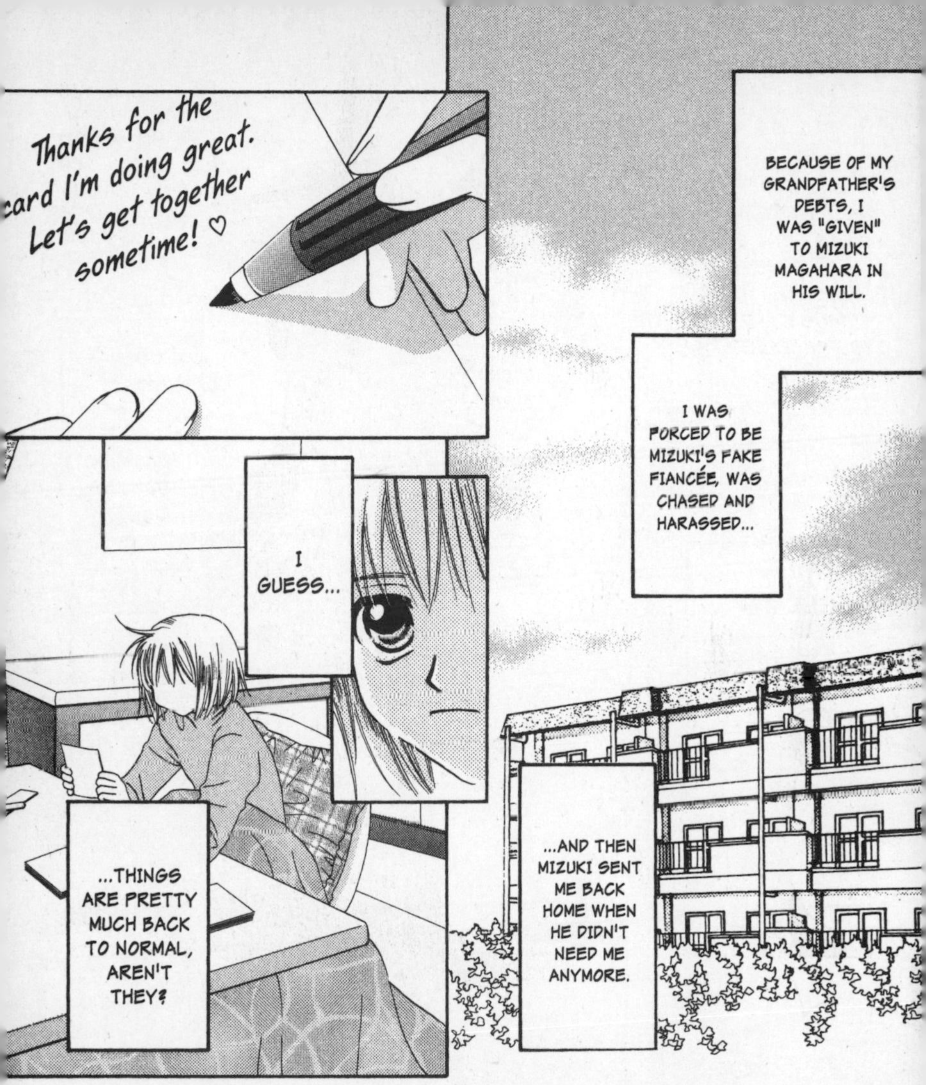
BECAUSE OF MY GRANDFATHER'S DEBTS, I WAS "GIVEN" TO MIZUKI MAGAHARA IN HIS WILL.
I WAS FORCED TO BE MIZUKI'S FAKE FIANCÉE, WAS CHASED AND HARASSED...
...AND THEN MIZUKI SENT ME BACK HOME WHEN HE DIDN'T NEED ME ANYMORE.
Thanks for the card I'm doing great. Let's get together sometime! ♡
I GUESS...
...THINGS ARE PRETTY MUCH BACK TO NORMAL, AREN'T THEY?

FUJITA'S SUMMER, 2002

EVERY YEAR, I PLAN TO RENOVATE MY BALCONY AND CLOSE IT IN SO MY WORKROOM WON'T BE SO TROPICAL... BUT I CAN NEVER DECIDE WHAT TO DO. THIS YEAR, WHEN I FINALLY DECIDED TO GO WITH A WOOD PANEL DESIGN, THE SUMMER WAS OVER! MAYBE NEXT YEAR...

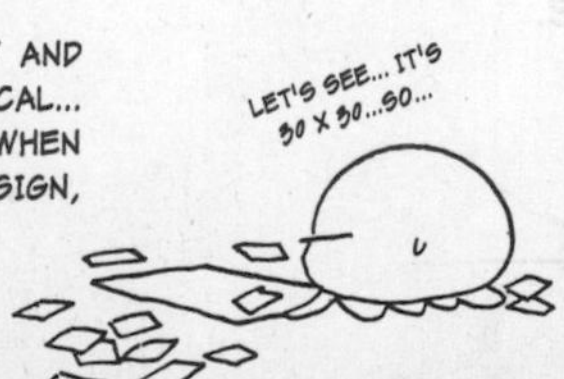
LET'S SEE... IT'S 30 X 30...SO...

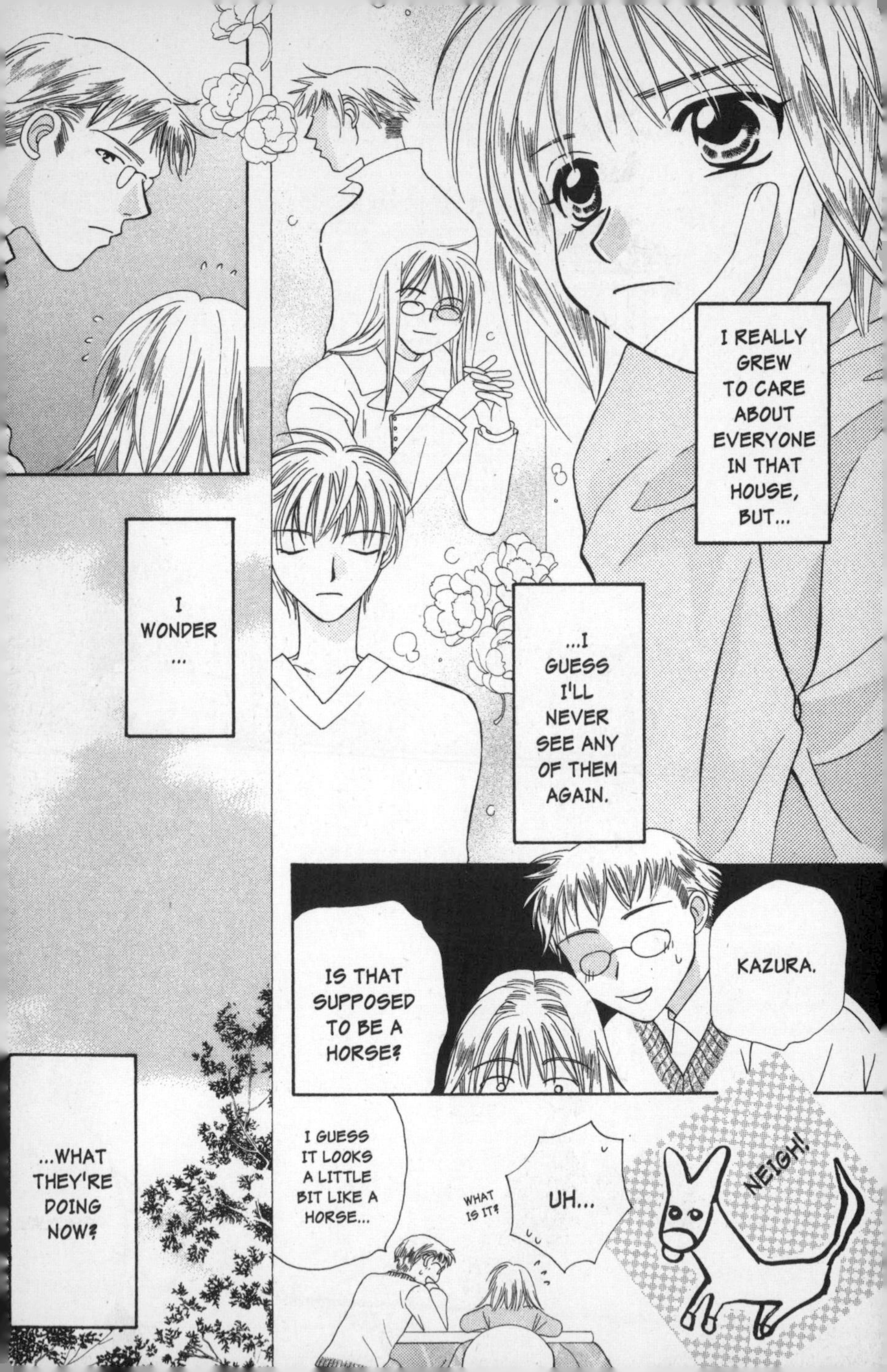
I REALLY GREW TO CARE ABOUT EVERYONE IN THAT HOUSE, BUT...
...I GUESS I'LL NEVER SEE ANY OF THEM AGAIN.
KAZURA.
IS THAT SUPPOSED TO BE A HORSE?
NEIGH!
UH...
WHAT IS IT?
I GUESS IT LOOKS A LITTLE BIT LIKE A HORSE...
I WONDER...
...WHAT THEY'RE DOING NOW?

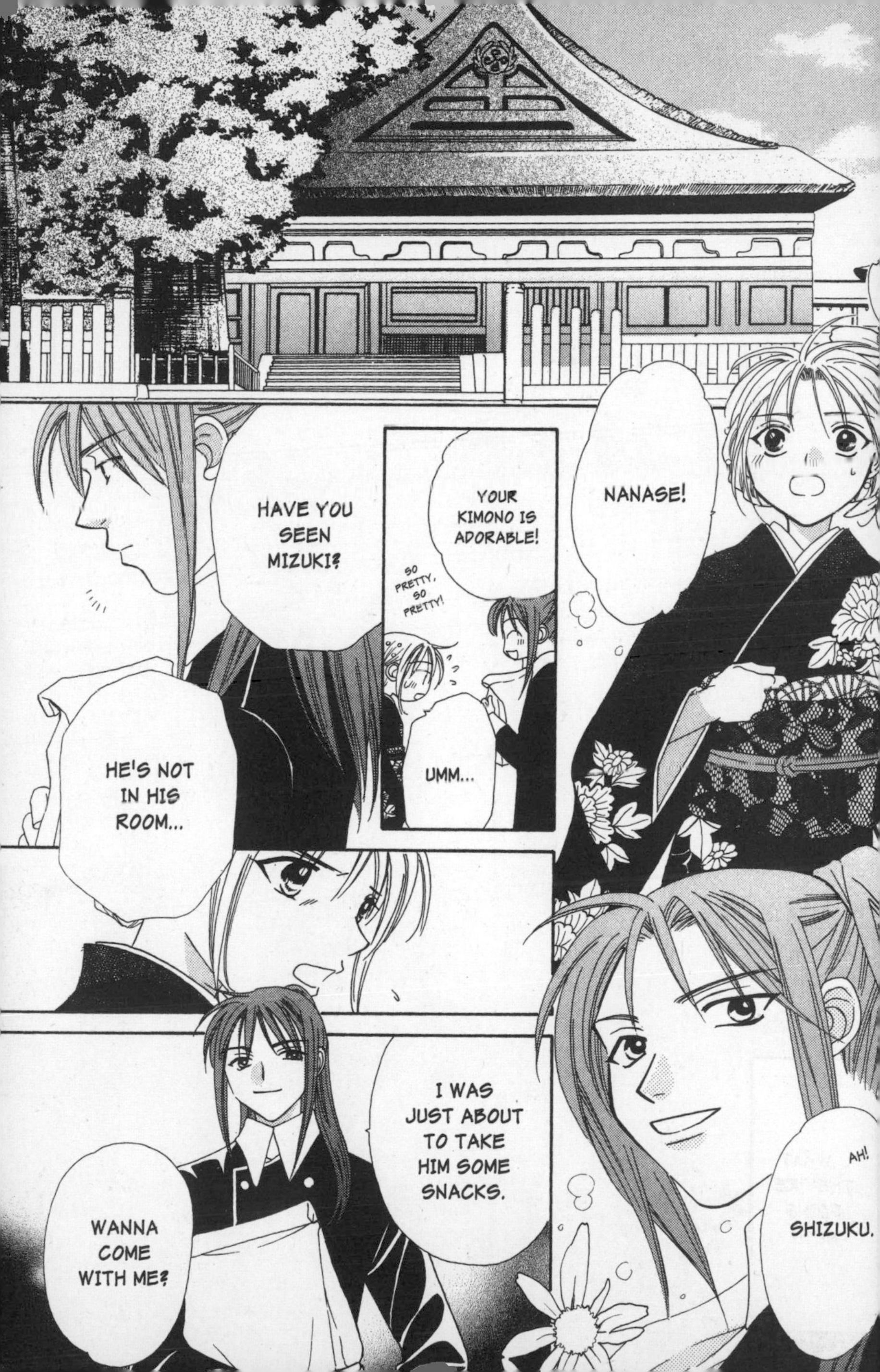
NANASE!
YOUR KIMONO IS ADORABLE!
SO PRETTY, SO PRETTY!
UMM...
HAVE YOU SEEN MIZUKI?
HE'S NOT IN HIS ROOM...
AH!
SHIZUKU.
I WAS JUST ABOUT TO TAKE HIM SOME SNACKS.
WANNA COME WITH ME?

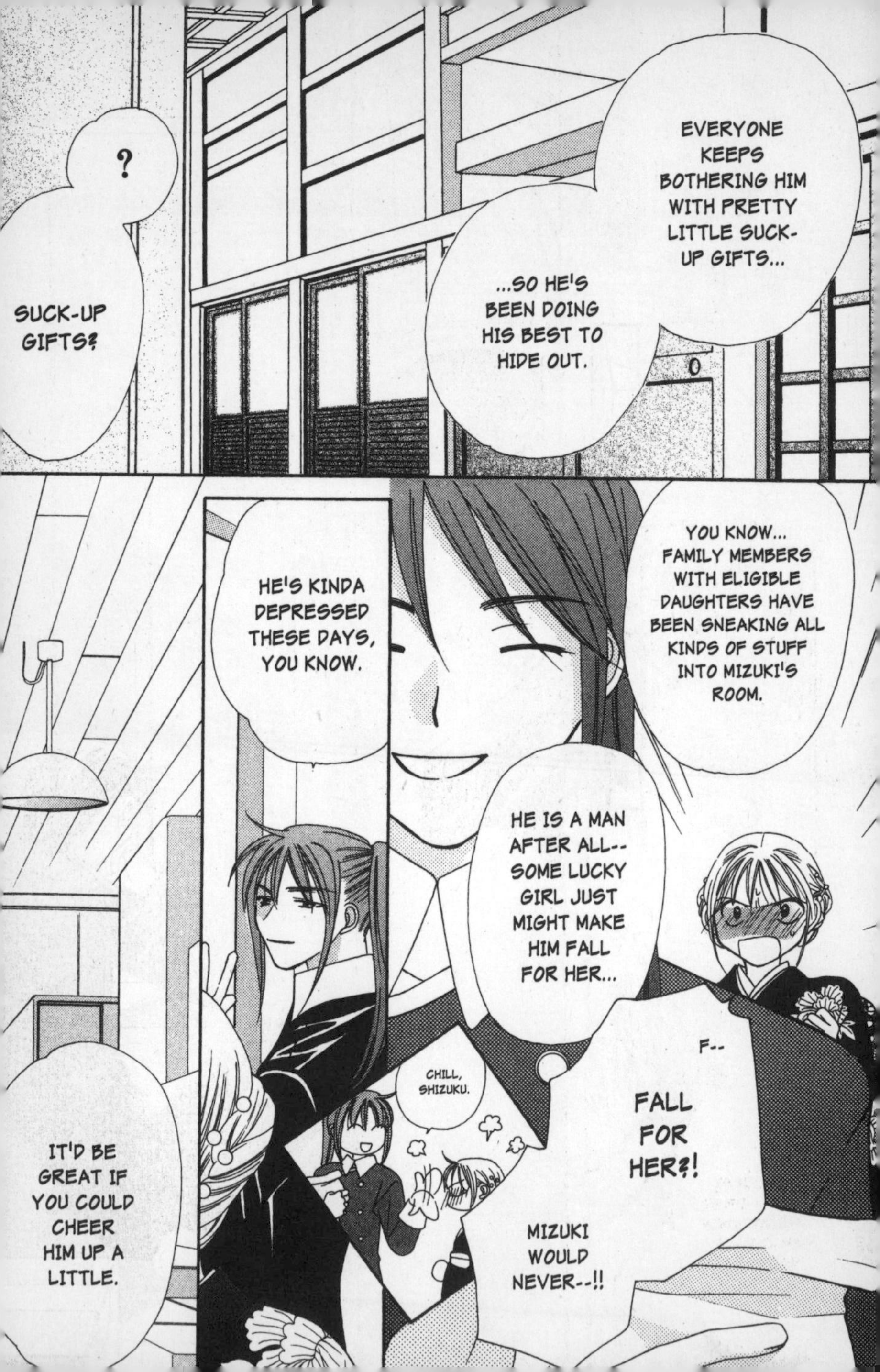
EVERYONE KEEPS BOTHERING HIM WITH PRETTY LITTLE SUCK-UP GIFTS...
...SO HE'S BEEN DOING HIS BEST TO HIDE OUT.
?
SUCK-UP GIFTS?
YOU KNOW... FAMILY MEMBERS WITH ELIGIBLE DAUGHTERS HAVE BEEN SNEAKING ALL KINDS OF STUFF INTO MIZUKI'S ROOM.
HE'S KINDA DEPRESSED THESE DAYS, YOU KNOW.
HE IS A MAN AFTER ALL-- SOME LUCKY GIRL JUST MIGHT MAKE HIM FALL FOR HER...
F--
FALL FOR HER?!
MIZUKI WOULD NEVER--!!
CHILL, SHIZUKU.
IT'D BE GREAT IF YOU COULD CHEER HIM UP A LITTLE.

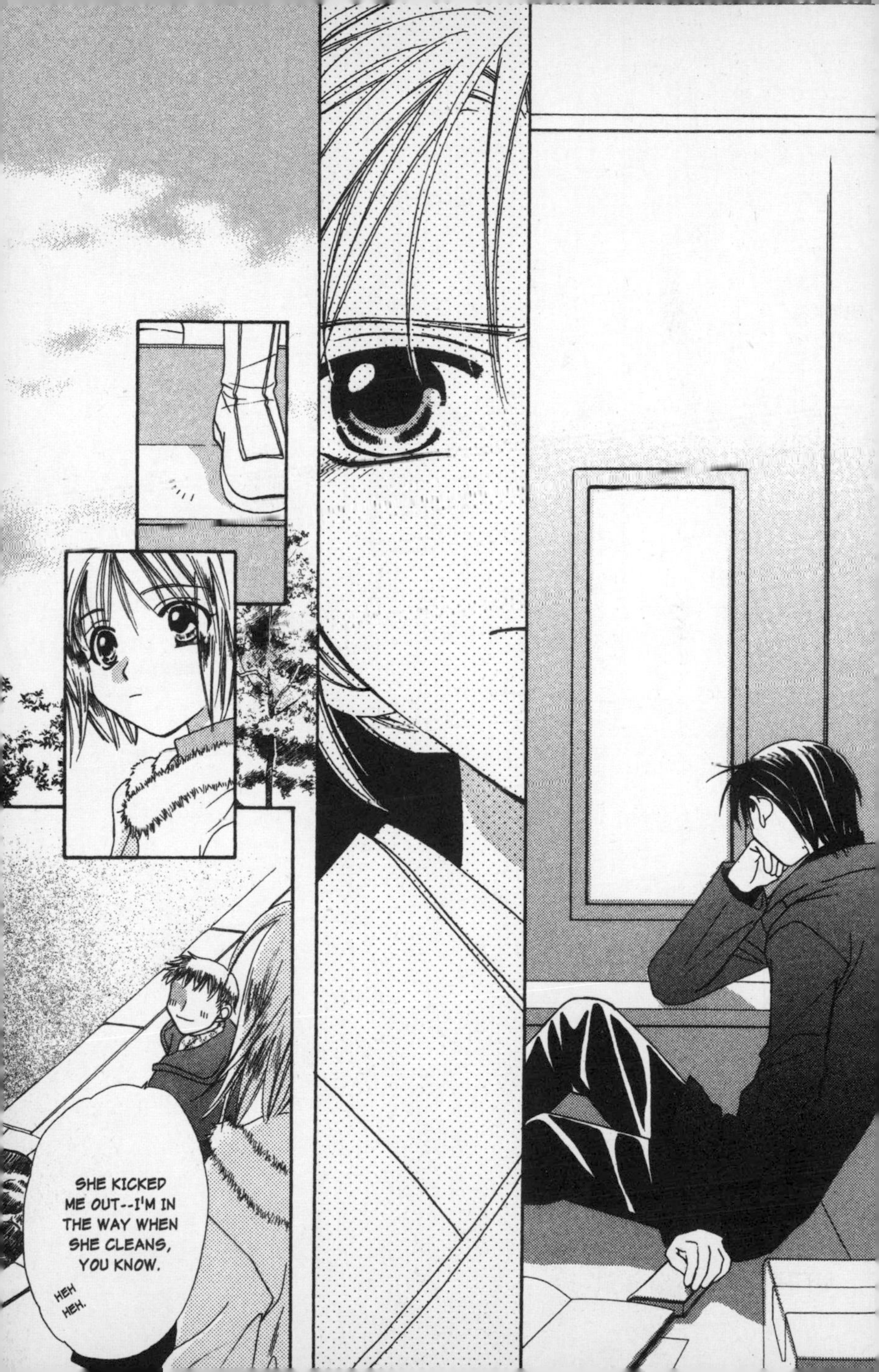
SHE KICKED ME OUT--I'M IN THE WAY WHEN SHE CLEANS, YOU KNOW.
HEH HEH.

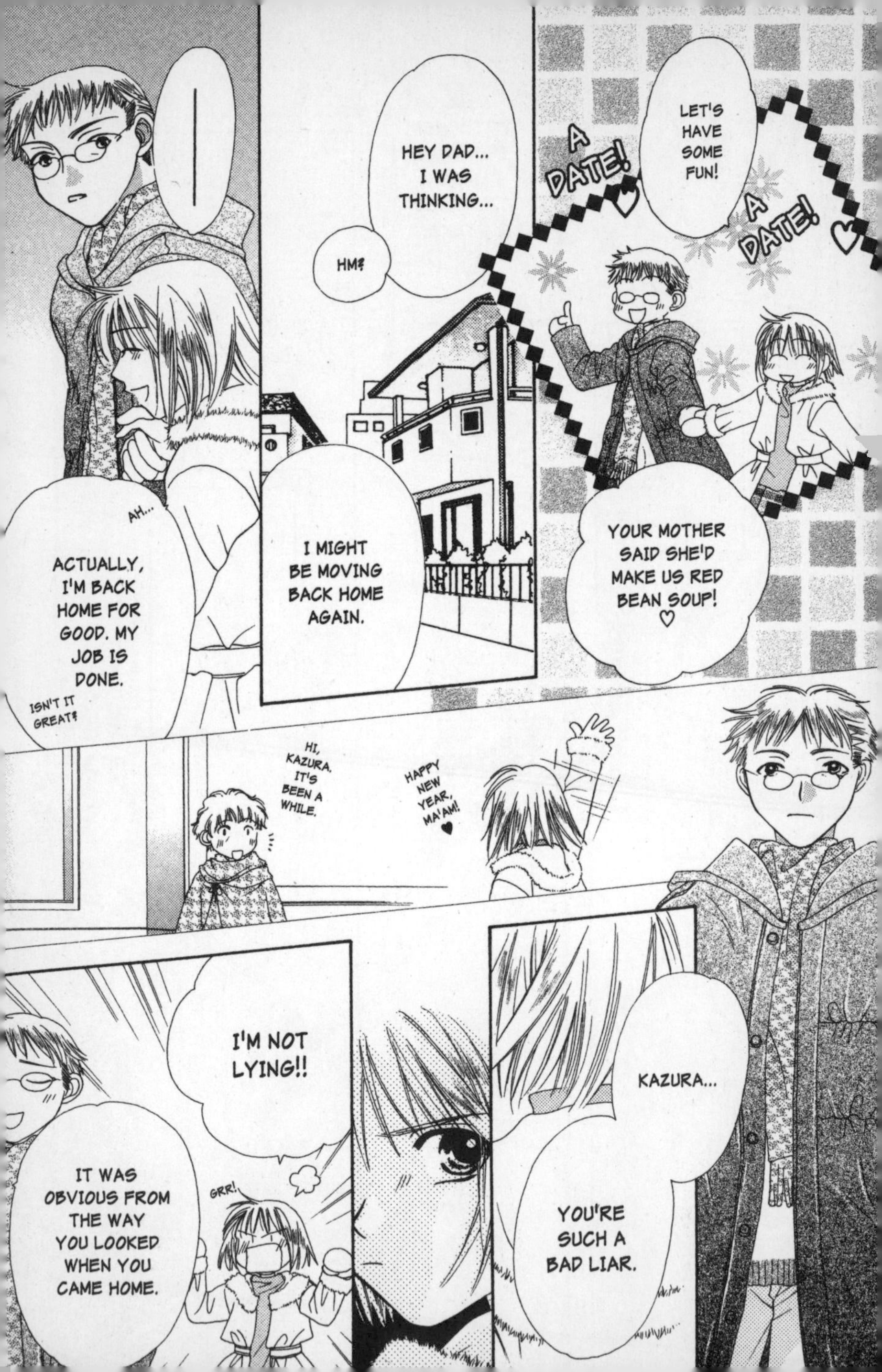
A DATE!
LET'S HAVE SOME FUN!
A DATE!
YOUR MOTHER SAID SHE'D MAKE US RED BEAN SOUP! ♡
HEY DAD... I WAS THINKING...
HM?
I MIGHT BE MOVING BACK HOME AGAIN.
—
AH...
ACTUALLY, I'M BACK HOME FOR GOOD. MY JOB IS DONE.
ISN'T IT GREAT?
HAPPY NEW YEAR, MA'AM! ♥
HI, KAZURA. IT'S BEEN A WHILE.
KAZURA...
YOU'RE SUCH A BAD LIAR.
I'M NOT LYING!!
GRR!
IT WAS OBVIOUS FROM THE WAY YOU LOOKED WHEN YOU CAME HOME.

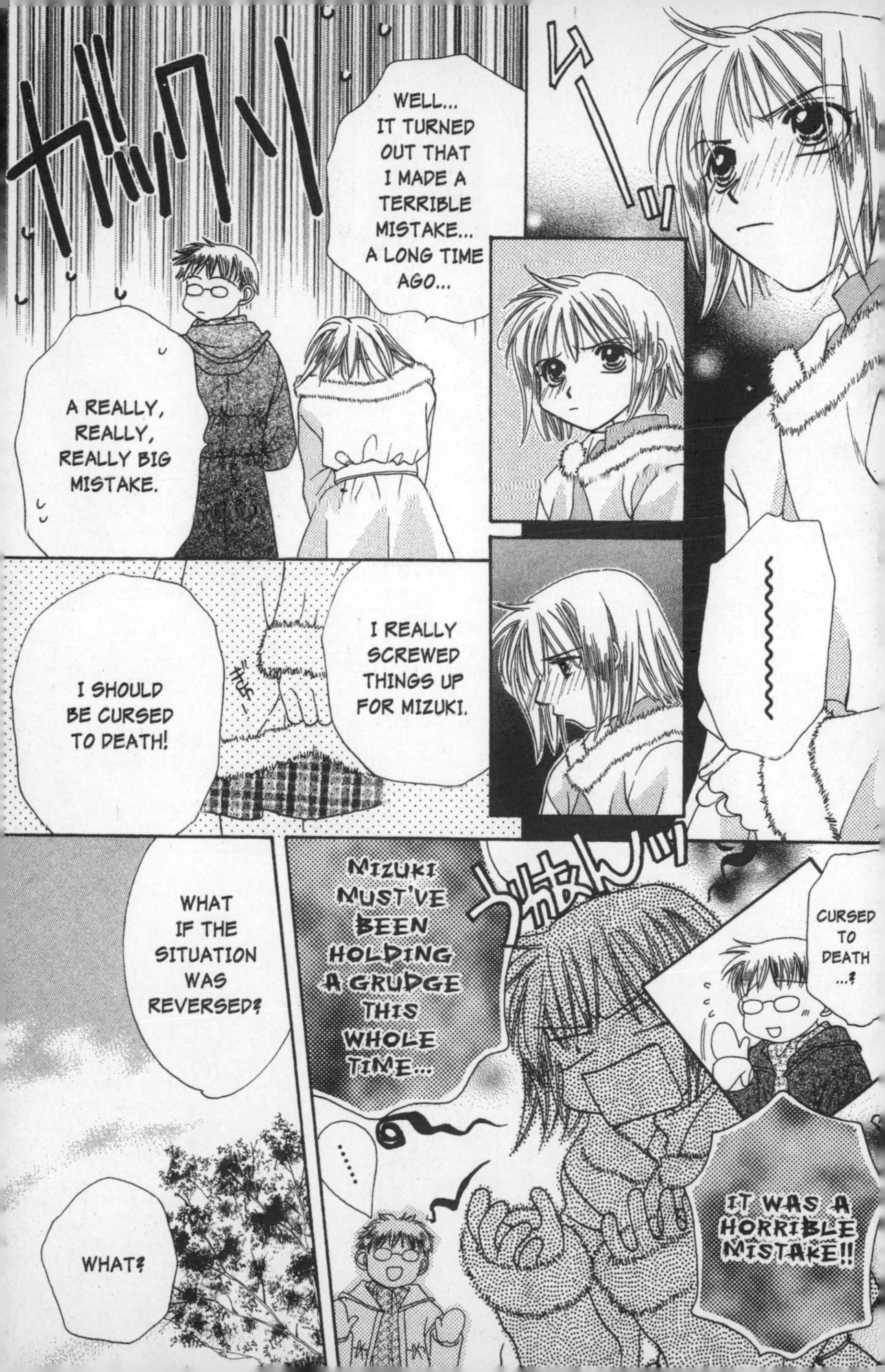

WELL... IT TURNED OUT THAT I MADE A TERRIBLE MISTAKE... A LONG TIME AGO...
A REALLY, REALLY, REALLY BIG MISTAKE.
I REALLY SCREWED THINGS UP FOR MIZUKI.
I SHOULD BE CURSED TO DEATH!
CURSED TO DEATH ...?
MIZUKI MUST'VE BEEN HOLDING A GRUDGE THIS WHOLE TIME...
IT WAS A HORRIBLE MISTAKE!!
......
WHAT IF THE SITUATION WAS REVERSED?
WHAT?

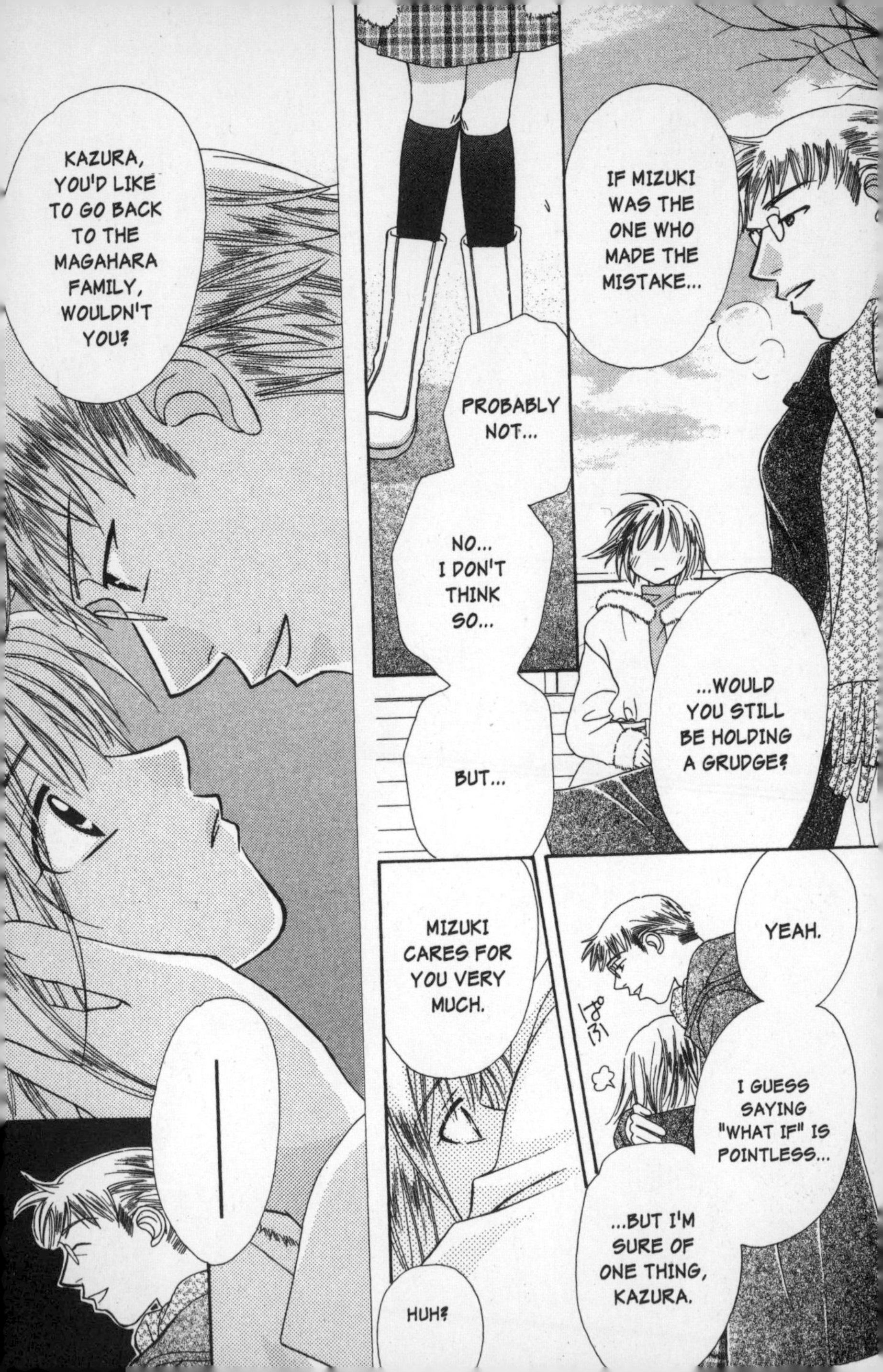
IF MIZUKI WAS THE ONE WHO MADE THE MISTAKE...
...WOULD YOU STILL BE HOLDING A GRUDGE?
PROBABLY NOT...
NO... I DON'T THINK SO...
BUT...
YEAH.
ぽふ
I GUESS SAYING "WHAT IF" IS POINTLESS...
...BUT I'M SURE OF ONE THING, KAZURA.
MIZUKI CARES FOR YOU VERY MUCH.
HUH?
KAZURA, YOU'D LIKE TO GO BACK TO THE MAGAHARA FAMILY, WOULDN'T YOU?
—

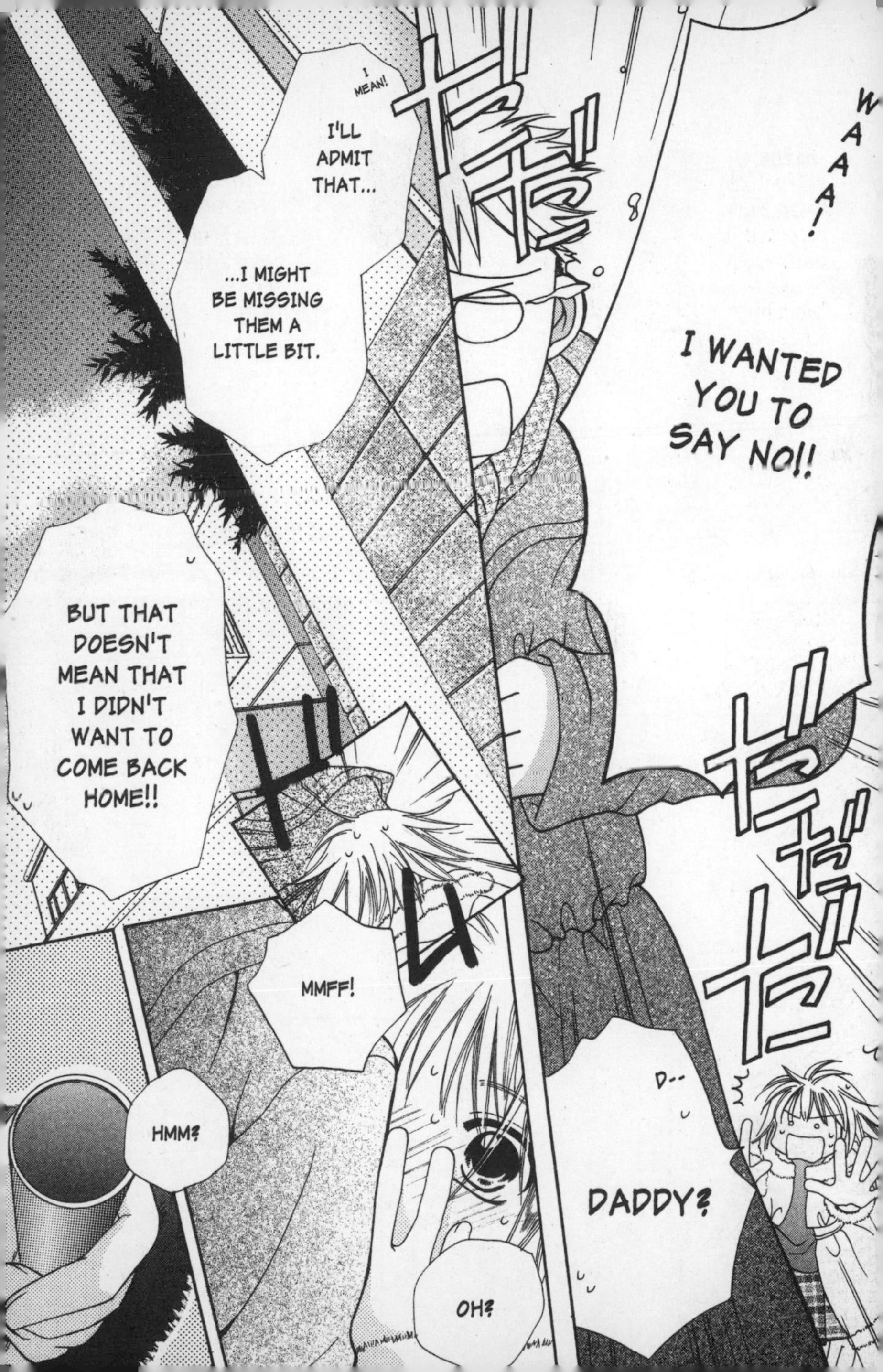
WAAAA!
I WANTED YOU TO SAY NO!!
I MEAN!
I'LL ADMIT THAT...
...I MIGHT BE MISSING THEM A LITTLE BIT.
BUT THAT DOESN'T MEAN THAT I DIDN'T WANT TO COME BACK HOME!!
D--
DADDY?
MMFF!
OH?
HMM?

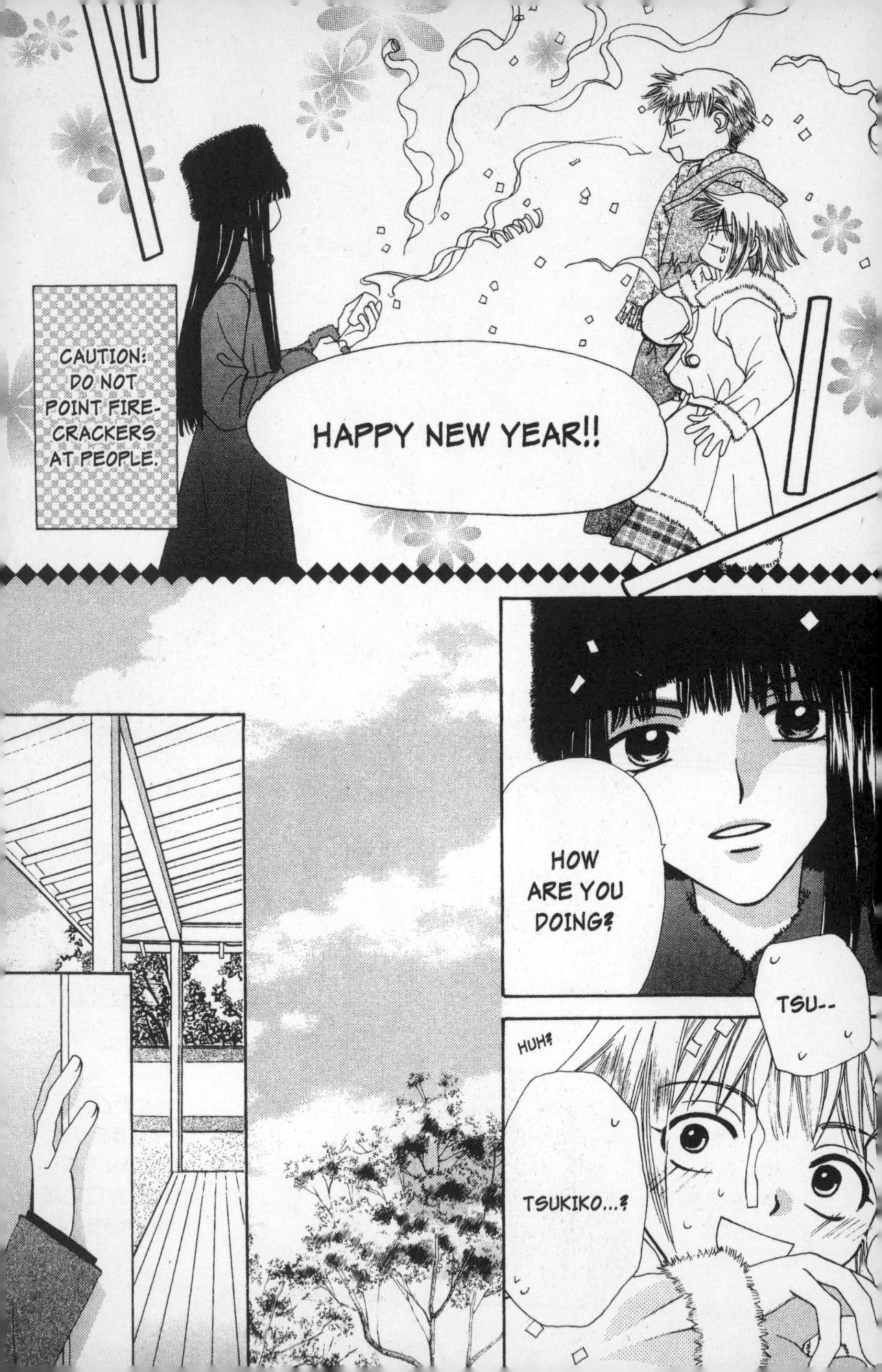
HAPPY NEW YEAR!!
CAUTION: DO NOT POINT FIRE-CRACKERS AT PEOPLE.
HOW ARE YOU DOING?
TSU--
HUH?
TSUKIKO...?

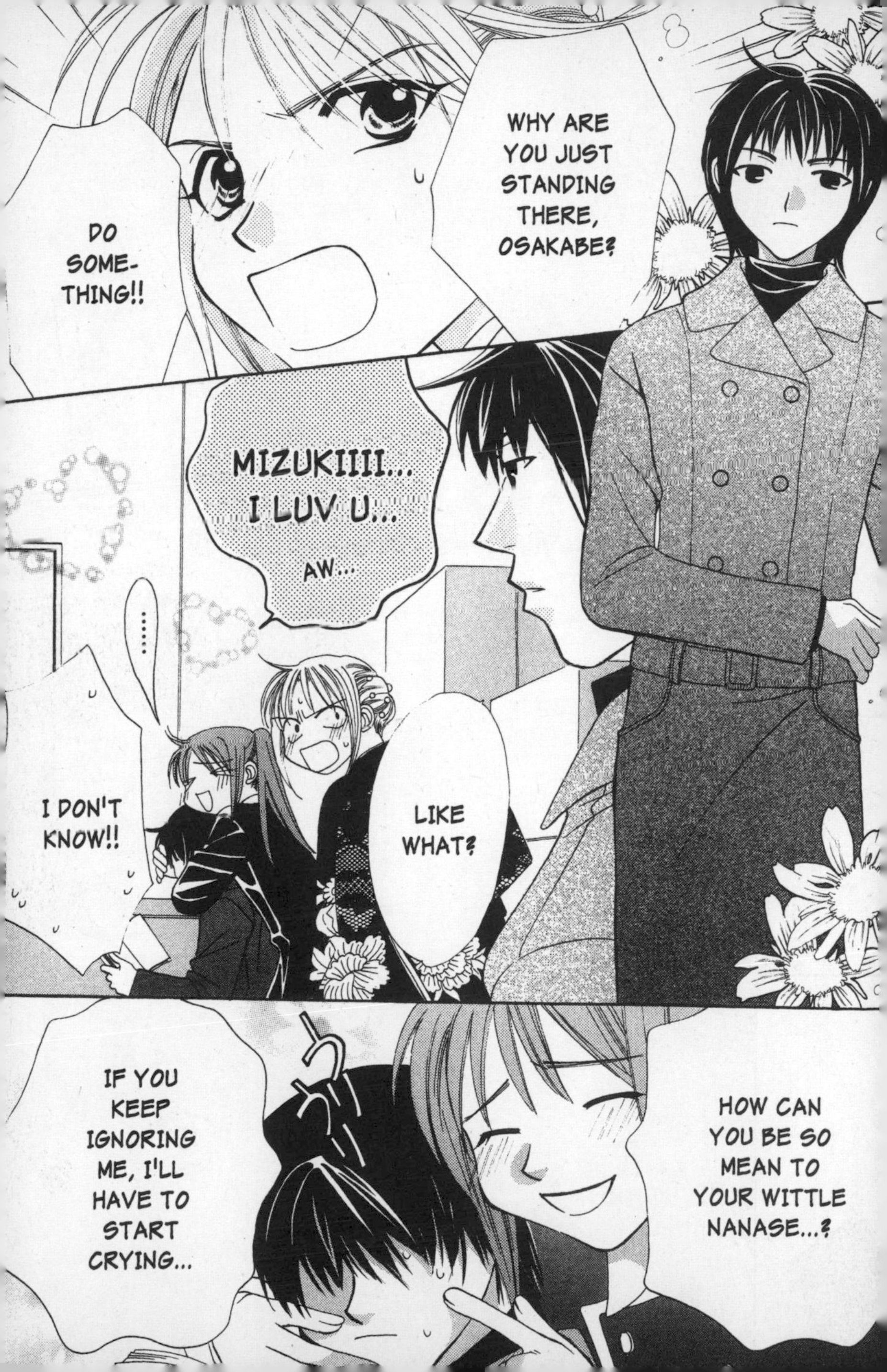
WHY ARE YOU JUST STANDING THERE, OSAKABE?
DO SOME-THING!!
MIZUKIIII... I LUV U...
AW...
......
LIKE WHAT?
I DON'T KNOW!!
HOW CAN YOU BE SO MEAN TO YOUR WITTLE NANASE...?
IF YOU KEEP IGNORING ME, I'LL HAVE TO START CRYING...

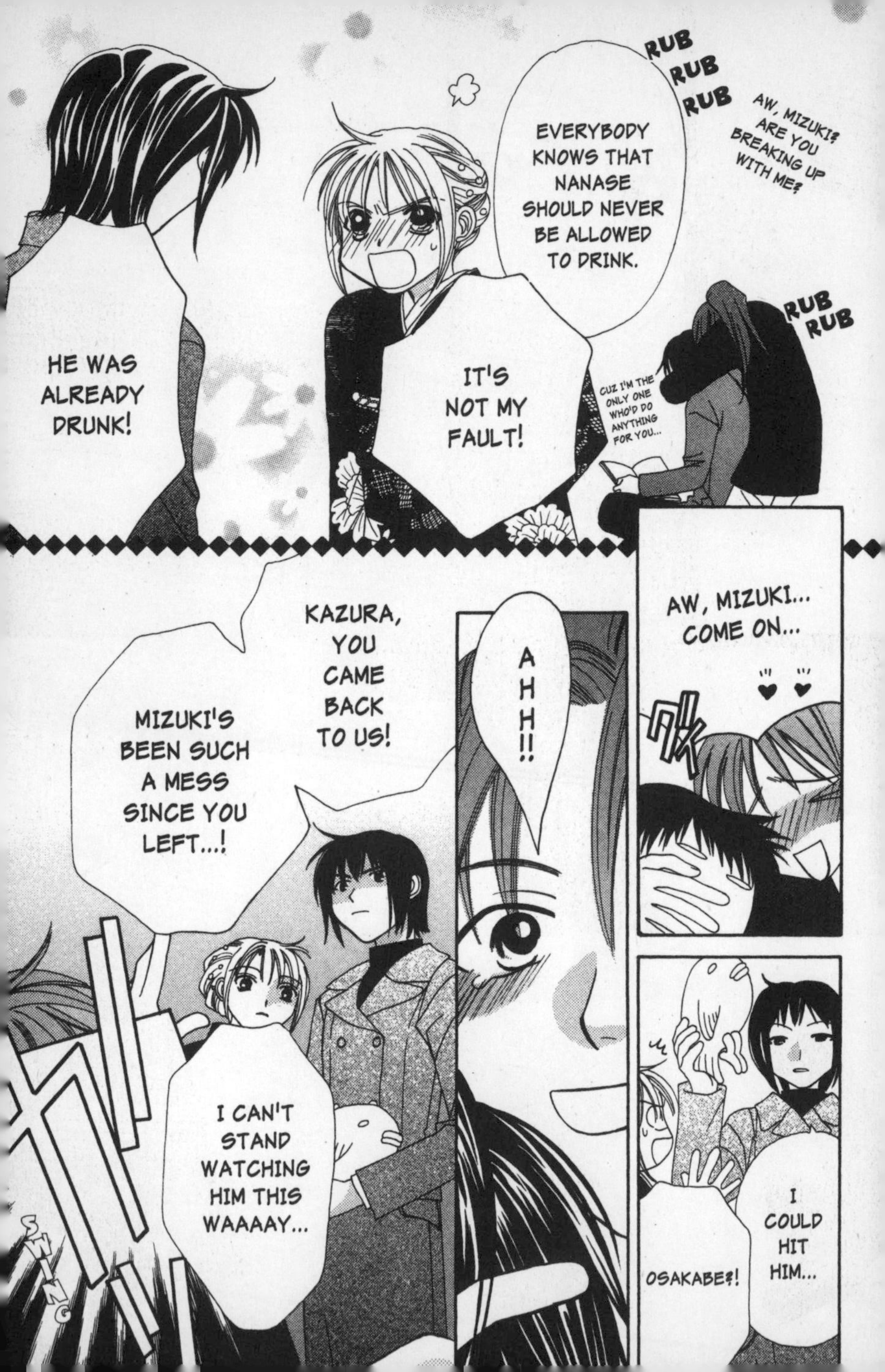
RUB RUB RUB
AW, MIZUKI? ARE YOU BREAKING UP WITH ME?
EVERYBODY KNOWS THAT NANASE SHOULD NEVER BE ALLOWED TO DRINK.
RUB RUB
CUZ I'M THE ONLY ONE WHO'D DO ANYTHING FOR YOU...
IT'S NOT MY FAULT!
HE WAS ALREADY DRUNK!
AW, MIZUKI... COME ON...
I COULD HIT HIM...
OSAKABE?!
AHH!!
KAZURA, YOU CAME BACK TO US!
MIZUKI'S BEEN SUCH A MESS SINCE YOU LEFT...!
I CAN'T STAND WATCHING HIM THIS WAAAAY...
SWING

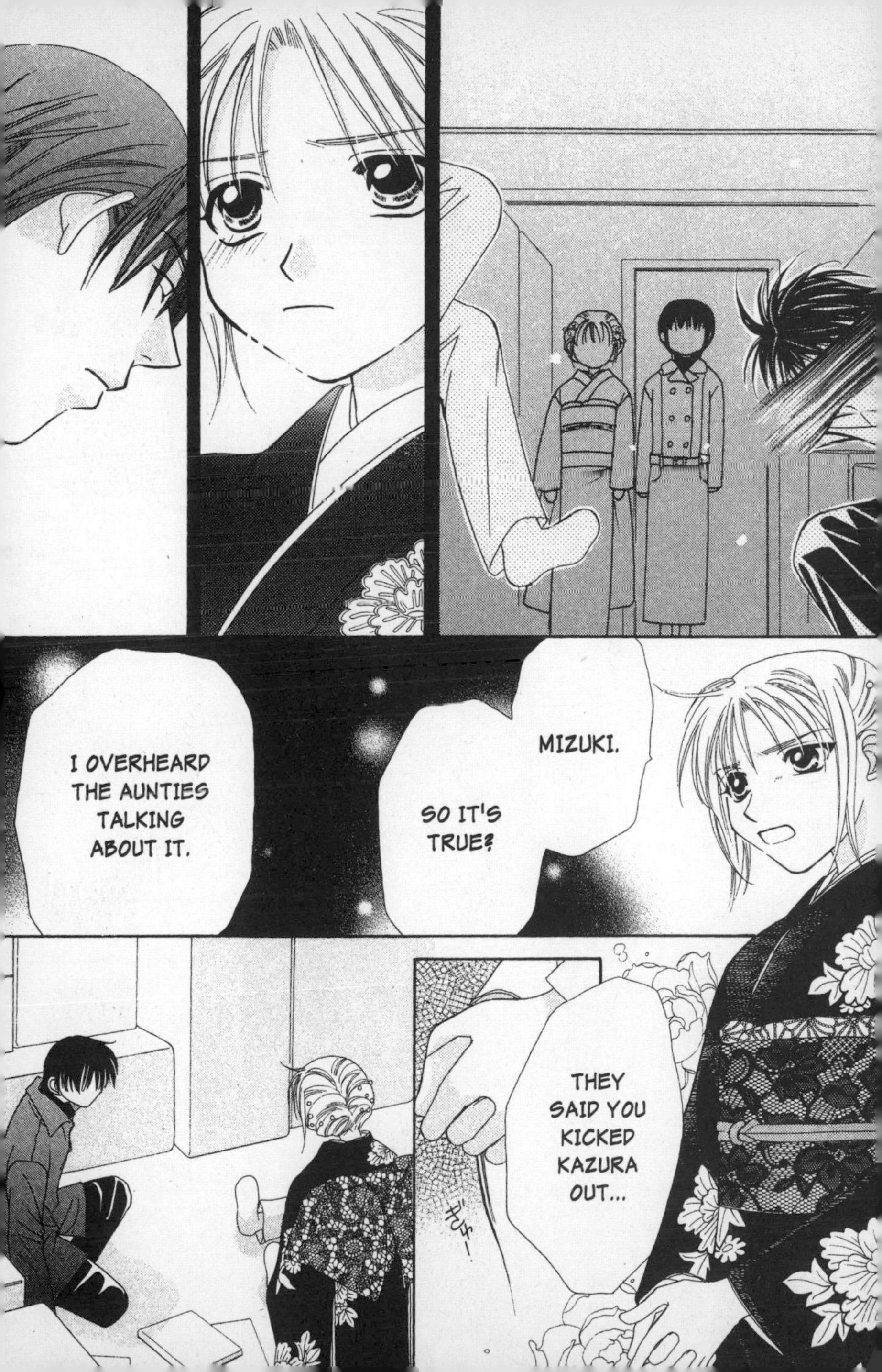
MIZUKI.
SO IT'S TRUE?
I OVERHEARD THE AUNTIES TALKING ABOUT IT.
THEY SAID YOU KICKED KAZURA OUT...

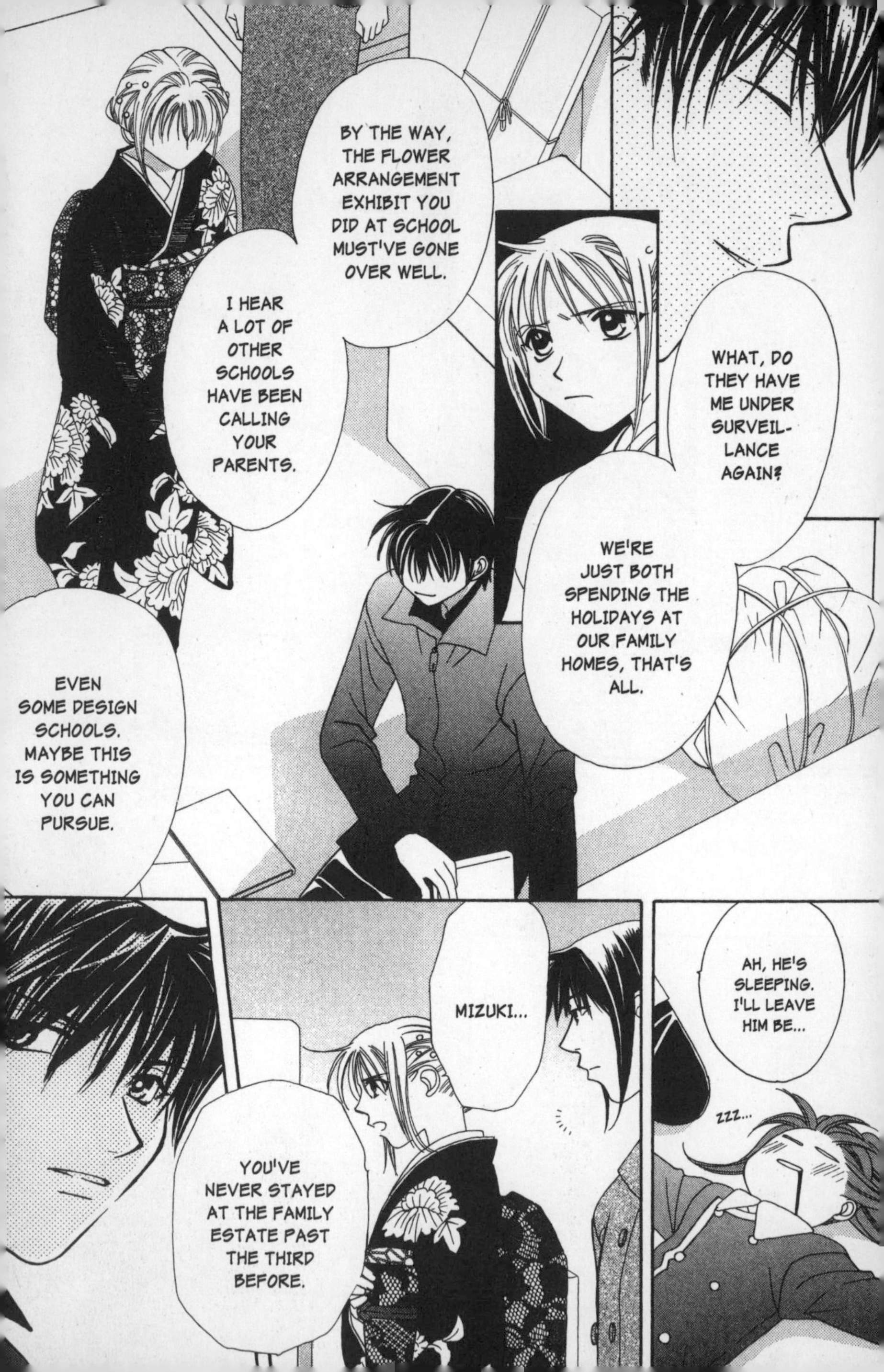
WHAT, DO THEY HAVE ME UNDER SURVEIL-LANCE AGAIN?
WE'RE JUST BOTH SPENDING THE HOLIDAYS AT OUR FAMILY HOMES, THAT'S ALL.
BY THE WAY, THE FLOWER ARRANGEMENT EXHIBIT YOU DID AT SCHOOL MUST'VE GONE OVER WELL.
I HEAR A LOT OF OTHER SCHOOLS HAVE BEEN CALLING YOUR PARENTS.
EVEN SOME DESIGN SCHOOLS. MAYBE THIS IS SOMETHING YOU CAN PURSUE.
AH, HE'S SLEEPING. I'LL LEAVE HIM BE...
ZZZ...
MIZUKI...
YOU'VE NEVER STAYED AT THE FAMILY ESTATE PAST THE THIRD BEFORE.

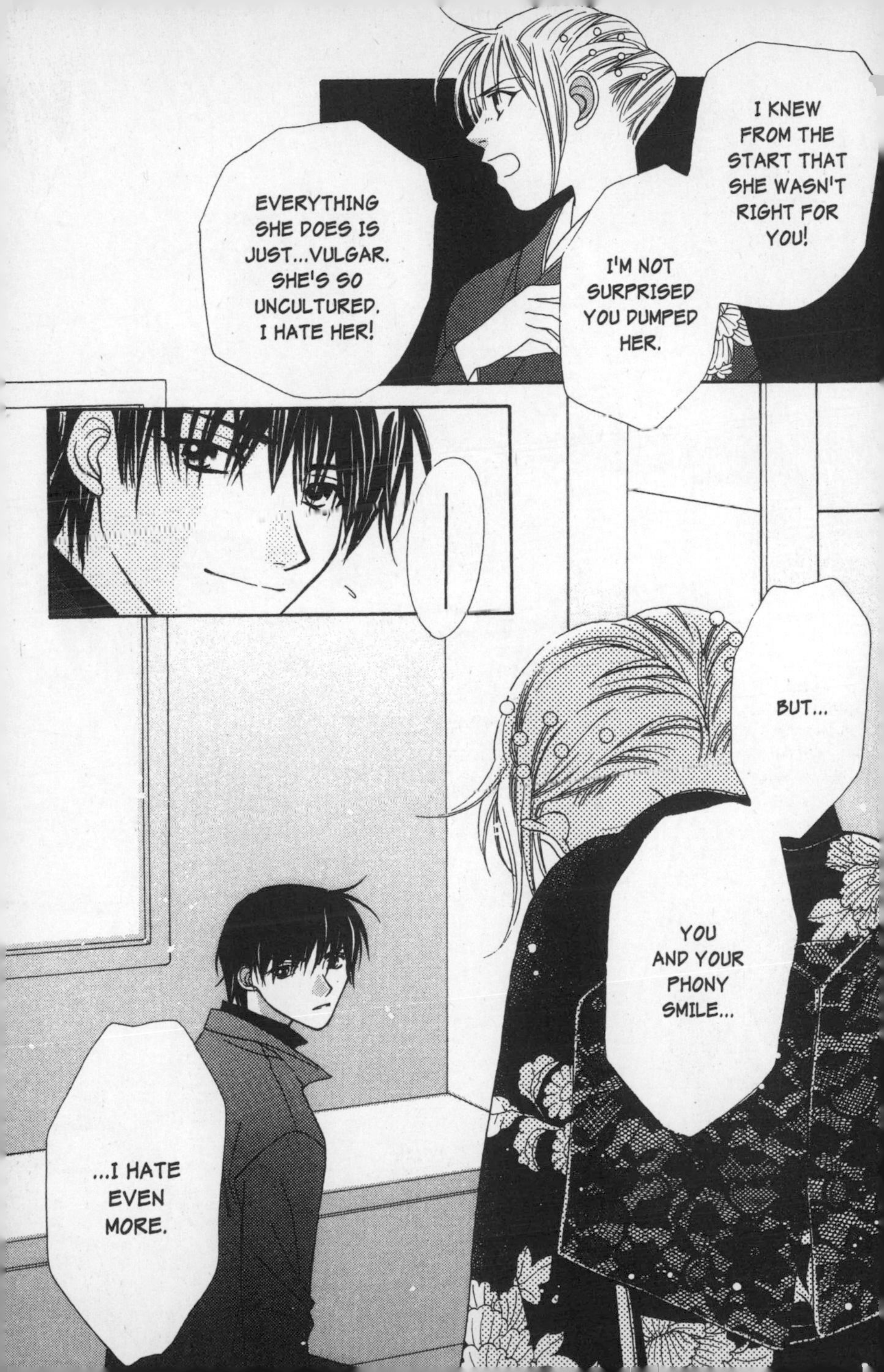
I KNEW FROM THE START THAT SHE WASN'T RIGHT FOR YOU!
I'M NOT SURPRISED YOU DUMPED HER.
EVERYTHING SHE DOES IS JUST...VULGAR. SHE'S SO UNCULTURED. I HATE HER!
BUT...
YOU AND YOUR PHONY SMILE...
...I HATE EVEN MORE.

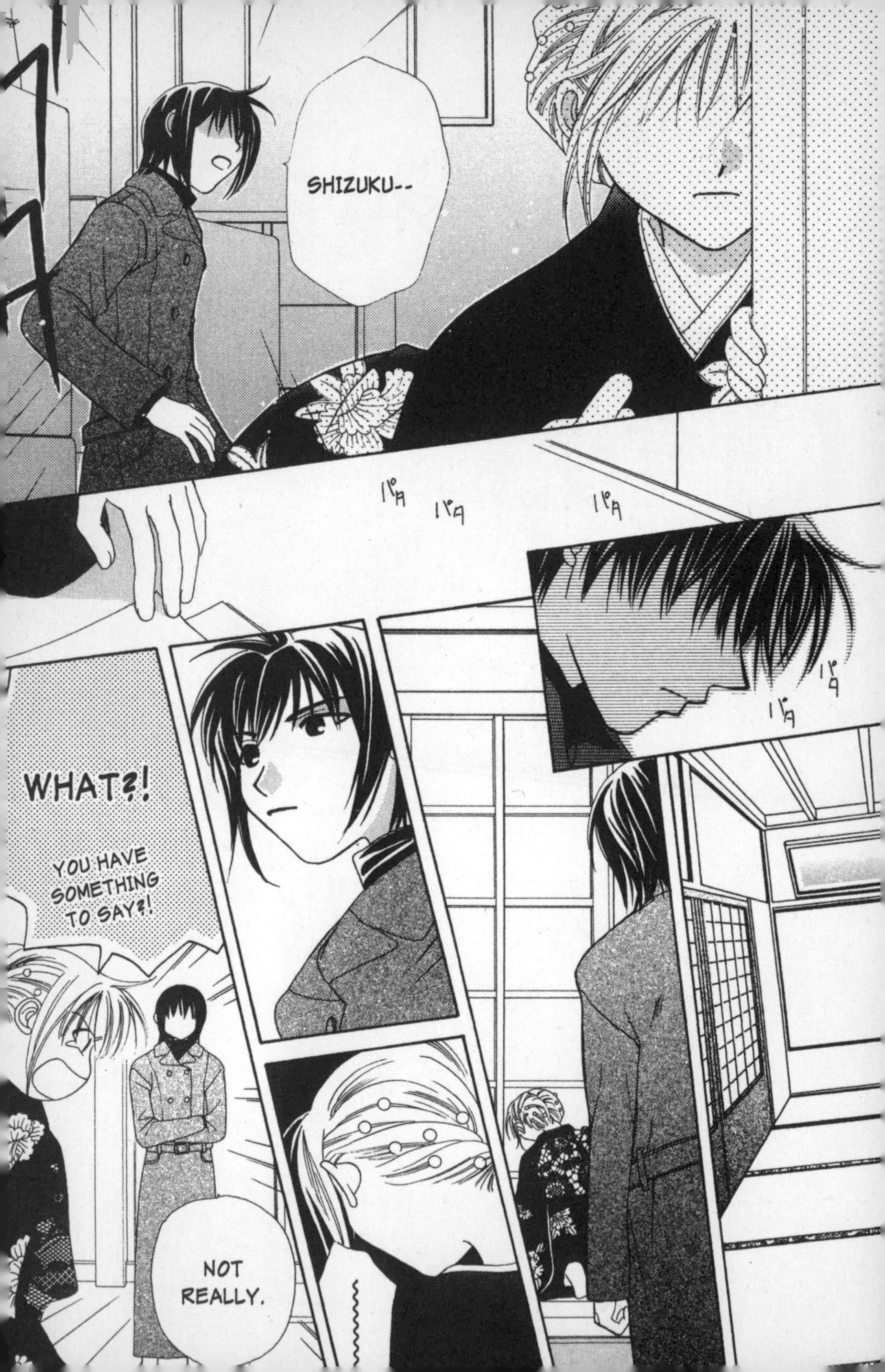
SHIZUKU--
パタ
パタ
パタ
パタ
パタ
WHAT?!
YOU HAVE SOMETHING TO SAY?!
NOT REALLY.

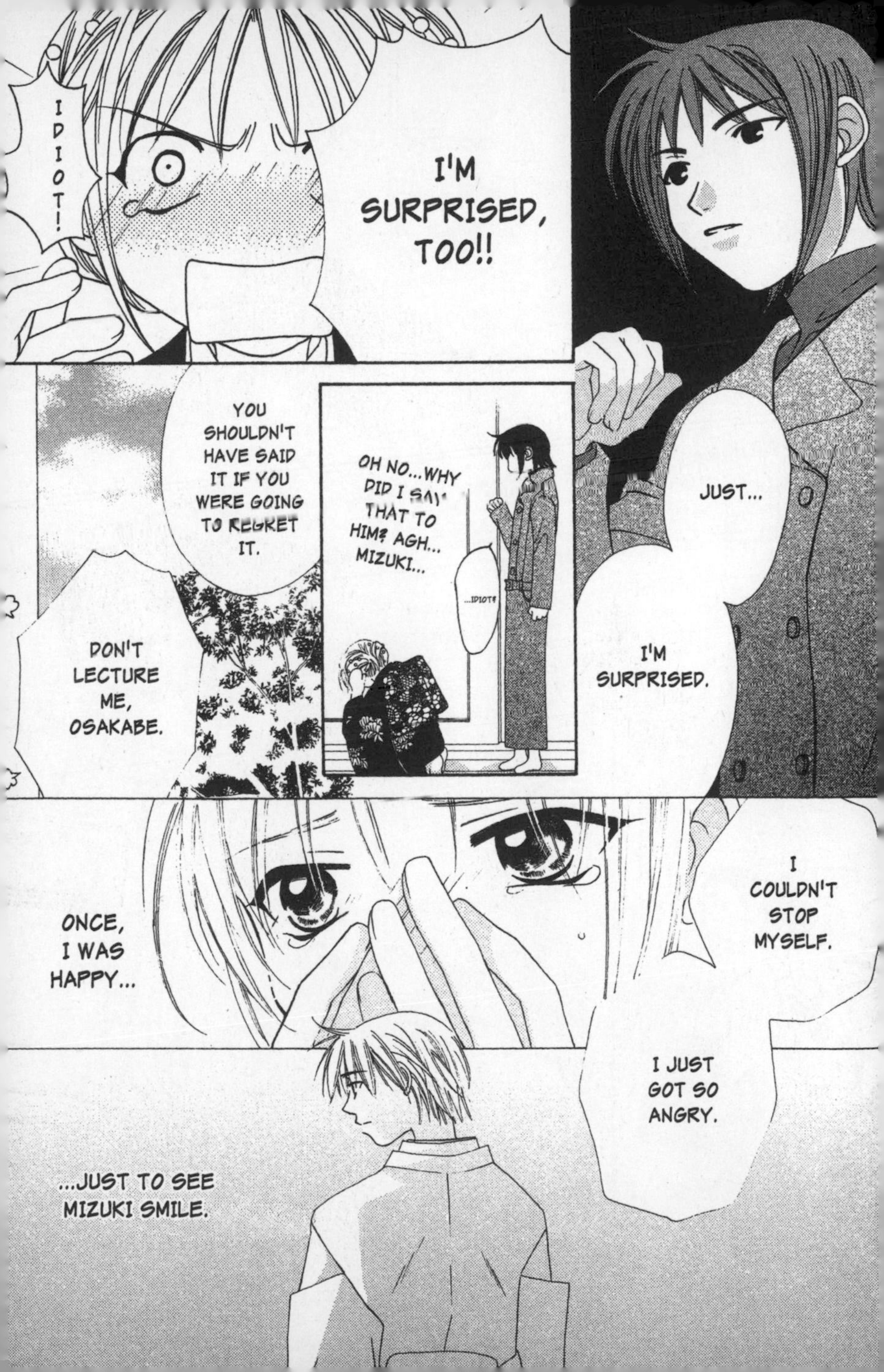
JUST...
I'M SURPRISED.
I'M SURPRISED, TOO!!
IDIOT!!
OH NO...WHY DID I SAY THAT TO HIM? AGH... MIZUKI...
...IDIOT?
YOU SHOULDN'T HAVE SAID IT IF YOU WERE GOING TO REGRET IT.
DON'T LECTURE ME, OSAKABE.
I COULDN'T STOP MYSELF.
ONCE, I WAS HAPPY...
I JUST GOT SO ANGRY.
...JUST TO SEE MIZUKI SMILE.

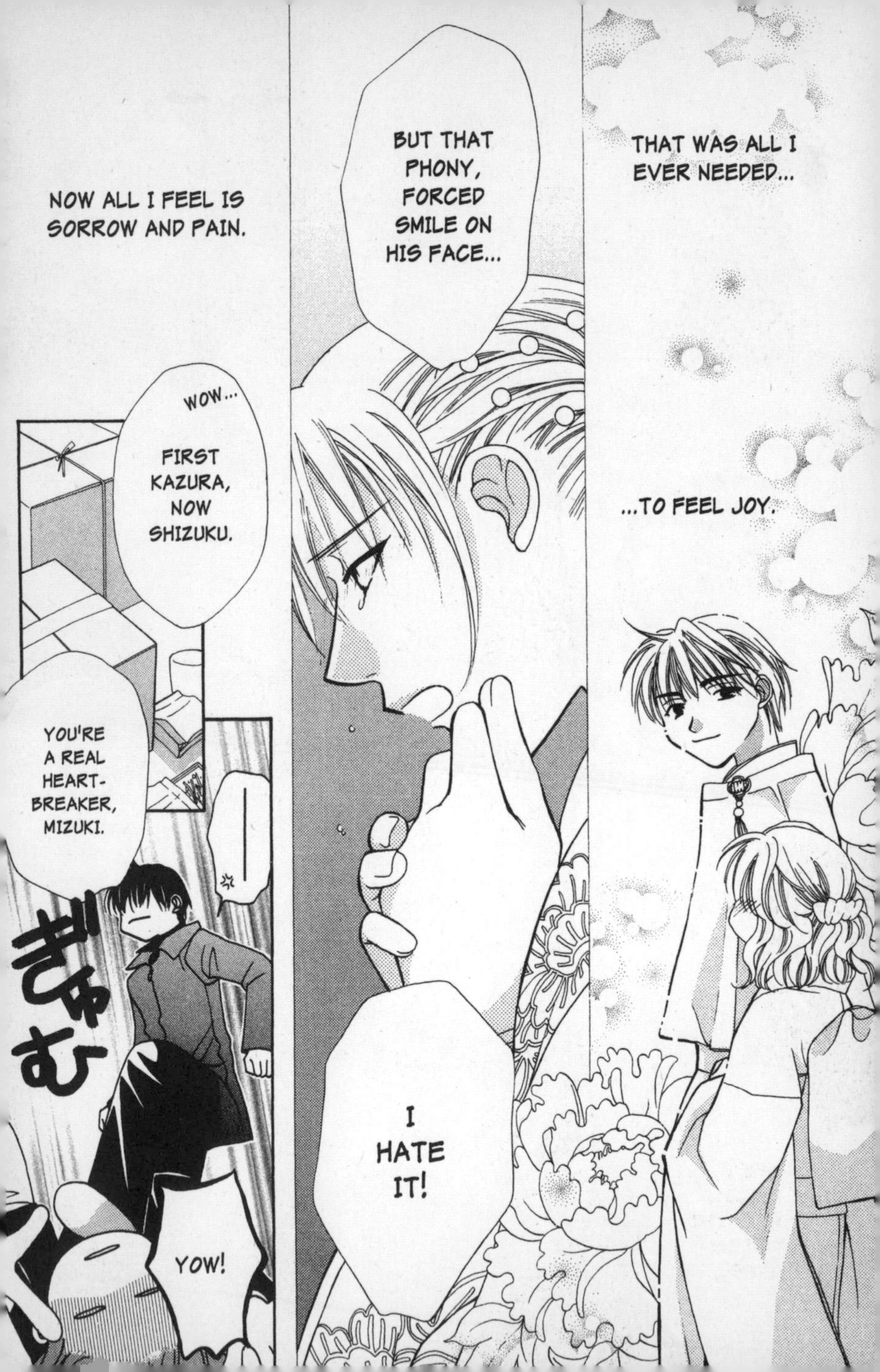
THAT WAS ALL I EVER NEEDED...
...TO FEEL JOY.
BUT THAT PHONY, FORCED SMILE ON HIS FACE...
I HATE IT!
NOW ALL I FEEL IS SORROW AND PAIN.
WOW... FIRST KAZURA, NOW SHIZUKU.
YOU'RE A REAL HEART-BREAKER, MIZUKI.
ぎゅむ
YOW!

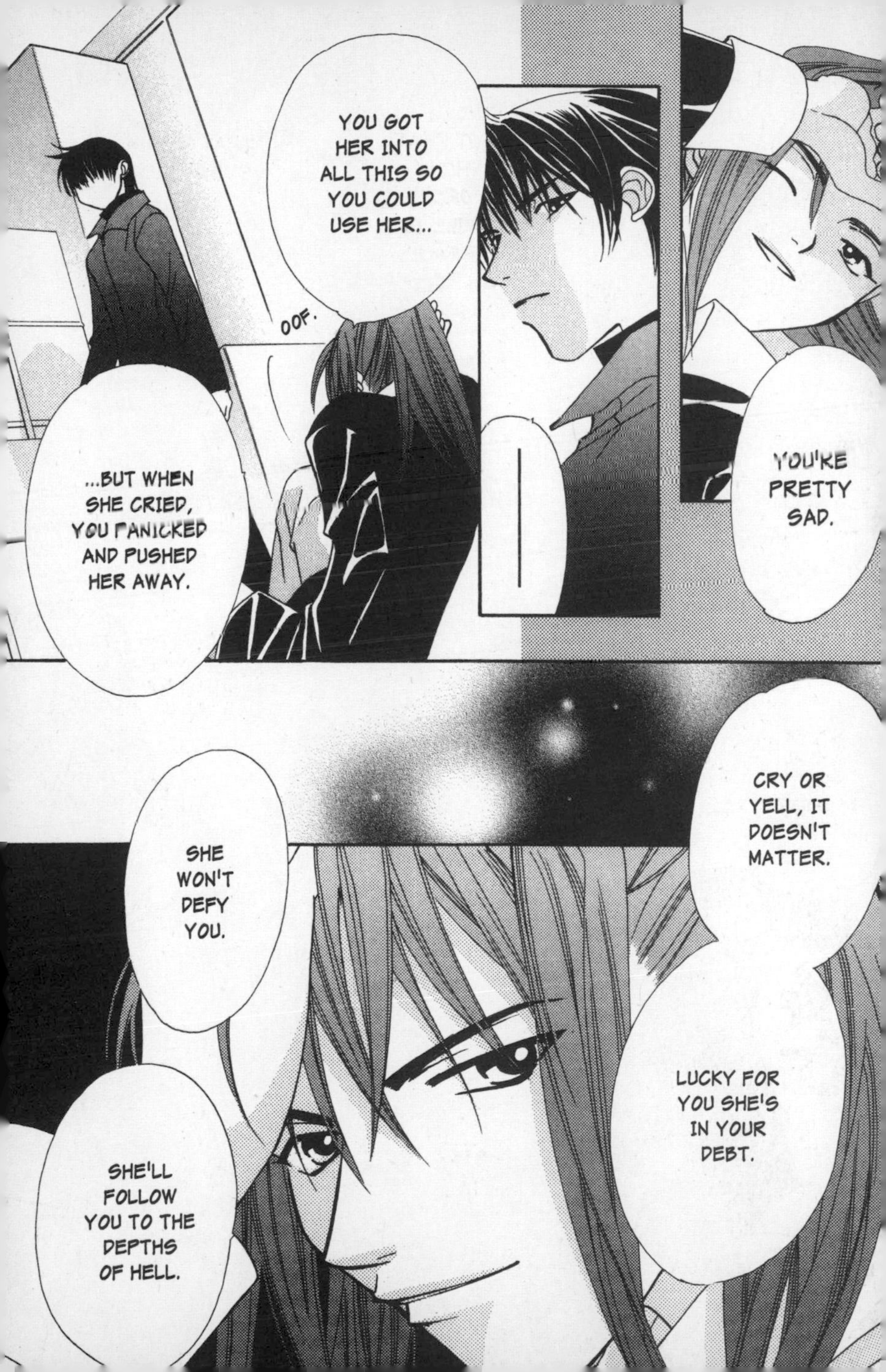
YOU'RE PRETTY SAD.
YOU GOT HER INTO ALL THIS SO YOU COULD USE HER...
OOF.
...BUT WHEN SHE CRIED, YOU PANICKED AND PUSHED HER AWAY.
CRY OR YELL, IT DOESN'T MATTER.
SHE WON'T DEFY YOU.
LUCKY FOR YOU SHE'S IN YOUR DEBT.
SHE'LL FOLLOW YOU TO THE DEPTHS OF HELL.

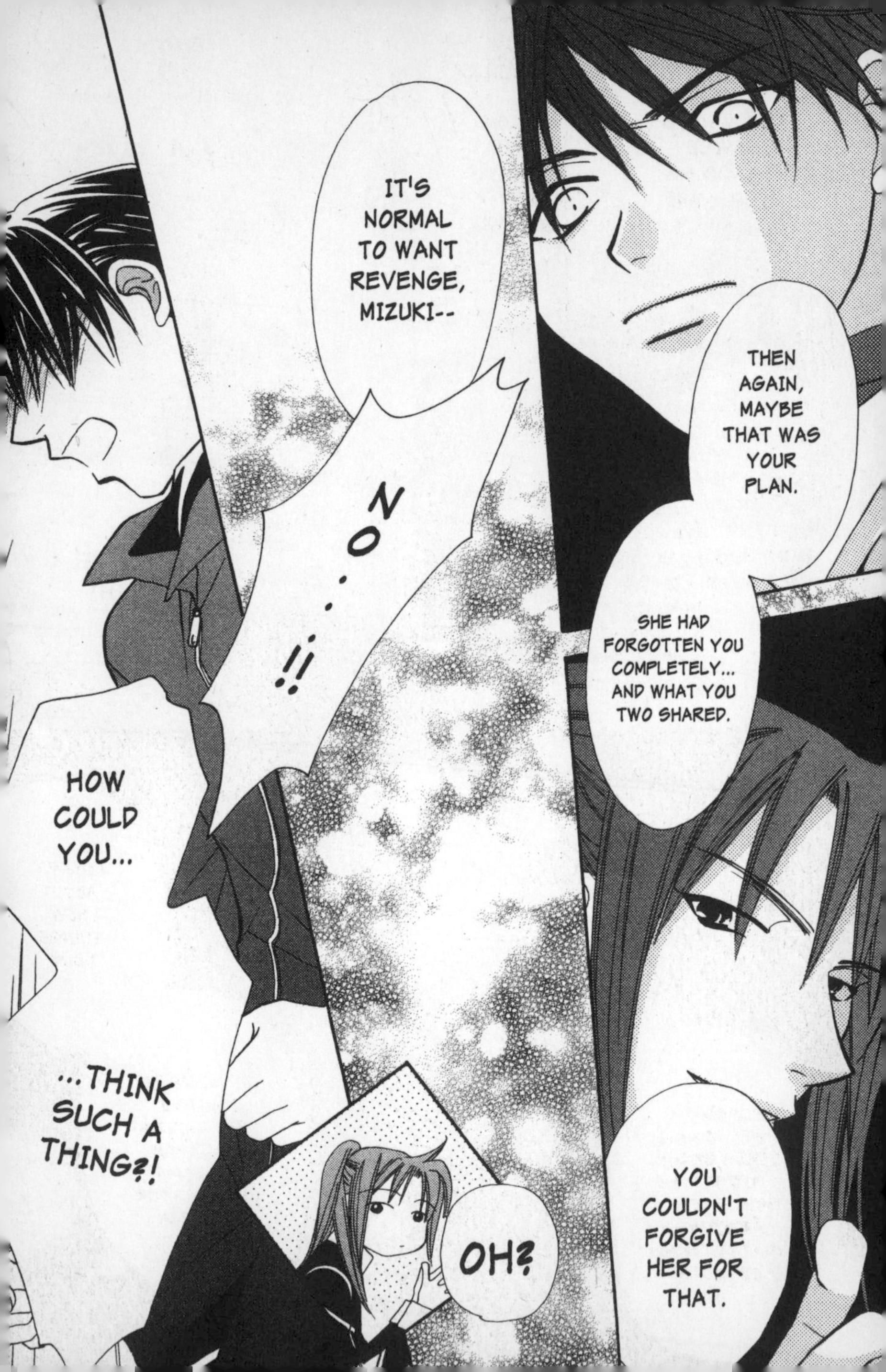
THEN AGAIN, MAYBE THAT WAS YOUR PLAN.
SHE HAD FORGOTTEN YOU COMPLETELY... AND WHAT YOU TWO SHARED.
YOU COULDN'T FORGIVE HER FOR THAT.
IT'S NORMAL TO WANT REVENGE, MIZUKI--
NO...!!
HOW COULD YOU...
...THINK SUCH A THING?!
OH?

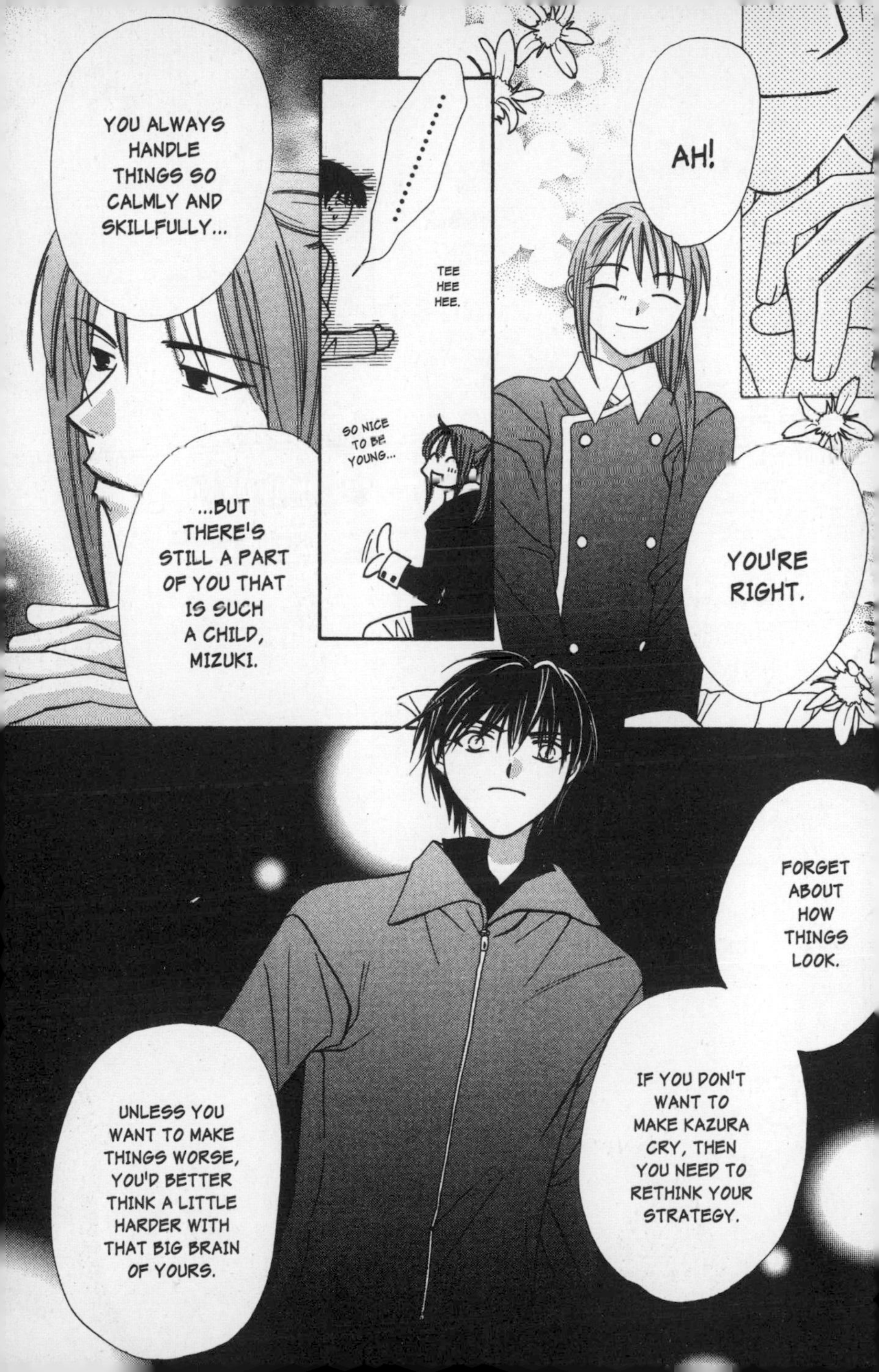
AH!
YOU'RE RIGHT.
......
TEE HEE HEE.
SO NICE TO BE YOUNG...
YOU ALWAYS HANDLE THINGS SO CALMLY AND SKILLFULLY...
...BUT THERE'S STILL A PART OF YOU THAT IS SUCH A CHILD, MIZUKI.
FORGET ABOUT HOW THINGS LOOK.
IF YOU DON'T WANT TO MAKE KAZURA CRY, THEN YOU NEED TO RETHINK YOUR STRATEGY.
UNLESS YOU WANT TO MAKE THINGS WORSE, YOU'D BETTER THINK A LITTLE HARDER WITH THAT BIG BRAIN OF YOURS.

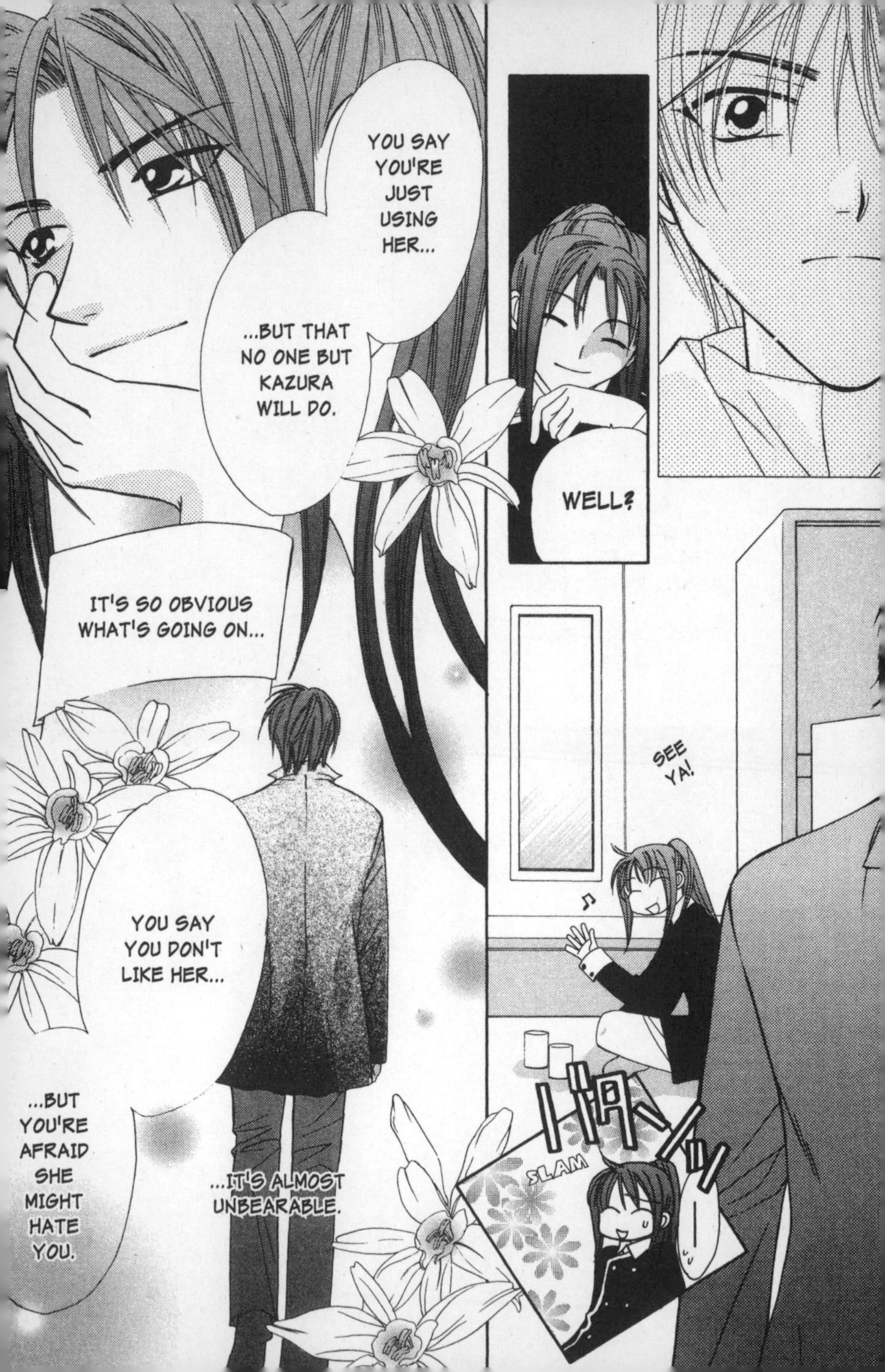
WELL?
SEE YA!
SLAM
YOU SAY YOU'RE JUST USING HER...
...BUT THAT NO ONE BUT KAZURA WILL DO.
IT'S SO OBVIOUS WHAT'S GOING ON...
YOU SAY YOU DON'T LIKE HER...
...BUT YOU'RE AFRAID SHE MIGHT HATE YOU.
...IT'S ALMOST UNBEARABLE.

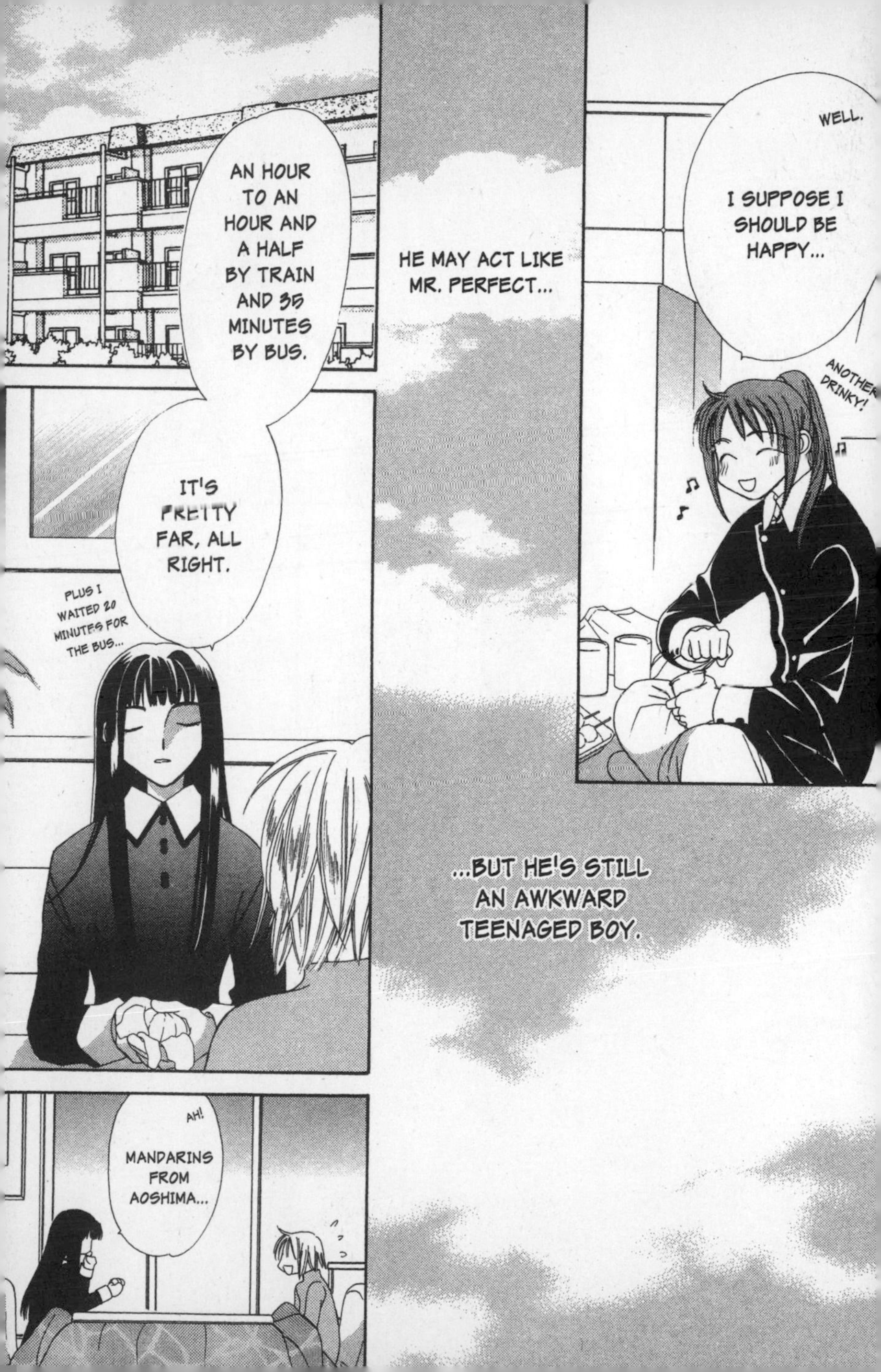
WELL.
I SUPPOSE I SHOULD BE HAPPY...
ANOTHER DRINKY!
HE MAY ACT LIKE MR. PERFECT...
AN HOUR TO AN HOUR AND A HALF BY TRAIN AND 35 MINUTES BY BUS.
IT'S PRETTY FAR, ALL RIGHT.
PLUS I WAITED 20 MINUTES FOR THE BUS...
...BUT HE'S STILL AN AWKWARD TEENAGED BOY.
AH!
MANDARINS FROM AOSHIMA...

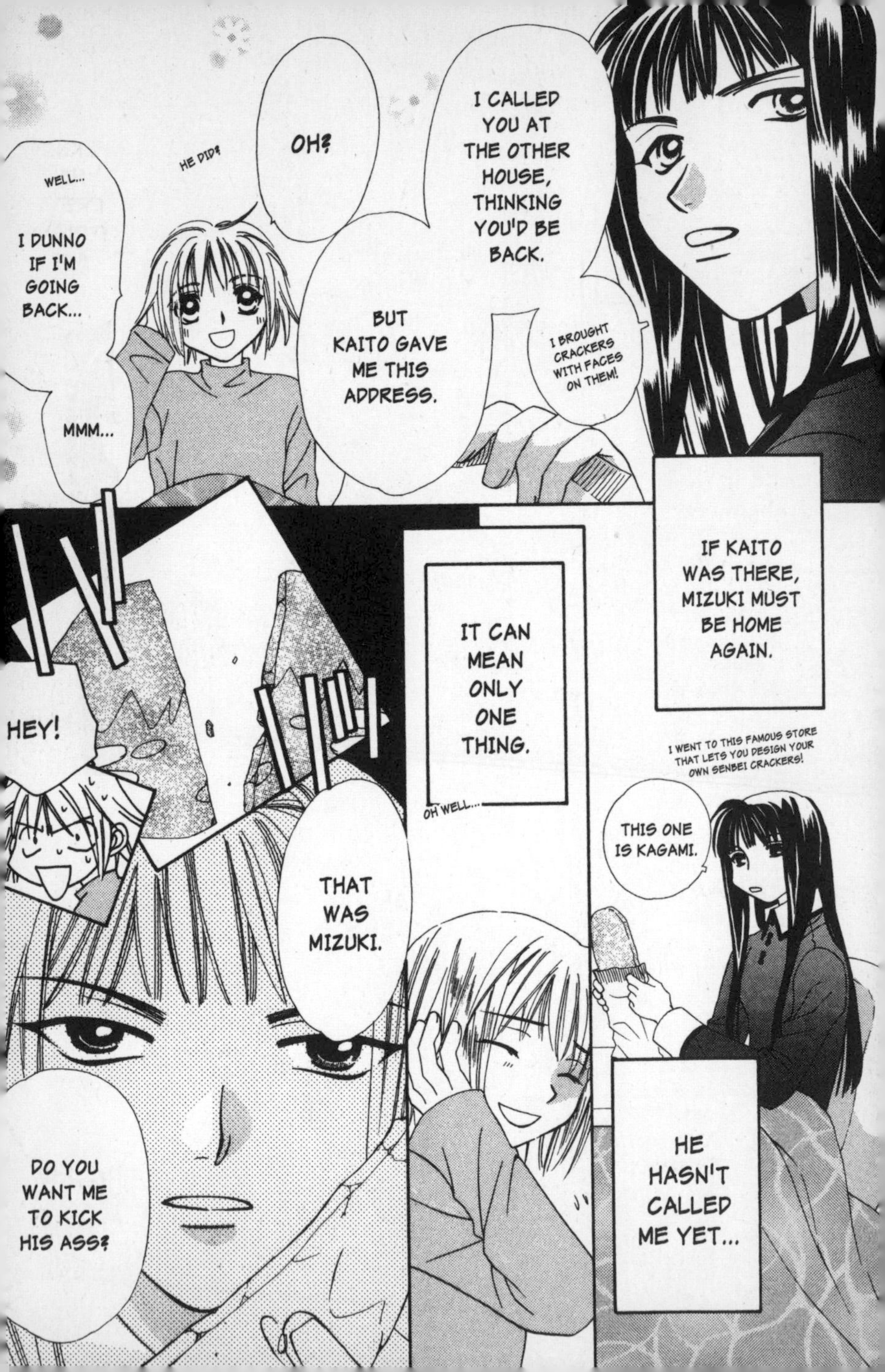
I CALLED YOU AT THE OTHER HOUSE, THINKING YOU'D BE BACK.
OH?
BUT KAITO GAVE ME THIS ADDRESS.
HE DID?
I BROUGHT CRACKERS WITH FACES ON THEM!
WELL...
I DUNNO IF I'M GOING BACK...
MMM...
IF KAITO WAS THERE, MIZUKI MUST BE HOME AGAIN.
I WENT TO THIS FAMOUS STORE THAT LETS YOU DESIGN YOUR OWN SENBEI CRACKERS!
THIS ONE IS KAGAMI.
HE HASN'T CALLED ME YET...
IT CAN MEAN ONLY ONE THING.
OH WELL...
HEY!
THAT WAS MIZUKI.
DO YOU WANT ME TO KICK HIS ASS?

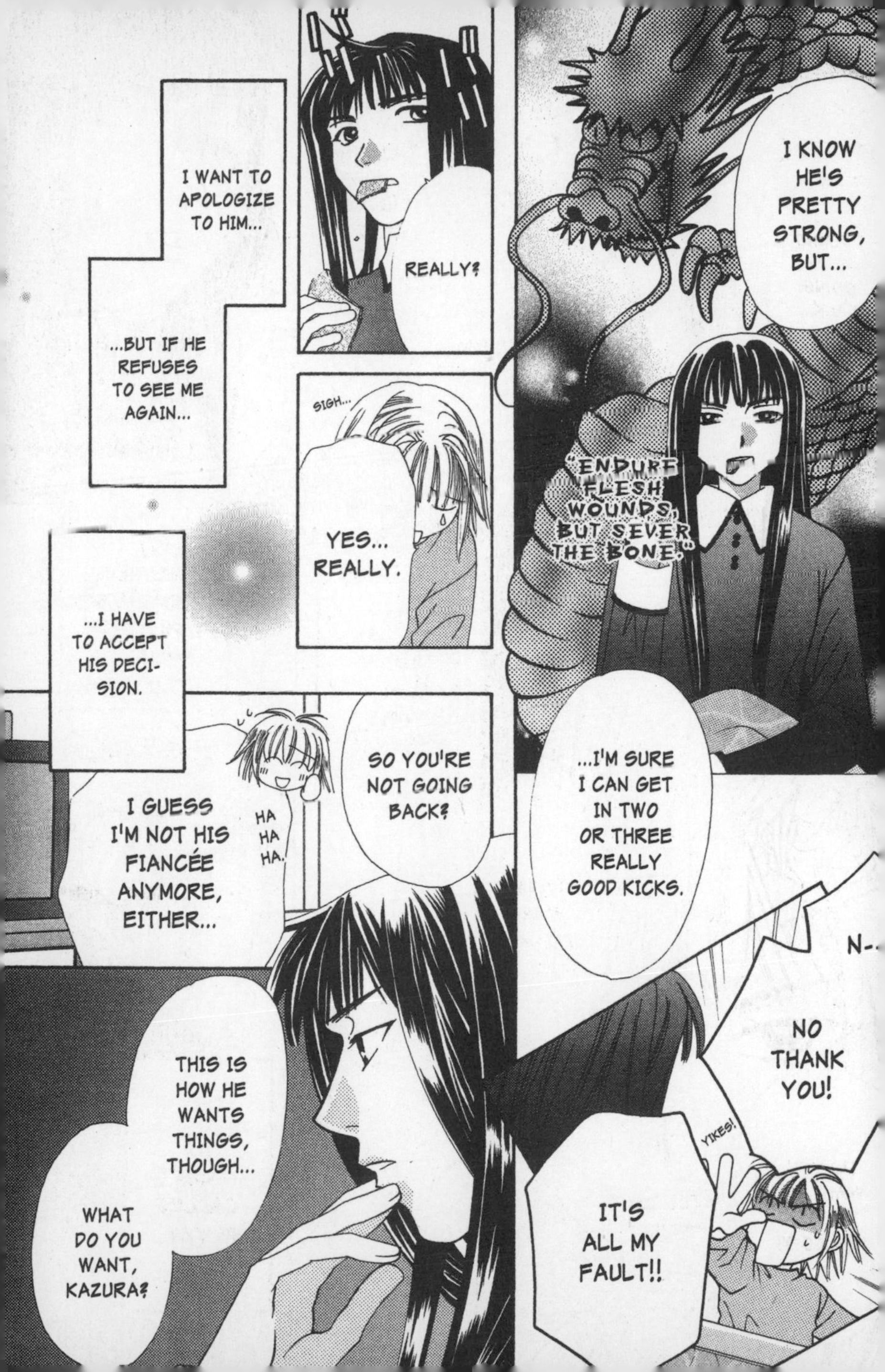
I KNOW HE'S PRETTY STRONG, BUT...
"ENDURE FLESH WOUNDS, BUT SEVER THE BONE."
...I'M SURE I CAN GET IN TWO OR THREE REALLY GOOD KICKS.
N-...
NO THANK YOU!
YIKES!
IT'S ALL MY FAULT!!
I WANT TO APOLOGIZE TO HIM...
REALLY?
...BUT IF HE REFUSES TO SEE ME AGAIN...
SIGH...
YES... REALLY.
...I HAVE TO ACCEPT HIS DECISION.
SO YOU'RE NOT GOING BACK?
I GUESS I'M NOT HIS FIANCÉE ANYMORE, EITHER...
HA HA HA.
THIS IS HOW HE WANTS THINGS, THOUGH...
WHAT DO YOU WANT, KAZURA?

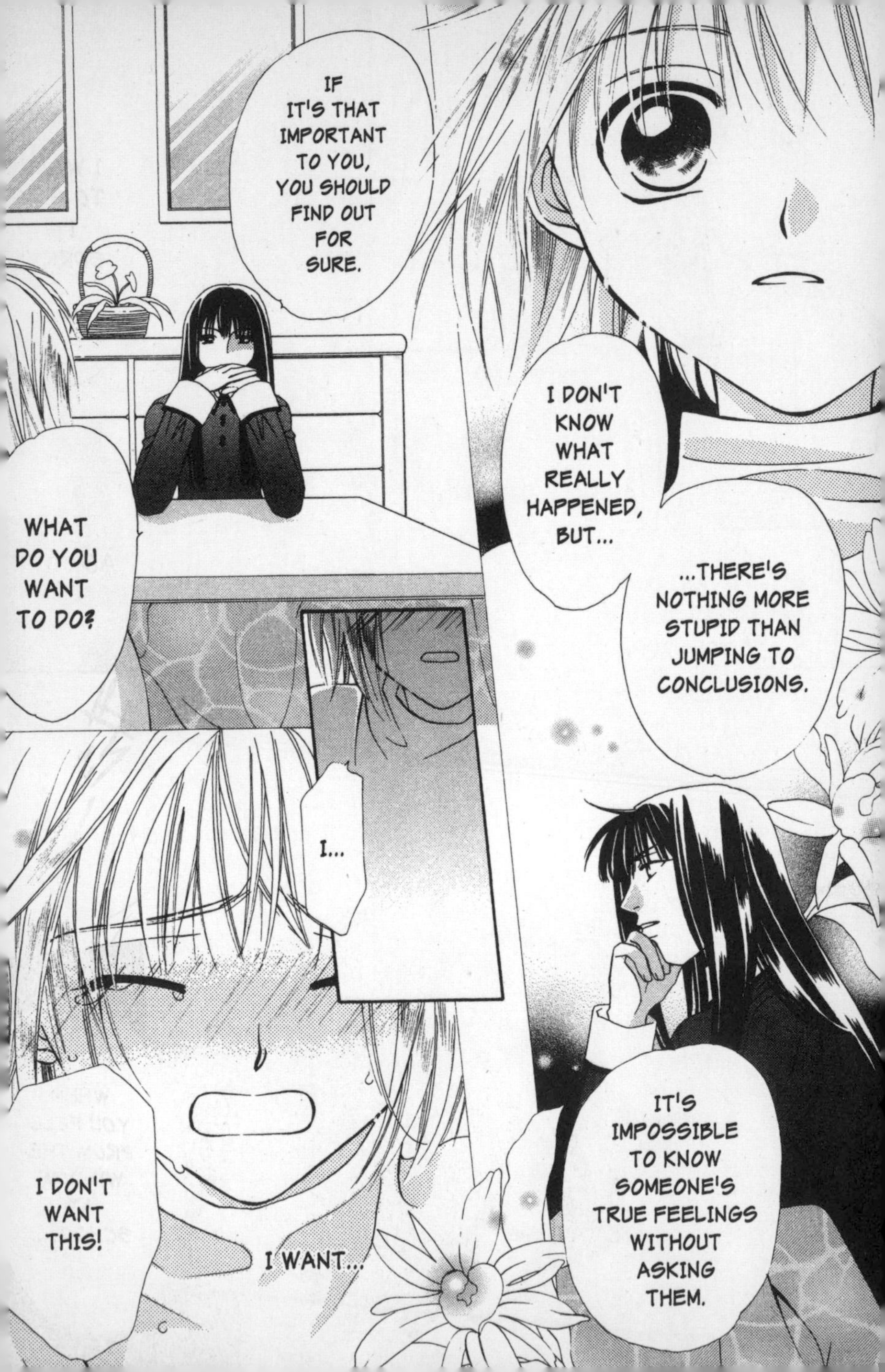
I DON'T KNOW WHAT REALLY HAPPENED, BUT...
...THERE'S NOTHING MORE STUPID THAN JUMPING TO CONCLUSIONS.
IT'S IMPOSSIBLE TO KNOW SOMEONE'S TRUE FEELINGS WITHOUT ASKING THEM.
IF IT'S THAT IMPORTANT TO YOU, YOU SHOULD FIND OUT FOR SURE.
WHAT DO YOU WANT TO DO?
I...
I DON'T WANT THIS!
I WANT...

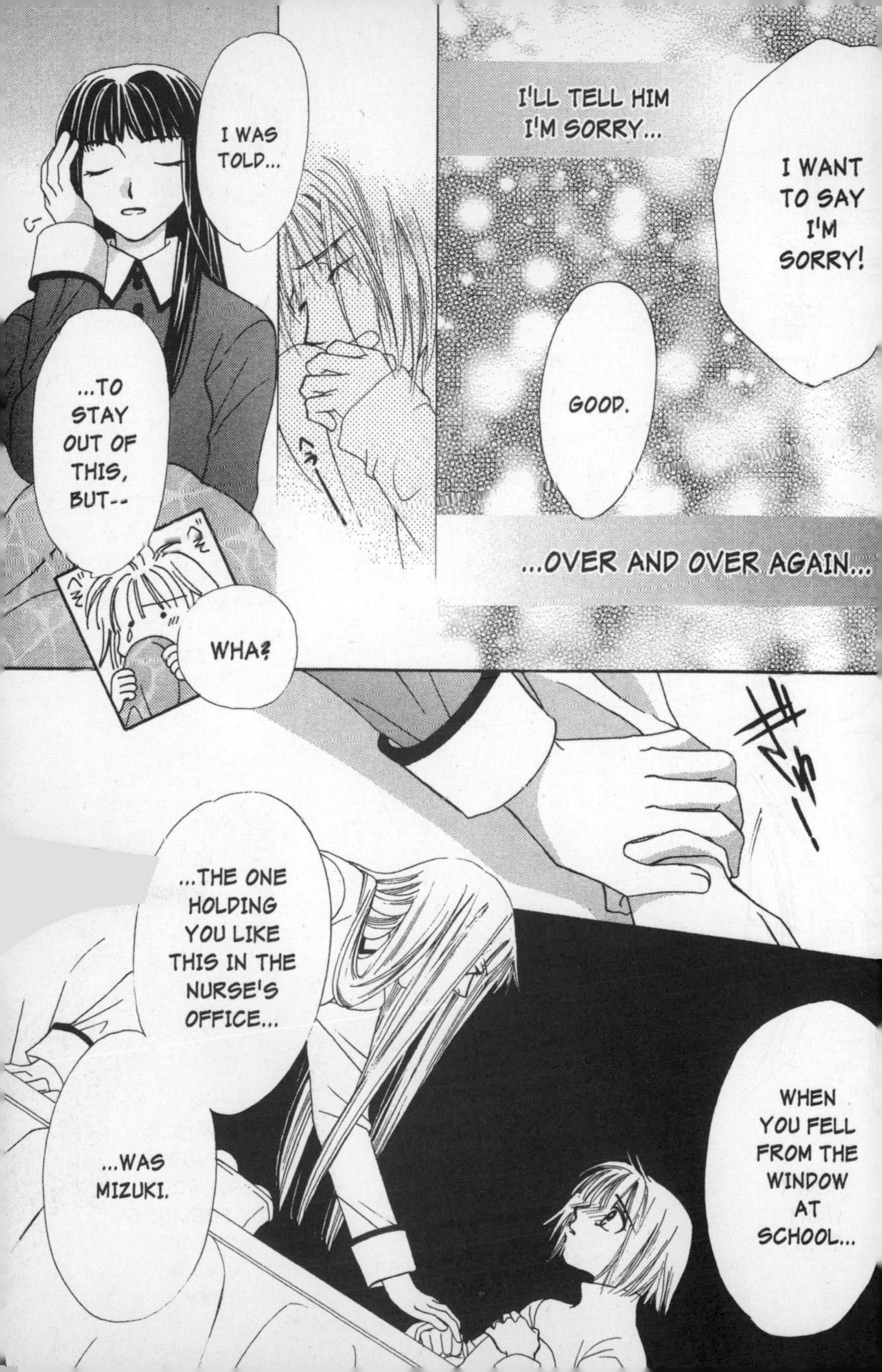
I WANT TO SAY I'M SORRY!
I'LL TELL HIM I'M SORRY...
GOOD.
...OVER AND OVER AGAIN...
I WAS TOLD...
...TO STAY OUT OF THIS, BUT--
WHA?
WHEN YOU FELL FROM THE WINDOW AT SCHOOL...
...THE ONE HOLDING YOU LIKE THIS IN THE NURSE'S OFFICE...
...WAS MIZUKI.

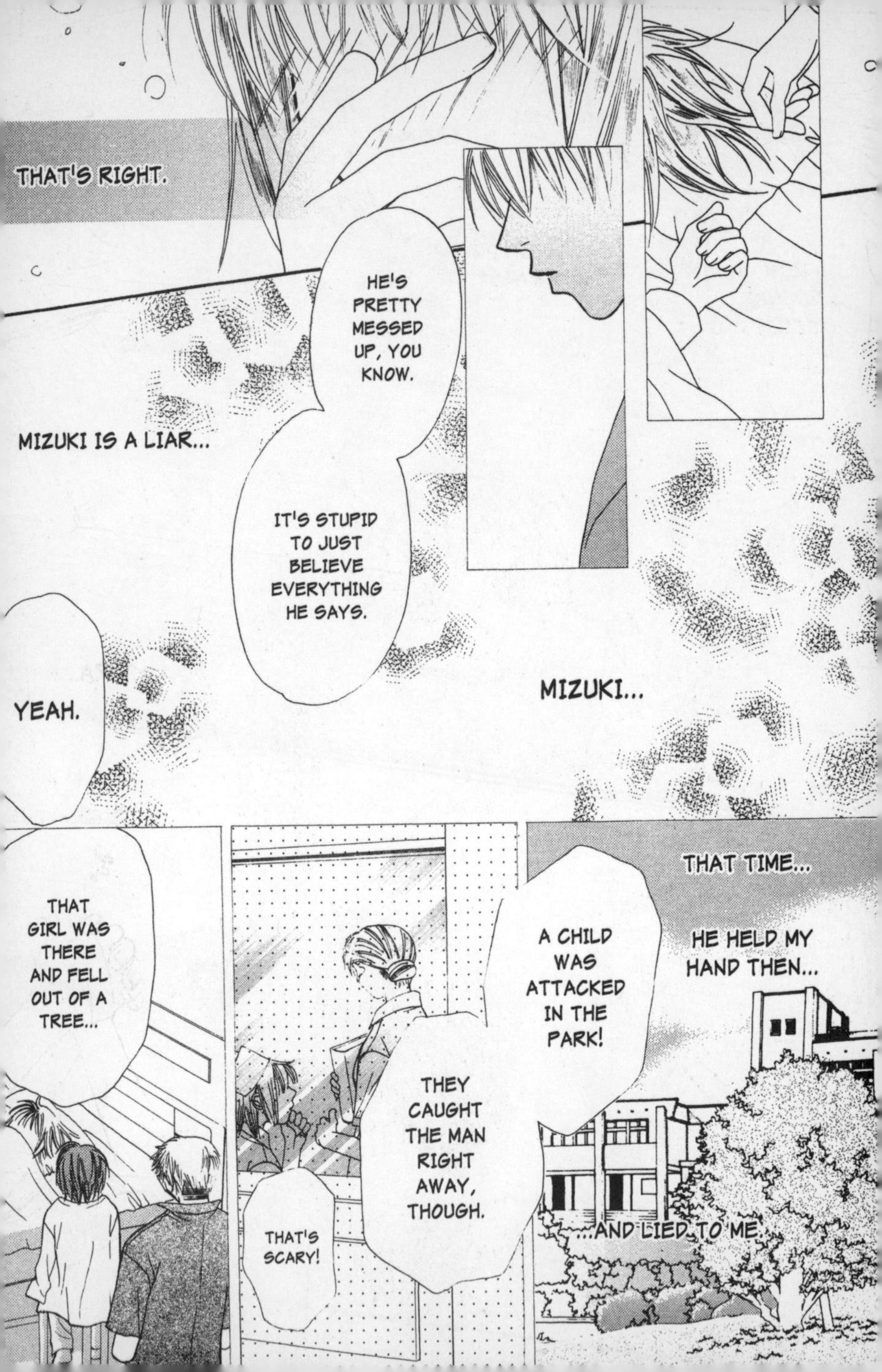
THAT'S RIGHT.
HE'S PRETTY MESSED UP, YOU KNOW.
IT'S STUPID TO JUST BELIEVE EVERYTHING HE SAYS.
MIZUKI...
MIZUKI IS A LIAR...
YEAH.
THAT TIME...
HE HELD MY HAND THEN...
A CHILD WAS ATTACKED IN THE PARK!
...AND LIED TO ME.
THEY CAUGHT THE MAN RIGHT AWAY, THOUGH.
THAT'S SCARY!
THAT GIRL WAS THERE AND FELL OUT OF A TREE...

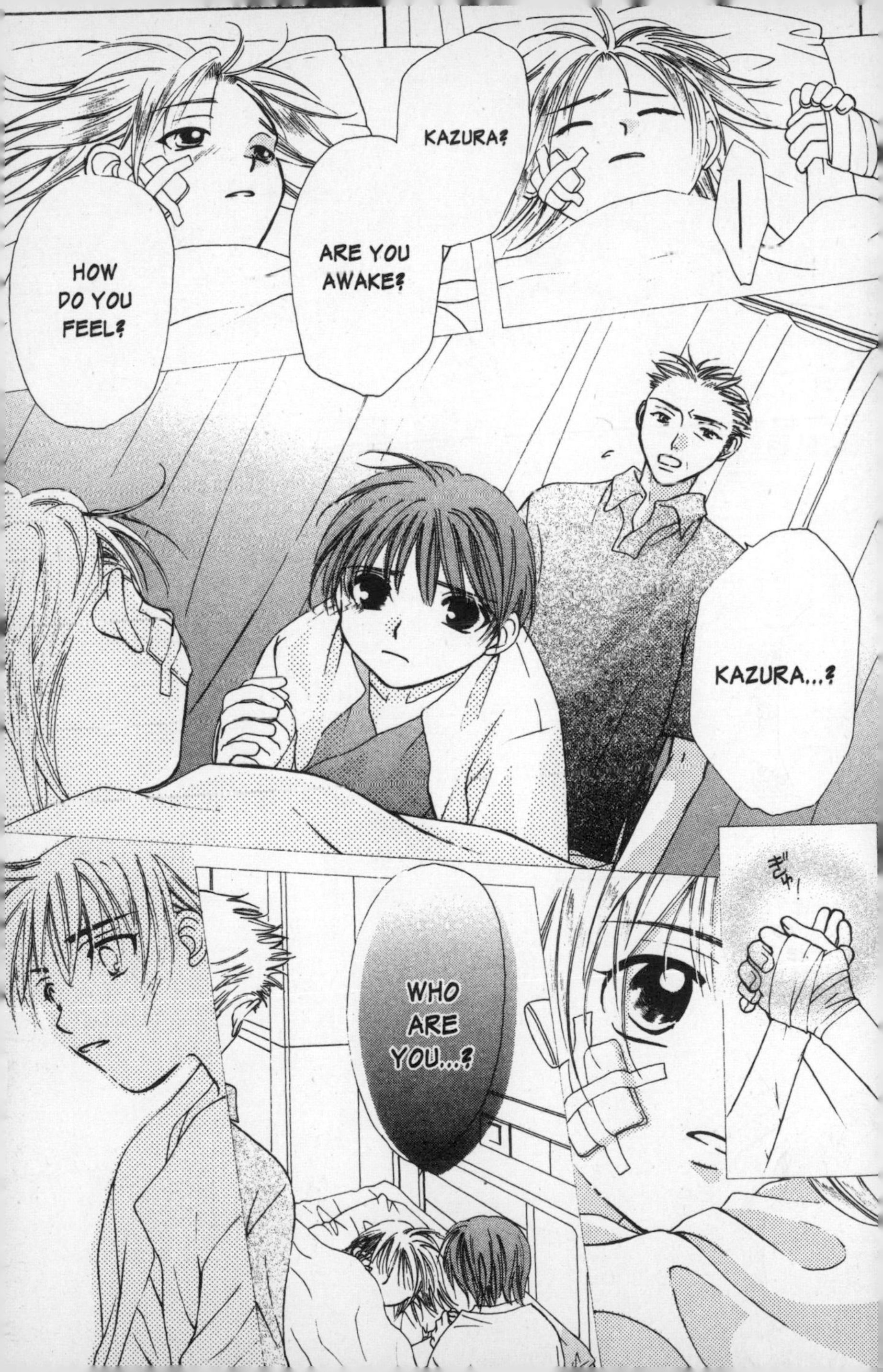

KAZURA?
ARE YOU AWAKE?
HOW DO YOU FEEL?
KAZURA...?
ぎゅ!
WHO ARE YOU...?

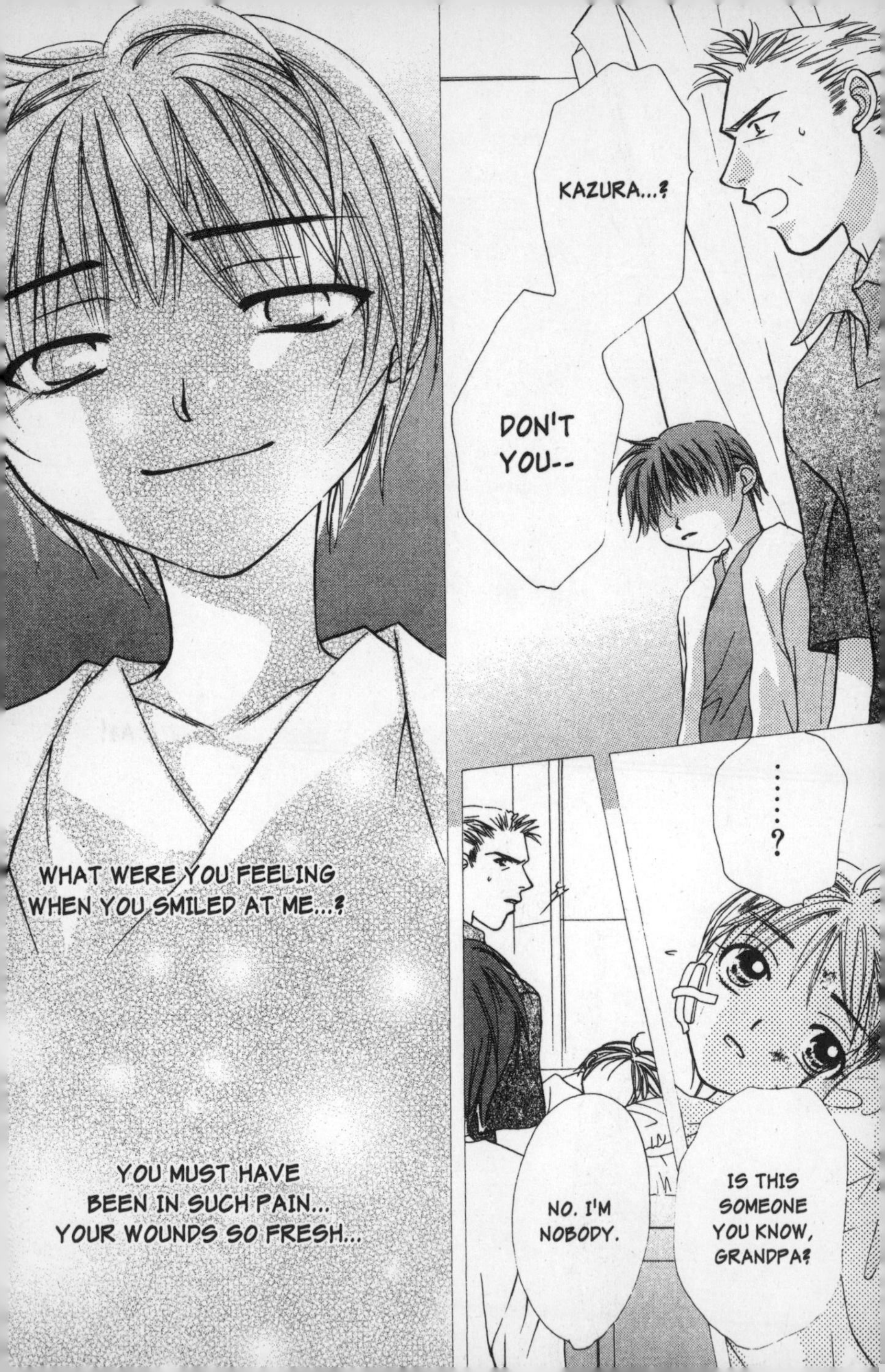
KAZURA...?
DON'T YOU--
......?
IS THIS SOMEONE YOU KNOW, GRANDPA?
NO. I'M NOBODY.
WHAT WERE YOU FEELING WHEN YOU SMILED AT ME...?
YOU MUST HAVE BEEN IN SUCH PAIN... YOUR WOUNDS SO FRESH...

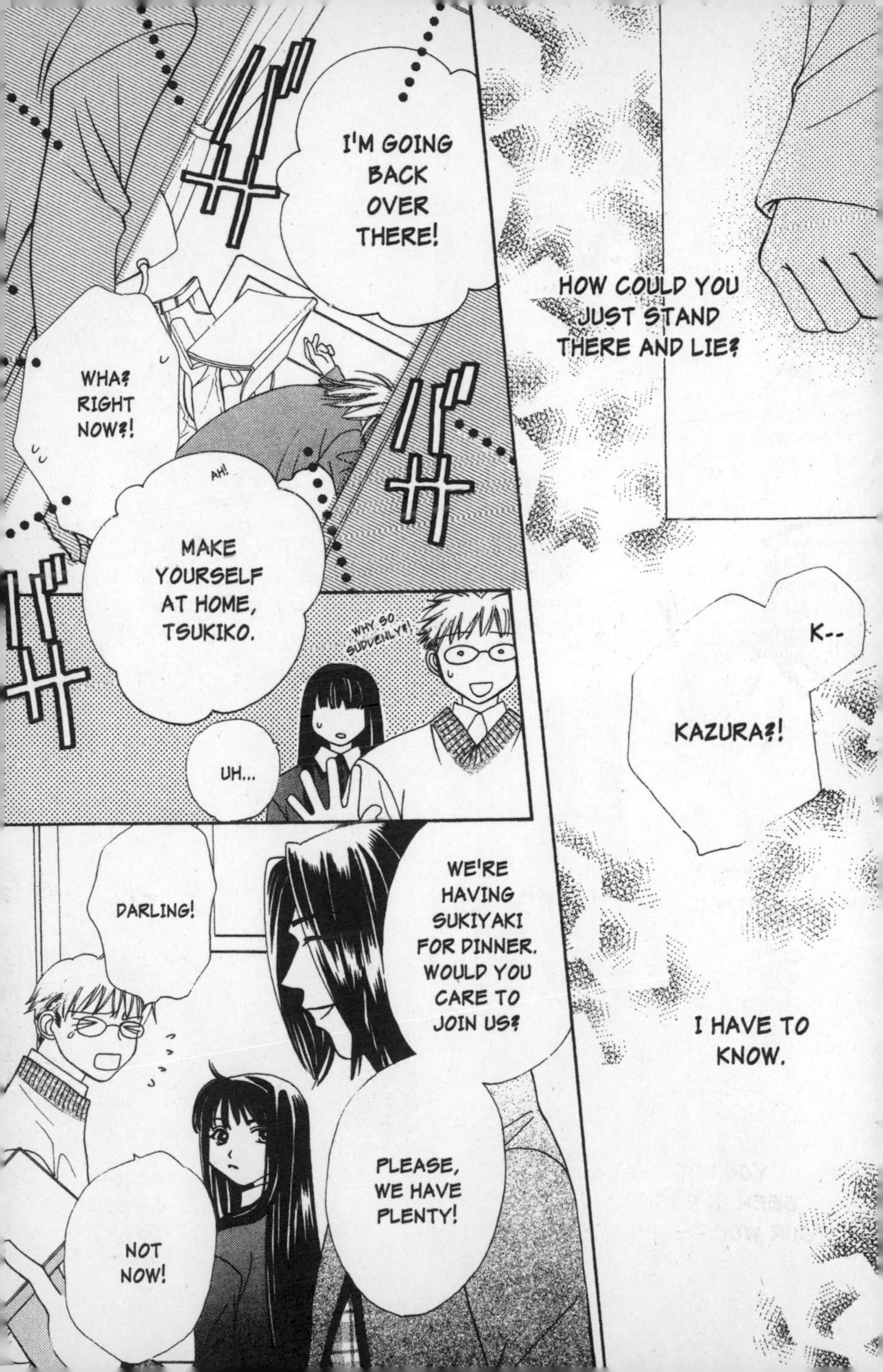
HOW COULD YOU JUST STAND THERE AND LIE?
K--
KAZURA?!
I HAVE TO KNOW.
I'M GOING BACK OVER THERE!
WHA? RIGHT NOW?!
AH!
MAKE YOURSELF AT HOME, TSUKIKO.
WHY SO SUDDENLY?!
UH...
WE'RE HAVING SUKIYAKI FOR DINNER. WOULD YOU CARE TO JOIN US?
DARLING!
PLEASE, WE HAVE PLENTY!
NOT NOW!

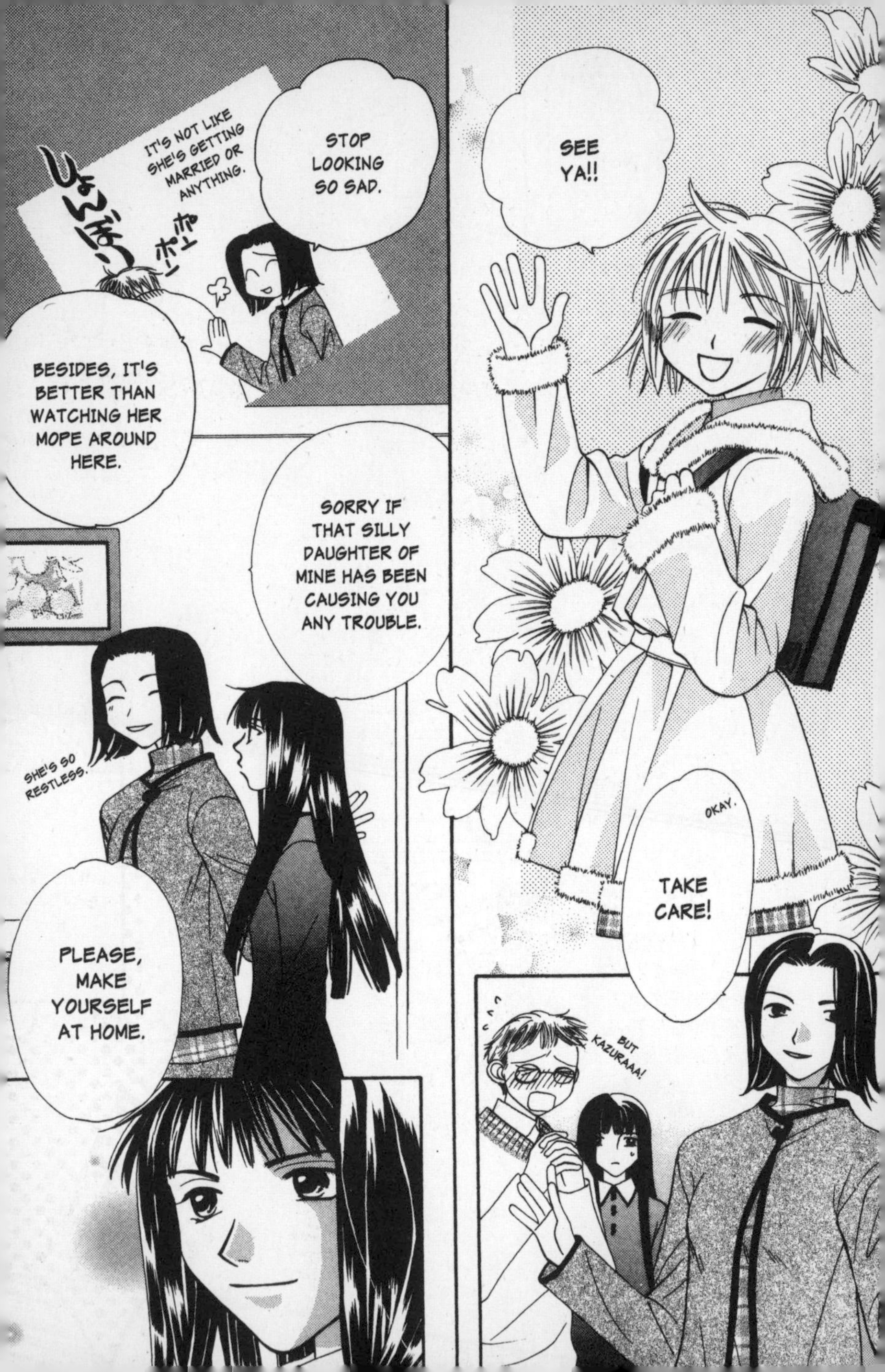
SEE YA!!
OKAY.
TAKE CARE!
BUT KAZURAAA!
IT'S NOT LIKE SHE'S GETTING MARRIED OR ANYTHING.
STOP LOOKING SO SAD.
しょんぼり
BESIDES, IT'S BETTER THAN WATCHING HER MOPE AROUND HERE.
SORRY IF THAT SILLY DAUGHTER OF MINE HAS BEEN CAUSING YOU ANY TROUBLE.
SHE'S SO RESTLESS.
PLEASE, MAKE YOURSELF AT HOME.

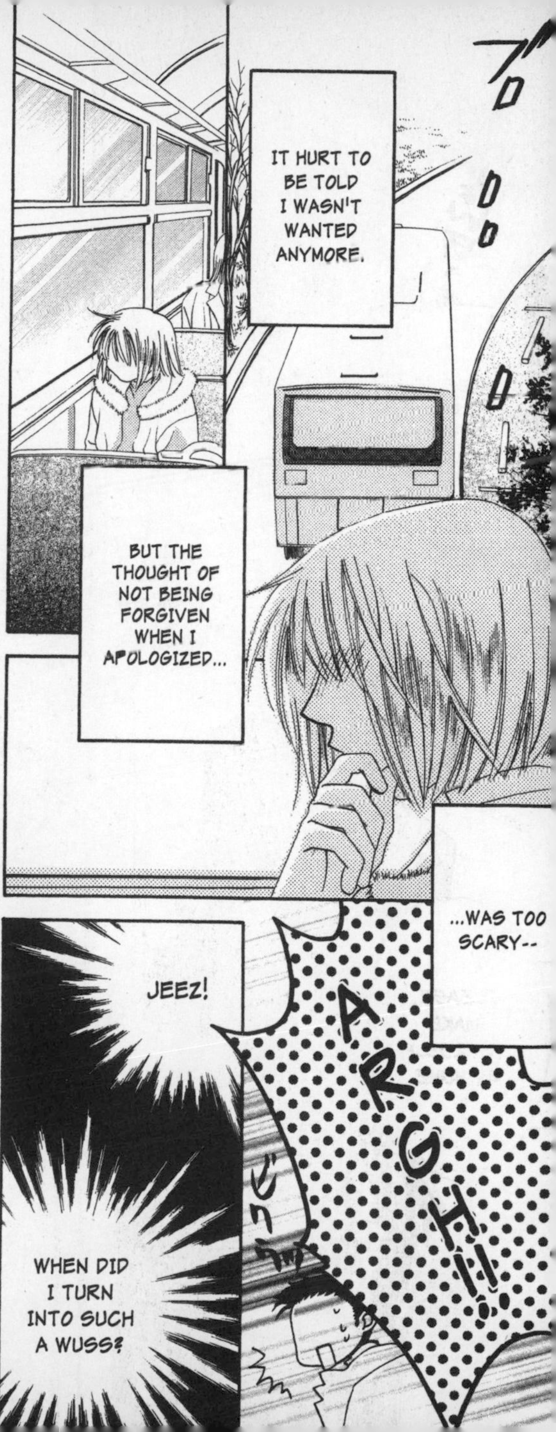
IT HURT TO BE TOLD I WASN'T WANTED ANYMORE.
BUT THE THOUGHT OF NOT BEING FORGIVEN WHEN I APOLOGIZED...
...WAS TOO SCARY--
ARGH!!
JEEZ!
WHEN DID I TURN INTO SUCH A WUSS?

IDIOTIC RAMBLINGS I

TO ALL MY READERS, NEW AND OLD...HI! THANKS FOR ALL YOUR SUPPORT. IT'S BECAUSE OF YOU THAT WE'VE MADE IT ALL THE WAY TO VOLUME FIVE. AND CAN YOU BELIEVE IT, THIS IS ALSO MY 20TH BOOK? I JUST WANT TO TELL YOU ALL...

I'M SO GRATEFUL!!

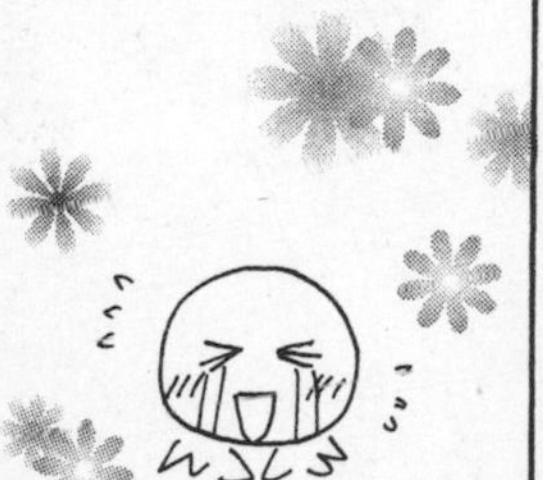

TO EVERYONE WHO'S CARED FOR ME, EVERYONE WHO'S HELPED ME, EVERYONE WHO'S KEPT AN EYE ON ME...

THANK YOU!!

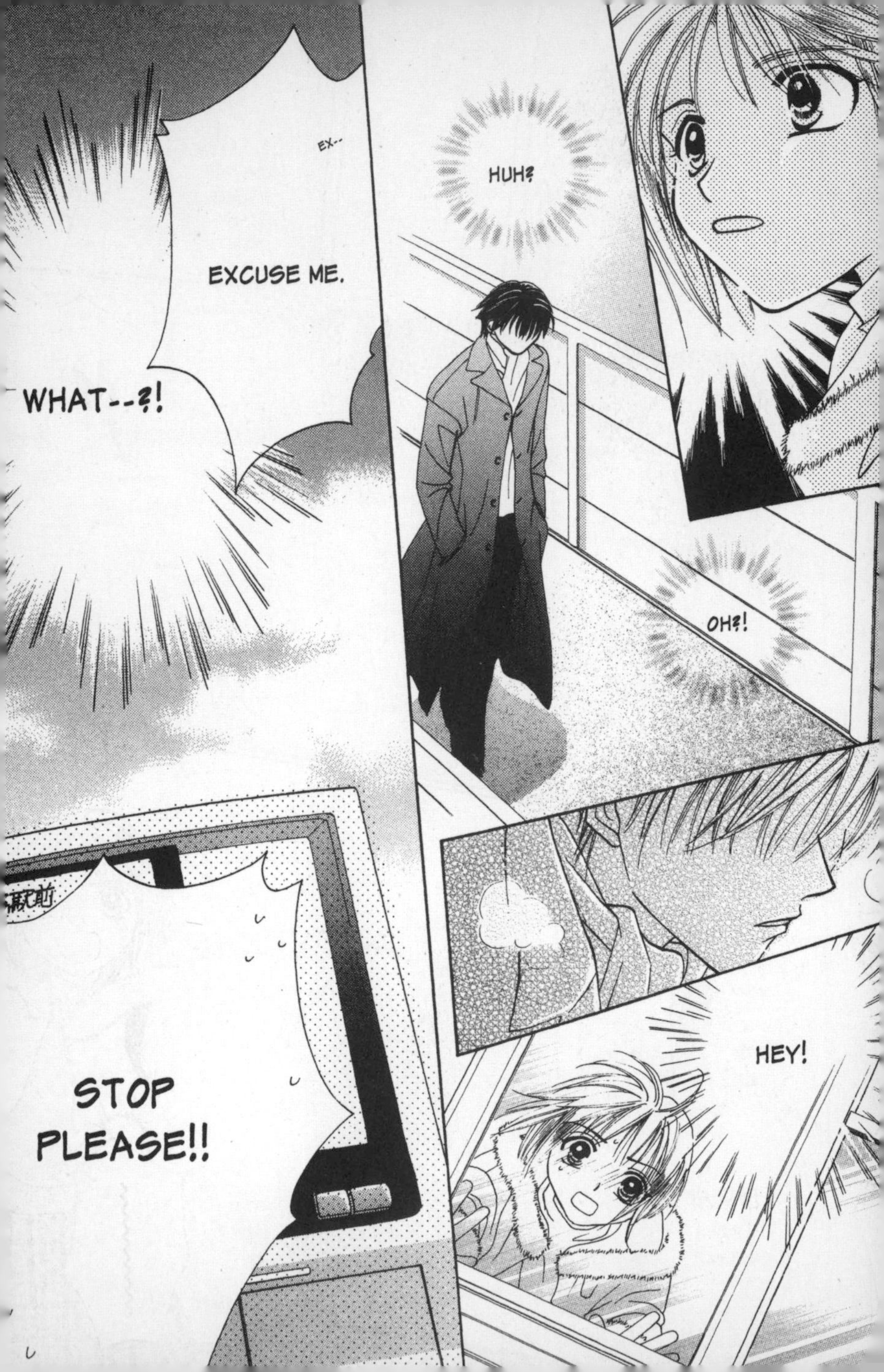
HUH?
OH?!
EX--
EXCUSE ME.
WHAT--?!
HEY!
STOP PLEASE!!

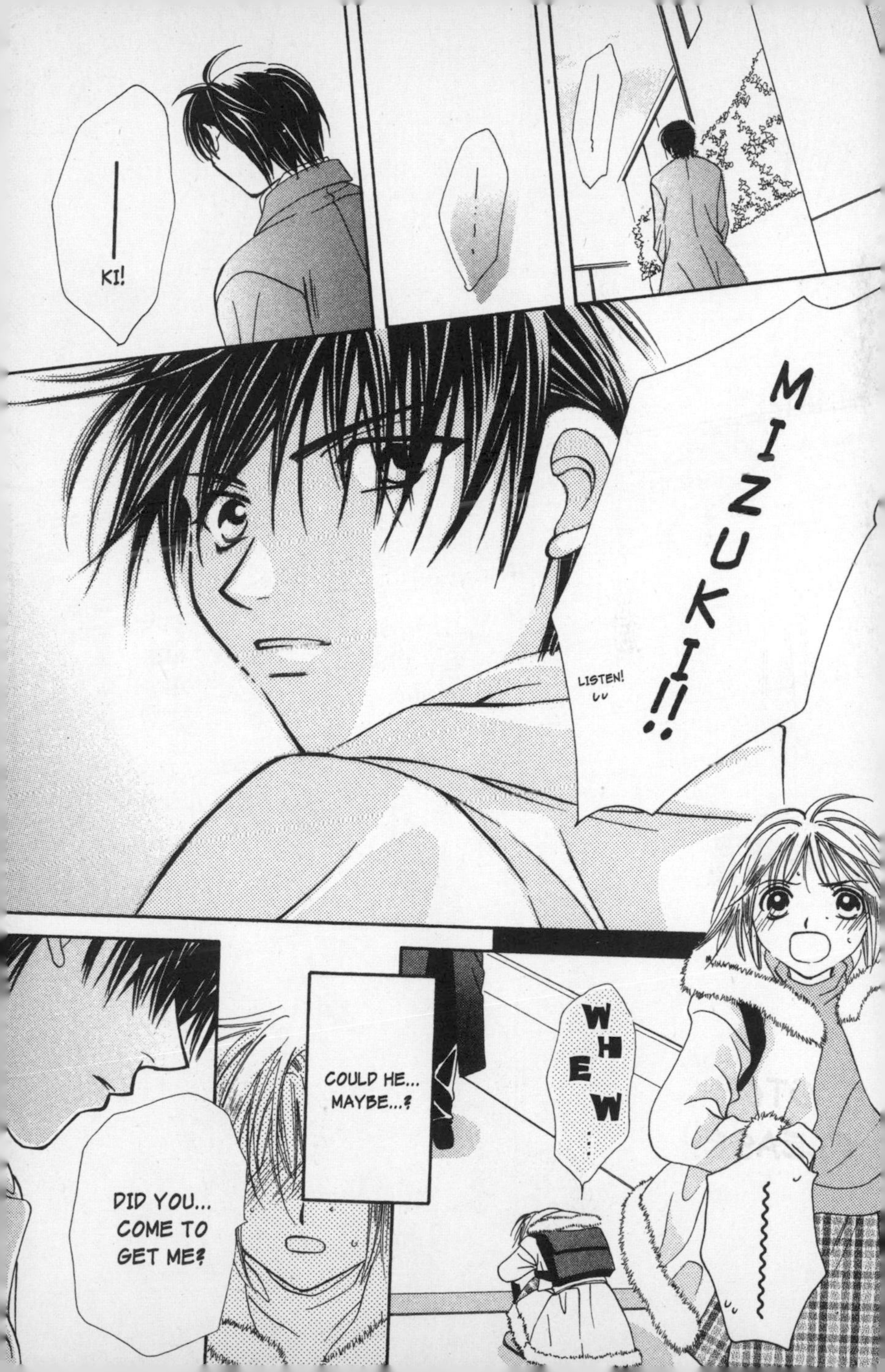
...
—KI!
MIZUKI!!
LISTEN!
WHEW...
COULD HE... MAYBE...?
DID YOU... COME TO GET ME?

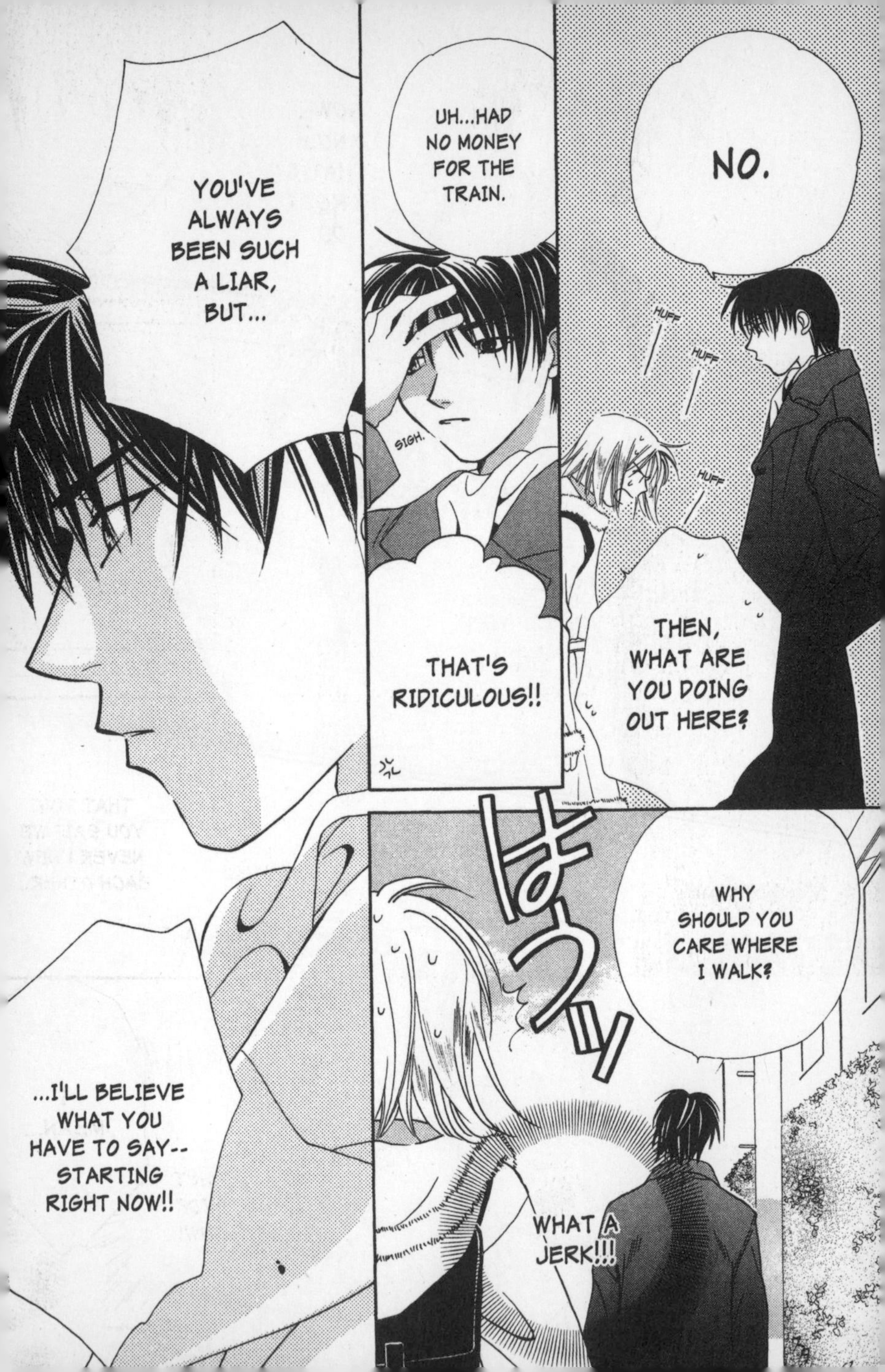
NO.
HUFF
HUFF
HUFF
THEN, WHAT ARE YOU DOING OUT HERE?
UH...HAD NO MONEY FOR THE TRAIN.
SIGH.
THAT'S RIDICULOUS!!
WHY SHOULD YOU CARE WHERE I WALK?
はっ
WHAT A JERK!!!
YOU'VE ALWAYS BEEN SUCH A LIAR, BUT...
...I'LL BELIEVE WHAT YOU HAVE TO SAY-- STARTING RIGHT NOW!!

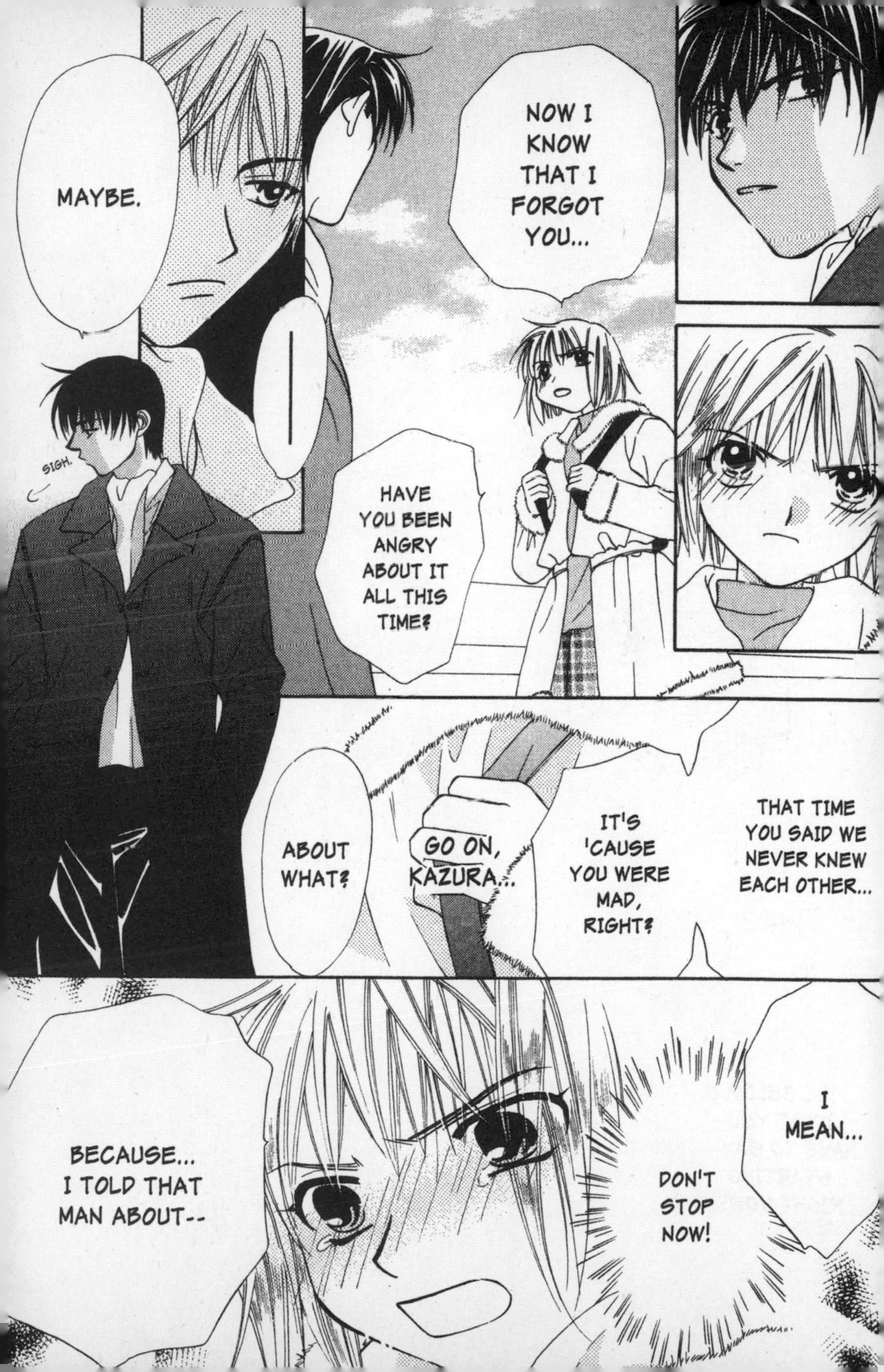
NOW I KNOW THAT I FORGOT YOU...
HAVE YOU BEEN ANGRY ABOUT IT ALL THIS TIME?
MAYBE.
SIGH.
THAT TIME YOU SAID WE NEVER KNEW EACH OTHER...
IT'S 'CAUSE YOU WERE MAD, RIGHT?
GO ON, KAZURA...
ABOUT WHAT?
I MEAN...
DON'T STOP NOW!
BECAUSE... I TOLD THAT MAN ABOUT--

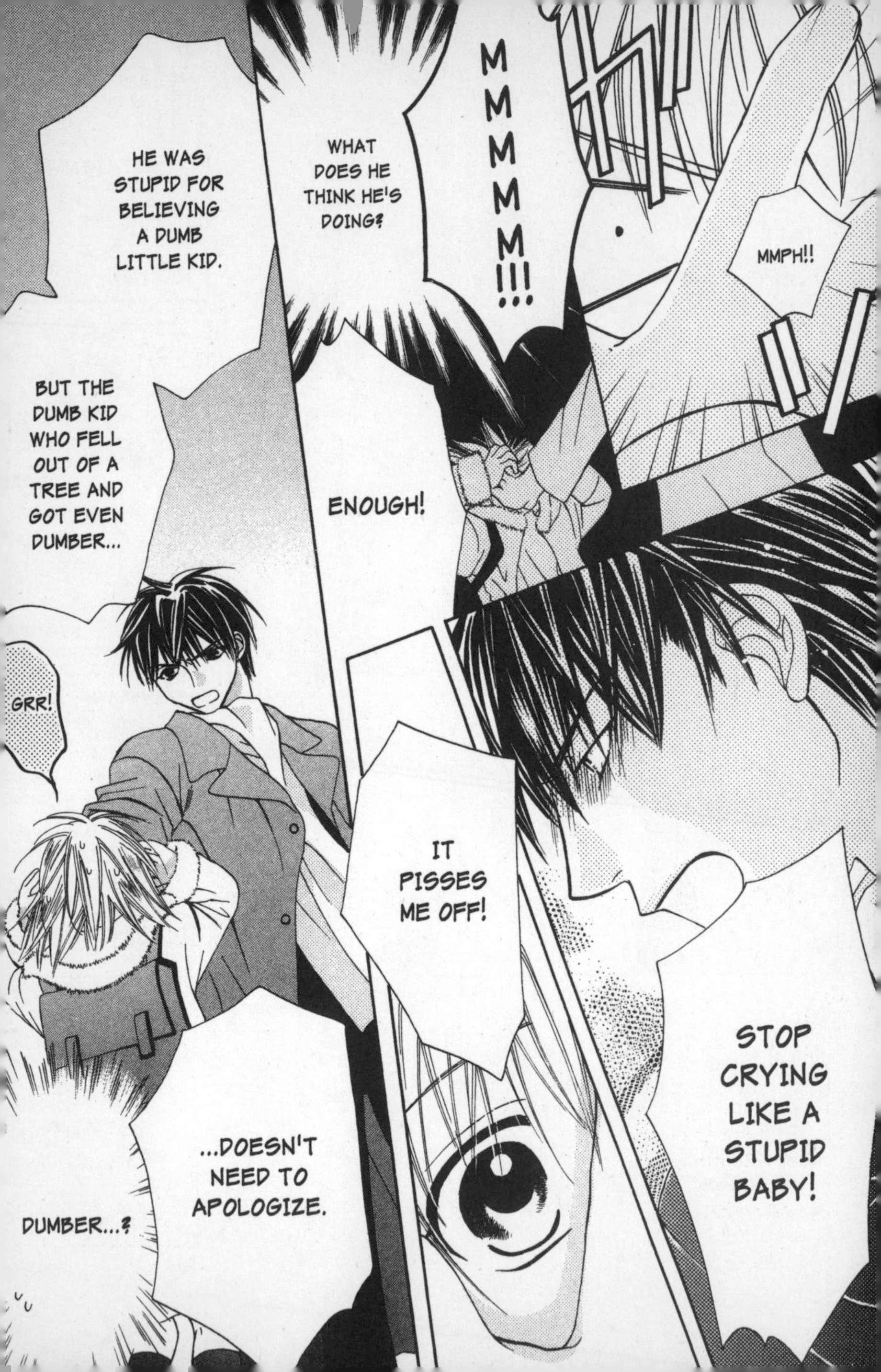
MMMMM!!!
MMPH!!
WHAT DOES HE THINK HE'S DOING?
HE WAS STUPID FOR BELIEVING A DUMB LITTLE KID.
ENOUGH!
IT PISSES ME OFF!
STOP CRYING LIKE A STUPID BABY!
BUT THE DUMB KID WHO FELL OUT OF A TREE AND GOT EVEN DUMBER...
GRR!
...DOESN'T NEED TO APOLOGIZE.
DUMBER...?

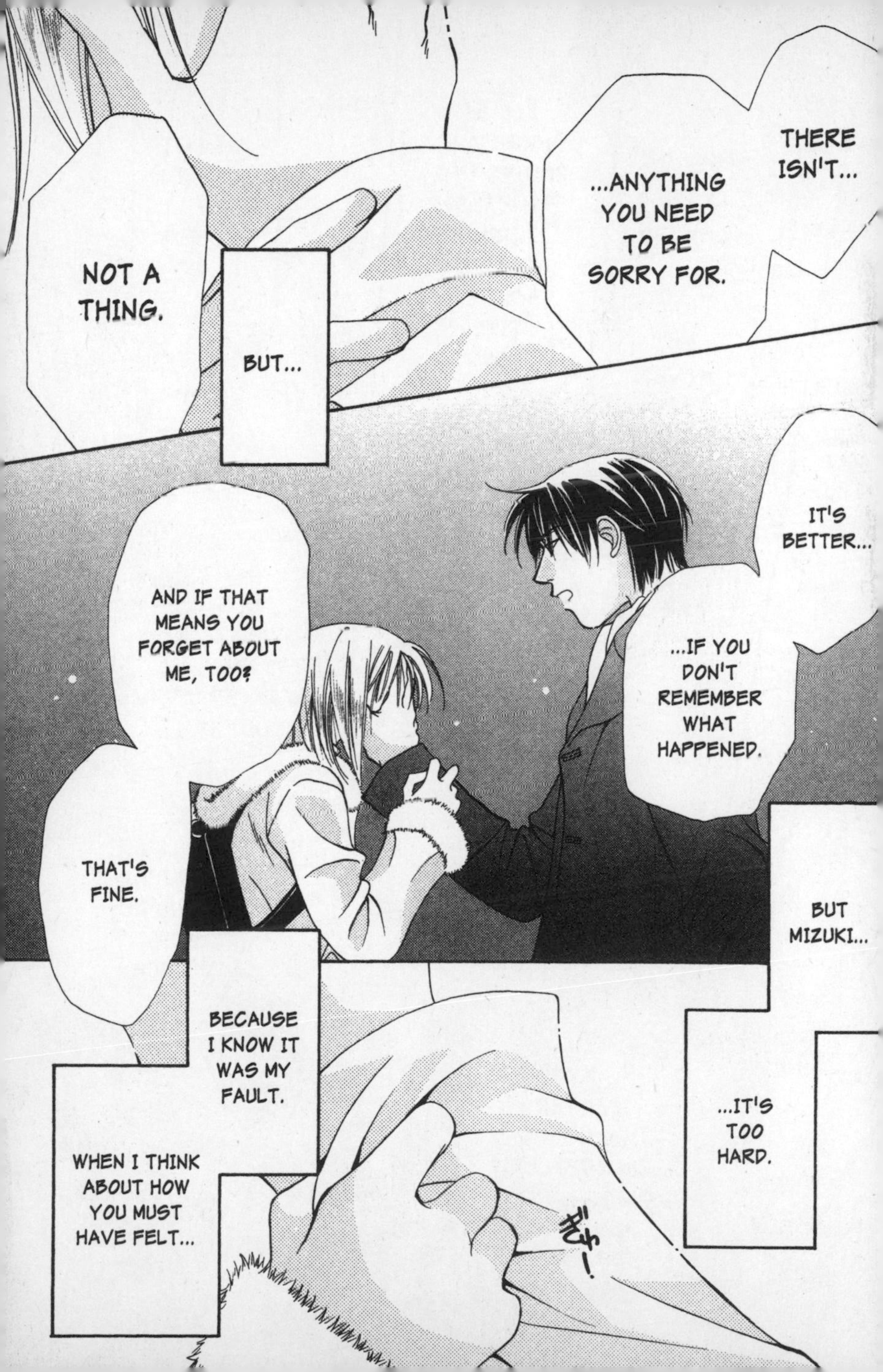
THERE ISN'T...
...ANYTHING YOU NEED TO BE SORRY FOR.
BUT...
NOT A THING.
IT'S BETTER...
...IF YOU DON'T REMEMBER WHAT HAPPENED.
AND IF THAT MEANS YOU FORGET ABOUT ME, TOO?
THAT'S FINE.
BUT MIZUKI...
...IT'S TOO HARD.
BECAUSE I KNOW IT WAS MY FAULT.
WHEN I THINK ABOUT HOW YOU MUST HAVE FELT...

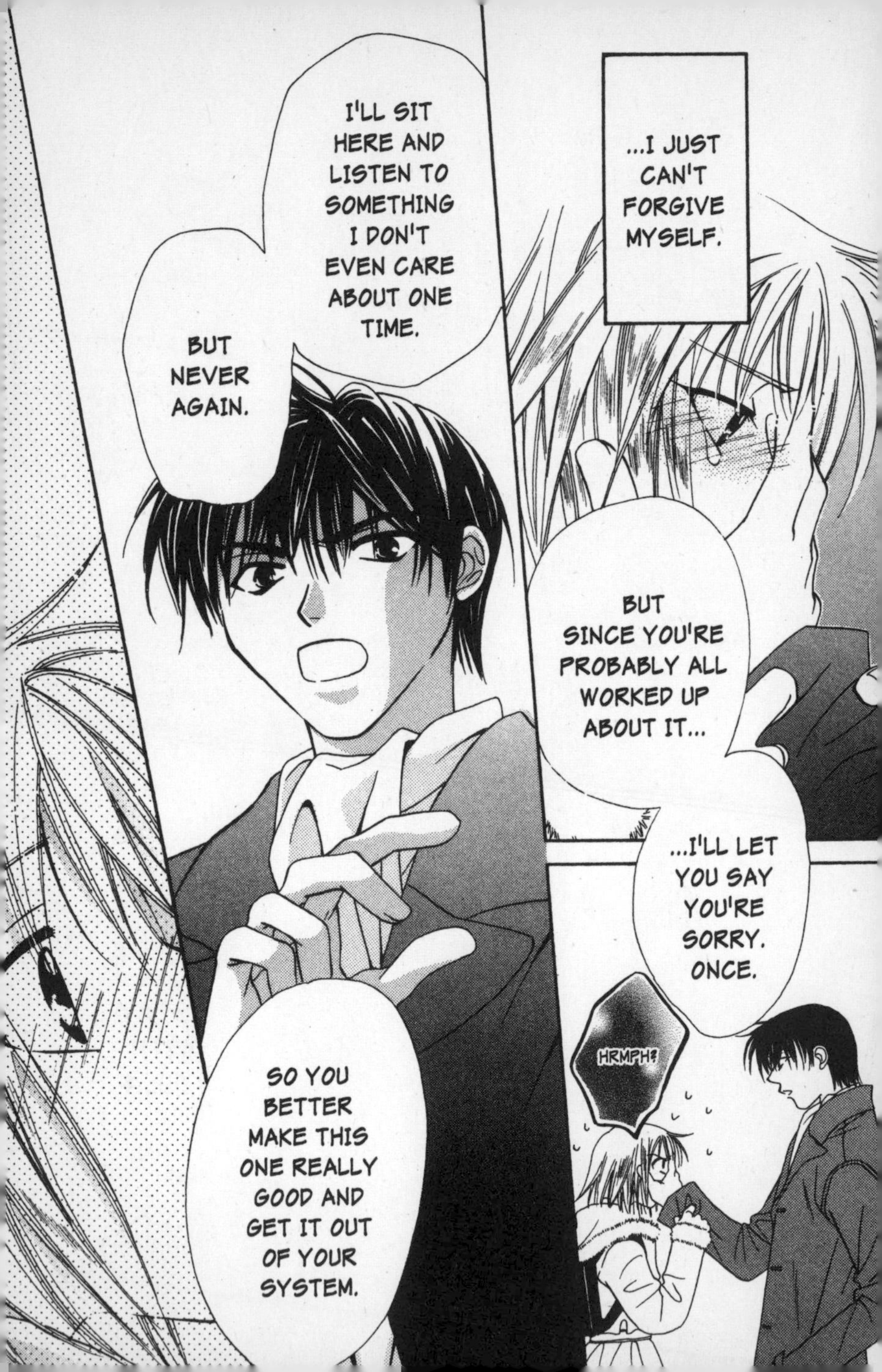
...I JUST CAN'T FORGIVE MYSELF.
BUT SINCE YOU'RE PROBABLY ALL WORKED UP ABOUT IT...
...I'LL LET YOU SAY YOU'RE SORRY. ONCE.
HRMPH?
I'LL SIT HERE AND LISTEN TO SOMETHING I DON'T EVEN CARE ABOUT ONE TIME.
BUT NEVER AGAIN.
SO YOU BETTER MAKE THIS ONE REALLY GOOD AND GET IT OUT OF YOUR SYSTEM.

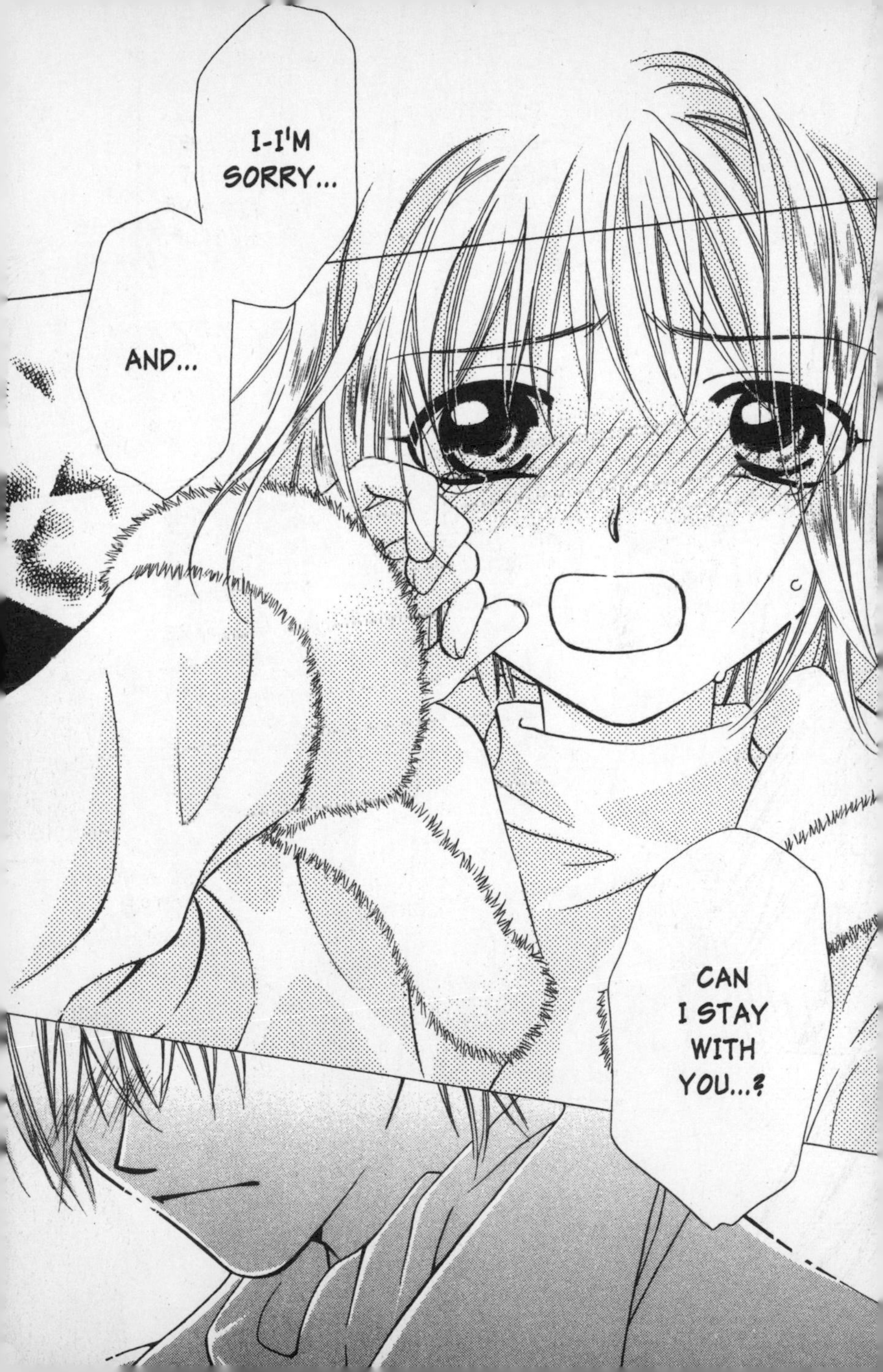
I-I'M SORRY...
AND...
CAN I STAY WITH YOU...?

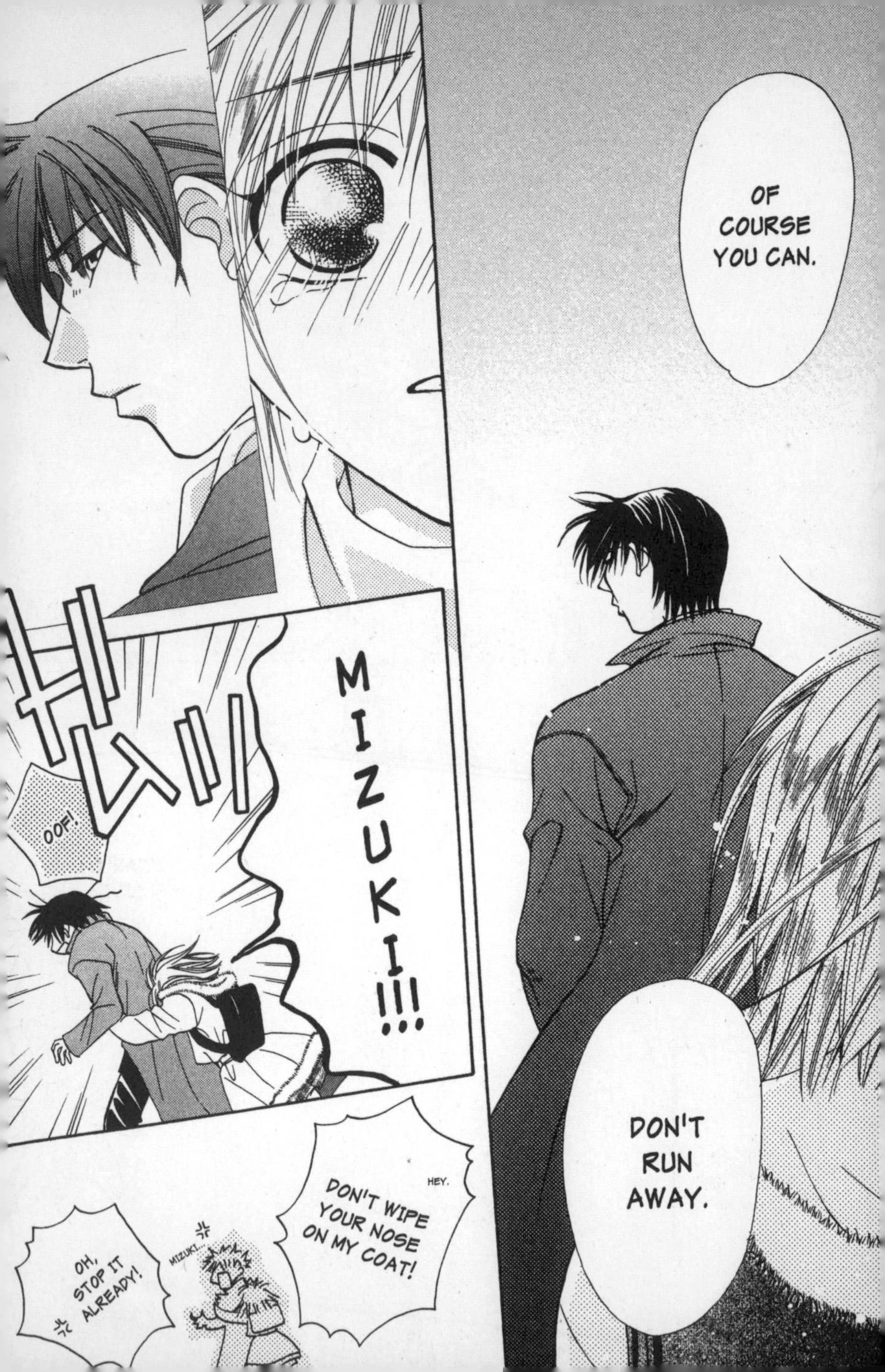
OF COURSE YOU CAN.
DON'T RUN AWAY.
MIZUKI!!!
OOF!
HEY.
DON'T WIPE YOUR NOSE ON MY COAT!
MIZUKI...
OH, STOP IT ALREADY!

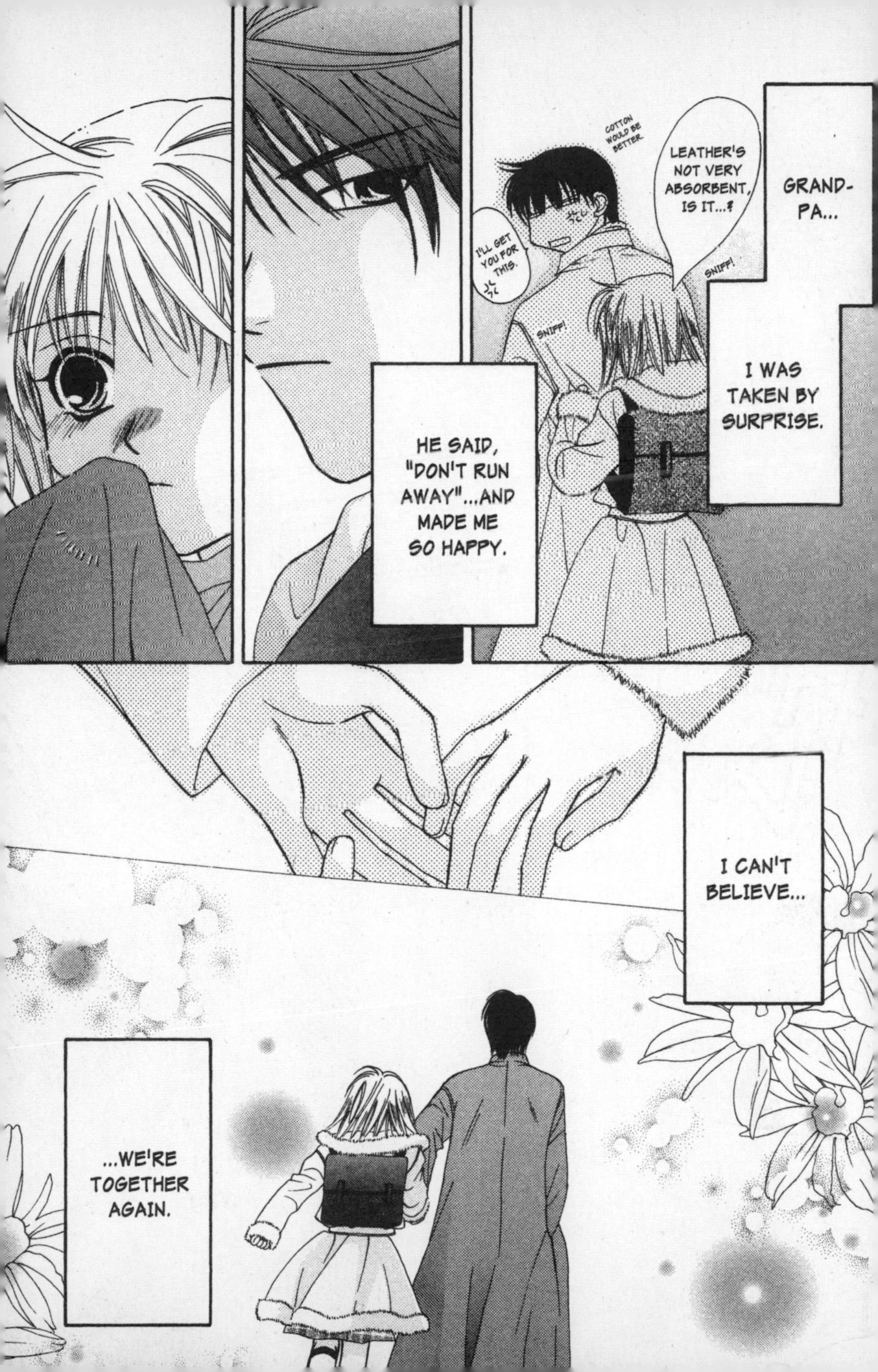
GRAND-PA...
LEATHER'S NOT VERY ABSORBENT, IS IT...?
COTTON WOULD BE BETTER.
SNIFF!
I WAS TAKEN BY SURPRISE.
I'LL GET YOU FOR THIS.
SNIFF!
HE SAID, "DON'T RUN AWAY"...AND MADE ME SO HAPPY.
I CAN'T BELIEVE...
...WE'RE TOGETHER AGAIN.

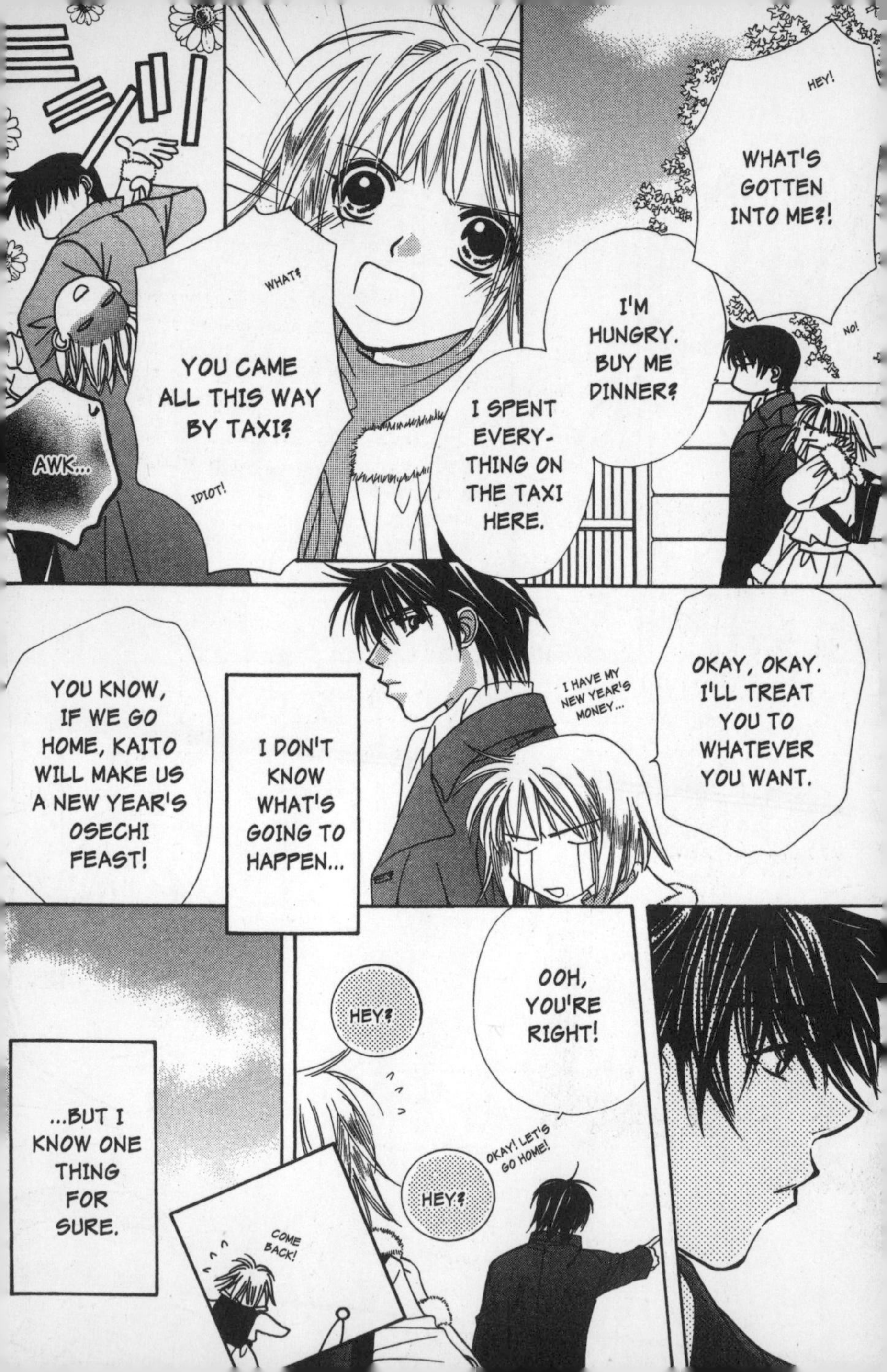
HEY!
WHAT'S GOTTEN INTO ME?!
NO!
I'M HUNGRY. BUY ME DINNER?
I SPENT EVERYTHING ON THE TAXI HERE.
WHAT?
YOU CAME ALL THIS WAY BY TAXI?
IDIOT!
AWK...
OKAY, OKAY. I'LL TREAT YOU TO WHATEVER YOU WANT.
I HAVE MY NEW YEAR'S MONEY...
YOU KNOW, IF WE GO HOME, KAITO WILL MAKE US A NEW YEAR'S OSECHI FEAST!
I DON'T KNOW WHAT'S GOING TO HAPPEN...
OOH, YOU'RE RIGHT!
HEY?
OKAY! LET'S GO HOME!
HEY?
COME BACK!
...BUT I KNOW ONE THING FOR SURE.

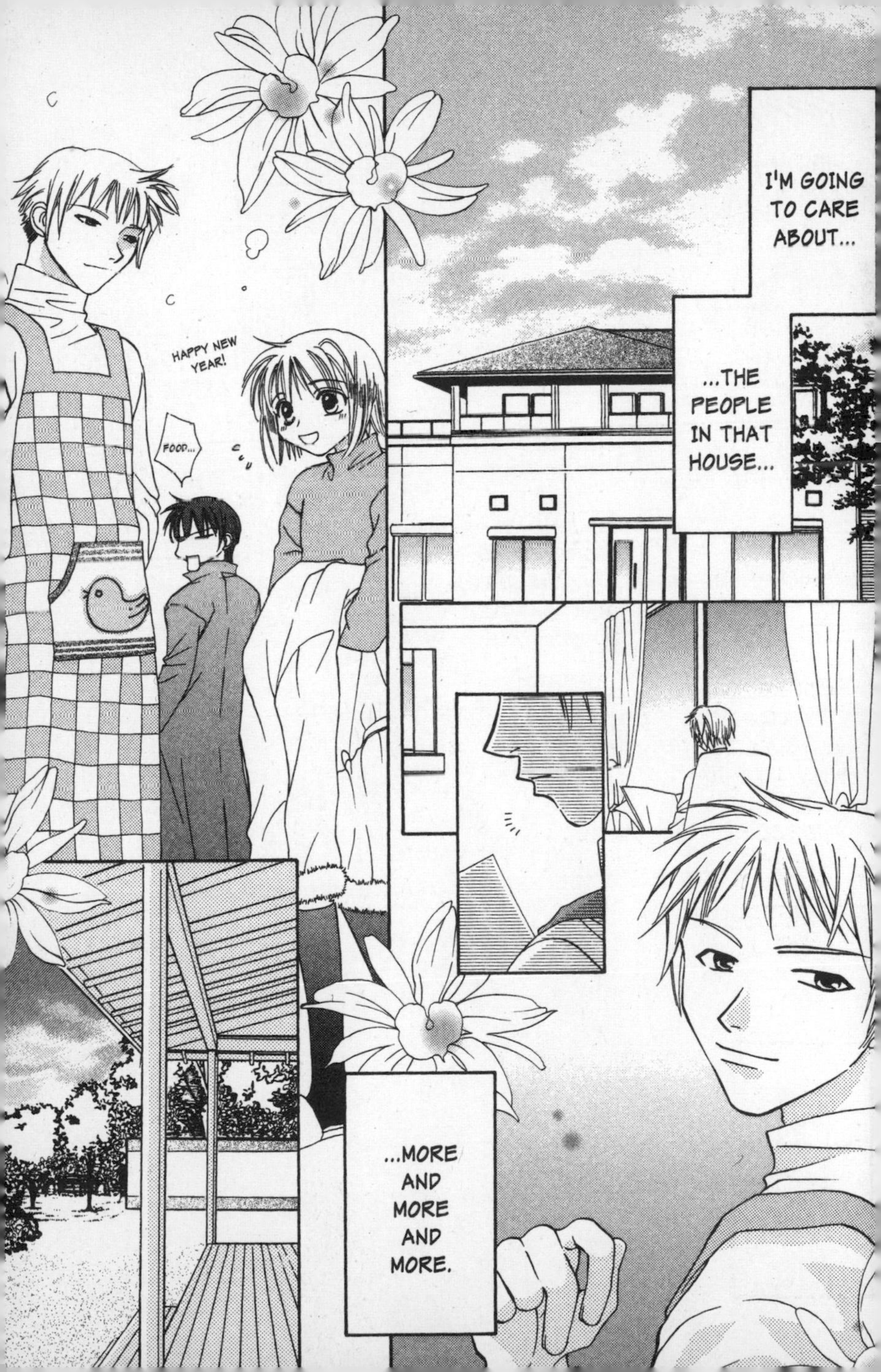
I'M GOING TO CARE ABOUT...
...THE PEOPLE IN THAT HOUSE...
HAPPY NEW YEAR!
FOOD...
...MORE AND MORE AND MORE.

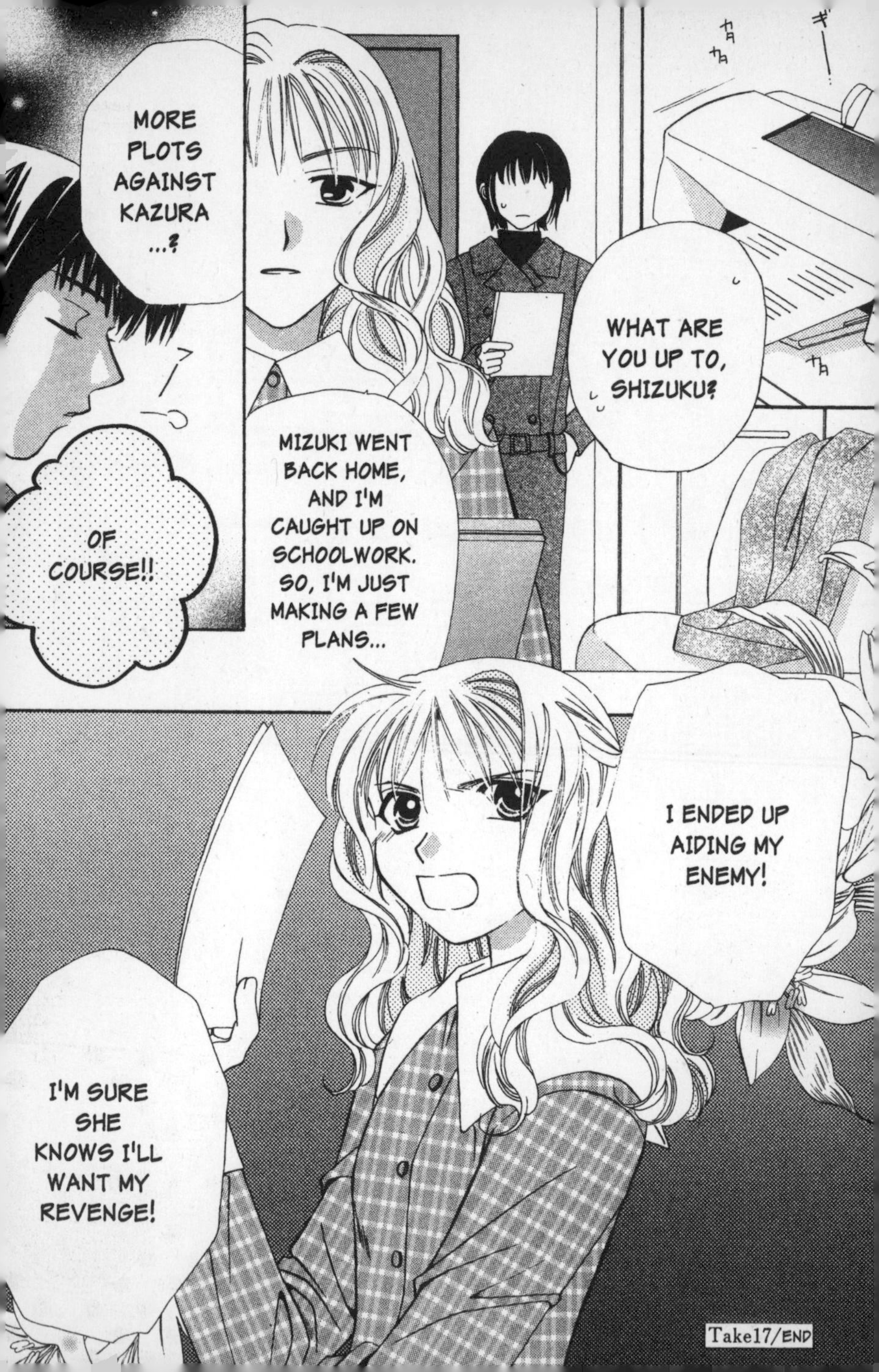ギー
カタカタ
WHAT ARE YOU UP TO, SHIZUKU?
MIZUKI WENT BACK HOME, AND I'M CAUGHT UP ON SCHOOLWORK. SO, I'M JUST MAKING A FEW PLANS...
MORE PLOTS AGAINST KAZURA ...?
OF COURSE!!
I ENDED UP AIDING MY ENEMY!
I'M SURE SHE KNOWS I'LL WANT MY REVENGE!
Take17/END

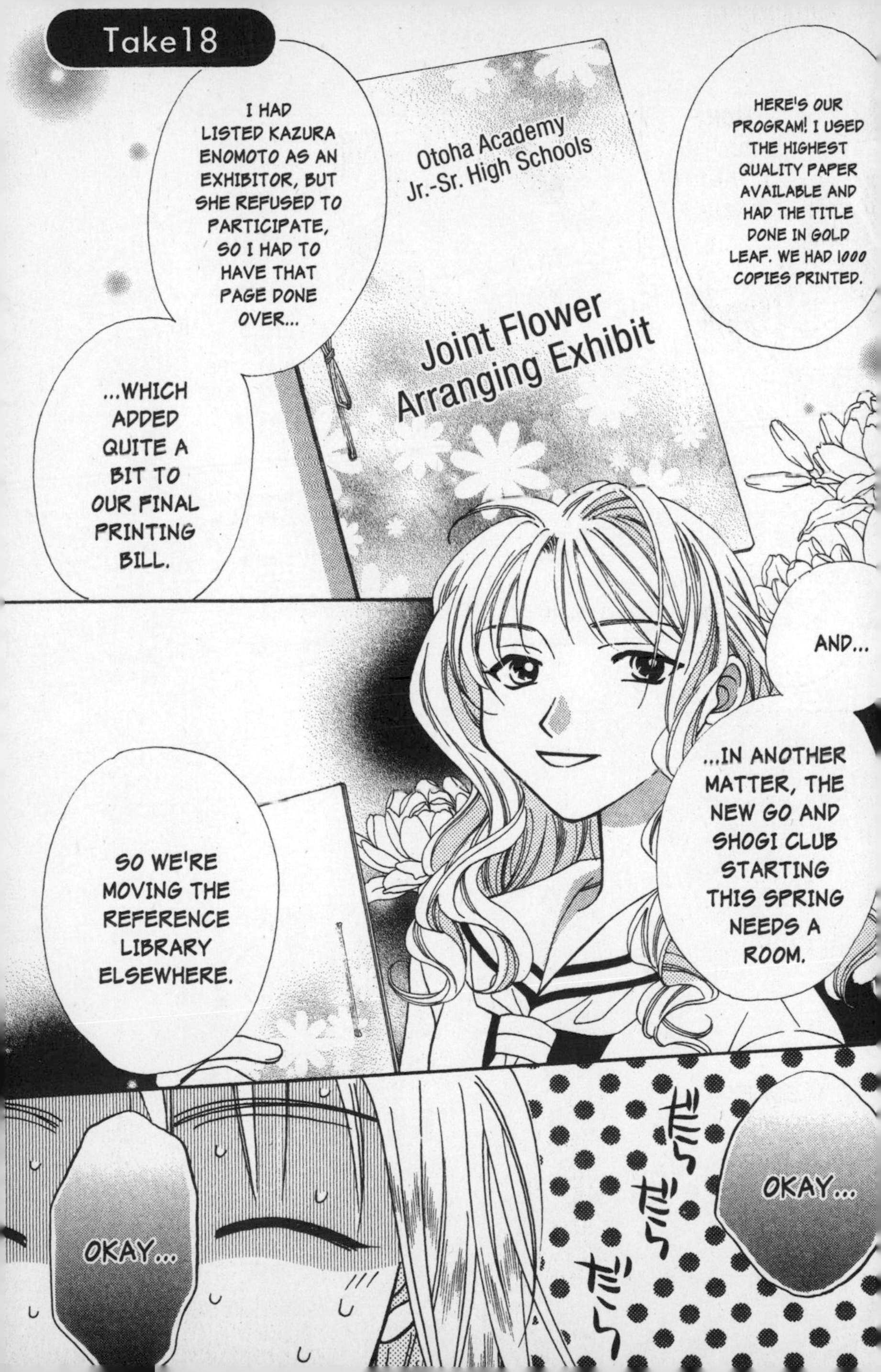
HERE'S OUR PROGRAM! I USED THE HIGHEST QUALITY PAPER AVAILABLE AND HAD THE TITLE DONE IN GOLD LEAF. WE HAD 1000 COPIES PRINTED.
Otoha Academy Jr.-Sr. High Schools
Joint Flower Arranging Exhibit
I HAD LISTED KAZURA ENOMOTO AS AN EXHIBITOR, BUT SHE REFUSED TO PARTICIPATE, SO I HAD TO HAVE THAT PAGE DONE OVER...
...WHICH ADDED QUITE A BIT TO OUR FINAL PRINTING BILL.
AND...
...IN ANOTHER MATTER, THE NEW GO AND SHOGI CLUB STARTING THIS SPRING NEEDS A ROOM.
SO WE'RE MOVING THE REFERENCE LIBRARY ELSEWHERE.
OKAY...
だらだらだら
OKAY...

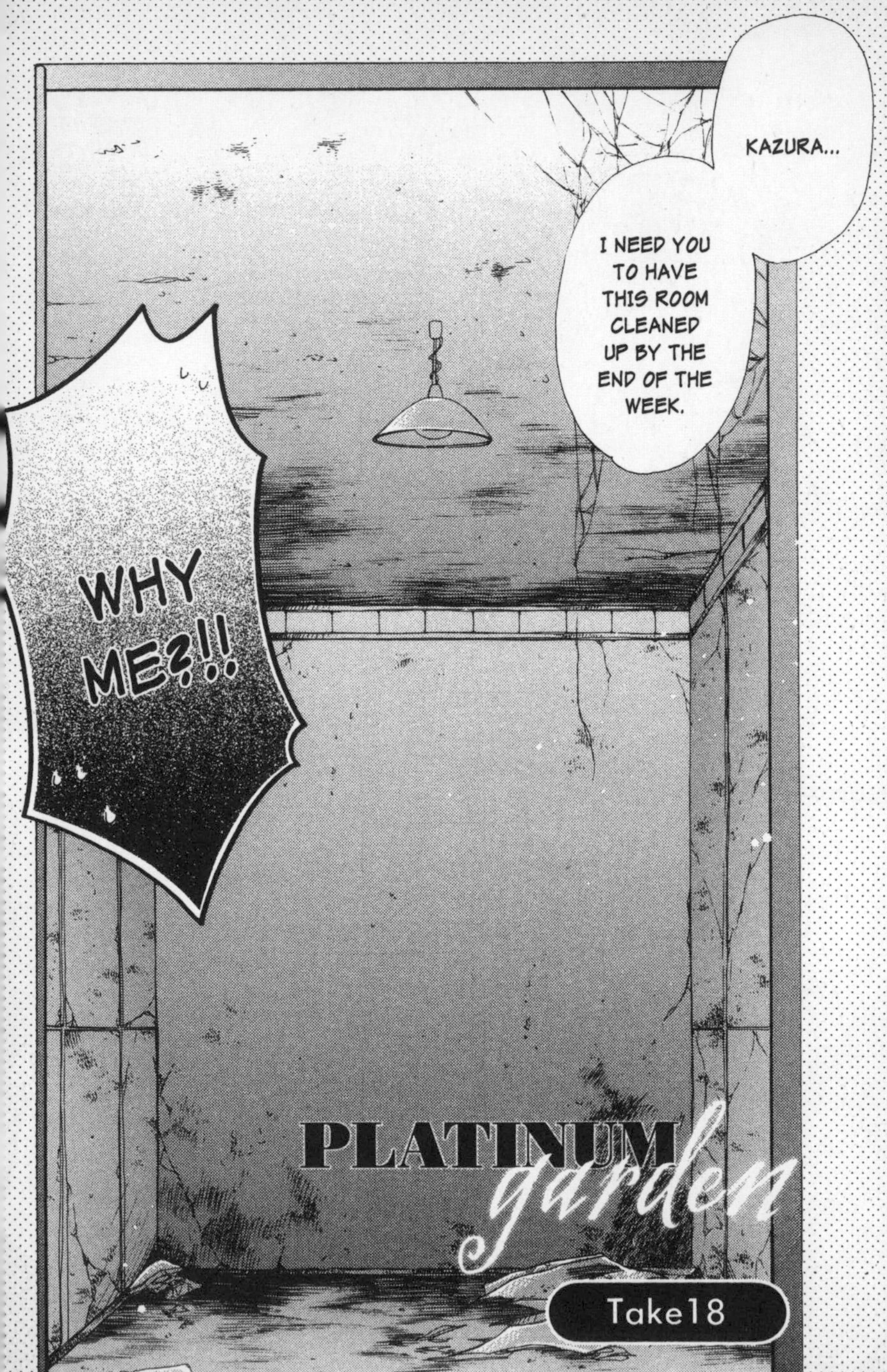
KAZURA...
I NEED YOU TO HAVE THIS ROOM CLEANED UP BY THE END OF THE WEEK.
WHY ME?!!
PLATINUM garden
Take18

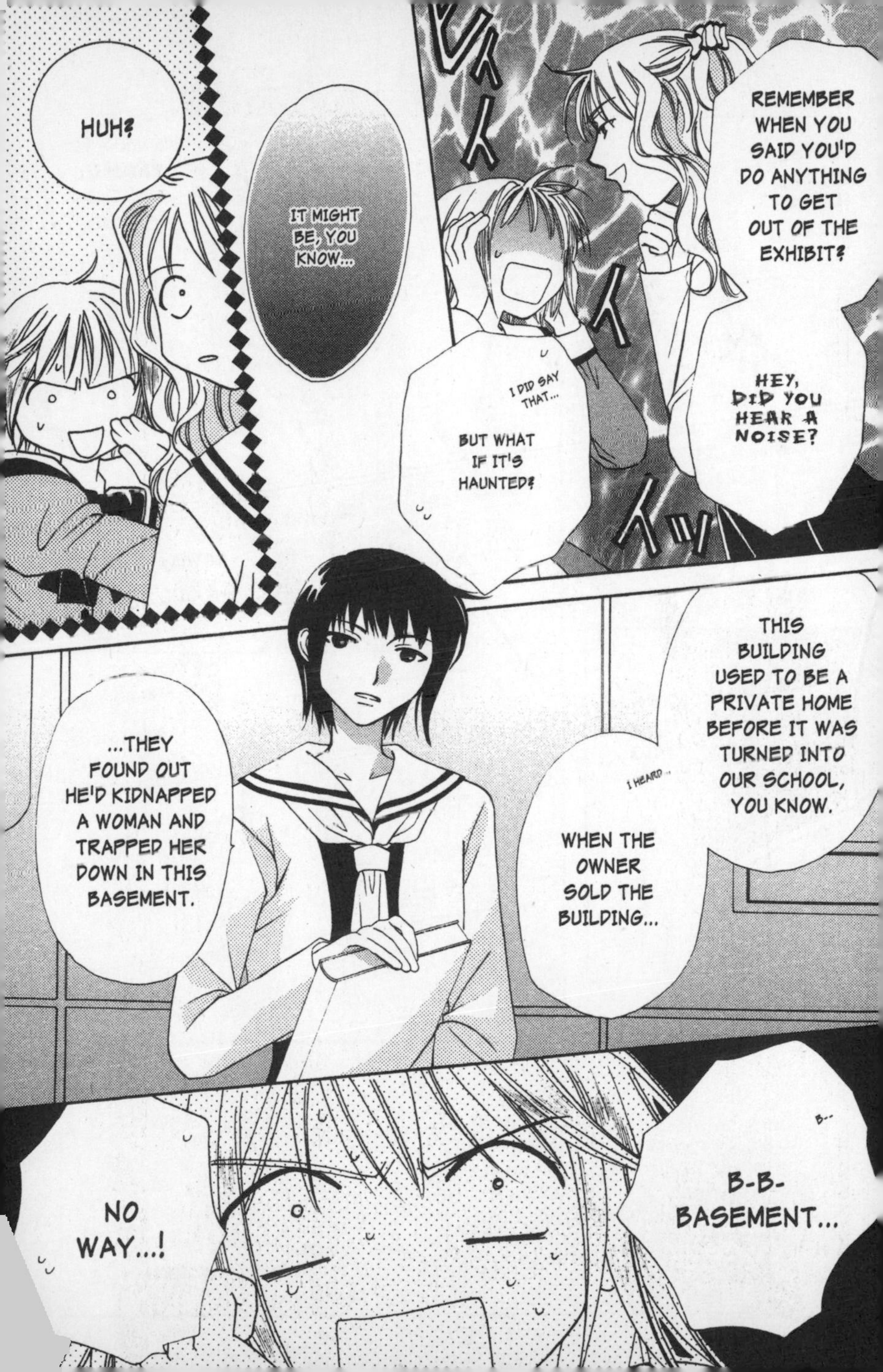
REMEMBER WHEN YOU SAID YOU'D DO ANYTHING TO GET OUT OF THE EXHIBIT?
HEY, DID YOU HEAR A NOISE?
I DID SAY THAT...
BUT WHAT IF IT'S HAUNTED?
IT MIGHT BE, YOU KNOW...
HUH?
THIS BUILDING USED TO BE A PRIVATE HOME BEFORE IT WAS TURNED INTO OUR SCHOOL, YOU KNOW.
I HEARD...
WHEN THE OWNER SOLD THE BUILDING...
...THEY FOUND OUT HE'D KIDNAPPED A WOMAN AND TRAPPED HER DOWN IN THIS BASEMENT.
B-..
B-B-BASEMENT...
NO WAY...!

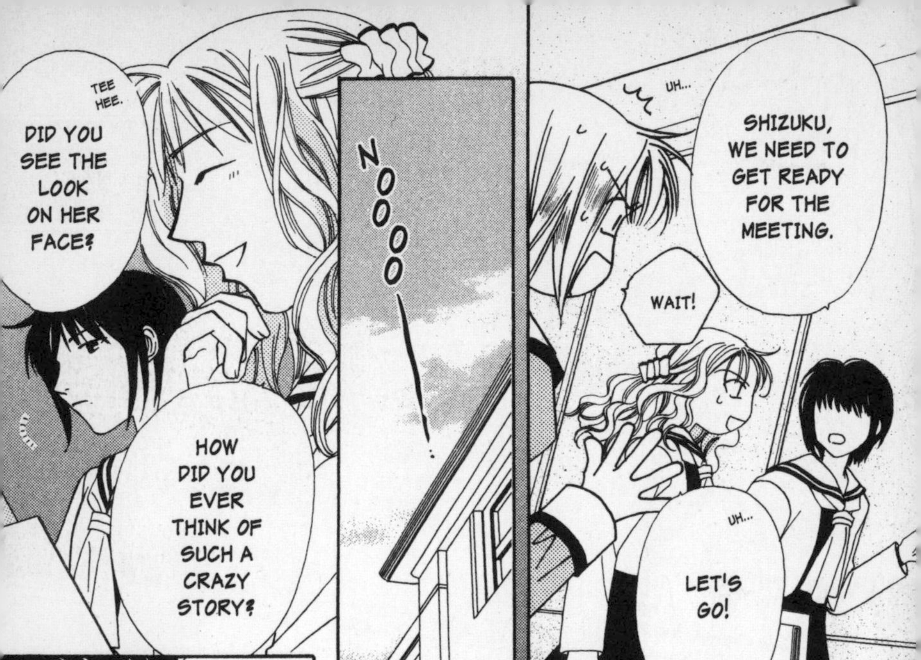
SHIZUKU, WE NEED TO GET READY FOR THE MEETING.
UH...
WAIT!
UH...
LET'S GO!
REMEMBER! YOU HAVE ONE WEEK!
BUT!
HEY!
HAVE FUN!
NOOOO—!
TEE HEE.
DID YOU SEE THE LOOK ON HER FACE?
HOW DID YOU EVER THINK OF SUCH A CRAZY STORY?
I DIDN'T. IT'S TRUE.
Random History You Don't Know vol. 14
WHA?!

FUJITA'S SUMMER, 2002

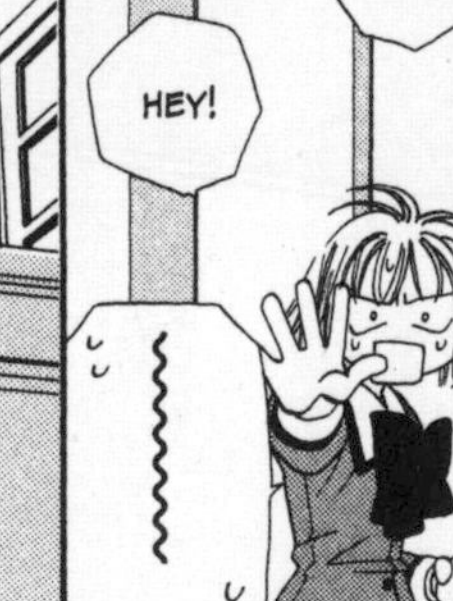
COFF...
UHHH...

I WAS REALLY SICK THIS SUMMER FOR THE FIRST TIME IN AGES. NORMALLY, I NEVER GET SICK AT ALL, SO I WAS PRETTY WORRIED...BUT I'M BACK TO MY USUAL TOUGH SELF! PLEASE TAKE CARE OF YOURSELVES AND STAY WELL!

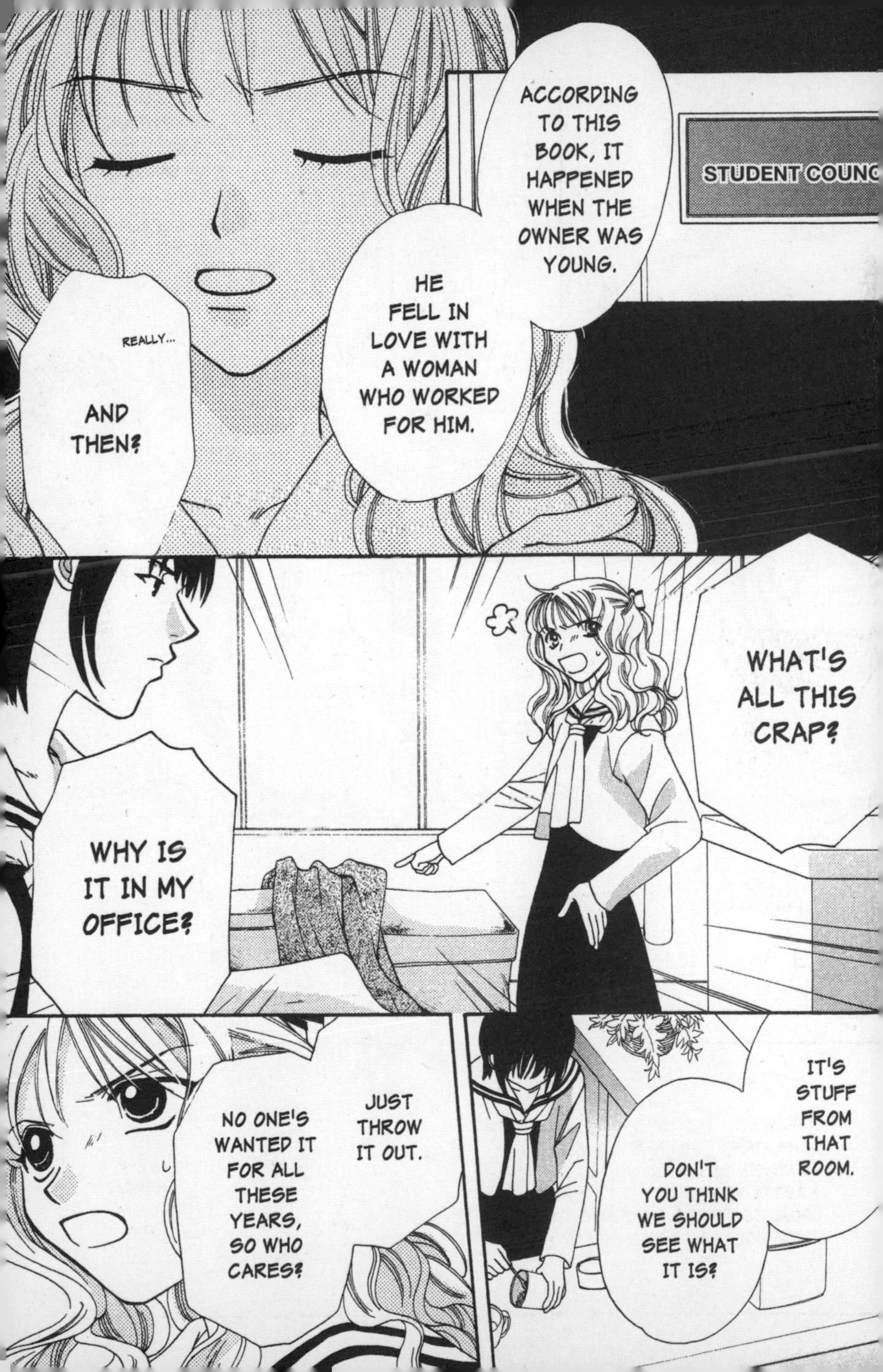
ACCORDING TO THIS BOOK, IT HAPPENED WHEN THE OWNER WAS YOUNG.
STUDENT COUNC
HE FELL IN LOVE WITH A WOMAN WHO WORKED FOR HIM.
REALLY...
AND THEN?
WHAT'S ALL THIS CRAP?
WHY IS IT IN MY OFFICE?
IT'S STUFF FROM THAT ROOM.
DON'T YOU THINK WE SHOULD SEE WHAT IT IS?
JUST THROW IT OUT.
NO ONE'S WANTED IT FOR ALL THESE YEARS, SO WHO CARES?

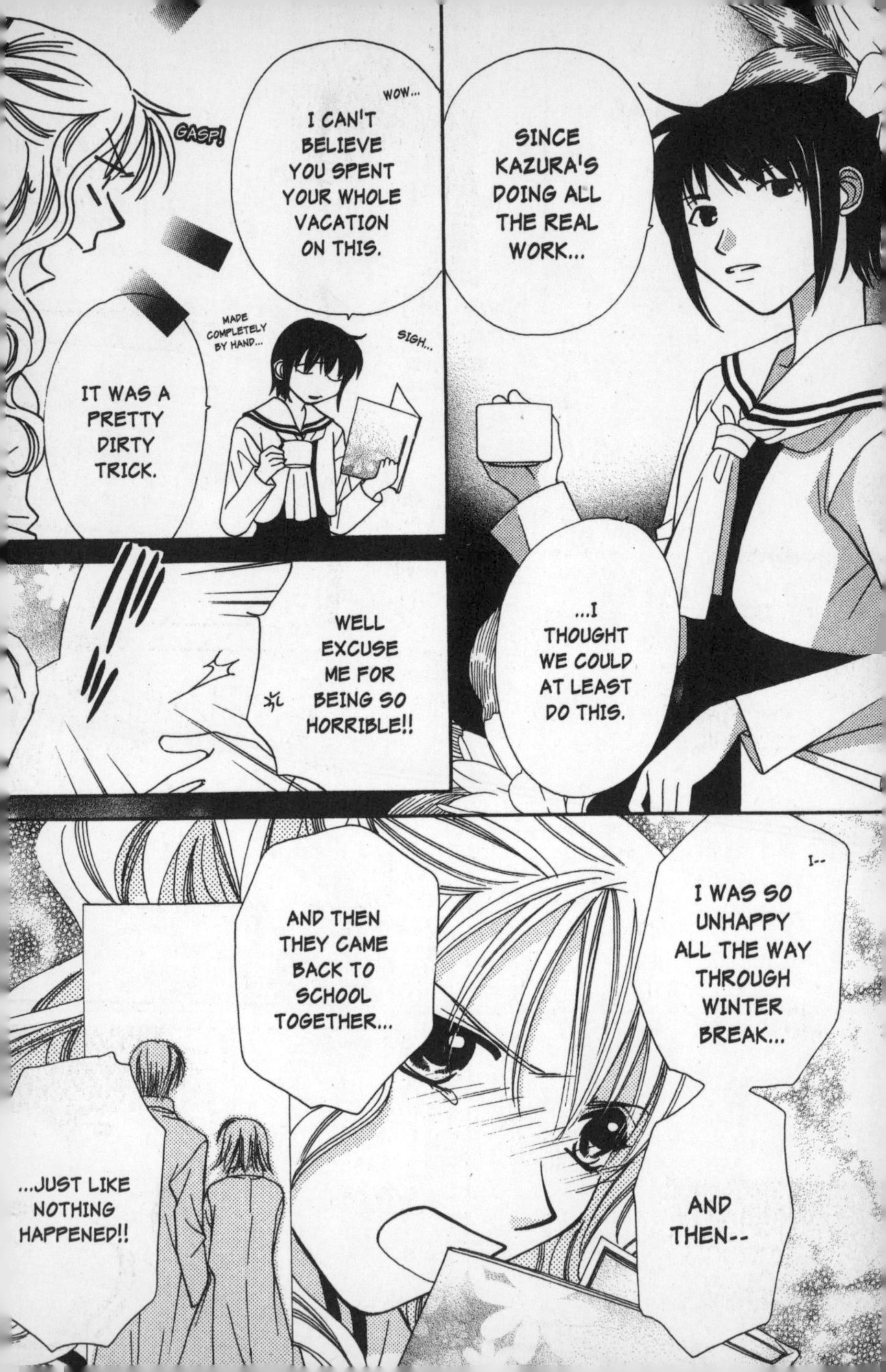
SINCE KAZURA'S DOING ALL THE REAL WORK...
...I THOUGHT WE COULD AT LEAST DO THIS.
WOW...
I CAN'T BELIEVE YOU SPENT YOUR WHOLE VACATION ON THIS.
SIGH...
GASP!
MADE COMPLETELY BY HAND...
IT WAS A PRETTY DIRTY TRICK.
WELL EXCUSE ME FOR BEING SO HORRIBLE!!
I--
I WAS SO UNHAPPY ALL THE WAY THROUGH WINTER BREAK...
AND THEN--
AND THEN THEY CAME BACK TO SCHOOL TOGETHER...
...JUST LIKE NOTHING HAPPENED!!

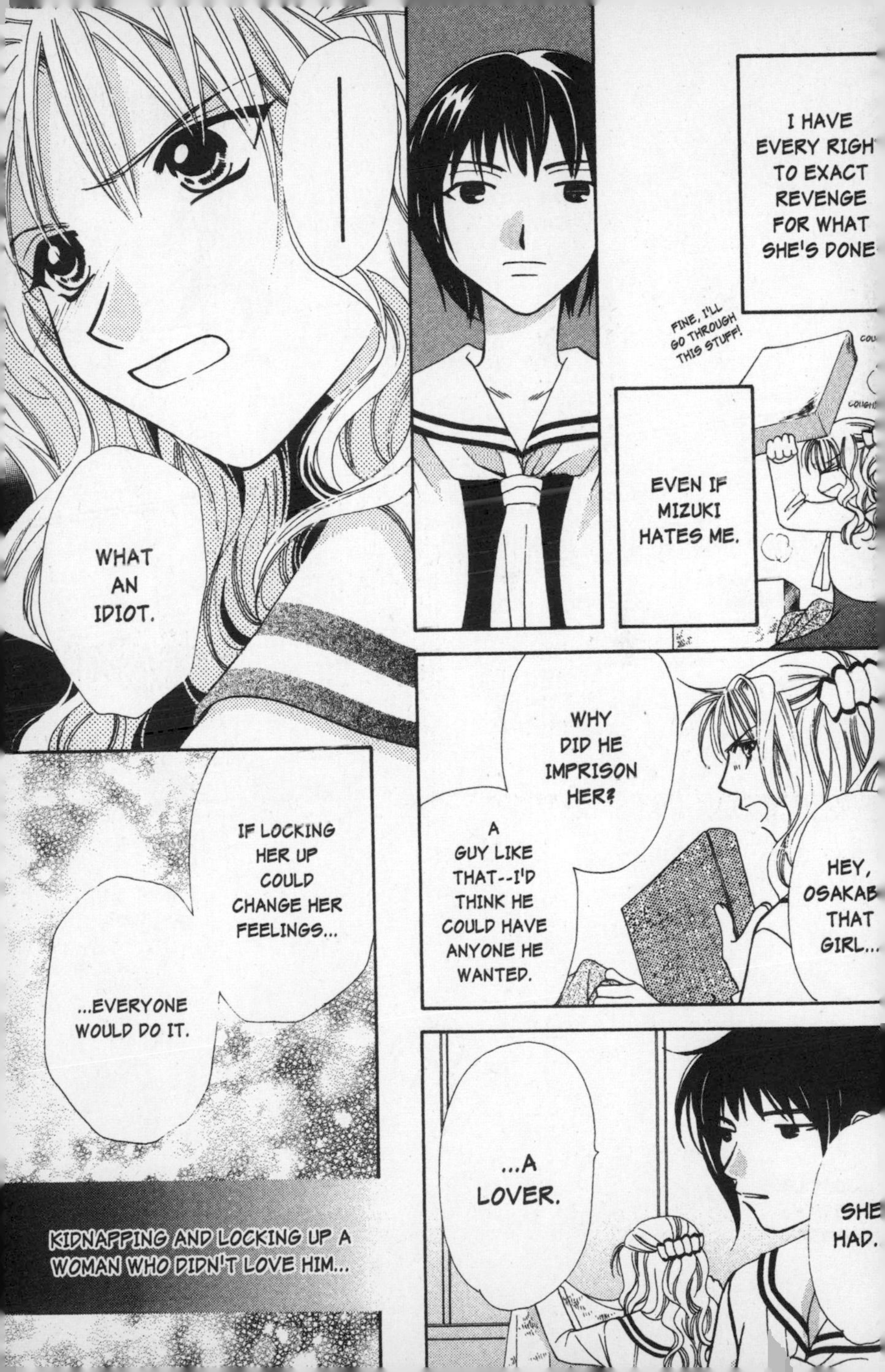
I HAVE EVERY RIGH TO EXACT REVENGE FOR WHAT SHE'S DONE
FINE, I'LL GO THROUGH THIS STUFF!
COUGH
EVEN IF MIZUKI HATES ME.
WHAT AN IDIOT.
HEY, OSAKAB THAT GIRL...
WHY DID HE IMPRISON HER?
A GUY LIKE THAT--I'D THINK HE COULD HAVE ANYONE HE WANTED.
SHE HAD.
...A LOVER.
IF LOCKING HER UP COULD CHANGE HER FEELINGS...
...EVERYONE WOULD DO IT.
KIDNAPPING AND LOCKING UP A WOMAN WHO DIDN'T LOVE HIM...

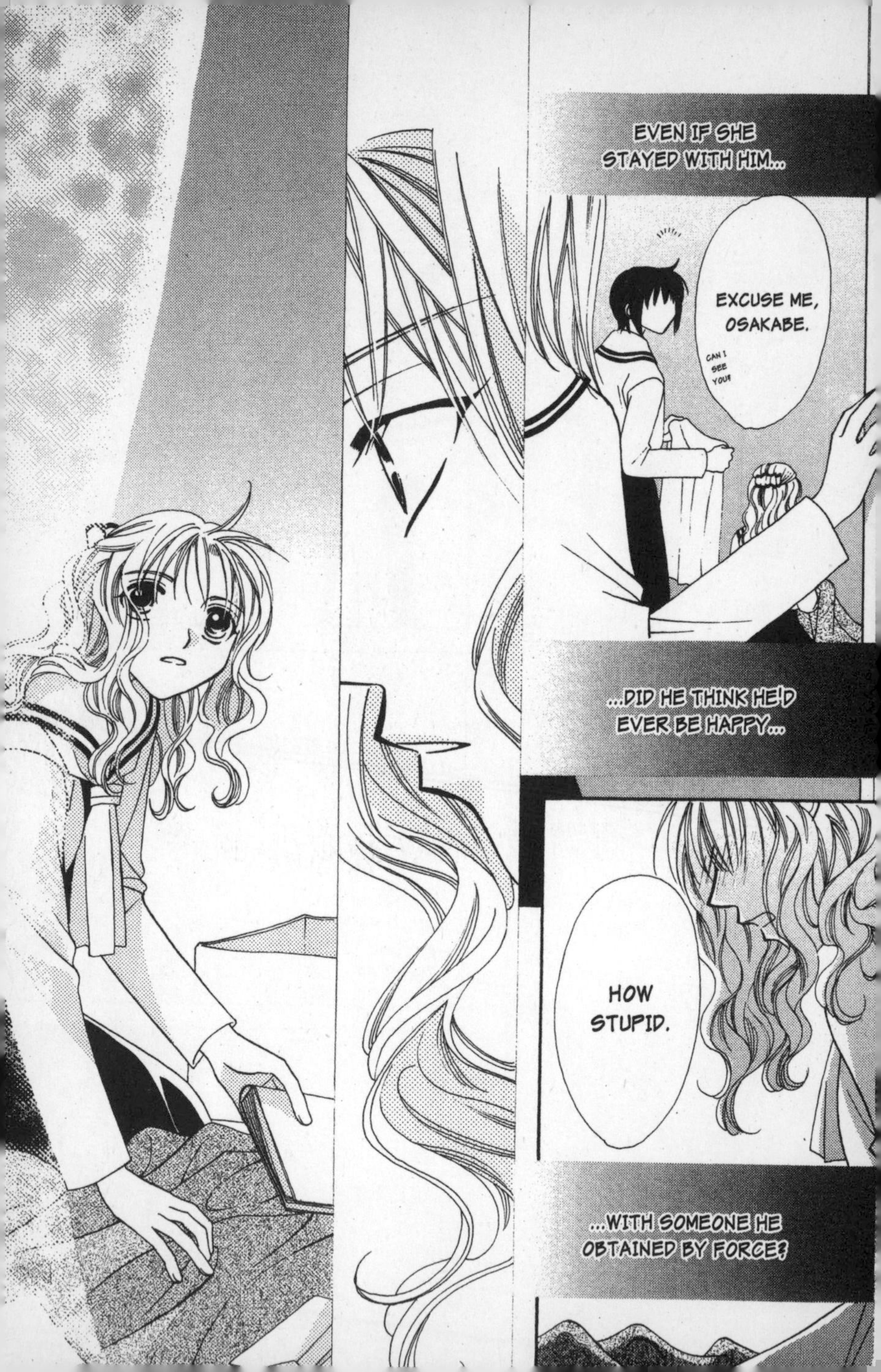
EVEN IF SHE STAYED WITH HIM...
EXCUSE ME, OSAKABE.
CAN I SEE YOU?
...DID HE THINK HE'D EVER BE HAPPY...
HOW STUPID.
...WITH SOMEONE HE OBTAINED BY FORCE?

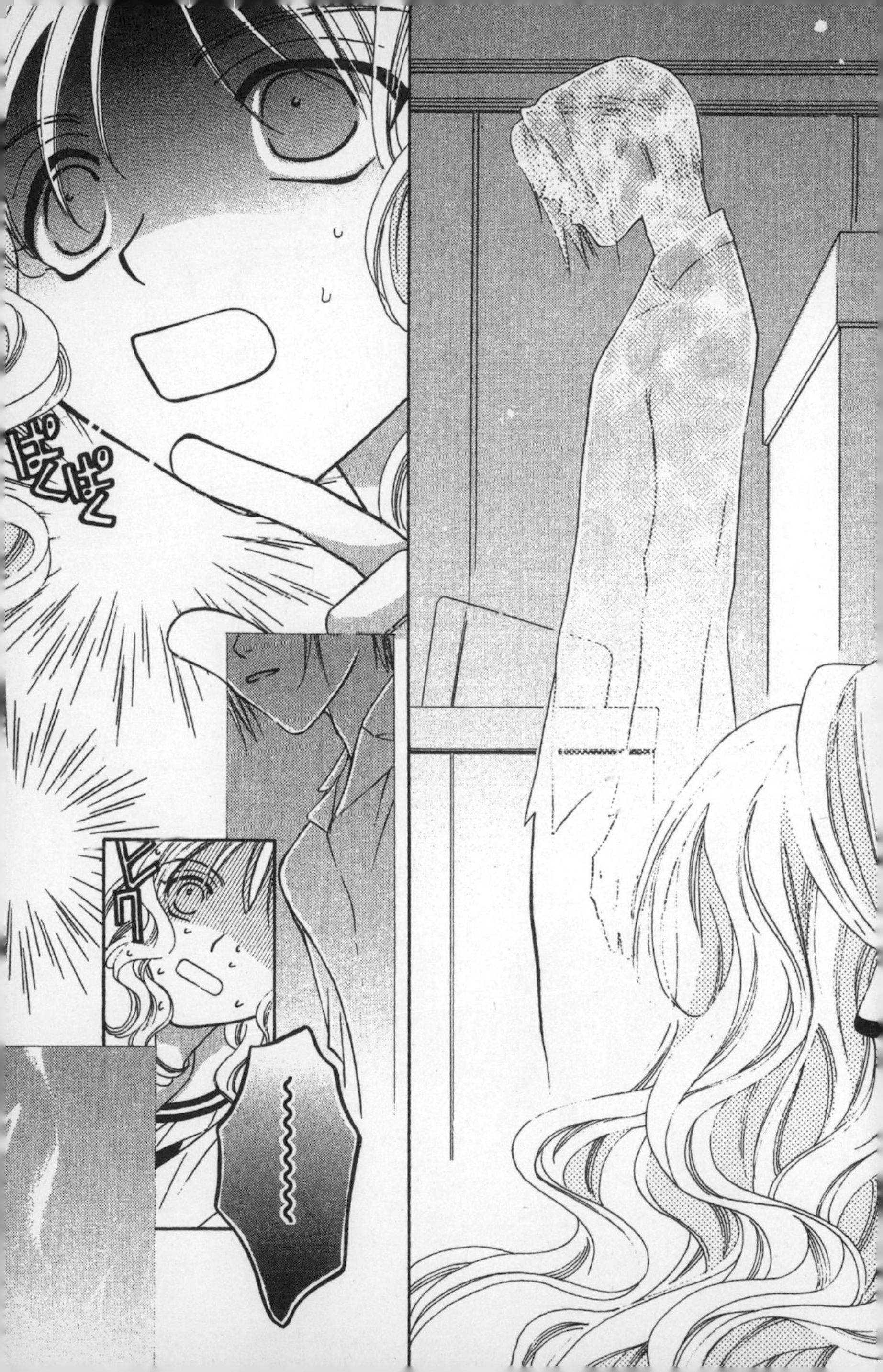
ぱくぱく
ヒク

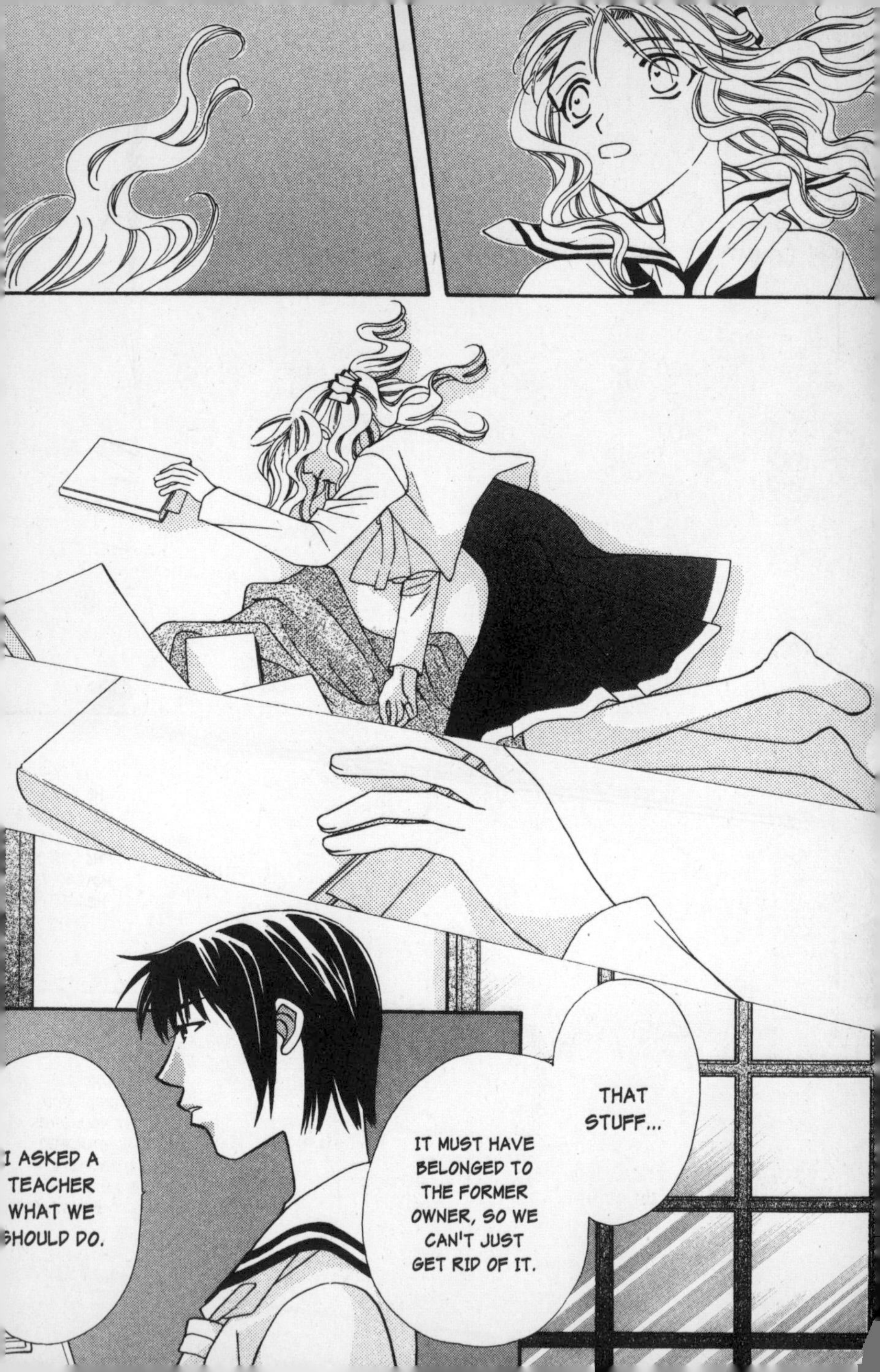
THAT STUFF...
IT MUST HAVE BELONGED TO THE FORMER OWNER, SO WE CAN'T JUST GET RID OF IT.
I ASKED A TEACHER WHAT WE SHOULD DO.

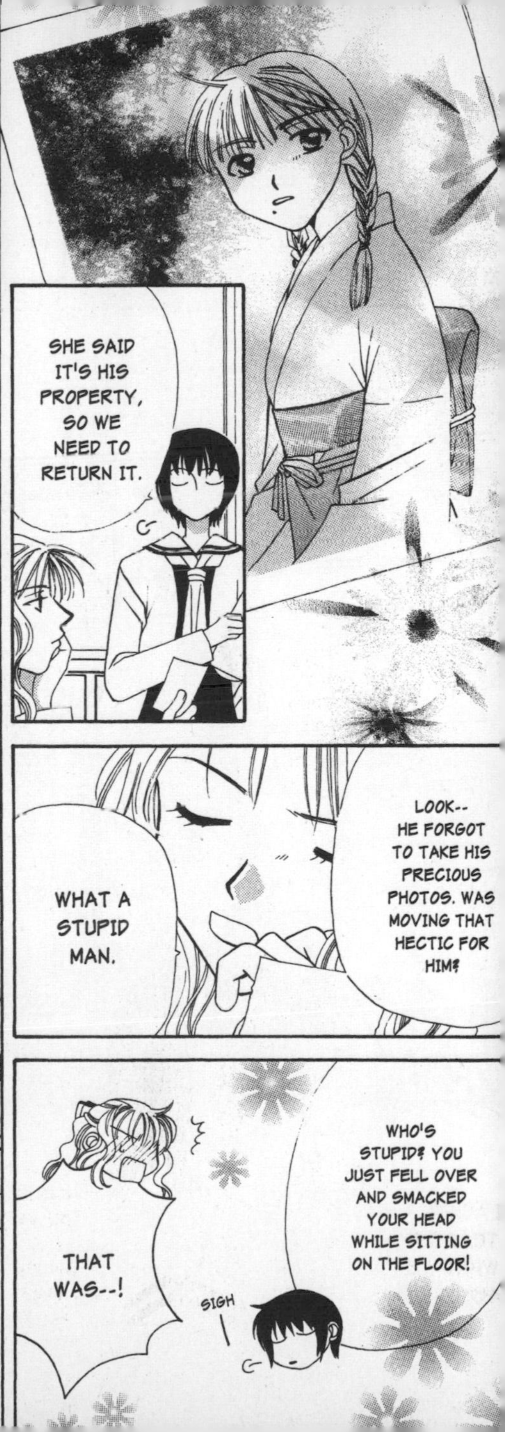
SHE SAID IT'S HIS PROPERTY, SO WE NEED TO RETURN IT.
LOOK-- HE FORGOT TO TAKE HIS PRECIOUS PHOTOS. WAS MOVING THAT HECTIC FOR HIM?
WHAT A STUPID MAN.
WHO'S STUPID? YOU JUST FELL OVER AND SMACKED YOUR HEAD WHILE SITTING ON THE FLOOR!
THAT WAS--!
SIGH

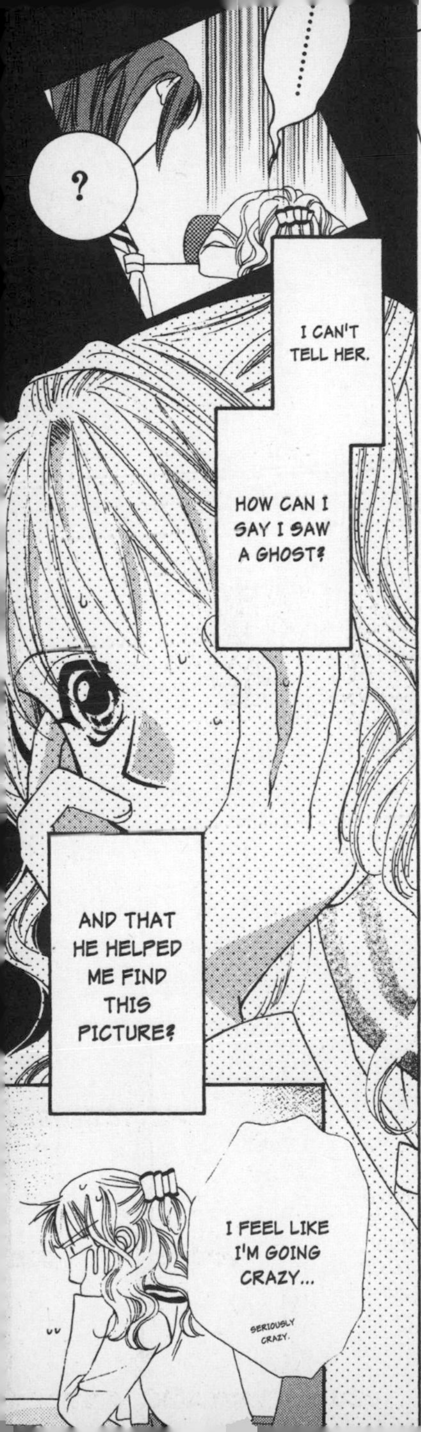
......
?
I CAN'T TELL HER.
HOW CAN I SAY I SAW A GHOST?
AND THAT HE HELPED ME FIND THIS PICTURE?
I FEEL LIKE I'M GOING CRAZY...
SERIOUSLY CRAZY.

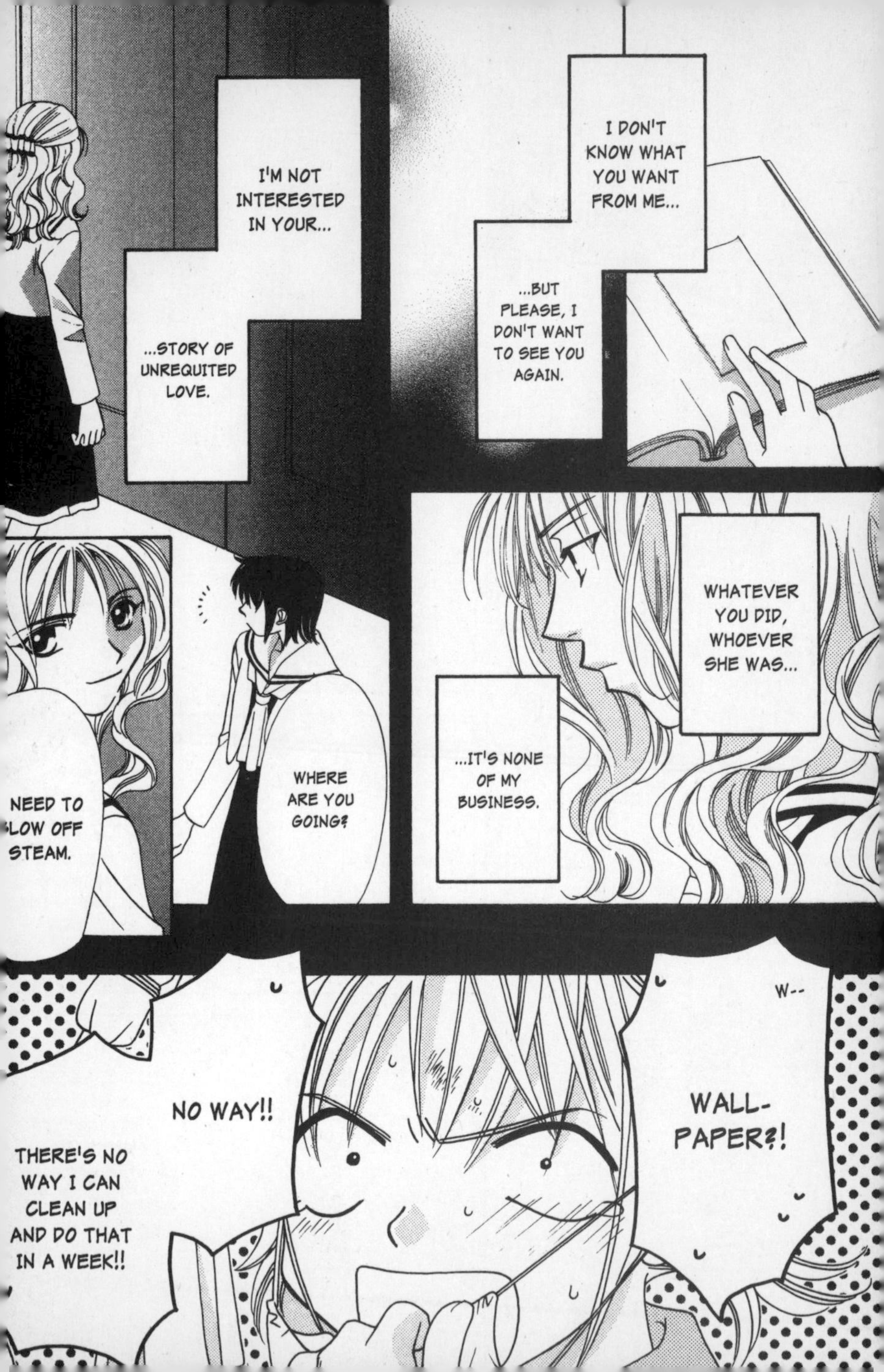
I DON'T KNOW WHAT YOU WANT FROM ME...
...BUT PLEASE, I DON'T WANT TO SEE YOU AGAIN.
I'M NOT INTERESTED IN YOUR...
...STORY OF UNREQUITED LOVE.
WHATEVER YOU DID, WHOEVER SHE WAS...
...IT'S NONE OF MY BUSINESS.
WHERE ARE YOU GOING?
NEED TO LOW OFF STEAM.
W--
WALL-PAPER?!
NO WAY!!
THERE'S NO WAY I CAN CLEAN UP AND DO THAT IN A WEEK!!

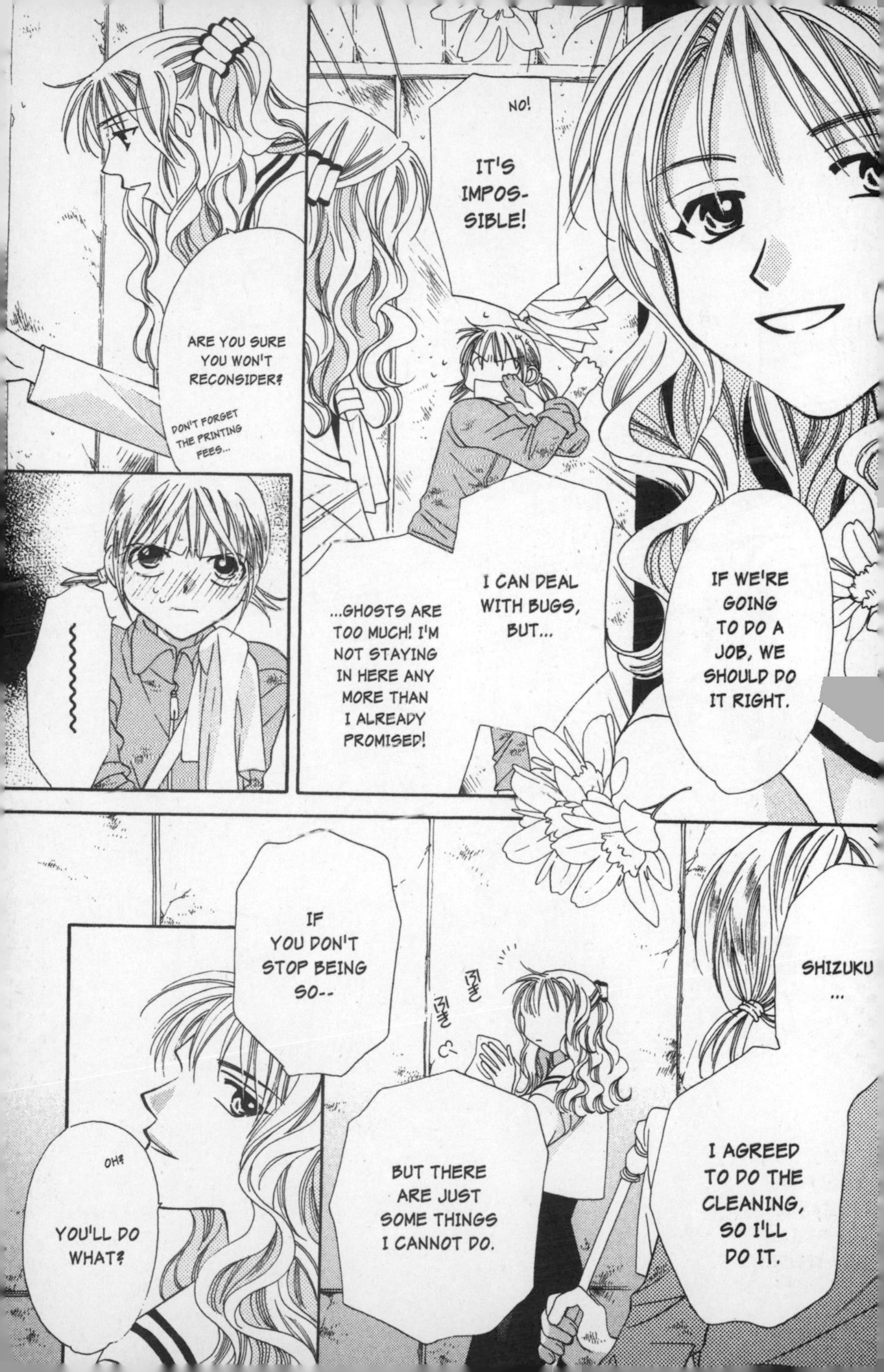
IF WE'RE GOING TO DO A JOB, WE SHOULD DO IT RIGHT.
NO!
IT'S IMPOS-SIBLE!
I CAN DEAL WITH BUGS, BUT...
...GHOSTS ARE TOO MUCH! I'M NOT STAYING IN HERE ANY MORE THAN I ALREADY PROMISED!
ARE YOU SURE YOU WON'T RECONSIDER?
DON'T FORGET THE PRINTING FEES...
SHIZUKU ...
I AGREED TO DO THE CLEANING, SO I'LL DO IT.
BUT THERE ARE JUST SOME THINGS I CANNOT DO.
IF YOU DON'T STOP BEING SO--
OH?
YOU'LL DO WHAT?

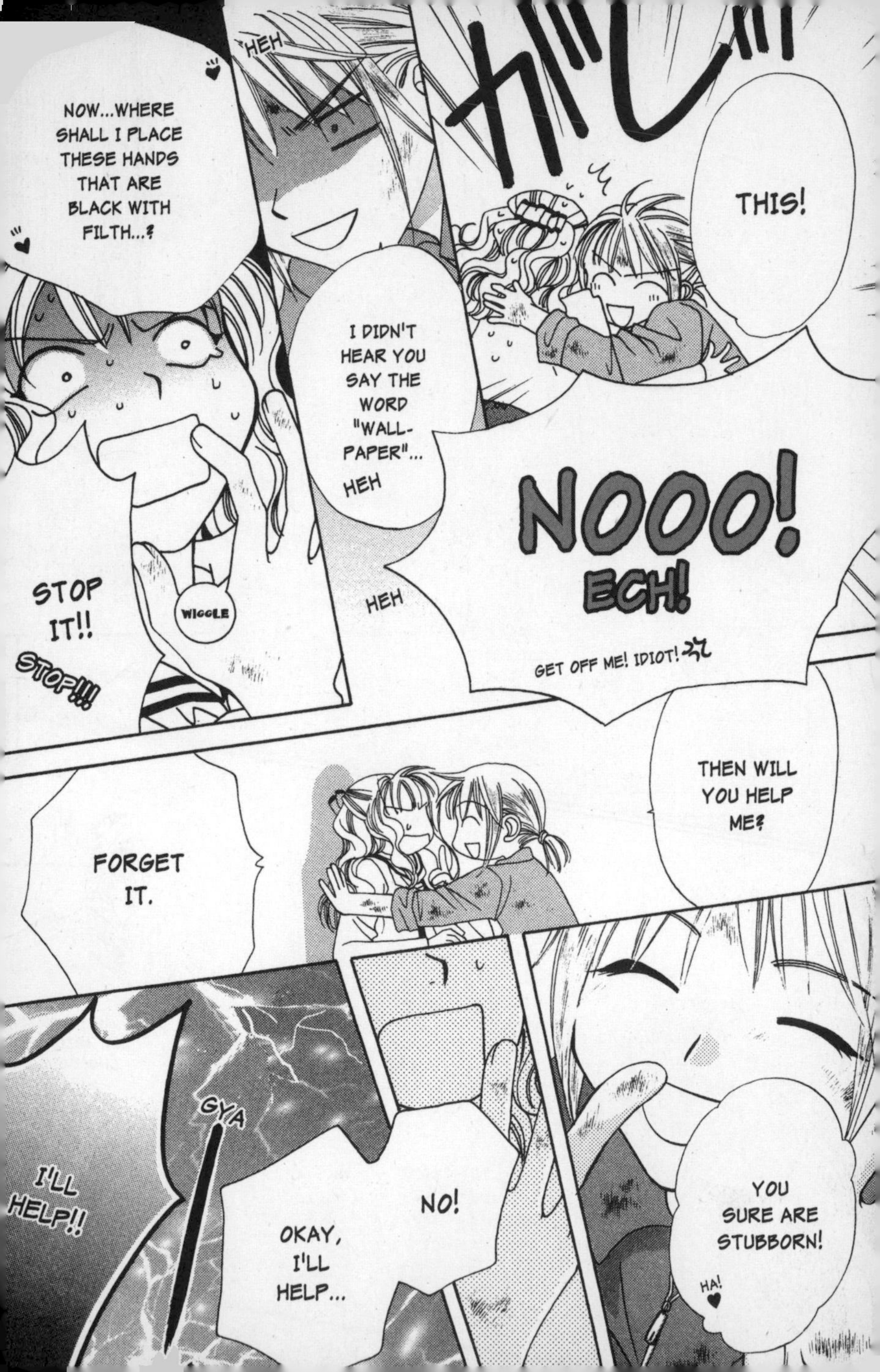
THIS!
NOOO!
ECH!
GET OFF ME! IDIOT!
HEH
I DIDN'T HEAR YOU SAY THE WORD "WALL-PAPER"... HEH
HEH
NOW...WHERE SHALL I PLACE THESE HANDS THAT ARE BLACK WITH FILTH...?
STOP IT!!
WIGGLE
STOP!!!
THEN WILL YOU HELP ME?
FORGET IT.
YOU SURE ARE STUBBORN!
HA!
NO!
OKAY, I'LL HELP...
GYA
I'LL HELP!!

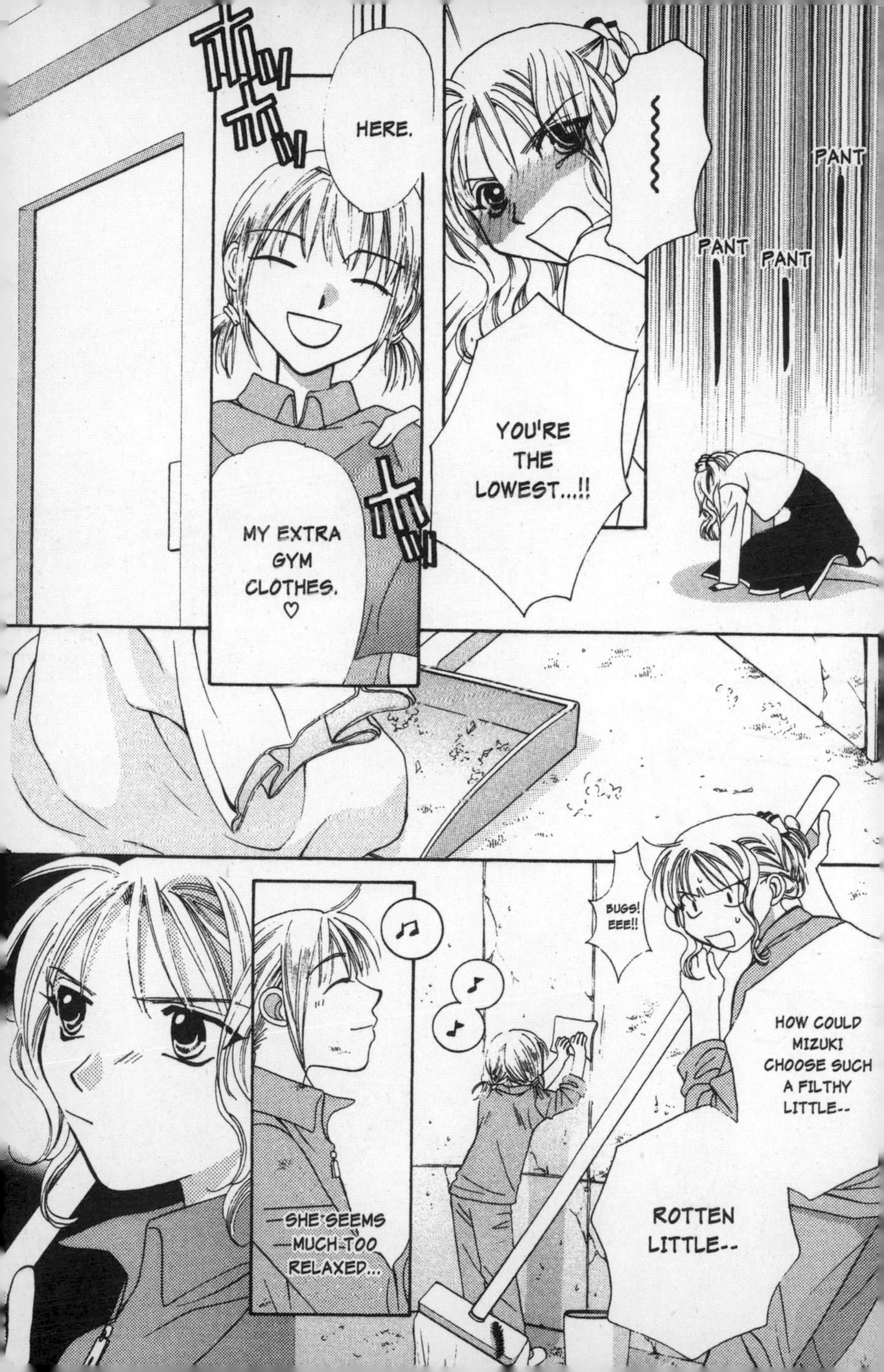
PANT
PANT PANT
YOU'RE THE LOWEST...!!
HERE.
MY EXTRA GYM CLOTHES. ♡
BUGS! EEE!!
HOW COULD MIZUKI CHOOSE SUCH A FILTHY LITTLE--
ROTTEN LITTLE--
♫
—SHE SEEMS —MUCH TOO RELAXED...

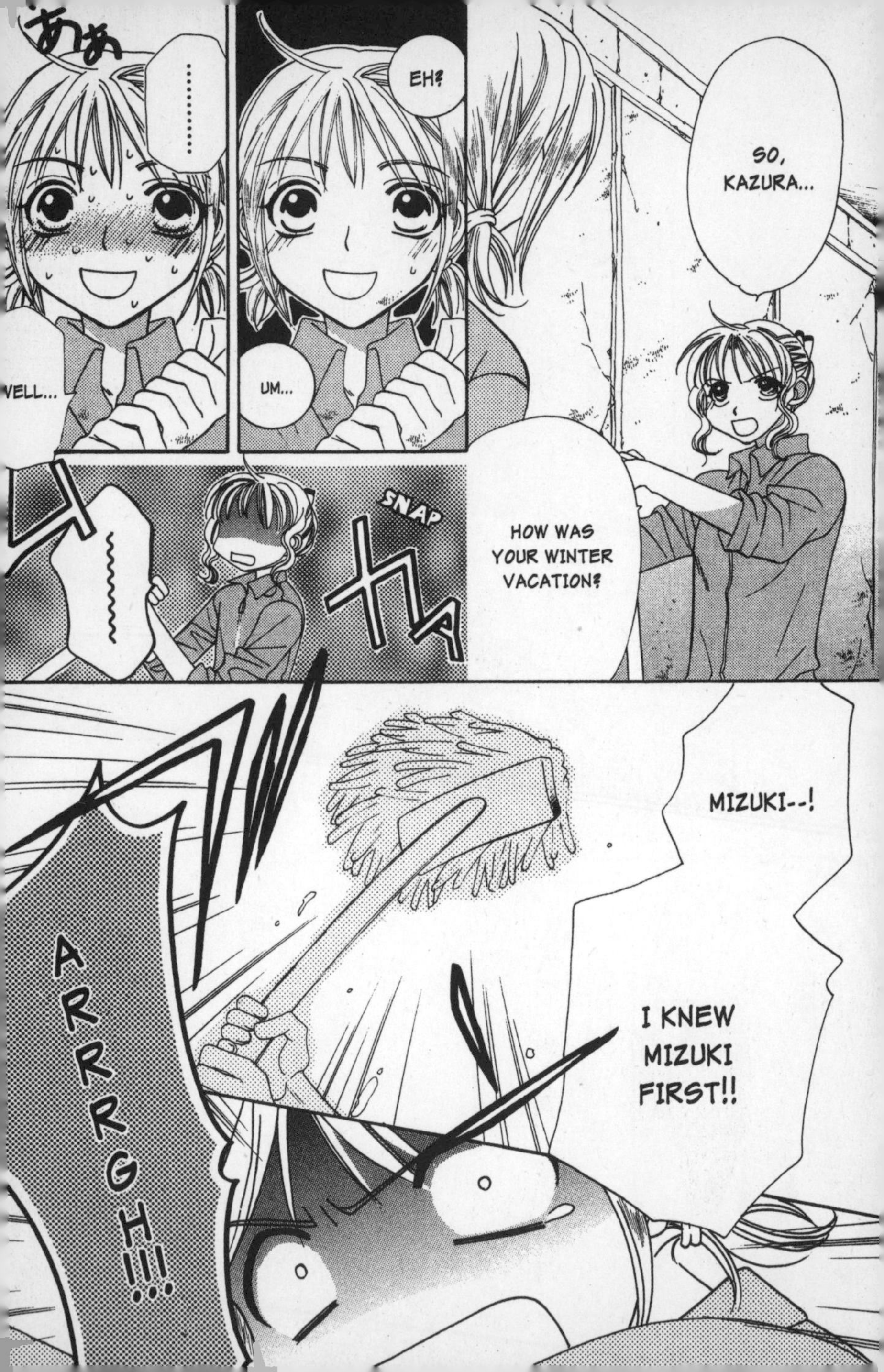

SO, KAZURA...
HOW WAS YOUR WINTER VACATION?
EH?
UM...
あぁ
......
VELL...
SNAP
MIZUKI--!
I KNEW MIZUKI FIRST!!
ARRRGH!!!

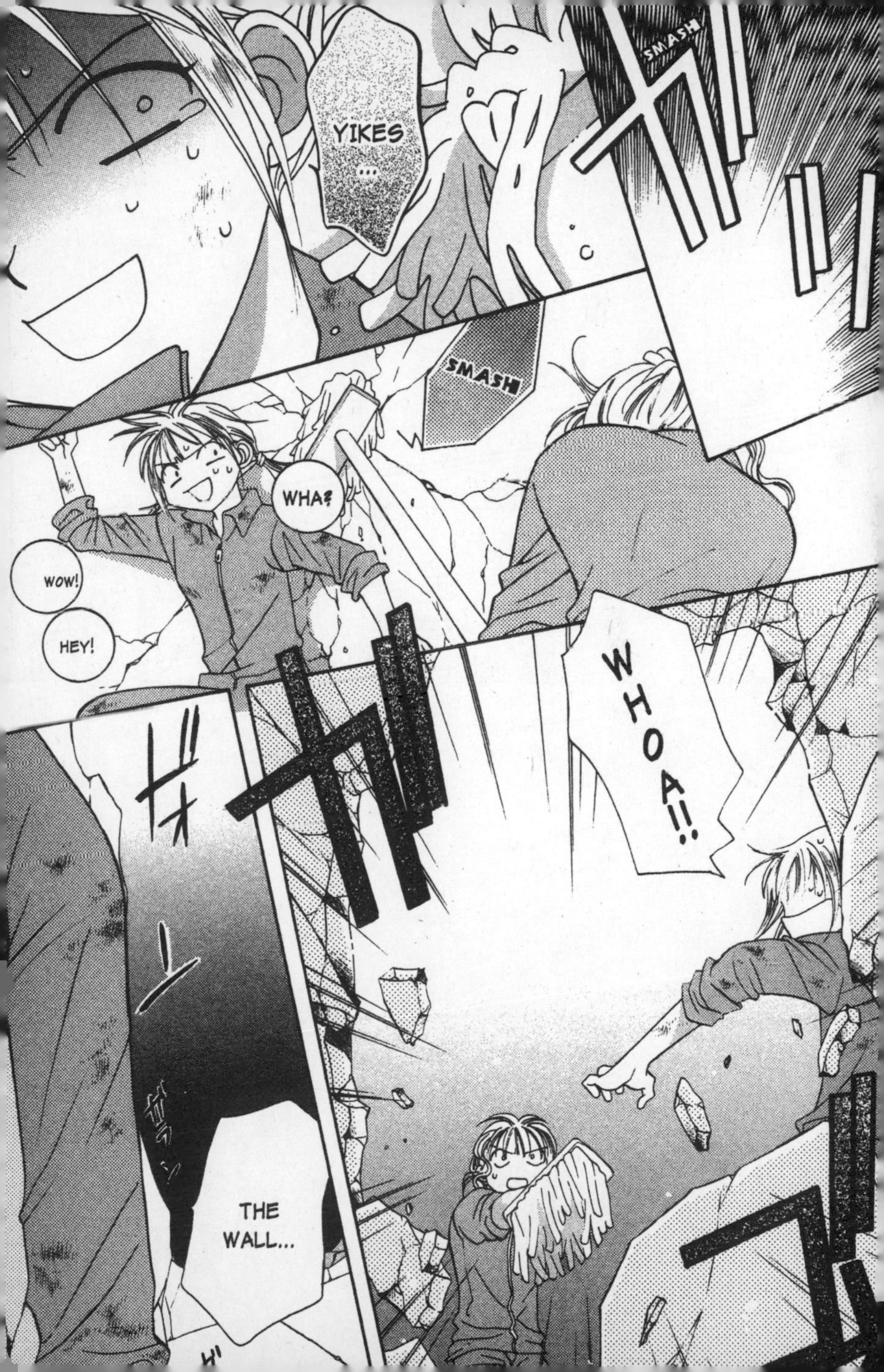
SMASH
YIKES ...
SMASH
WHA?
WOW!
HEY!
WHOA!!
THE WALL...

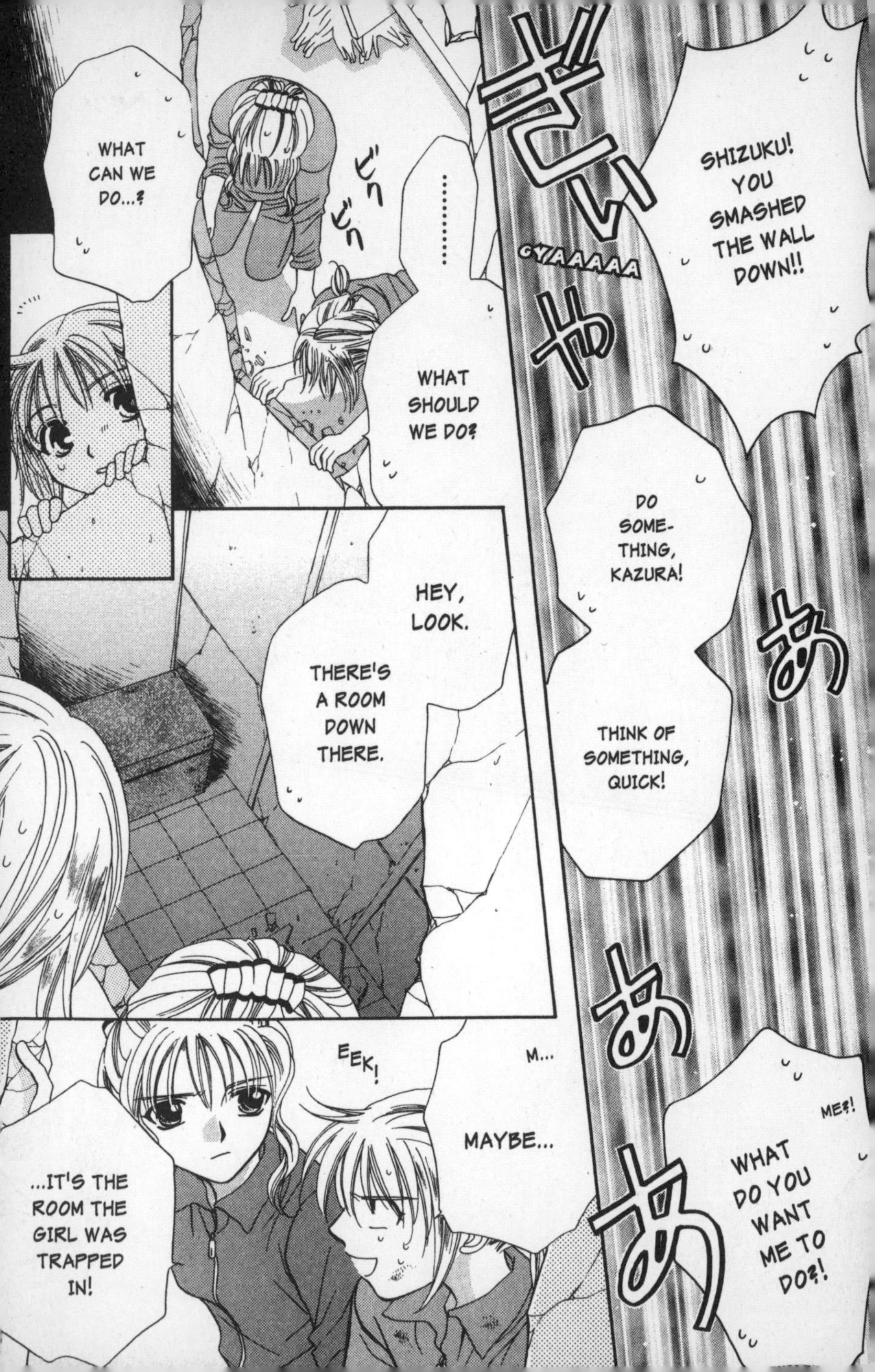
SHIZUKU! YOU SMASHED THE WALL DOWN!!
ぎゃあああ
GYAAAAAA
DO SOME-THING, KAZURA!
THINK OF SOMETHING, QUICK!
ME?!
WHAT DO YOU WANT ME TO DO?!
......
WHAT SHOULD WE DO?
ビクビク
WHAT CAN WE DO...?
HEY, LOOK.
THERE'S A ROOM DOWN THERE.
M...
MAYBE...
EEK!
...IT'S THE ROOM THE GIRL WAS TRAPPED IN!

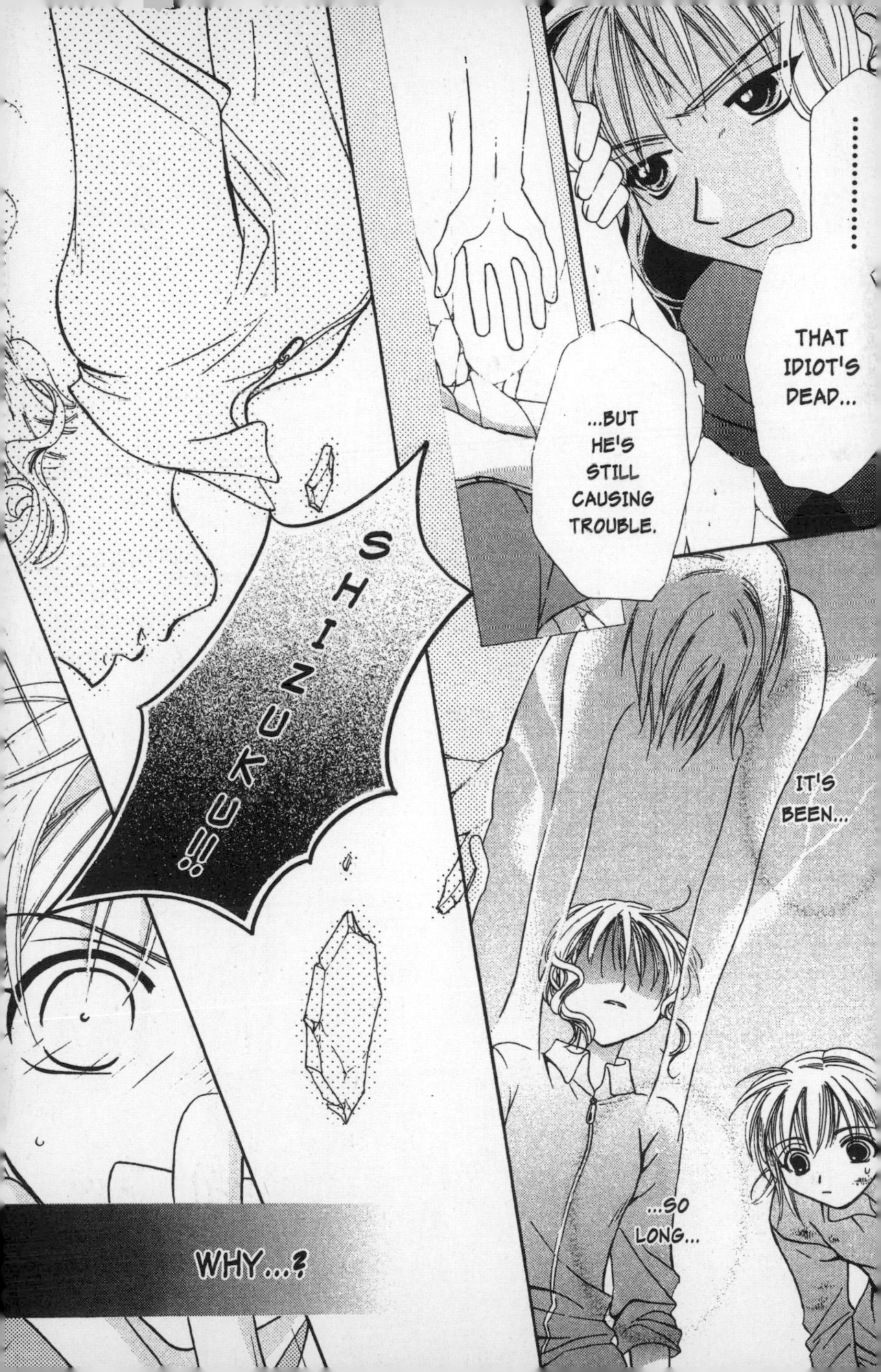

......
THAT IDIOT'S DEAD...
...BUT HE'S STILL CAUSING TROUBLE.
IT'S BEEN...
...SO LONG...
SHIZUKU!!
WHY...?

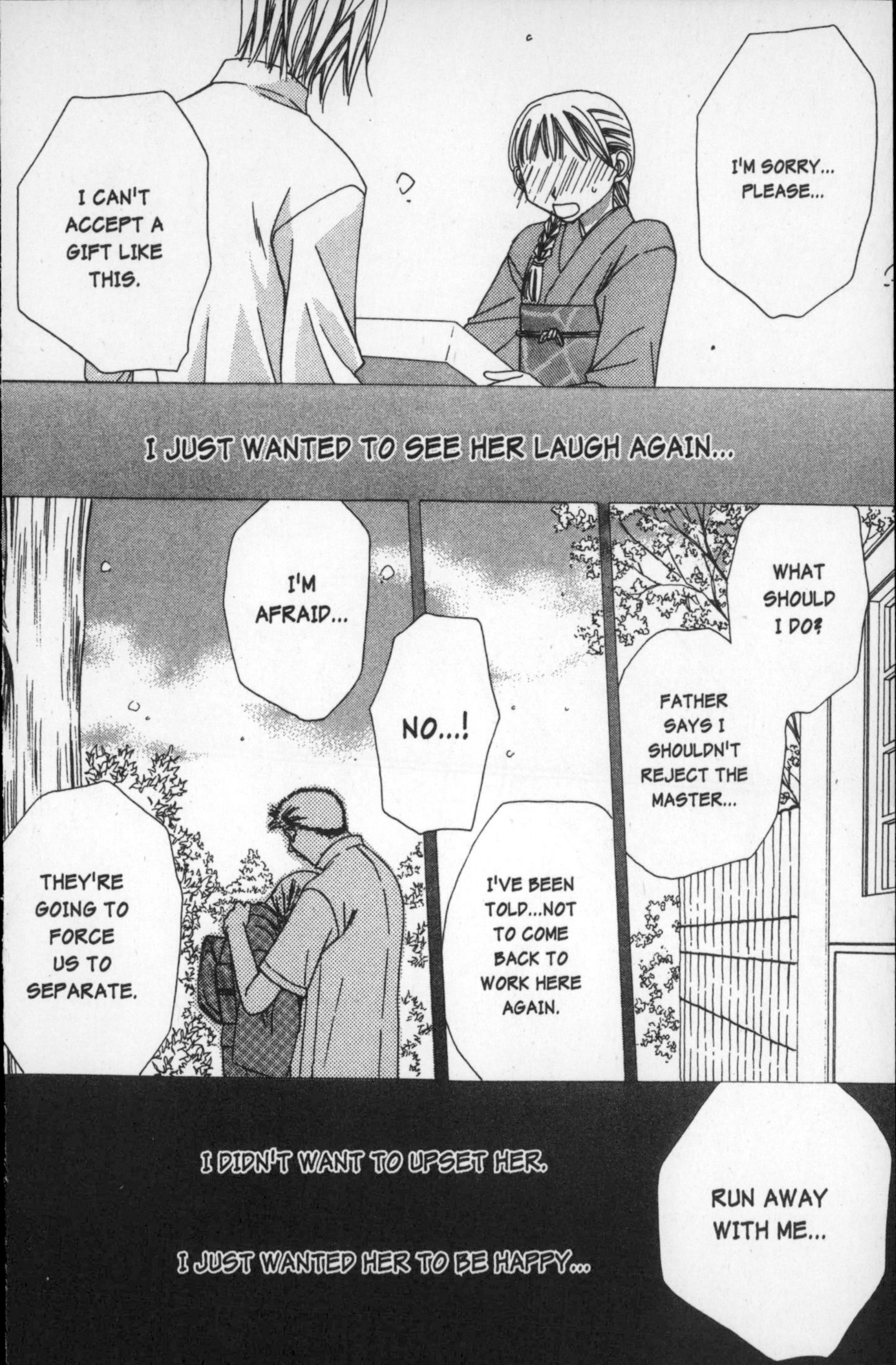
I'M SORRY... PLEASE...
I CAN'T ACCEPT A GIFT LIKE THIS.
I JUST WANTED TO SEE HER LAUGH AGAIN...
WHAT SHOULD I DO?
FATHER SAYS I SHOULDN'T REJECT THE MASTER...
NO...!
I'VE BEEN TOLD...NOT TO COME BACK TO WORK HERE AGAIN.
I'M AFRAID...
THEY'RE GOING TO FORCE US TO SEPARATE.
RUN AWAY WITH ME...
I DIDN'T WANT TO UPSET HER.
I JUST WANTED HER TO BE HAPPY...

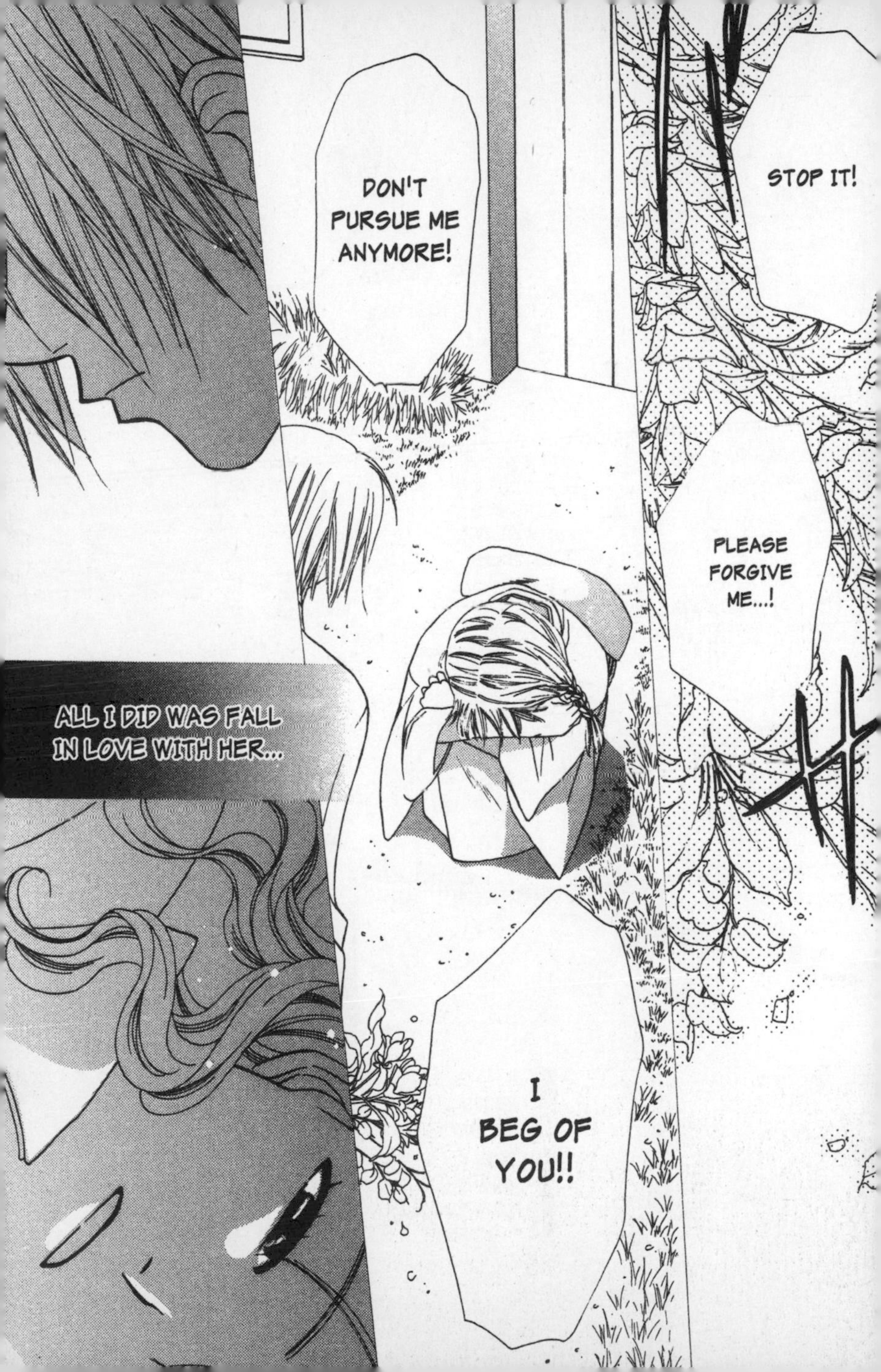
STOP IT!
PLEASE FORGIVE ME...!
DON'T PURSUE ME ANYMORE!
I BEG OF YOU!!
ALL I DID WAS FALL IN LOVE WITH HER...

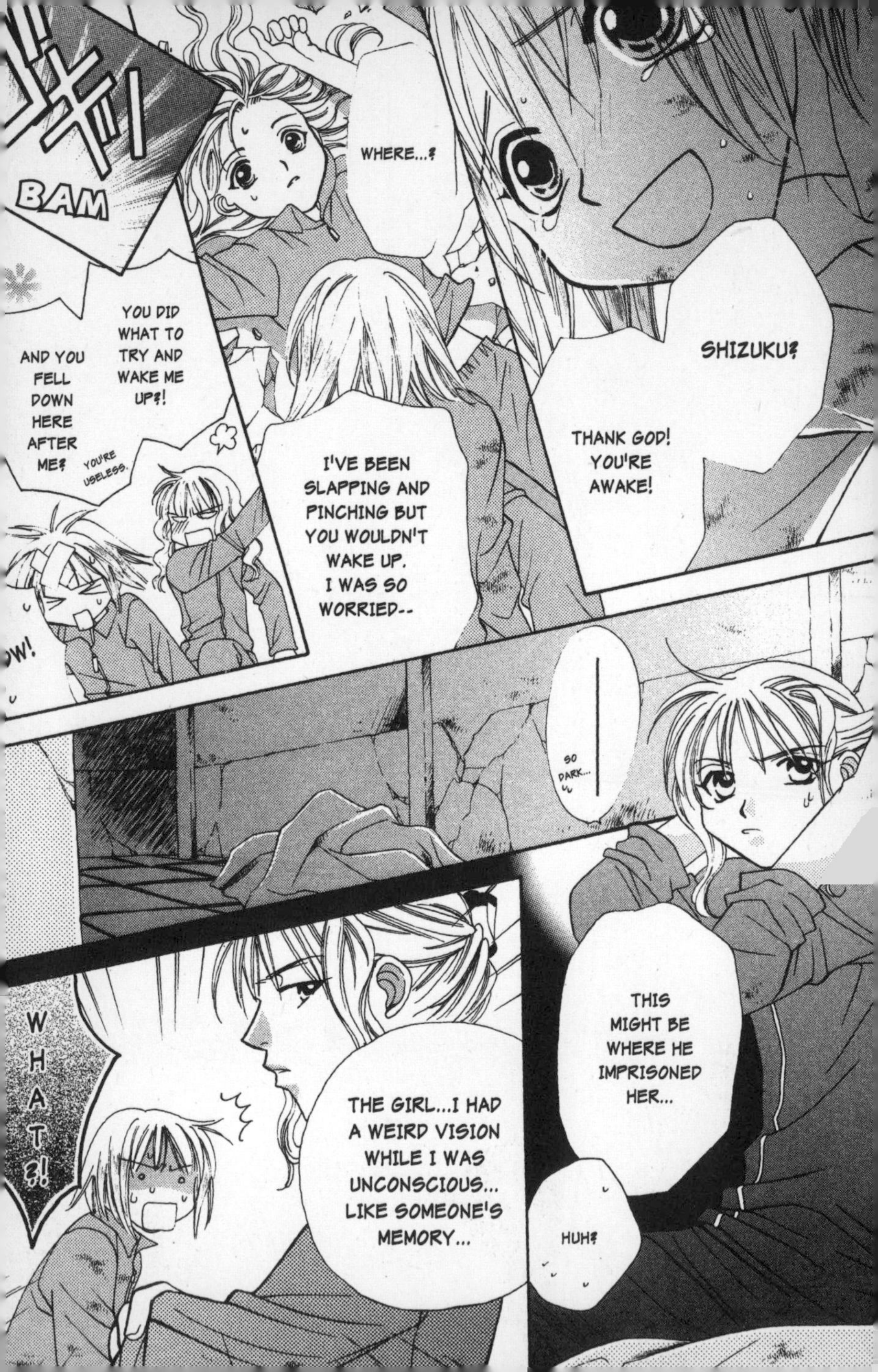
SHIZUKU?
THANK GOD! YOU'RE AWAKE!
WHERE...?
I'VE BEEN SLAPPING AND PINCHING BUT YOU WOULDN'T WAKE UP. I WAS SO WORRIED--
BAM
YOU DID WHAT TO TRY AND WAKE ME UP?!
AND YOU FELL DOWN HERE AFTER ME?
YOU'RE USELESS.
OW!
SO DARK...
THIS MIGHT BE WHERE HE IMPRISONED HER...
HUH?
THE GIRL...I HAD A WEIRD VISION WHILE I WAS UNCONSCIOUS... LIKE SOMEONE'S MEMORY...
WHAT?!

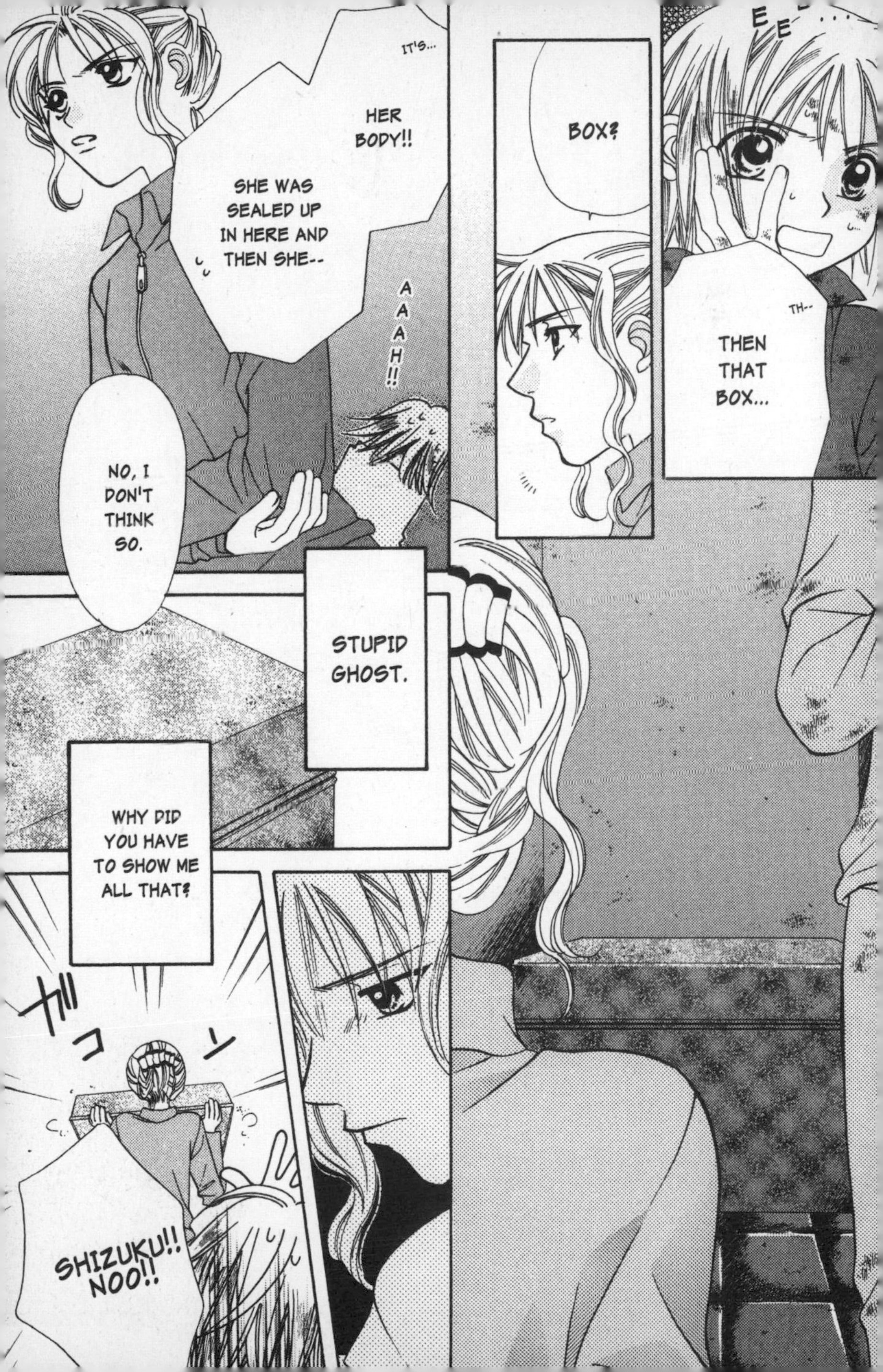

EE...
TH--
THEN THAT BOX...
BOX?
IT'S...
HER BODY!!
SHE WAS SEALED UP IN HERE AND THEN SHE--
AAAAH!!
NO, I DON'T THINK SO.
STUPID GHOST.
WHY DID YOU HAVE TO SHOW ME ALL THAT?
ガコン
SHIZUKU!! NOO!!

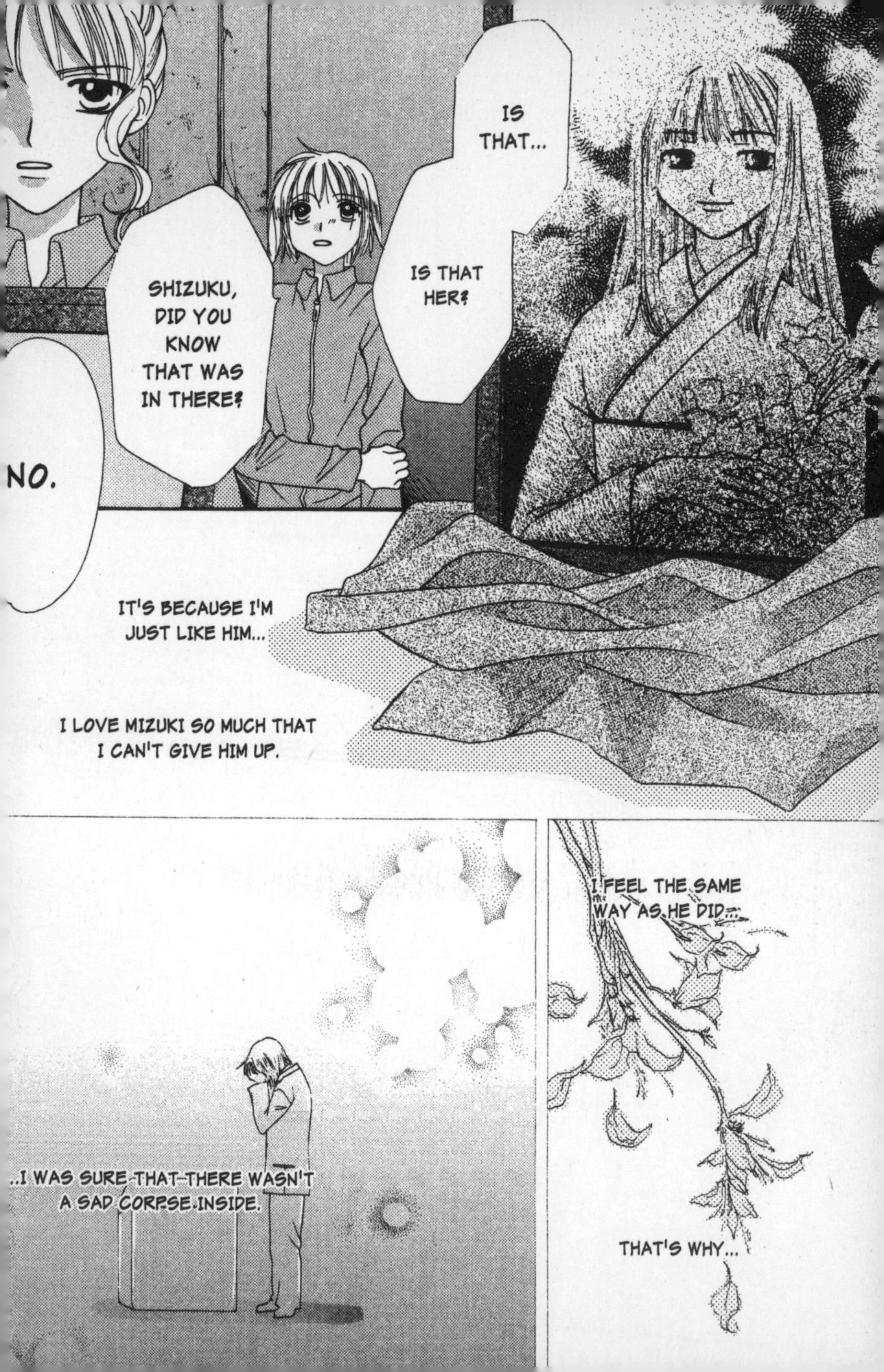
IS THAT...
IS THAT HER?
SHIZUKU, DID YOU KNOW THAT WAS IN THERE?
NO.
IT'S BECAUSE I'M JUST LIKE HIM...
I LOVE MIZUKI SO MUCH THAT I CAN'T GIVE HIM UP.
I FEEL THE SAME WAY AS HE DID...
THAT'S WHY...
...I WAS SURE THAT THERE WASN'T A SAD CORPSE INSIDE.

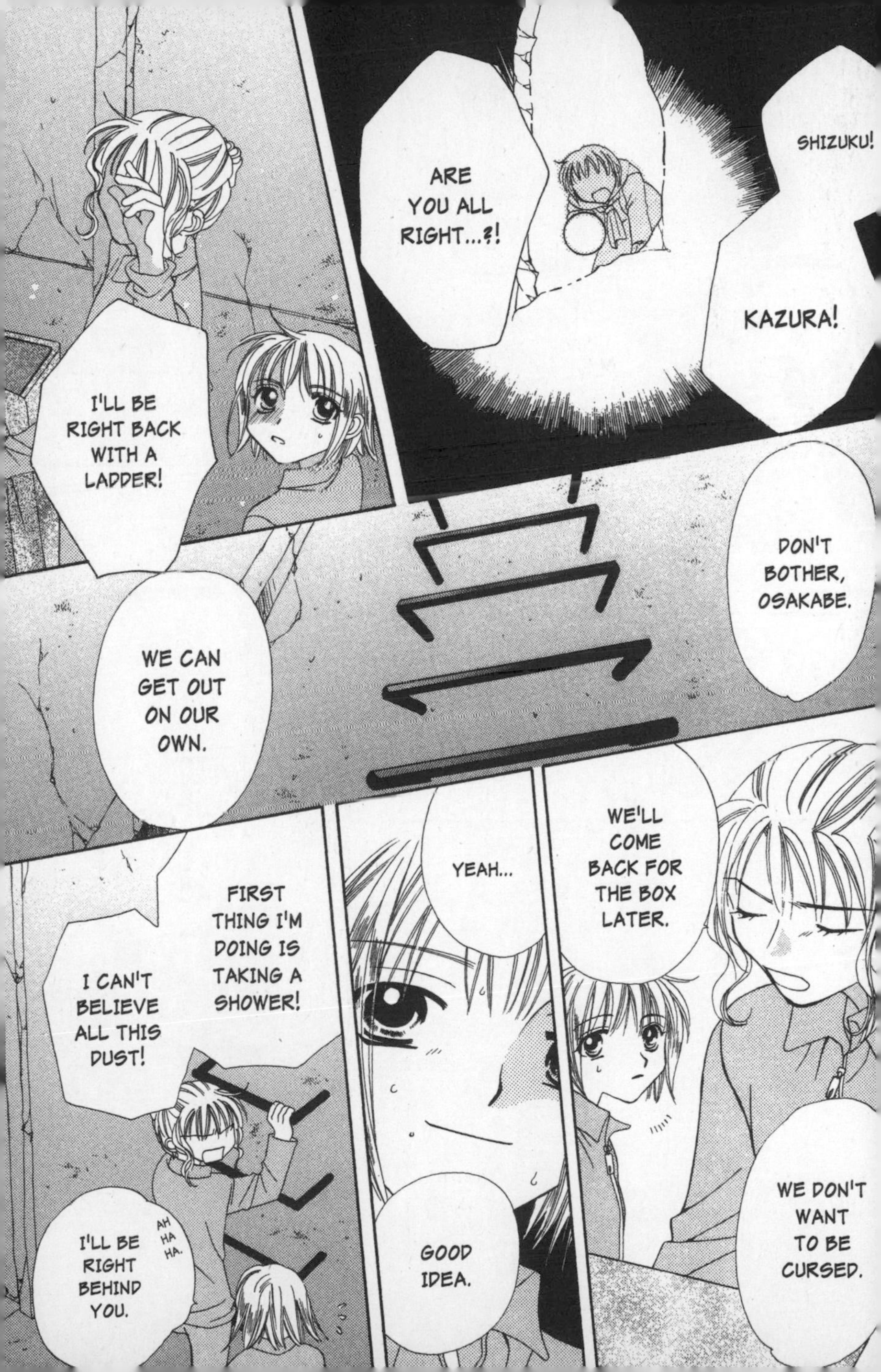
SHIZUKU!
KAZURA!
ARE YOU ALL RIGHT...?!
I'LL BE RIGHT BACK WITH A LADDER!
DON'T BOTHER, OSAKABE.
WE CAN GET OUT ON OUR OWN.
WE'LL COME BACK FOR THE BOX LATER.
WE DON'T WANT TO BE CURSED.
YEAH...
GOOD IDEA.
FIRST THING I'M DOING IS TAKING A SHOWER!
I CAN'T BELIEVE ALL THIS DUST!
AH HA HA.
I'LL BE RIGHT BEHIND YOU.

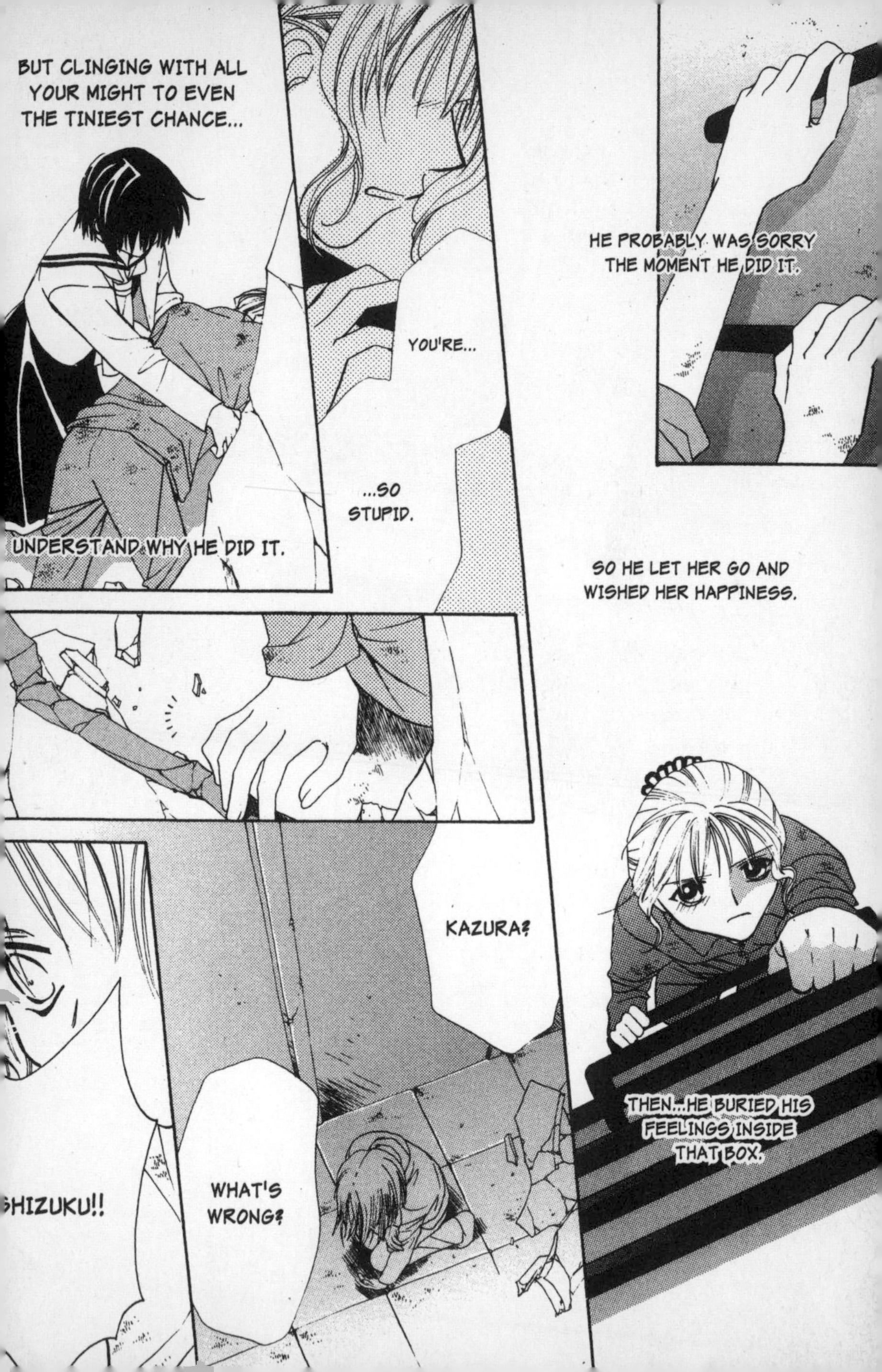
HE PROBABLY WAS SORRY THE MOMENT HE DID IT.
YOU'RE...
...SO STUPID.
BUT CLINGING WITH ALL YOUR MIGHT TO EVEN THE TINIEST CHANCE...
UNDERSTAND WHY HE DID IT.
SO HE LET HER GO AND WISHED HER HAPPINESS.
THEN...HE BURIED HIS FEELINGS INSIDE THAT BOX.
KAZURA?
WHAT'S WRONG?
HIZUKU!!

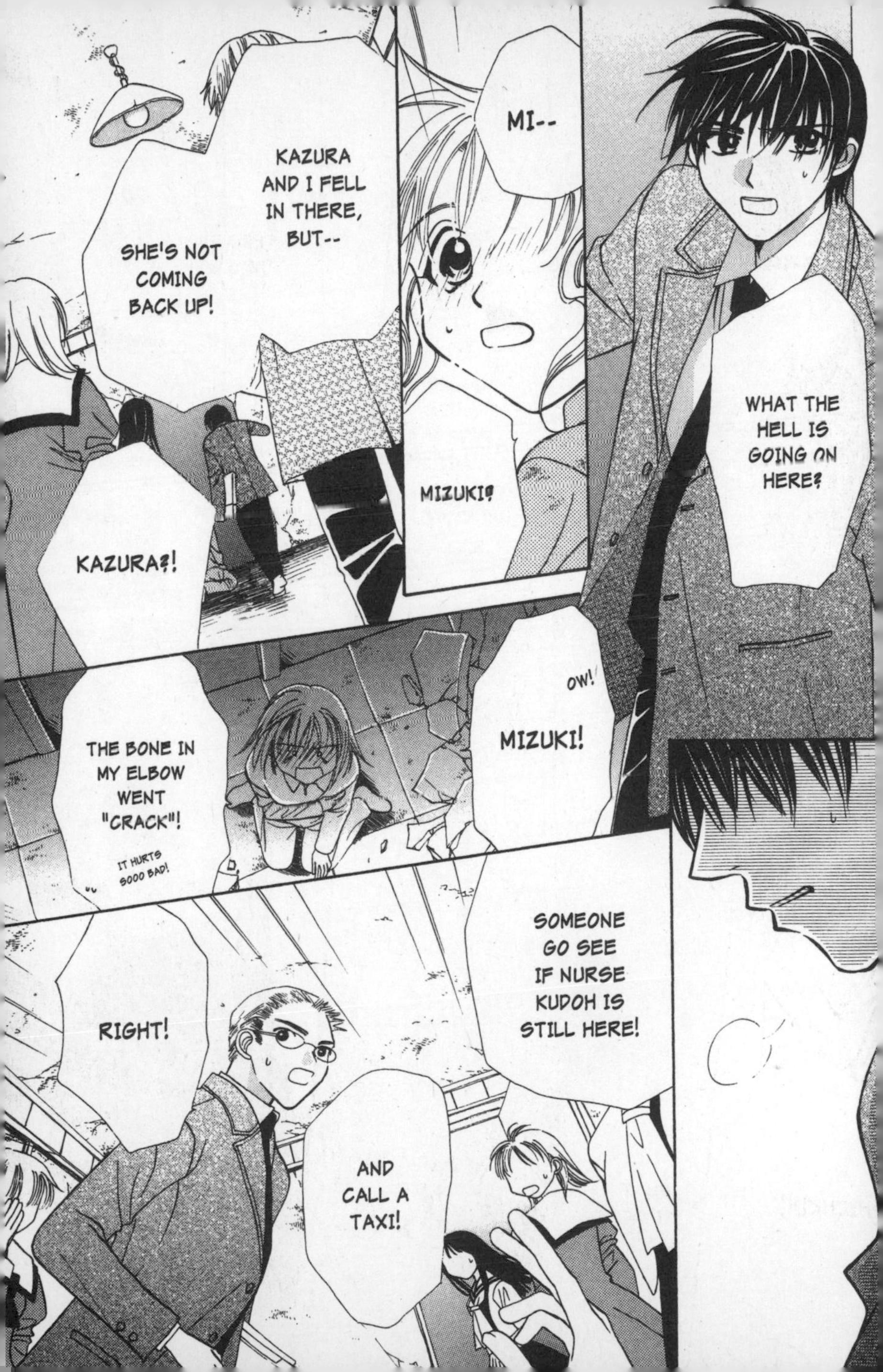
WHAT THE HELL IS GOING ON HERE?
MI--
MIZUKI!?
KAZURA AND I FELL IN THERE, BUT--
SHE'S NOT COMING BACK UP!
KAZURA?!
OW!
MIZUKI!
THE BONE IN MY ELBOW WENT "CRACK"!
IT HURTS SOOO BAD!
SOMEONE GO SEE IF NURSE KUDOH IS STILL HERE!
AND CALL A TAXI!
RIGHT!

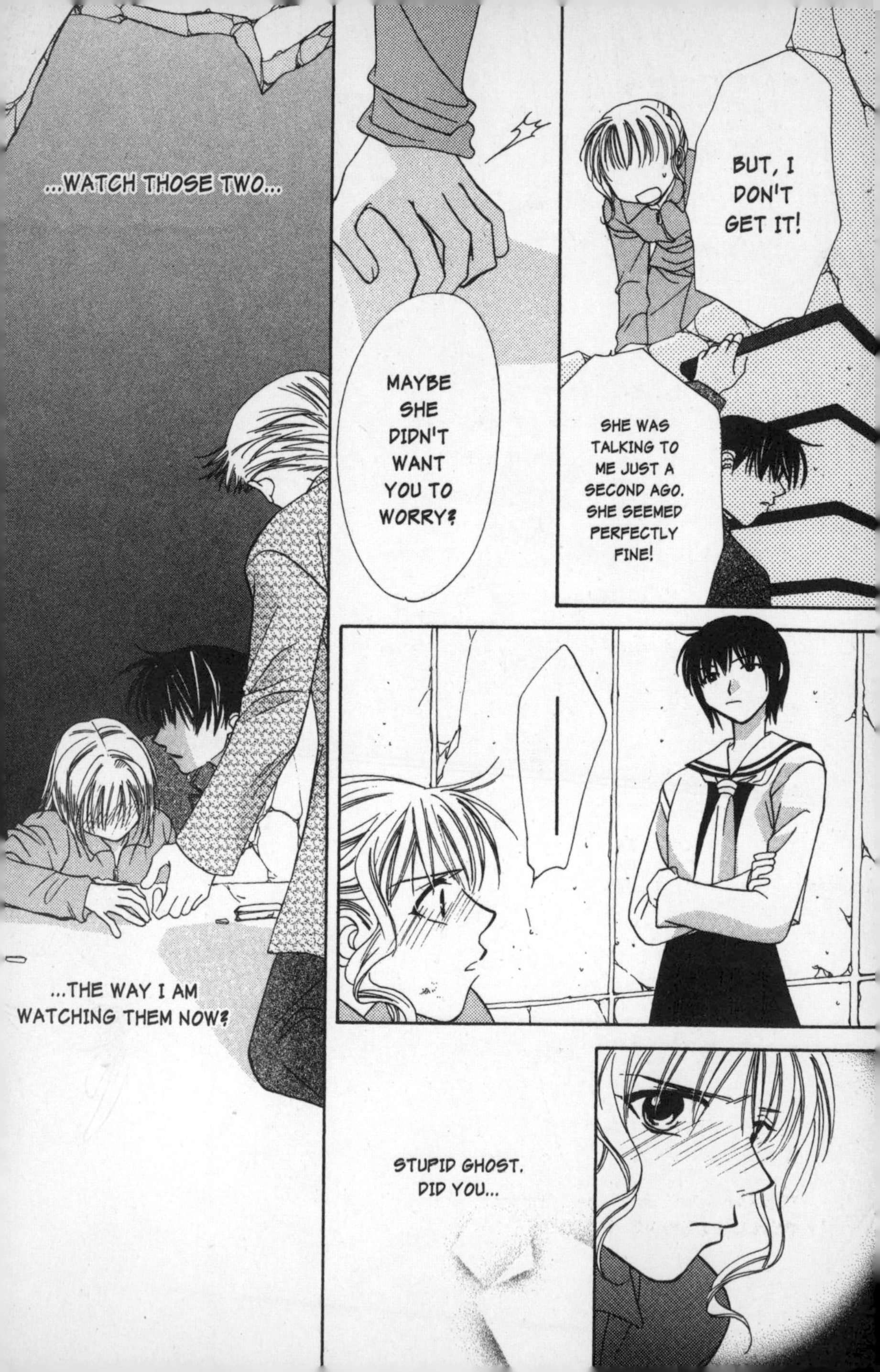
BUT, I DON'T GET IT!
SHE WAS TALKING TO ME JUST A SECOND AGO. SHE SEEMED PERFECTLY FINE!
MAYBE SHE DIDN'T WANT YOU TO WORRY?
STUPID GHOST. DID YOU...
...WATCH THOSE TWO...
...THE WAY I AM WATCHING THEM NOW?

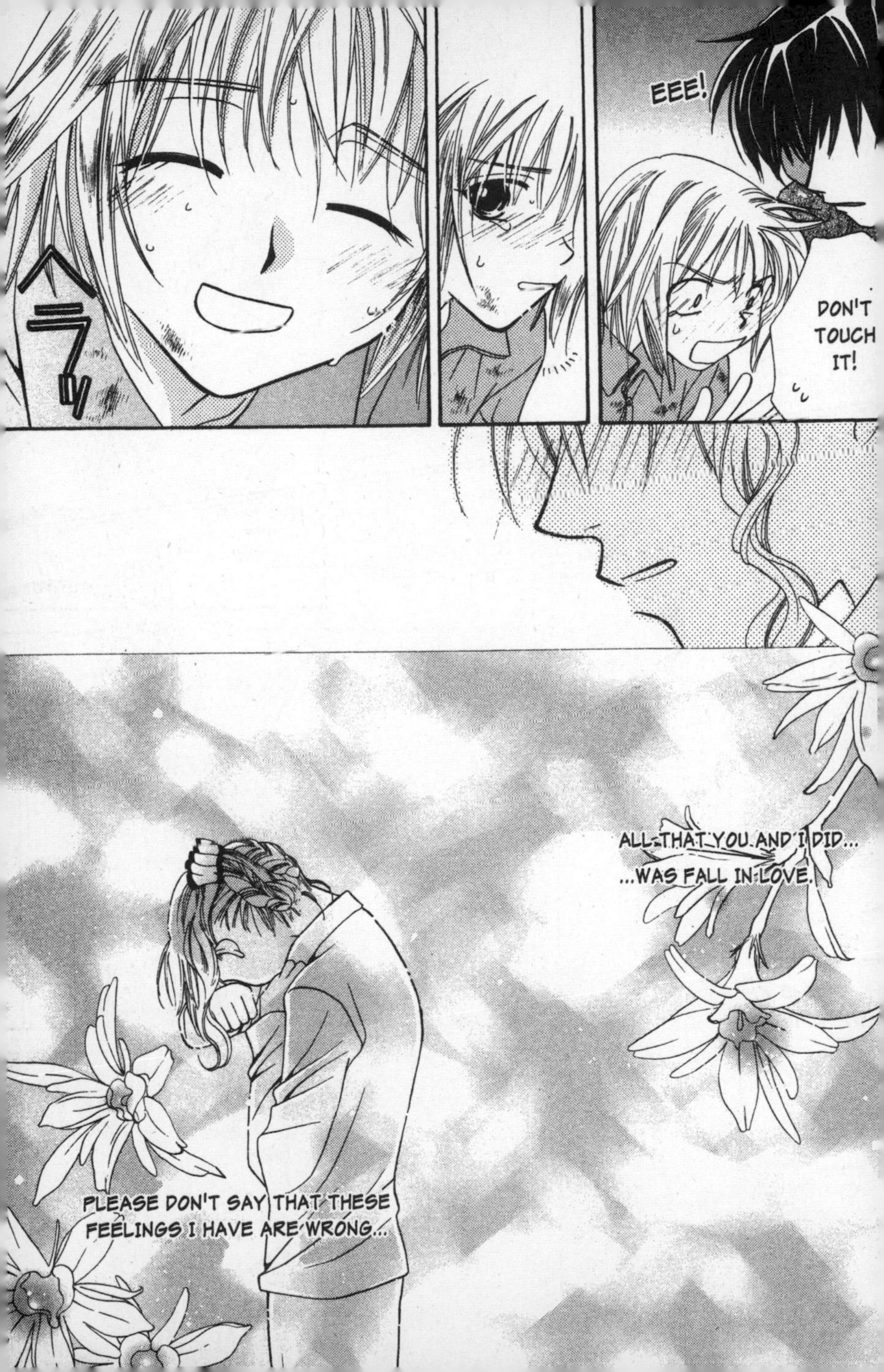
EEE!
DON'T TOUCH IT!
ヘラッ
ALL THAT YOU AND I DID...
...WAS FALL IN LOVE.
PLEASE DON'T SAY THAT THESE FEELINGS I HAVE ARE WRONG...

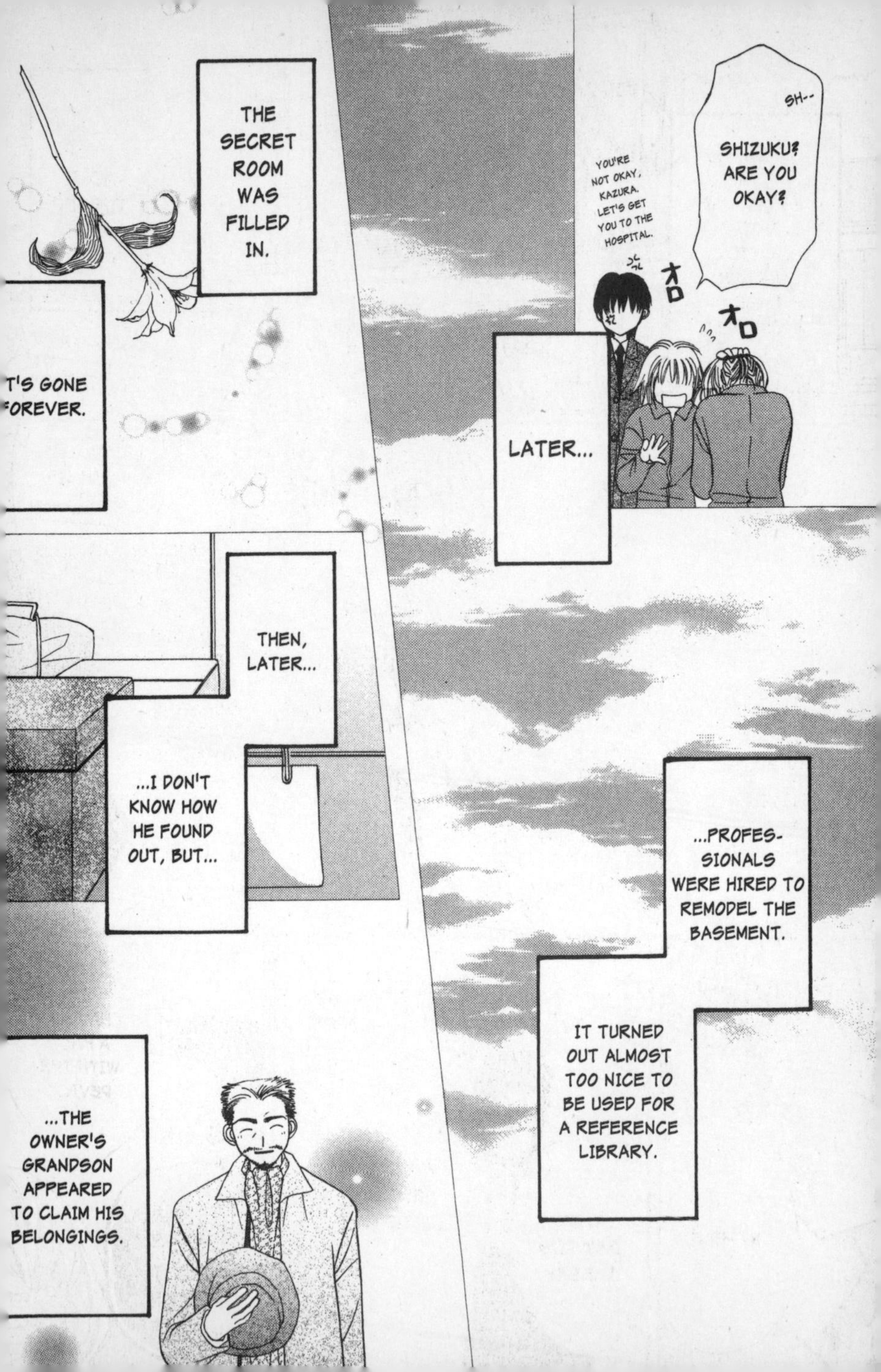
SH--
SHIZUKU? ARE YOU OKAY?
YOU'RE NOT OKAY, KAZURA. LET'S GET YOU TO THE HOSPITAL.
オロ
オロ
LATER...
THE SECRET ROOM WAS FILLED IN.
T'S GONE FOREVER.
...PROFES-SIONALS WERE HIRED TO REMODEL THE BASEMENT.
IT TURNED OUT ALMOST TOO NICE TO BE USED FOR A REFERENCE LIBRARY.
THEN, LATER...
...I DON'T KNOW HOW HE FOUND OUT, BUT...
...THE OWNER'S GRANDSON APPEARED TO CLAIM HIS BELONGINGS.

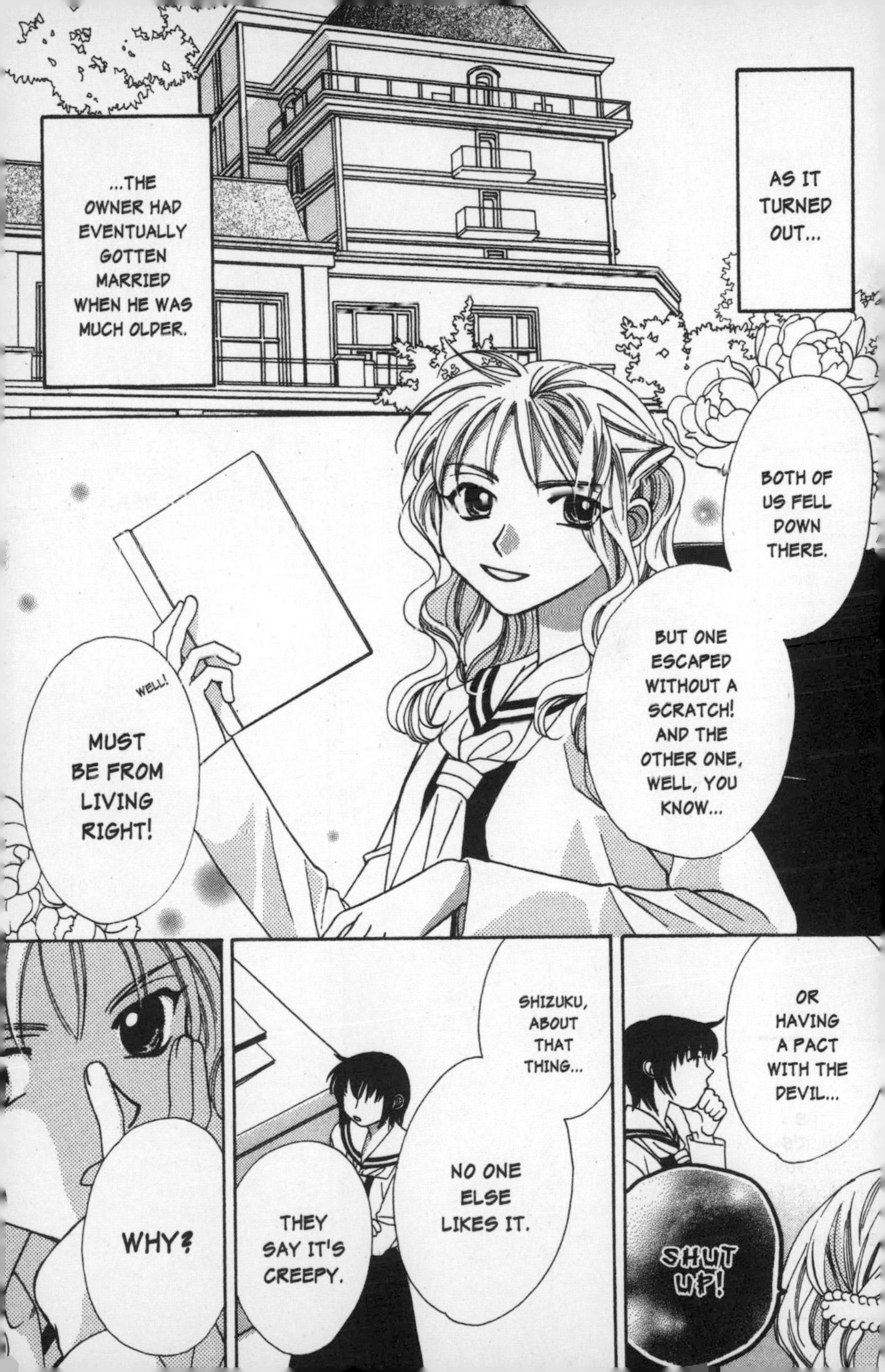
AS IT TURNED OUT...
...THE OWNER HAD EVENTUALLY GOTTEN MARRIED WHEN HE WAS MUCH OLDER.
BOTH OF US FELL DOWN THERE.
BUT ONE ESCAPED WITHOUT A SCRATCH! AND THE OTHER ONE, WELL, YOU KNOW...
WELL!
MUST BE FROM LIVING RIGHT!
OR HAVING A PACT WITH THE DEVIL...
SHUT UP!
SHIZUKU, ABOUT THAT THING...
NO ONE ELSE LIKES IT.
THEY SAY IT'S CREEPY.
WHY?

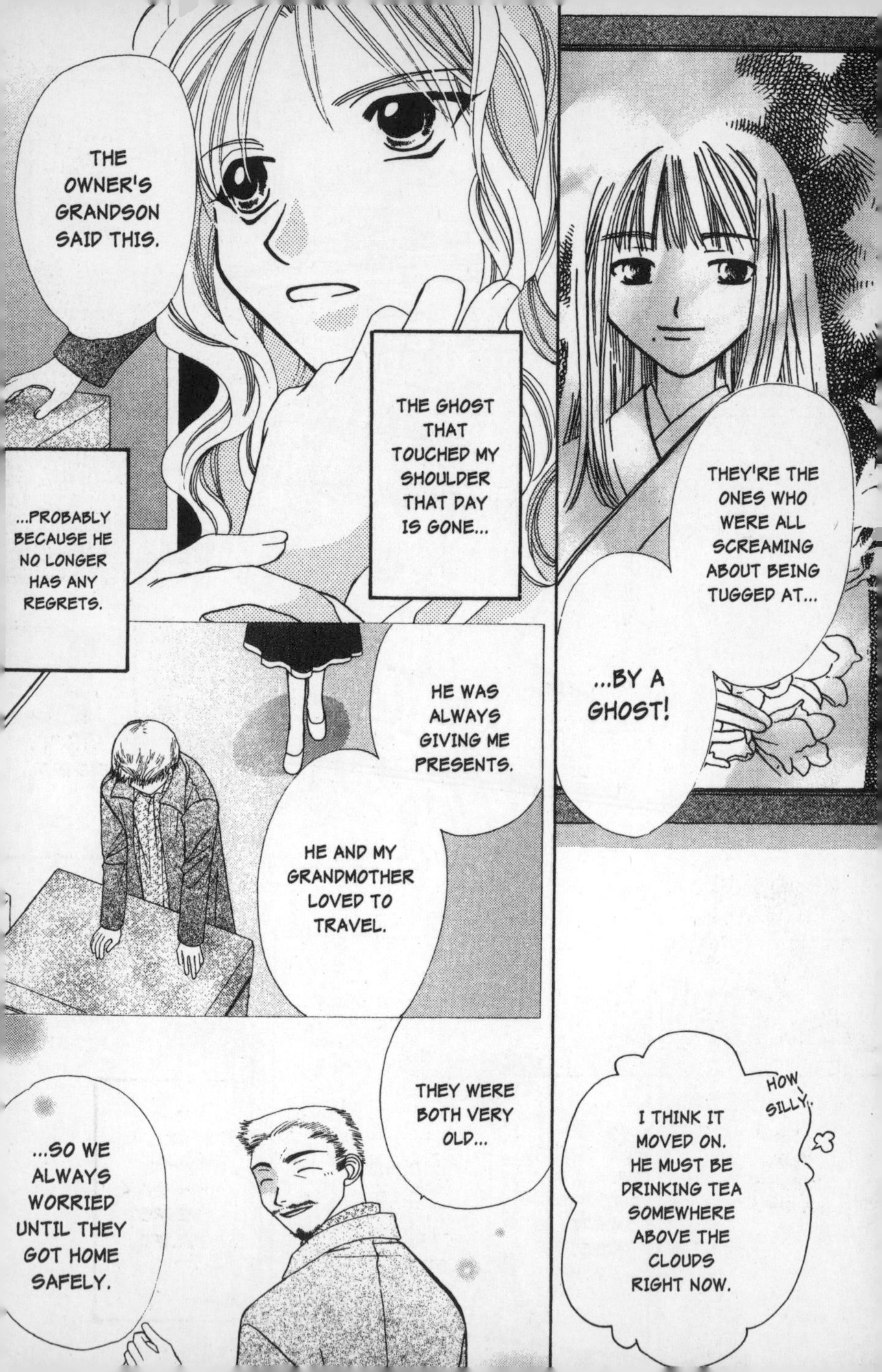
THEY'RE THE ONES WHO WERE ALL SCREAMING ABOUT BEING TUGGED AT...
...BY A GHOST!
I THINK IT MOVED ON. HE MUST BE DRINKING TEA SOMEWHERE ABOVE THE CLOUDS RIGHT NOW.
HOW SILLY.
THE GHOST THAT TOUCHED MY SHOULDER THAT DAY IS GONE...
...PROBABLY BECAUSE HE NO LONGER HAS ANY REGRETS.
THE OWNER'S GRANDSON SAID THIS.
HE WAS ALWAYS GIVING ME PRESENTS.
HE AND MY GRANDMOTHER LOVED TO TRAVEL.
THEY WERE BOTH VERY OLD...
...SO WE ALWAYS WORRIED UNTIL THEY GOT HOME SAFELY.

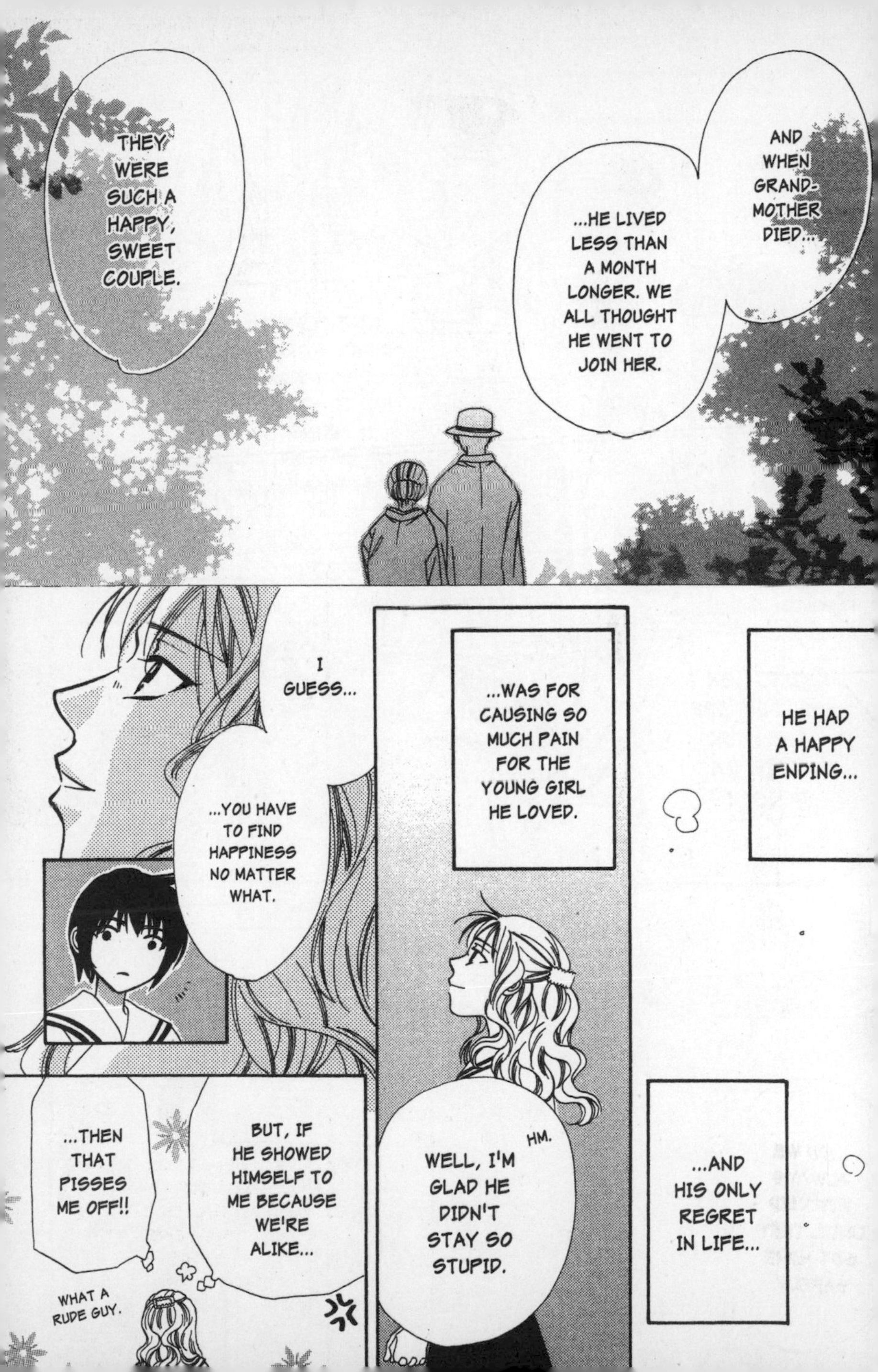
AND WHEN GRAND-MOTHER DIED...
...HE LIVED LESS THAN A MONTH LONGER. WE ALL THOUGHT HE WENT TO JOIN HER.
THEY WERE SUCH A HAPPY, SWEET COUPLE.
HE HAD A HAPPY ENDING...
...AND HIS ONLY REGRET IN LIFE...
...WAS FOR CAUSING SO MUCH PAIN FOR THE YOUNG GIRL HE LOVED.
HM.
WELL, I'M GLAD HE DIDN'T STAY SO STUPID.
I GUESS...
...YOU HAVE TO FIND HAPPINESS NO MATTER WHAT.
BUT, IF HE SHOWED HIMSELF TO ME BECAUSE WE'RE ALIKE...
...THEN THAT PISSES ME OFF!!
WHAT A RUDE GUY.

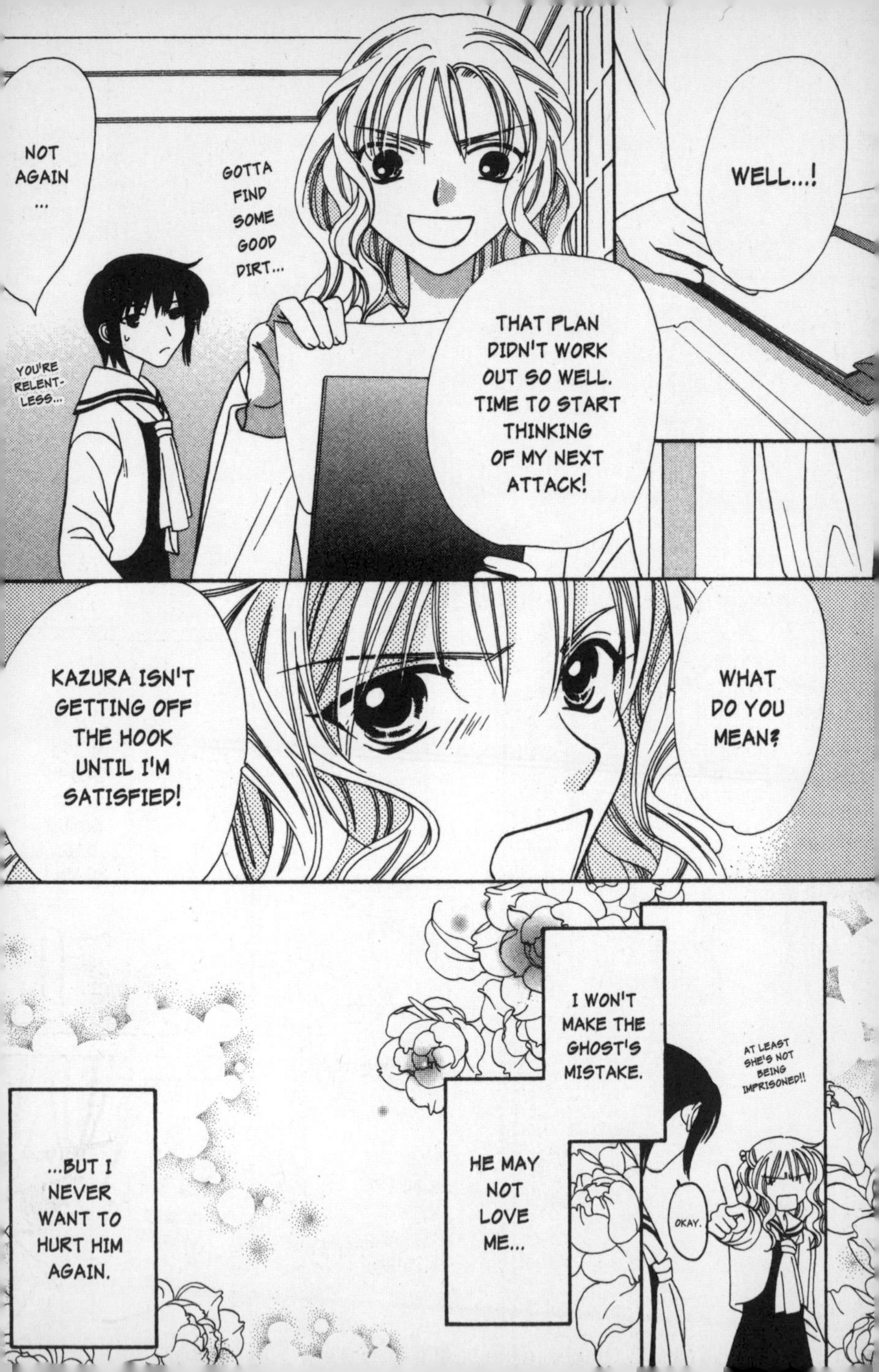

WELL...!
THAT PLAN DIDN'T WORK OUT SO WELL. TIME TO START THINKING OF MY NEXT ATTACK!
GOTTA FIND SOME GOOD DIRT...
NOT AGAIN ...
YOU'RE RELENT-LESS...
WHAT DO YOU MEAN?
KAZURA ISN'T GETTING OFF THE HOOK UNTIL I'M SATISFIED!
AT LEAST SHE'S NOT BEING IMPRISONED!!
OKAY.
I WON'T MAKE THE GHOST'S MISTAKE.
HE MAY NOT LOVE ME...
...BUT I NEVER WANT TO HURT HIM AGAIN.

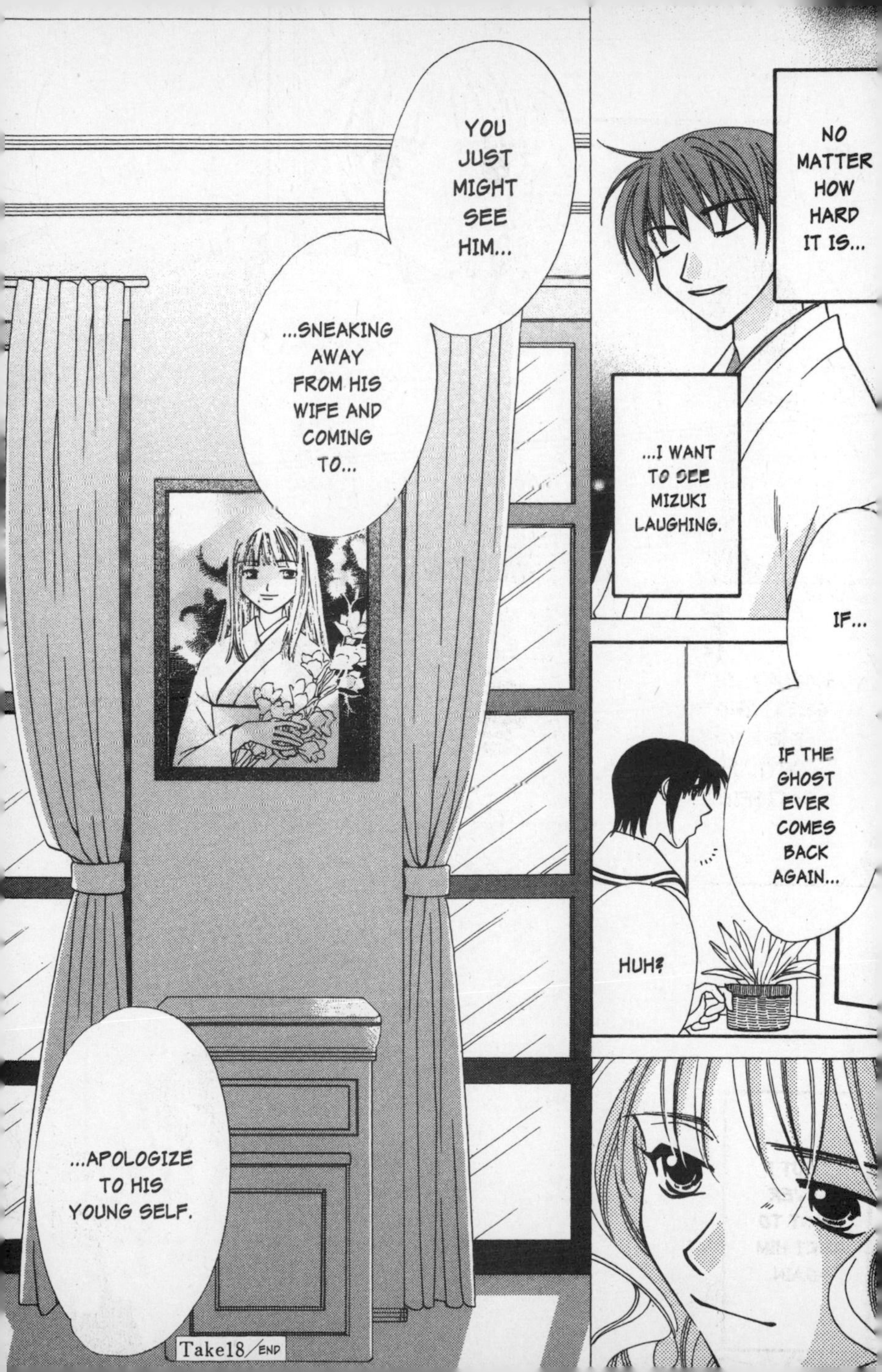
NO MATTER HOW HARD IT IS...
...I WANT TO SEE MIZUKI LAUGHING.
IF...
IF THE GHOST EVER COMES BACK AGAIN...
...
HUH?
YOU JUST MIGHT SEE HIM...
...SNEAKING AWAY FROM HIS WIFE AND COMING TO...
...APOLOGIZE TO HIS YOUNG SELF.
Take18/END

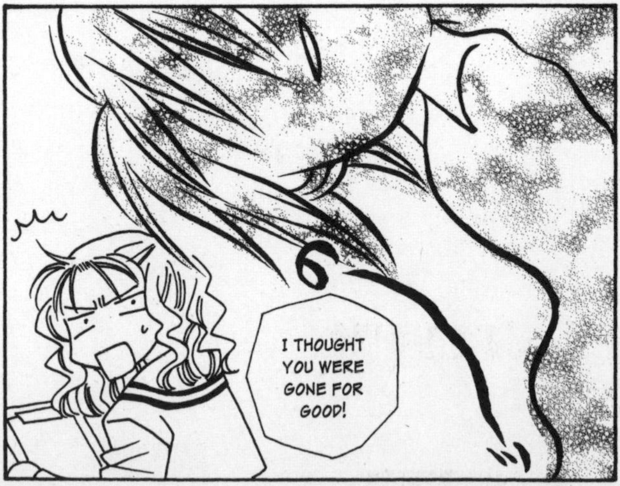
I THOUGHT YOU WERE GONE FOR GOOD!

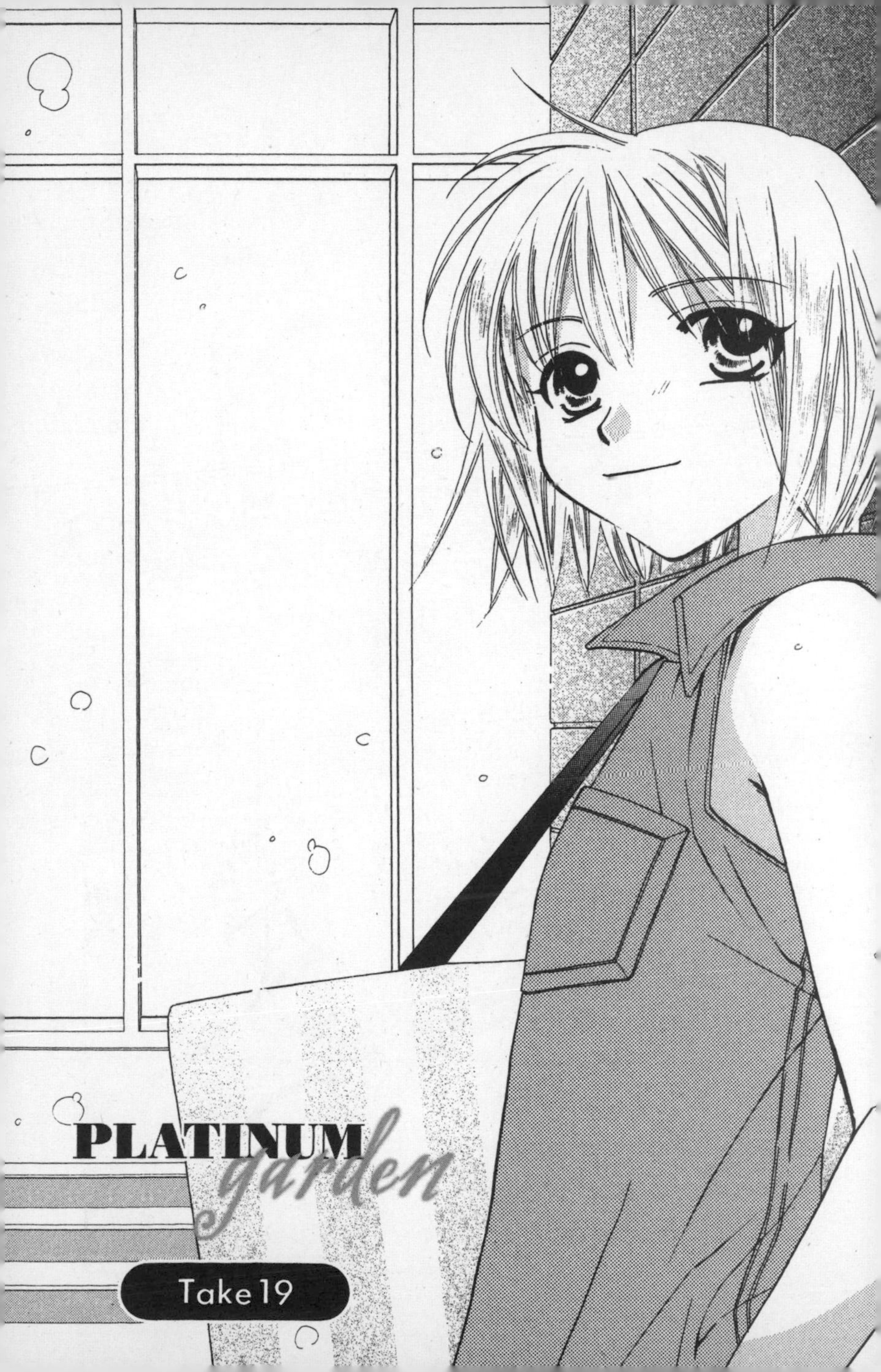
PLATINUM
garden
Take 19

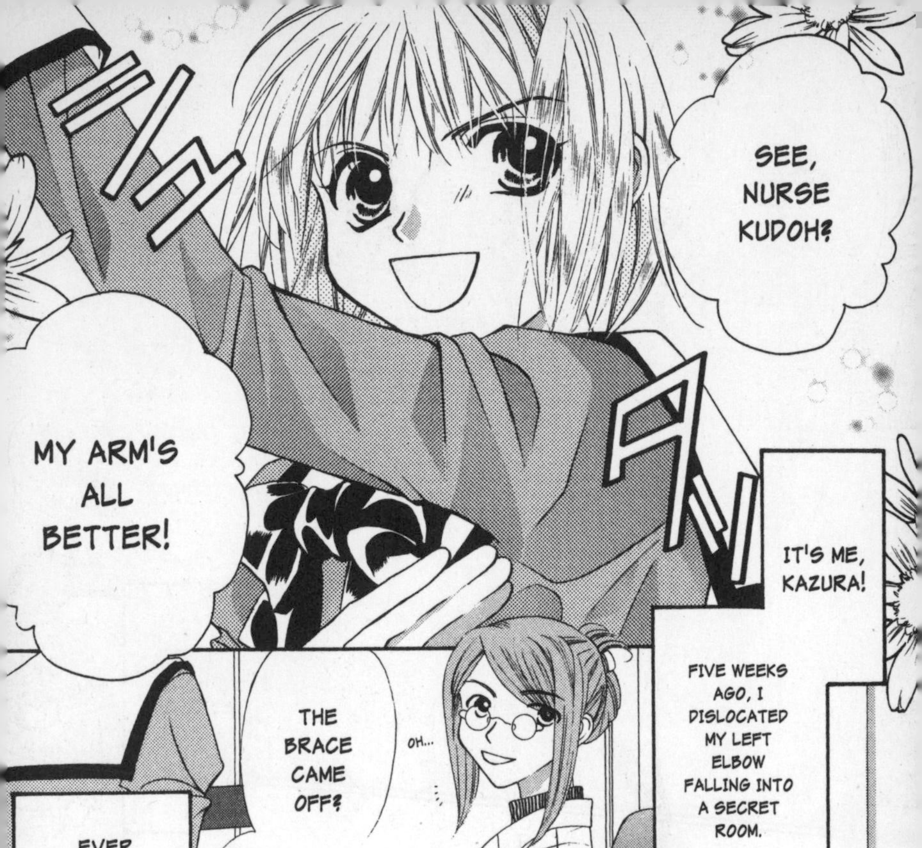
SEE, NURSE KUDOH?
IT'S ME, KAZURA!
MY ARM'S ALL BETTER!
FIVE WEEKS AGO, I DISLOCATED MY LEFT ELBOW FALLING INTO A SECRET ROOM.
OH...
THE BRACE CAME OFF?
CONGRATU-LATIONS!
EVER SINCE, I'VE BEEN A REGULAR AT THE NURSE'S OFFICE.

FUJITA'S SUMMER, 2002

THE PROGRAM I USE TO DO ALL
MY WRITING HAS BEEN ACTING UP LATELY...
NOTHING TERRIBLE HAS HAPPENED SO FAR...
BUT IF I LOSE A SCRIPT I'LL BE IN TROUBLE!!

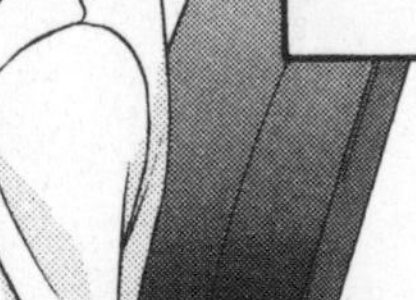
NO!!!

DEAR N*C, PLEASE PUT OUT AN UPGRADE SOON!

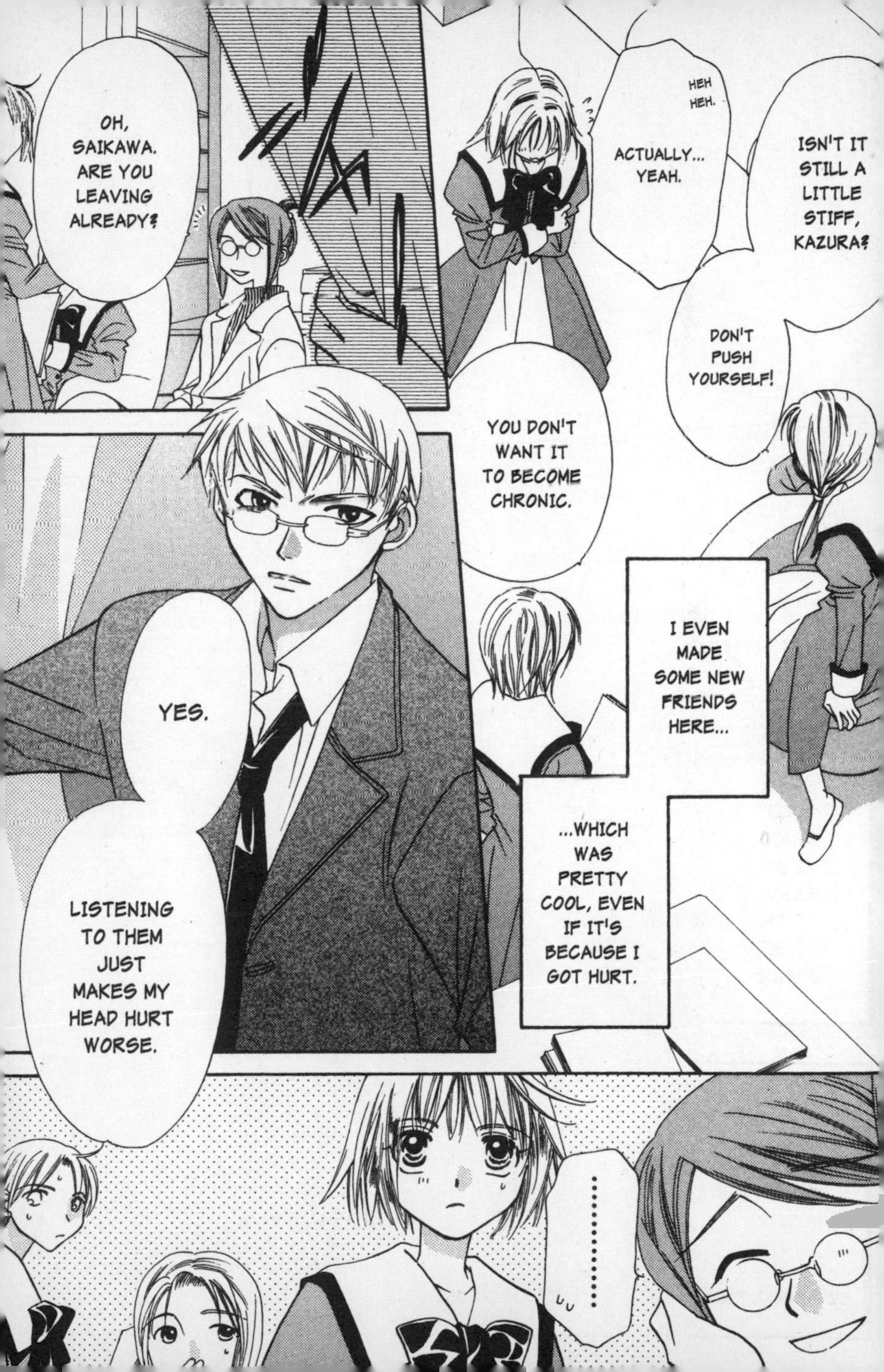

ISN'T IT STILL A LITTLE STIFF, KAZURA?
HEH HEH.
ACTUALLY... YEAH.
DON'T PUSH YOURSELF!
YOU DON'T WANT IT TO BECOME CHRONIC.
I EVEN MADE SOME NEW FRIENDS HERE...
...WHICH WAS PRETTY COOL, EVEN IF IT'S BECAUSE I GOT HURT.
OH, SAIKAWA. ARE YOU LEAVING ALREADY?
YES.
LISTENING TO THEM JUST MAKES MY HEAD HURT WORSE.
......

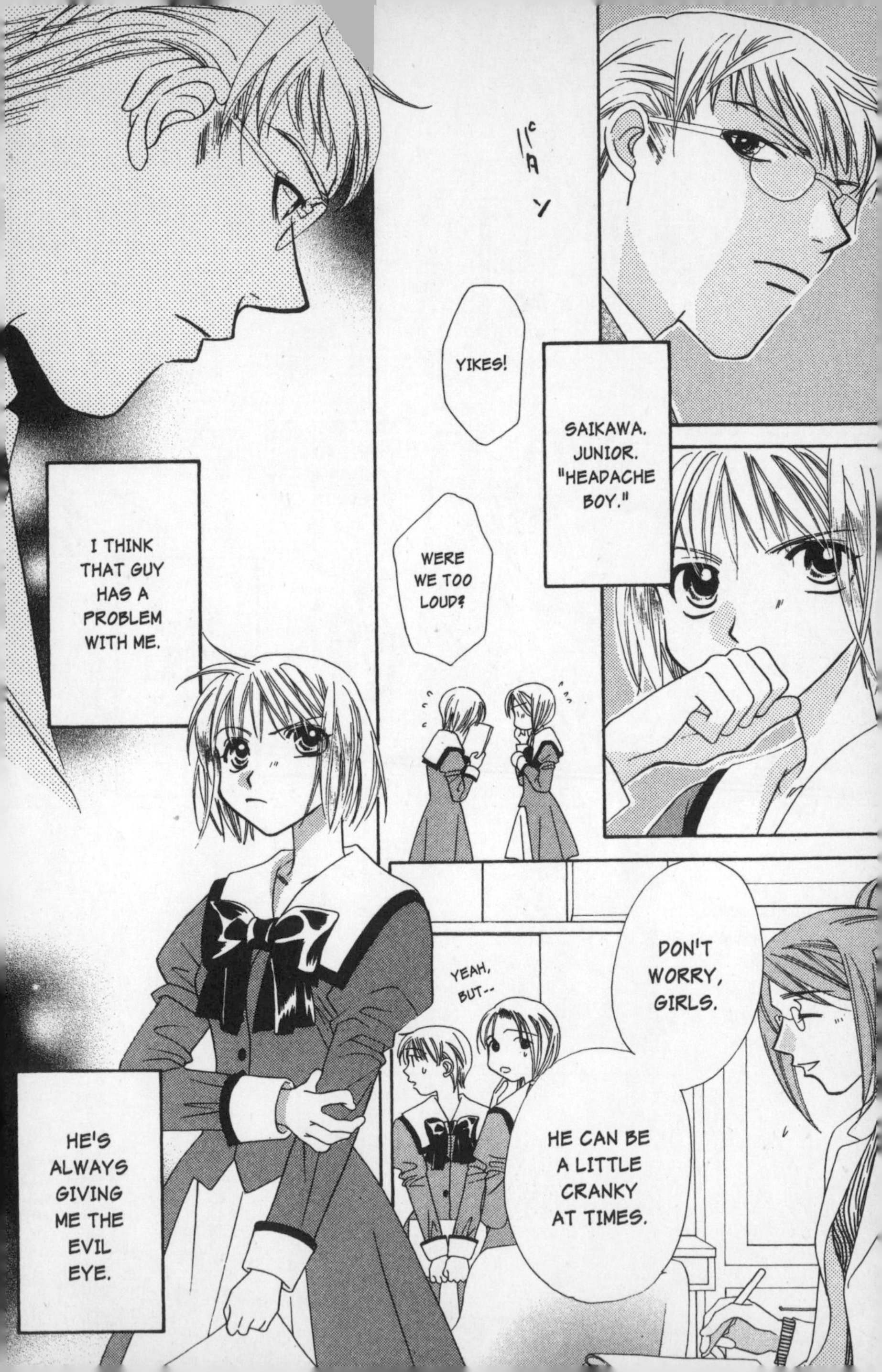
SAIKAWA. JUNIOR. "HEADACHE BOY."
YIKES!
WERE WE TOO LOUD?
I THINK THAT GUY HAS A PROBLEM WITH ME.
DON'T WORRY, GIRLS.
HE CAN BE A LITTLE CRANKY AT TIMES.
YEAH, BUT--
HE'S ALWAYS GIVING ME THE EVIL EYE.

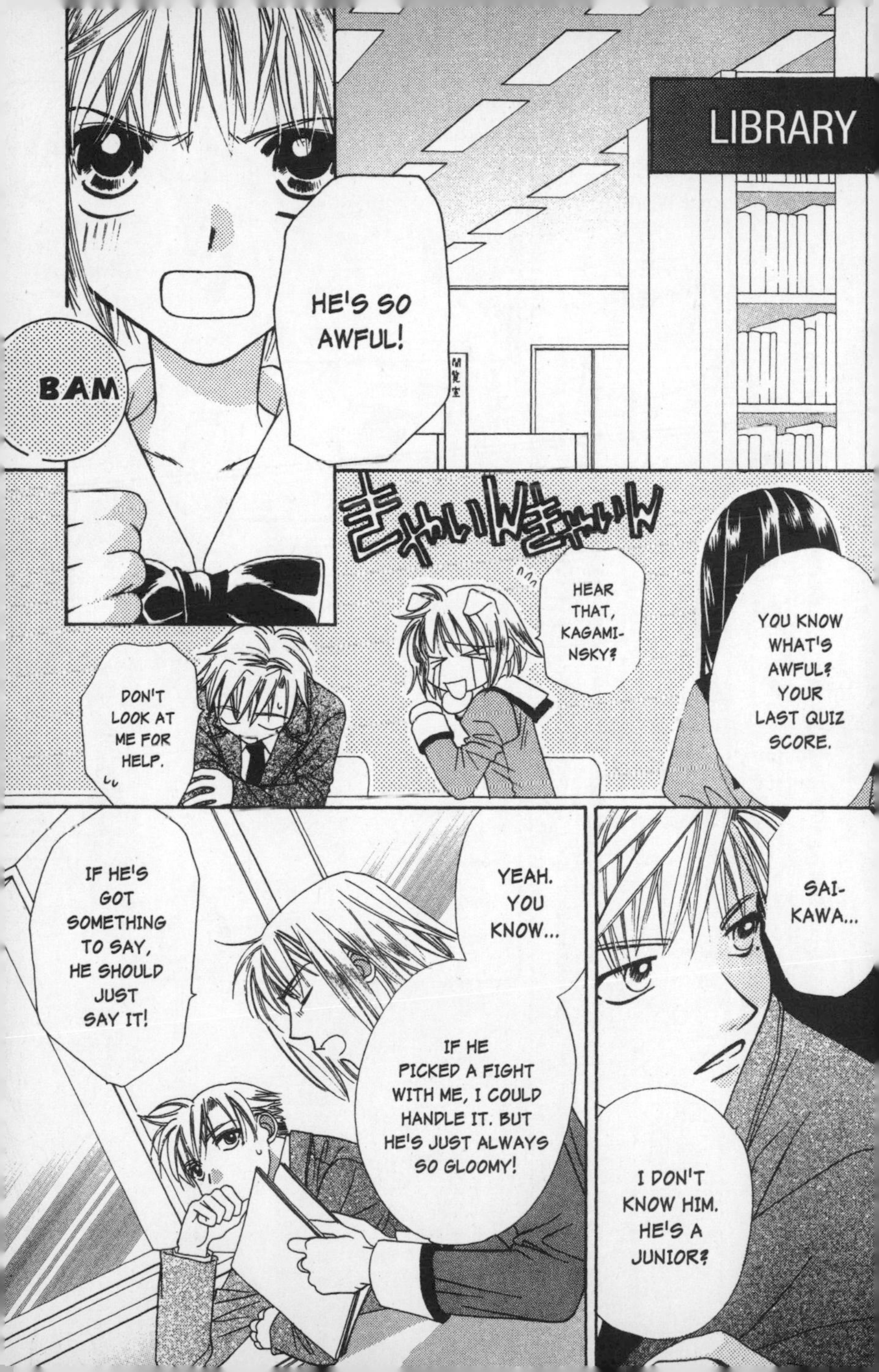
LIBRARY
HE'S SO AWFUL!
BAM
HEAR THAT, KAGAMINSKY?
YOU KNOW WHAT'S AWFUL? YOUR LAST QUIZ SCORE.
DON'T LOOK AT ME FOR HELP.
SAI-KAWA...
I DON'T KNOW HIM. HE'S A JUNIOR?
YEAH. YOU KNOW...
IF HE'S GOT SOMETHING TO SAY, HE SHOULD JUST SAY IT!
IF HE PICKED A FIGHT WITH ME, I COULD HANDLE IT. BUT HE'S JUST ALWAYS SO GLOOMY!

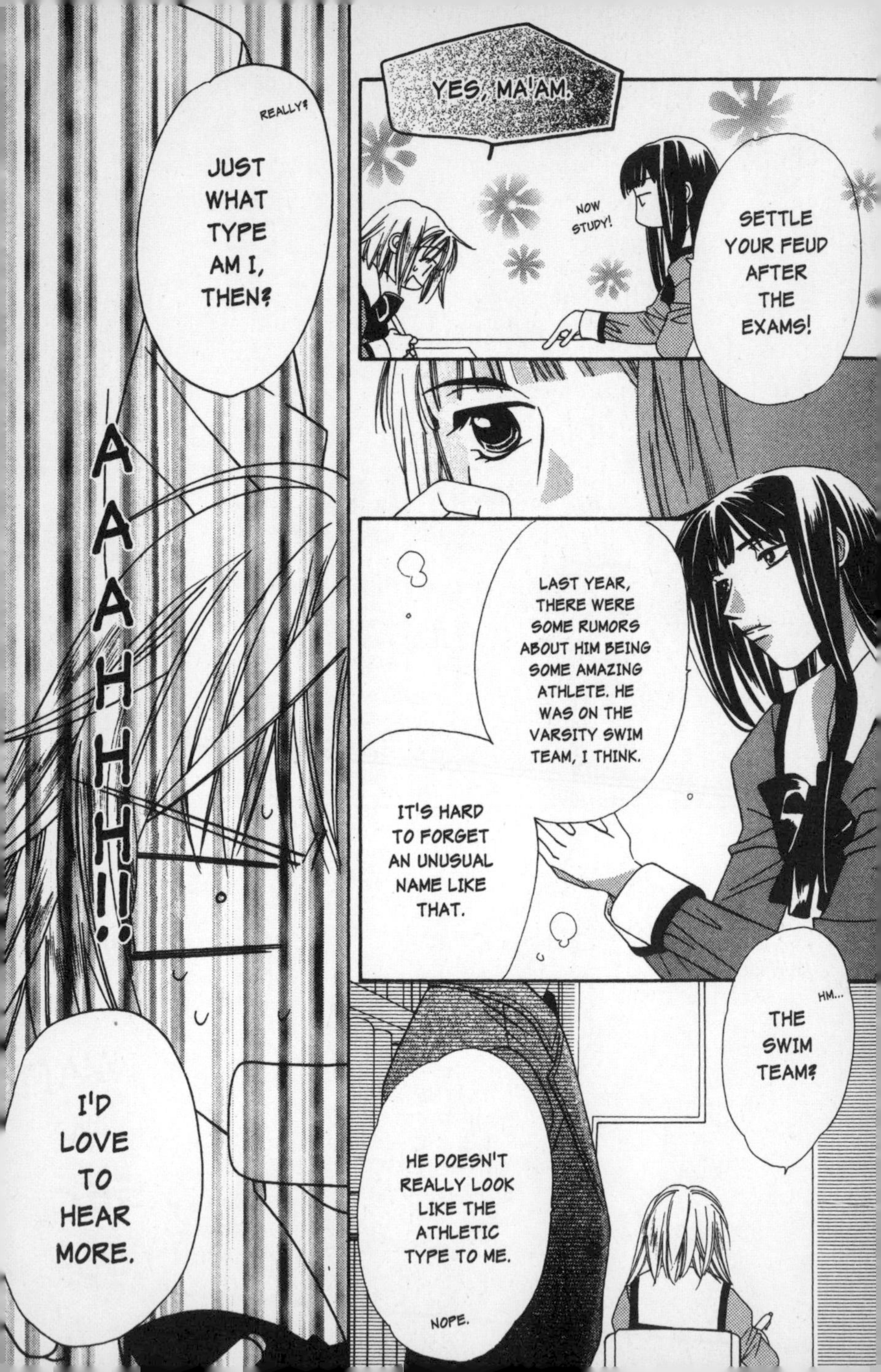
YES, MA'AM.
SETTLE YOUR FEUD AFTER THE EXAMS!
NOW STUDY!
LAST YEAR, THERE WERE SOME RUMORS ABOUT HIM BEING SOME AMAZING ATHLETE. HE WAS ON THE VARSITY SWIM TEAM, I THINK.
IT'S HARD TO FORGET AN UNUSUAL NAME LIKE THAT.
HM...
THE SWIM TEAM?
HE DOESN'T REALLY LOOK LIKE THE ATHLETIC TYPE TO ME.
NOPE.
REALLY?
JUST WHAT TYPE AM I, THEN?
AAAHHH!!
I'D LOVE TO HEAR MORE.

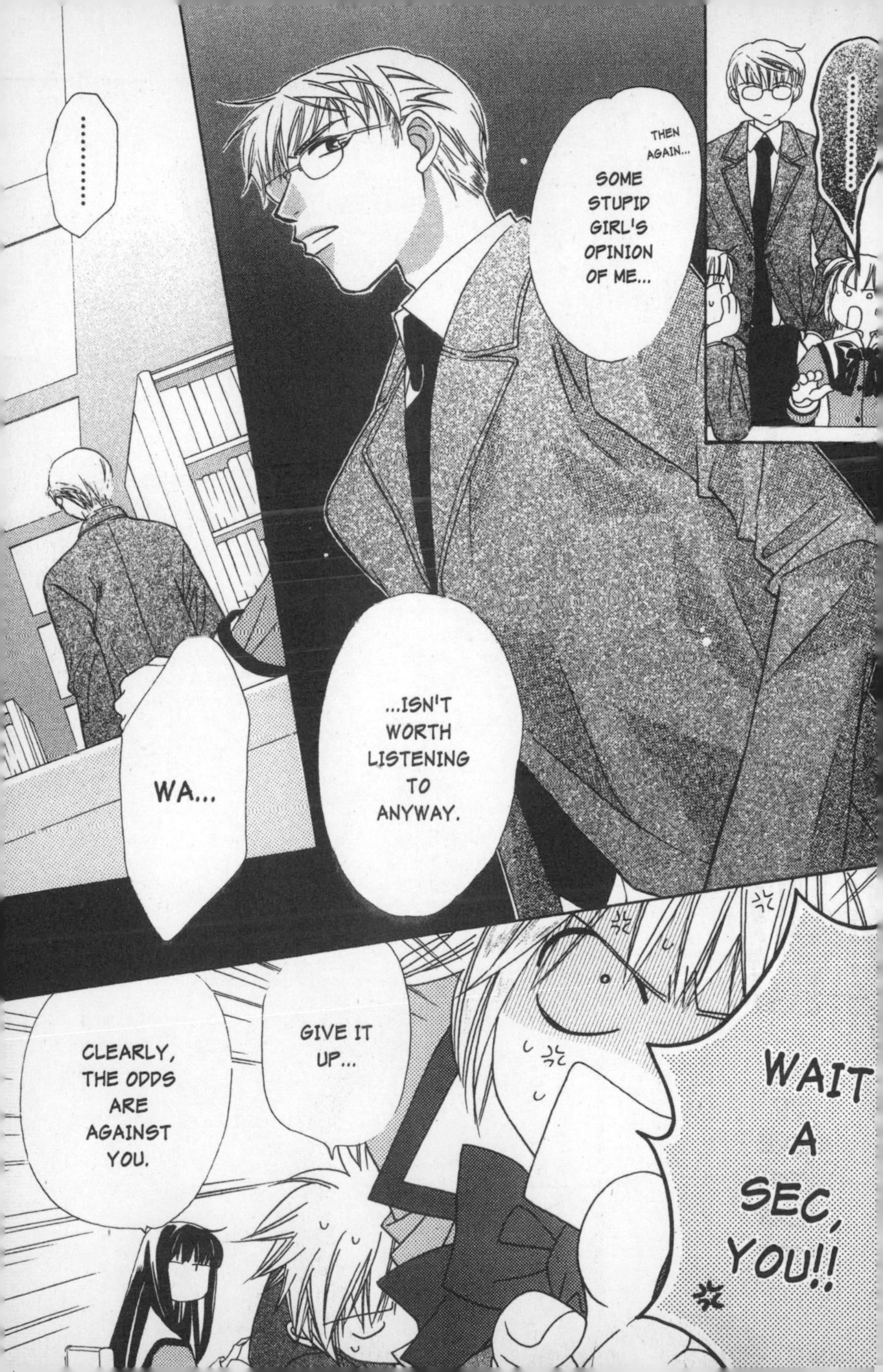

......
THEN AGAIN...
SOME STUPID GIRL'S OPINION OF ME...
...ISN'T WORTH LISTENING TO ANYWAY.
......
WA...
WAIT A SEC, YOU!!
GIVE IT UP...
CLEARLY, THE ODDS ARE AGAINST YOU.

OKAY, WE SHOULDN'T HAVE BEEN TALKING ABOUT HIM.
BUT WHEN YOU THINK ABOUT IT, IT'S HIS OWN FAULT!
I'VE HAD IT WITH HIM!
CHOKED
NEXT TIME, I'M GONNA JUMP RIGHT ON HIM AND CHOKE HIM!

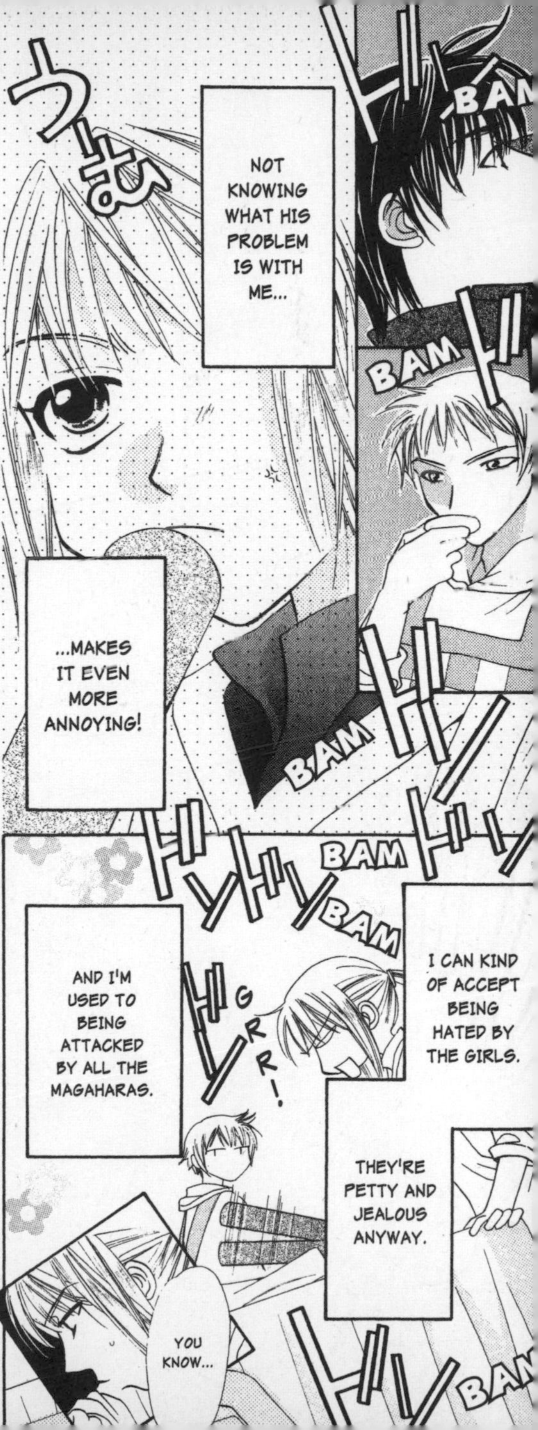
BAM
BAM
うむ
NOT KNOWING WHAT HIS PROBLEM IS WITH ME...
...MAKES IT EVEN MORE ANNOYING!
BAM
BAM
BAM
I CAN KIND OF ACCEPT BEING HATED BY THE GIRLS.
THEY'RE PETTY AND JEALOUS ANYWAY.
AND I'M USED TO BEING ATTACKED BY ALL THE MAGAHARAS.
GRR!
YOU KNOW...
BAM

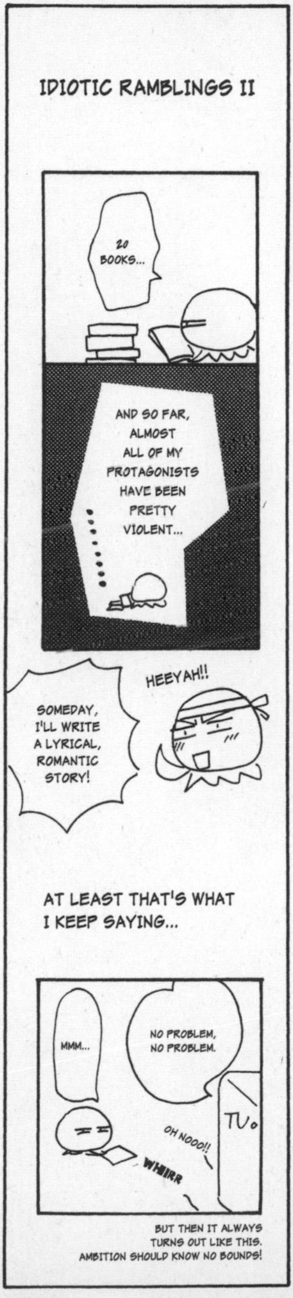
IDIOTIC RAMBLINGS II
20 BOOKS...
AND SO FAR, ALMOST ALL OF MY PROTAGONISTS HAVE BEEN PRETTY VIOLENT...
SOMEDAY, I'LL WRITE A LYRICAL, ROMANTIC STORY!
HEEYAH!!
AT LEAST THAT'S WHAT I KEEP SAYING...
NO PROBLEM, NO PROBLEM.
MMM...
TU。
OH NOOO!!
WHIRR
BUT THEN IT ALWAYS TURNS OUT LIKE THIS. AMBITION SHOULD KNOW NO BOUNDS!

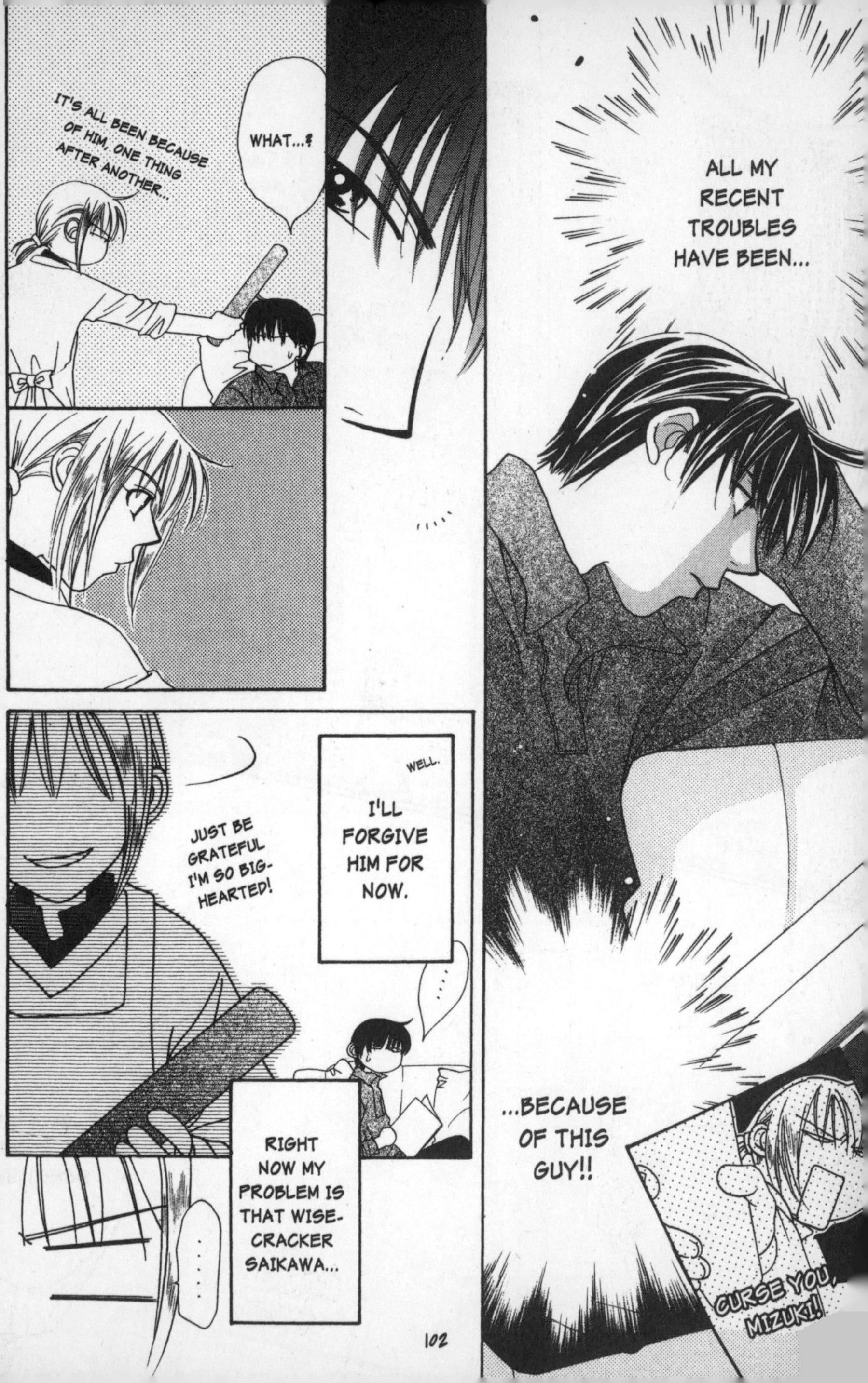

ALL MY RECENT TROUBLES HAVE BEEN...
...BECAUSE OF THIS GUY!!
CURSE YOU, MIZUKI!!
WHAT...?
IT'S ALL BEEN BECAUSE OF HIM, ONE THING AFTER ANOTHER...
WELL.
I'LL FORGIVE HIM FOR NOW.
JUST BE GRATEFUL I'M SO BIG-HEARTED!
...
RIGHT NOW MY PROBLEM IS THAT WISE-CRACKER SAIKAWA...
......

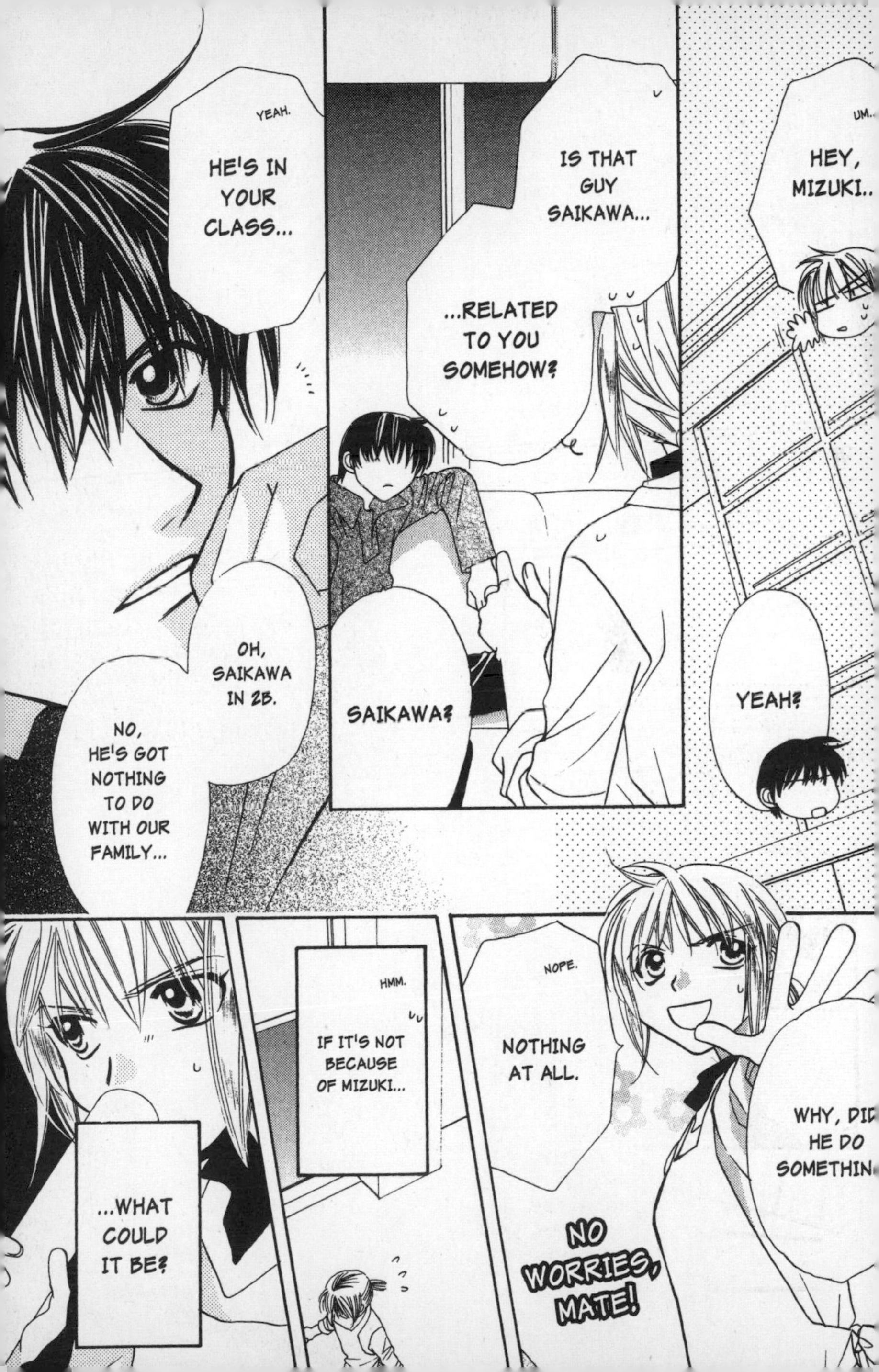
UM..
HEY, MIZUKI..
YEAH?
IS THAT GUY SAIKAWA...
...RELATED TO YOU SOMEHOW?
SAIKAWA?
YEAH.
HE'S IN YOUR CLASS...
OH, SAIKAWA IN 2B.
NO, HE'S GOT NOTHING TO DO WITH OUR FAMILY...
WHY, DID HE DO SOMETHIN
NOPE.
NOTHING AT ALL.
NO WORRIES, MATE!
HMM.
IF IT'S NOT BECAUSE OF MIZUKI...
...WHAT COULD IT BE?

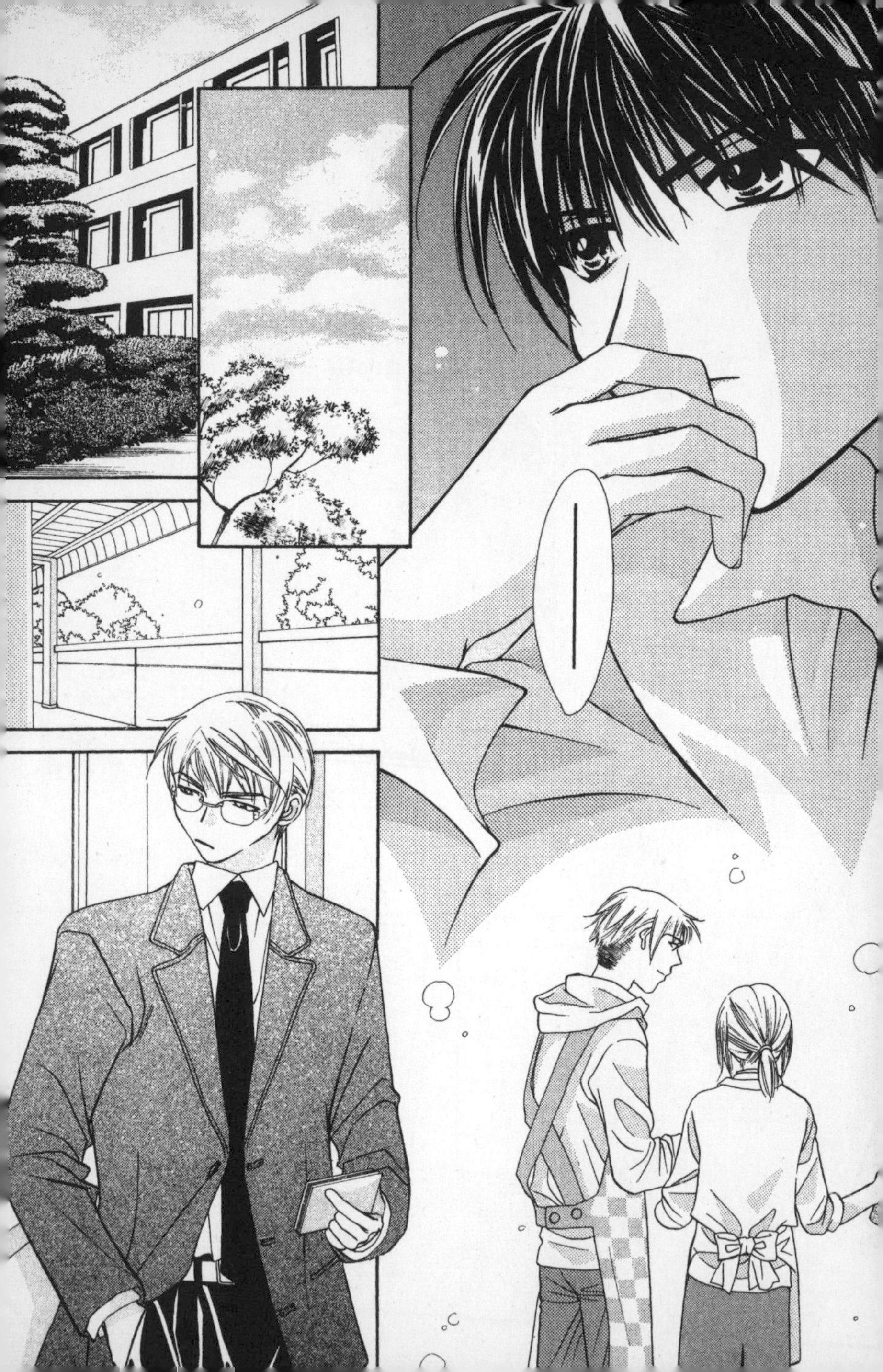

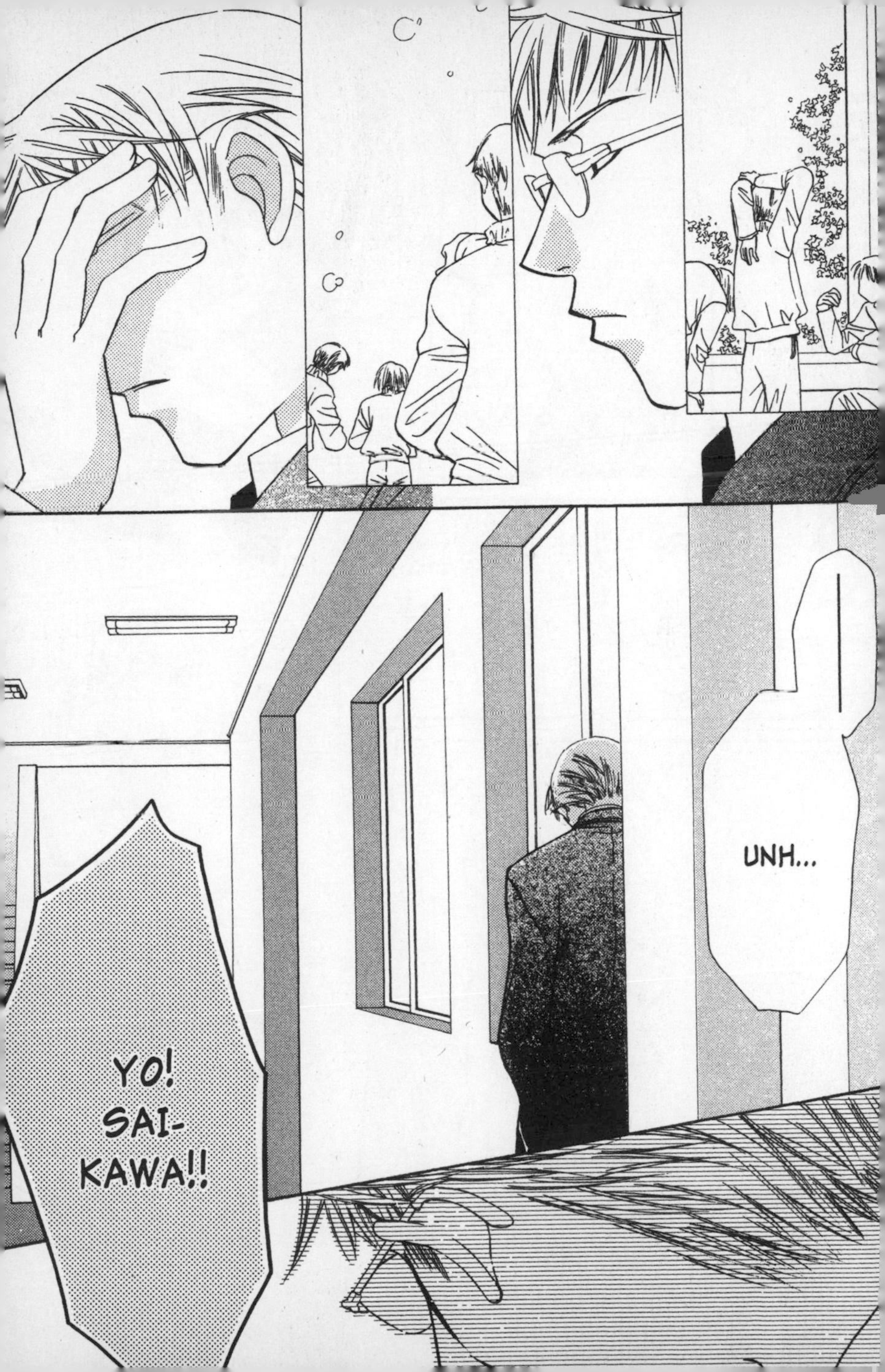
UNH...
YO! SAI-KAWA!!

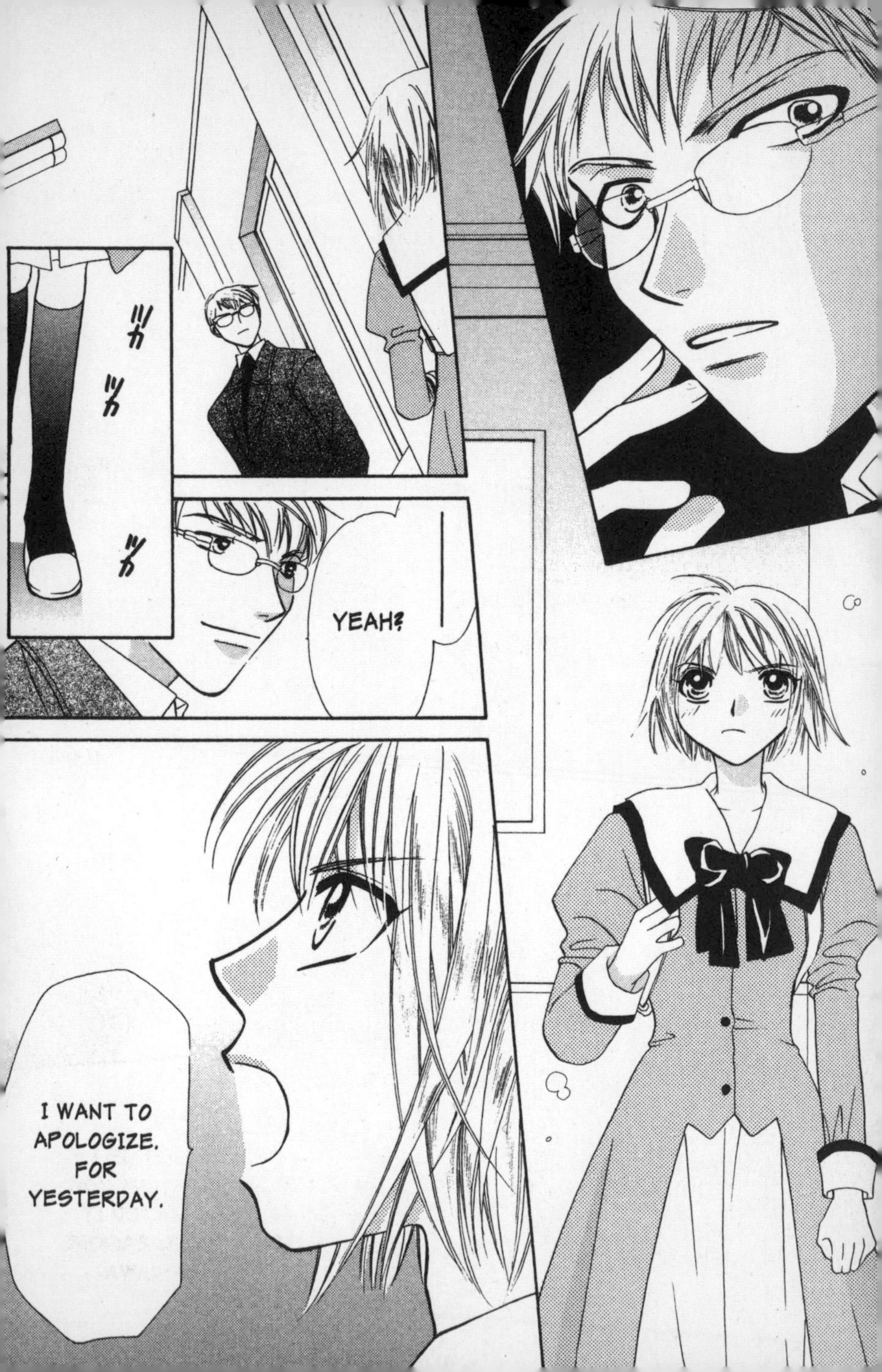
ツカ
ツカ
ツカ
YEAH?
I WANT TO APOLOGIZE. FOR YESTERDAY.

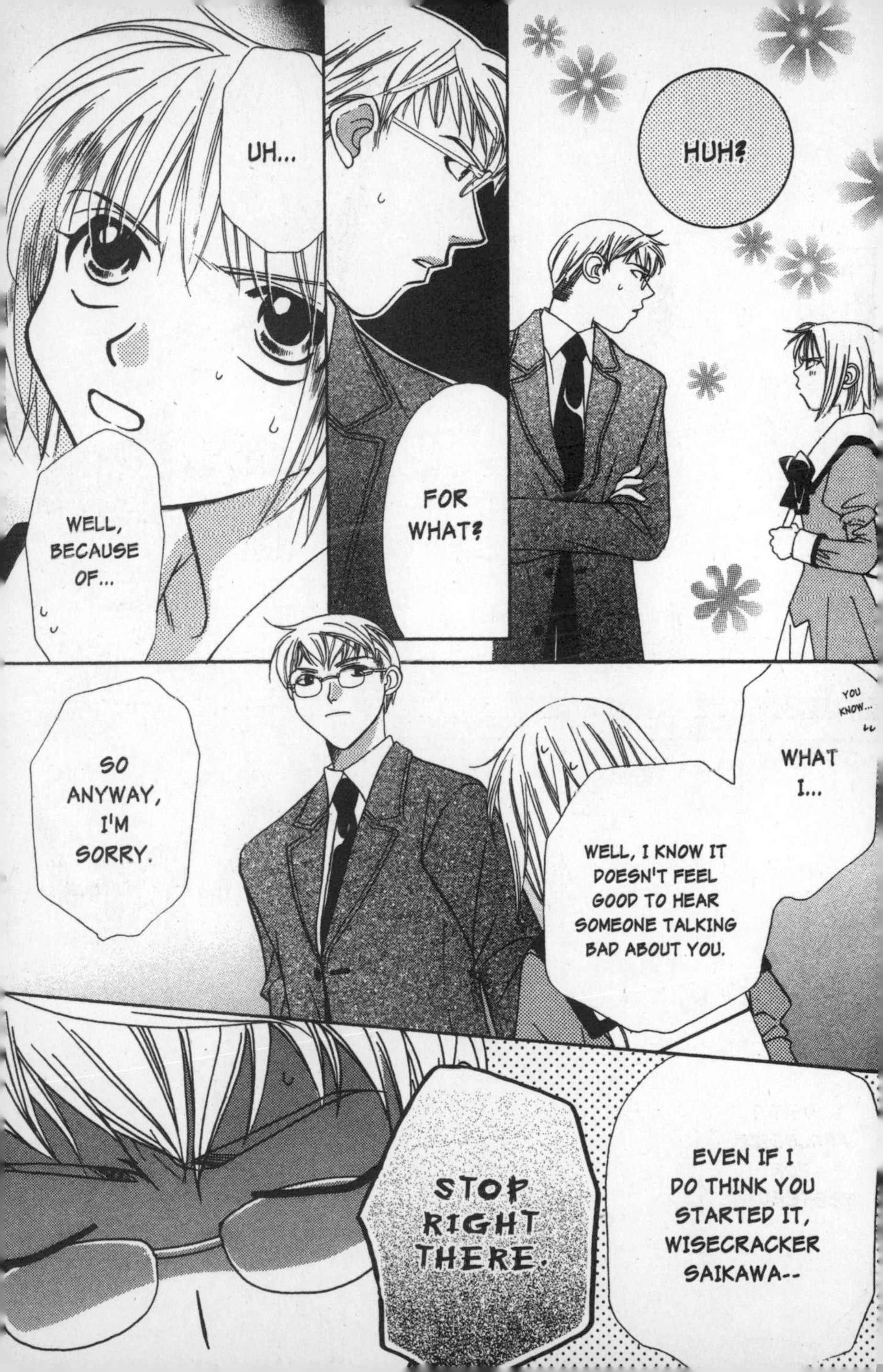
HUH?
FOR WHAT?
UH...
WELL, BECAUSE OF...
YOU KNOW...
WHAT I...
WELL, I KNOW IT DOESN'T FEEL GOOD TO HEAR SOMEONE TALKING BAD ABOUT YOU.
SO ANYWAY, I'M SORRY.
EVEN IF I DO THINK YOU STARTED IT, WISECRACKER SAIKAWA--
STOP RIGHT THERE.

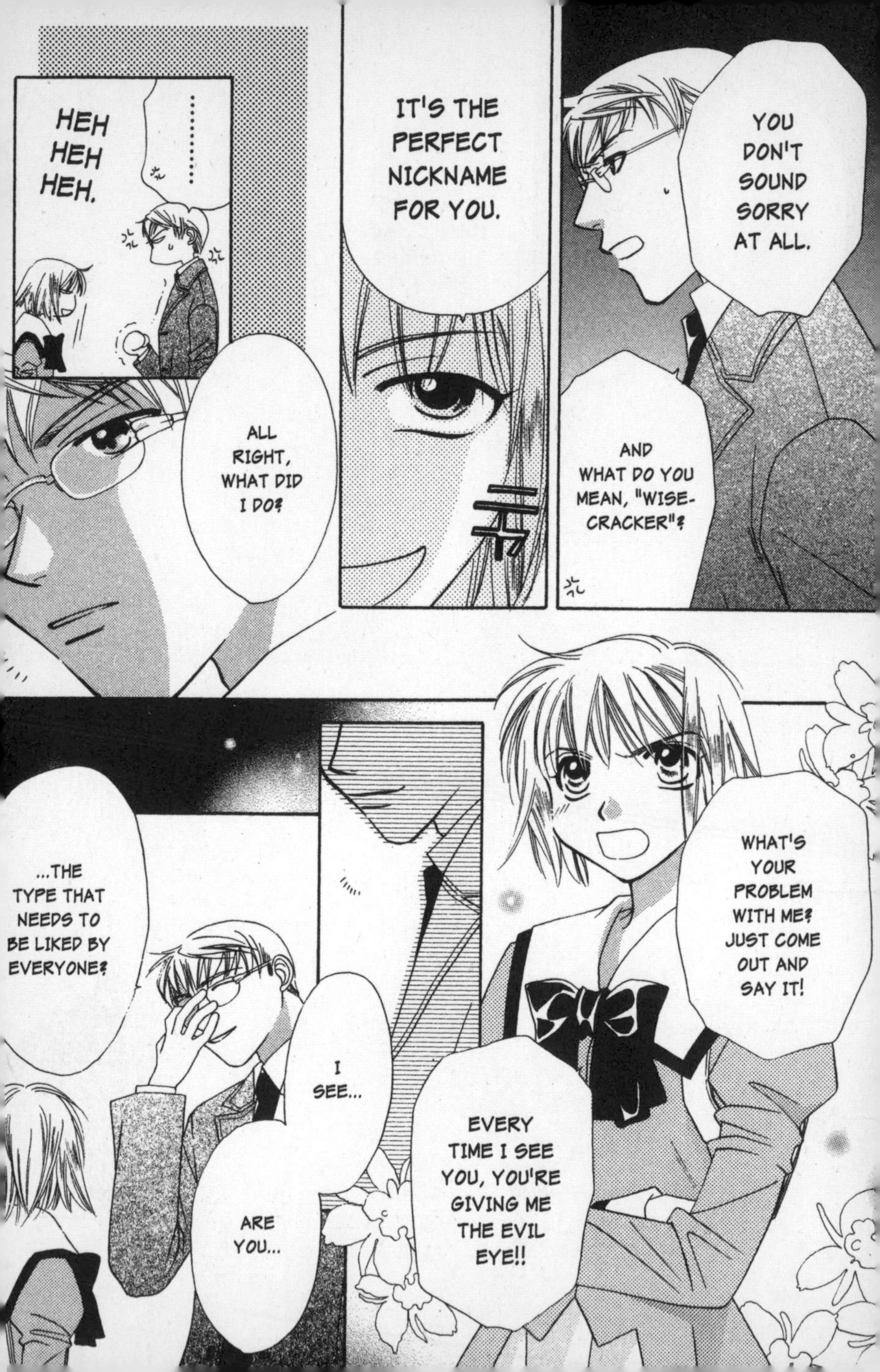
YOU DON'T SOUND SORRY AT ALL.
AND WHAT DO YOU MEAN, "WISE-CRACKER"?
IT'S THE PERFECT NICKNAME FOR YOU.
......
HEH HEH HEH.
ALL RIGHT, WHAT DID I DO?
WHAT'S YOUR PROBLEM WITH ME? JUST COME OUT AND SAY IT!
EVERY TIME I SEE YOU, YOU'RE GIVING ME THE EVIL EYE!!
I SEE...
ARE YOU...
...THE TYPE THAT NEEDS TO BE LIKED BY EVERYONE?

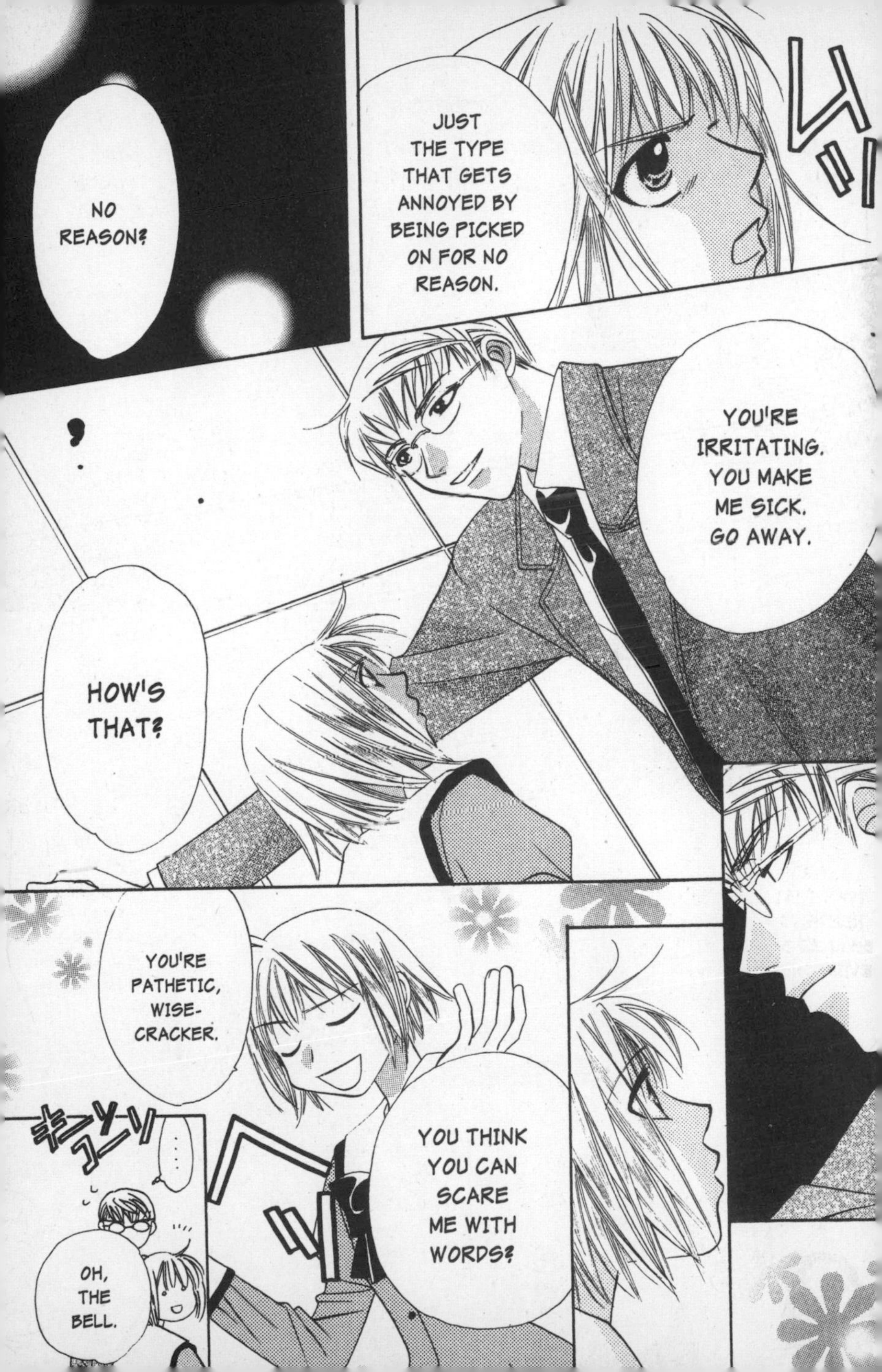
JUST THE TYPE THAT GETS ANNOYED BY BEING PICKED ON FOR NO REASON.
NO REASON?
YOU'RE IRRITATING. YOU MAKE ME SICK. GO AWAY.
HOW'S THAT?
YOU'RE PATHETIC, WISE-CRACKER.
YOU THINK YOU CAN SCARE ME WITH WORDS?
OH, THE BELL.

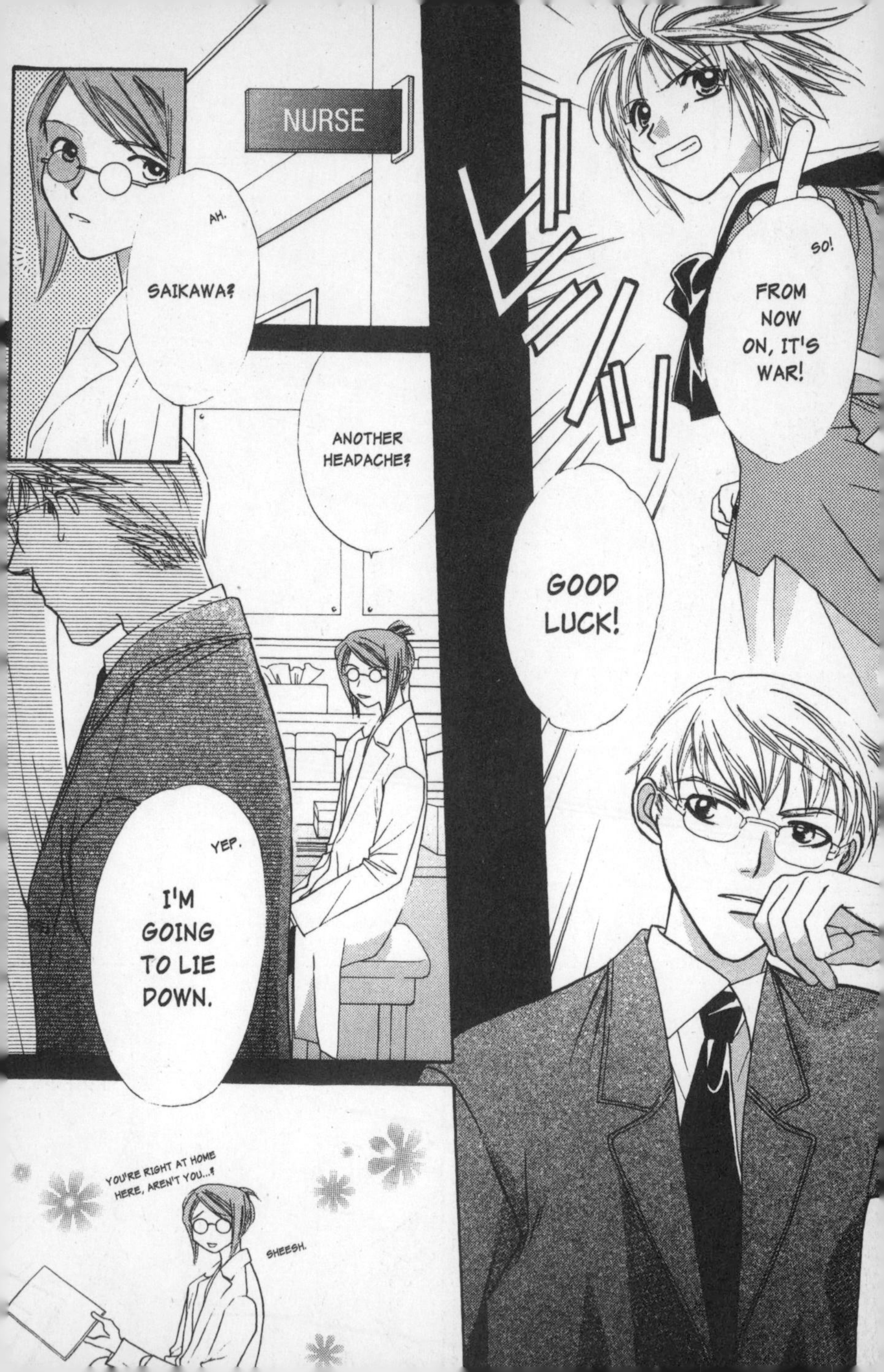
SO! FROM NOW ON, IT'S WAR!
GOOD LUCK!
NURSE
AH. SAIKAWA?
ANOTHER HEADACHE?
YEP. I'M GOING TO LIE DOWN.
YOU'RE RIGHT AT HOME HERE, AREN'T YOU...?
SHEESH.

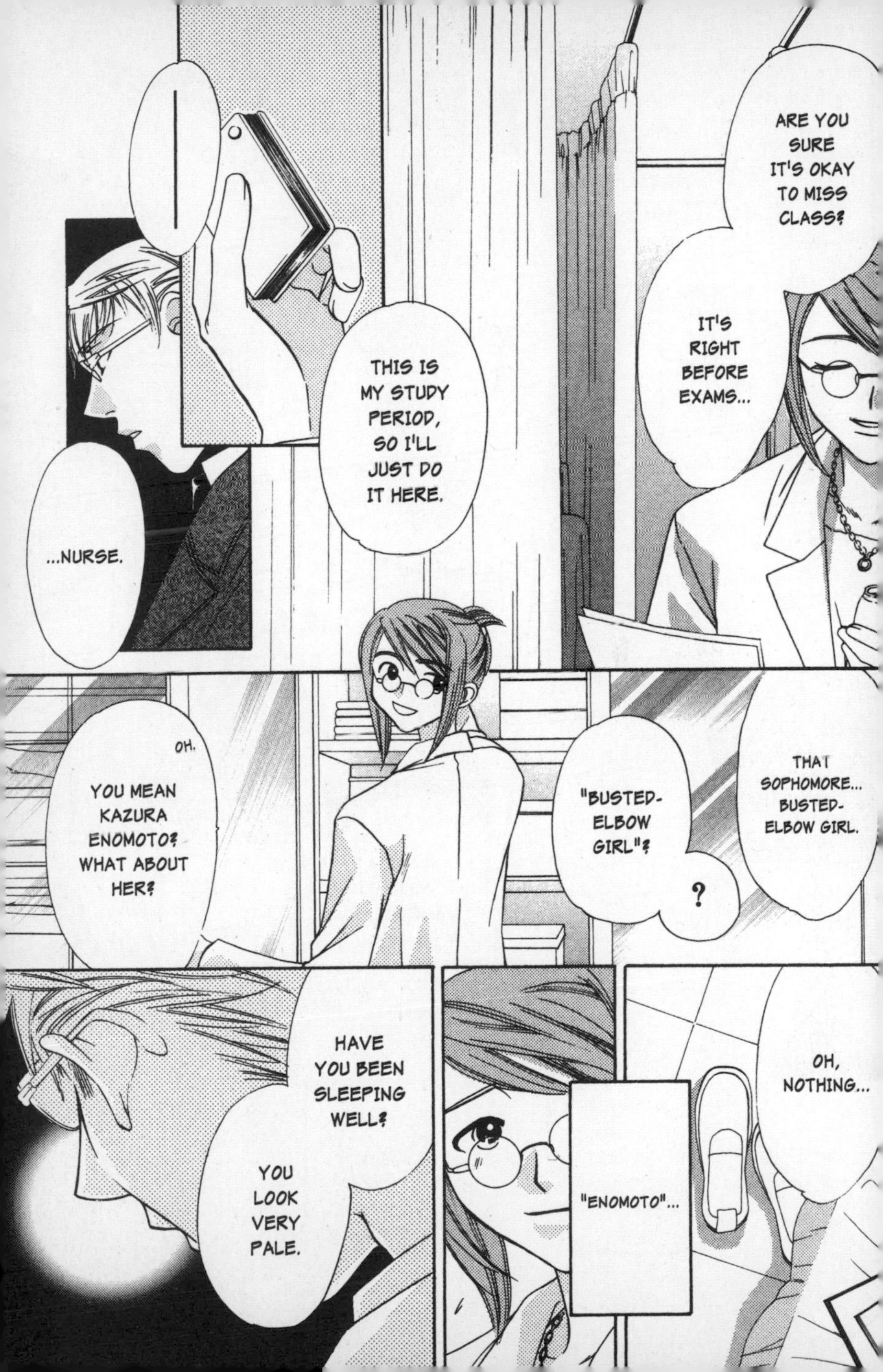
ARE YOU SURE IT'S OKAY TO MISS CLASS?
IT'S RIGHT BEFORE EXAMS...
THIS IS MY STUDY PERIOD, SO I'LL JUST DO IT HERE.
...NURSE.
THAT SOPHOMORE... BUSTED-ELBOW GIRL.
"BUSTED-ELBOW GIRL"?
?
OH.
YOU MEAN KAZURA ENOMOTO? WHAT ABOUT HER?
OH, NOTHING...
"ENOMOTO"...
HAVE YOU BEEN SLEEPING WELL?
YOU LOOK VERY PALE.

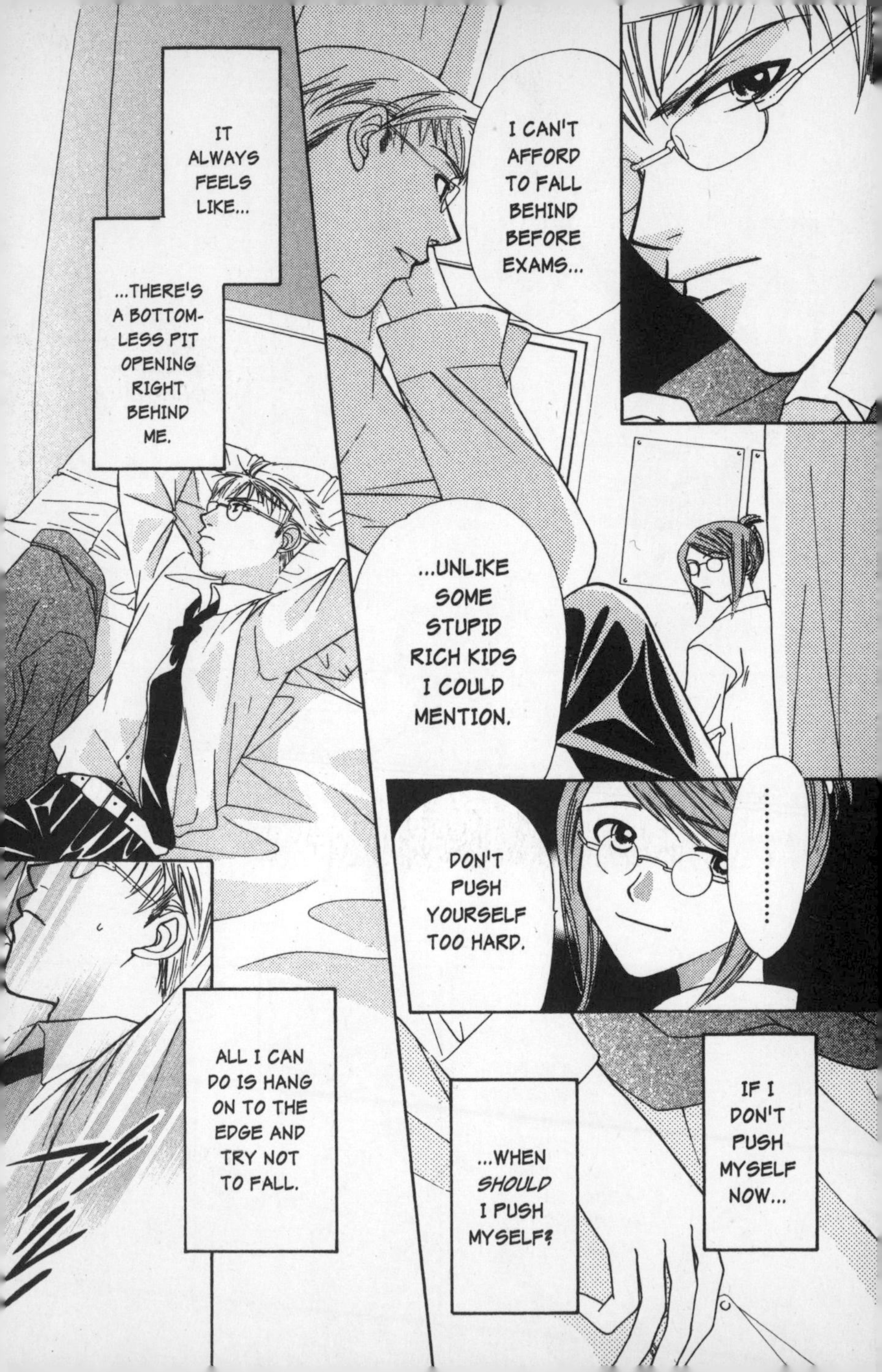
I CAN'T AFFORD TO FALL BEHIND BEFORE EXAMS...
...UNLIKE SOME STUPID RICH KIDS I COULD MENTION.
......
DON'T PUSH YOURSELF TOO HARD.
IF I DON'T PUSH MYSELF NOW...
...WHEN *SHOULD* I PUSH MYSELF?
IT ALWAYS FEELS LIKE...
...THERE'S A BOTTOM-LESS PIT OPENING RIGHT BEHIND ME.
ALL I CAN DO IS HANG ON TO THE EDGE AND TRY NOT TO FALL.

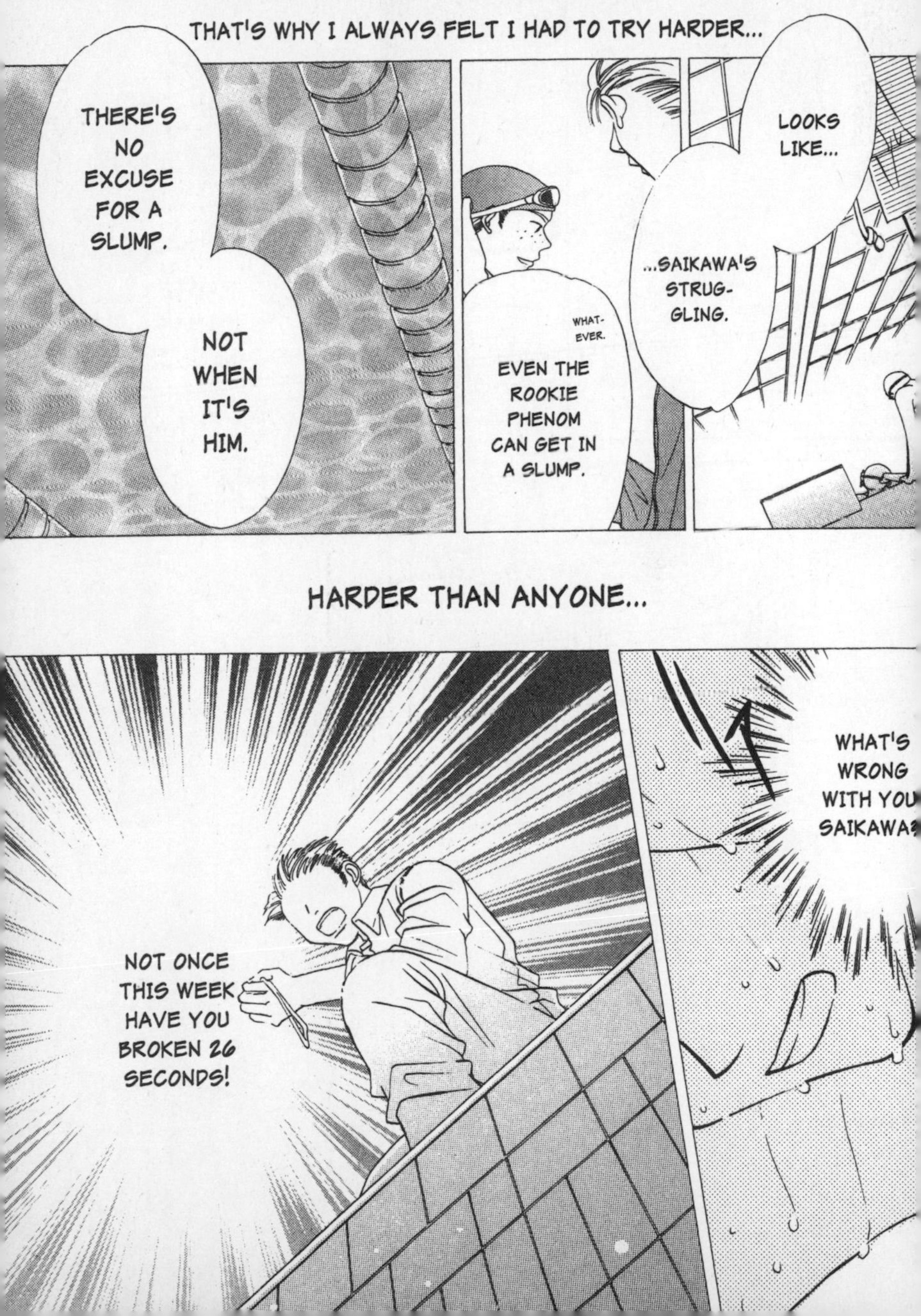
THAT'S WHY I ALWAYS FELT I HAD TO TRY HARDER...
LOOKS LIKE...
...SAIKAWA'S STRUG-GLING.
WHAT-EVER.
EVEN THE ROOKIE PHENOM CAN GET IN A SLUMP.
THERE'S NO EXCUSE FOR A SLUMP.
NOT WHEN IT'S HIM.
HARDER THAN ANYONE...
WHAT'S WRONG WITH YOU SAIKAWA?
NOT ONCE THIS WEEK HAVE YOU BROKEN 26 SECONDS!

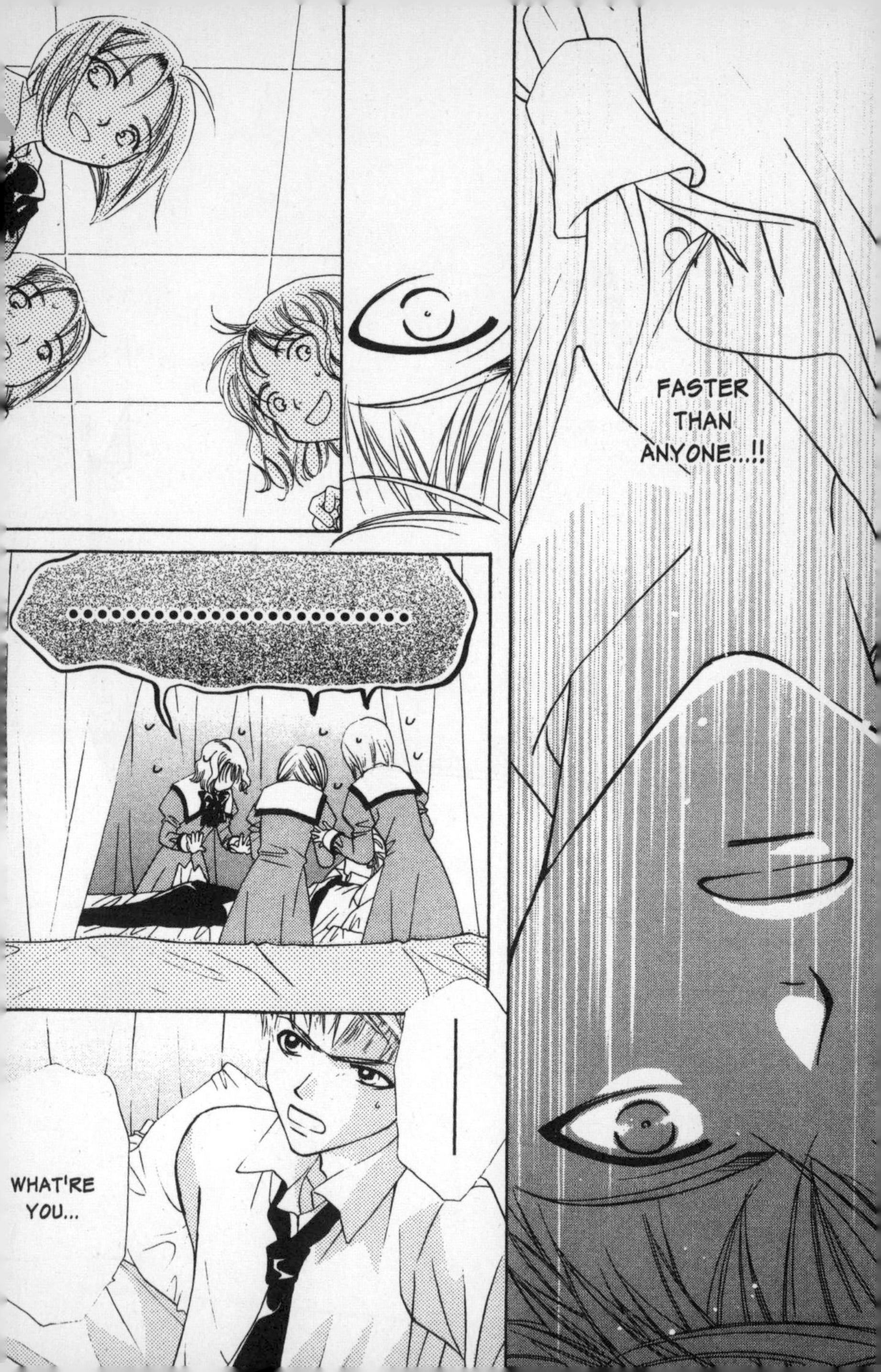
FASTER THAN ANYONE...!!
....
WHAT'RE YOU...

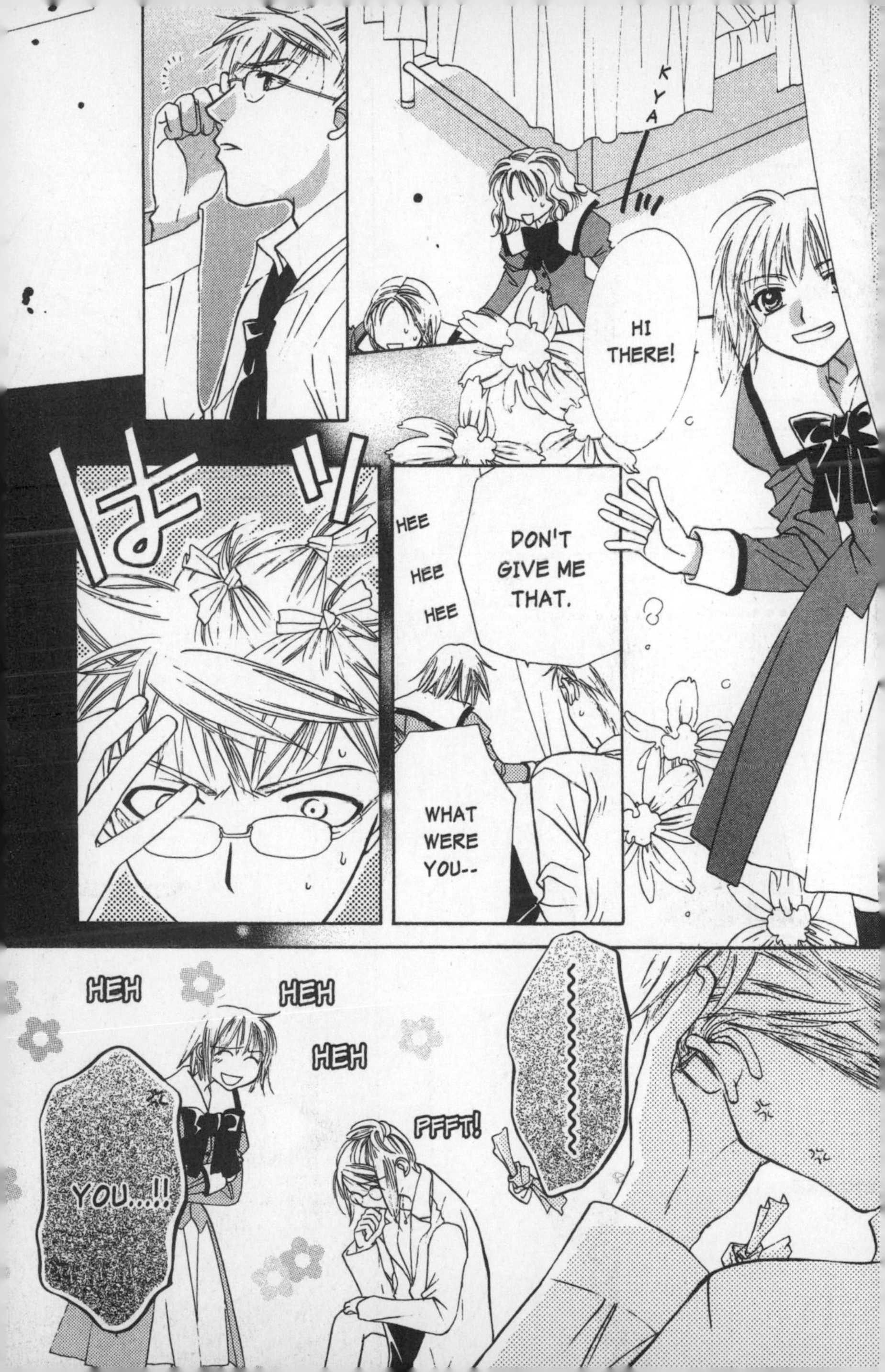
KYA
HI THERE!
DON'T GIVE ME THAT.
HEE HEE HEE
WHAT WERE YOU--
はッ
HEH HEH HEH
PFFT!
YOU...!!

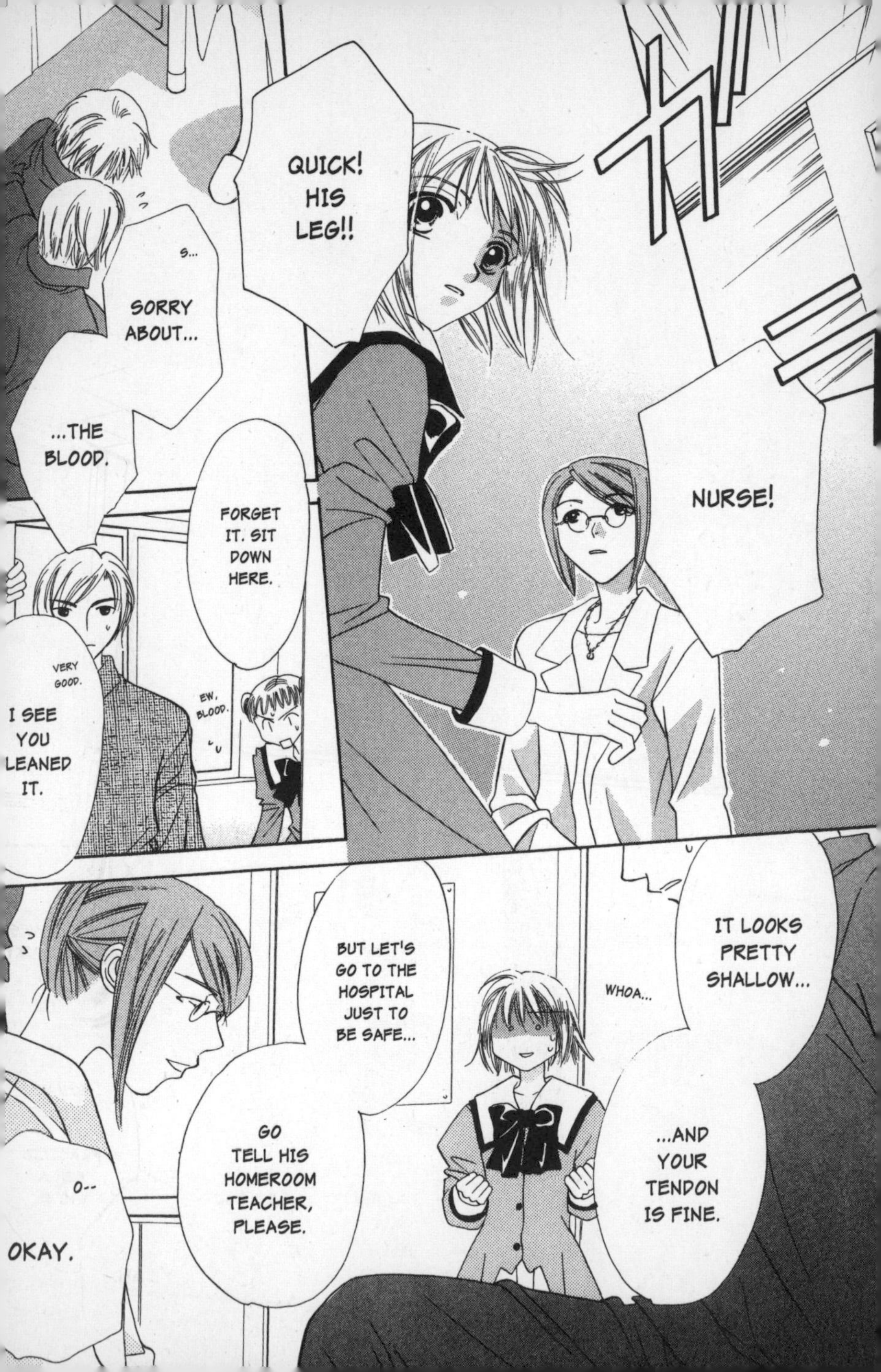
NURSE!
QUICK! HIS LEG!!
S...
SORRY ABOUT...
...THE BLOOD.
FORGET IT. SIT DOWN HERE.
EW, BLOOD.
VERY GOOD.
I SEE YOU LEANED IT.
IT LOOKS PRETTY SHALLOW...
...AND YOUR TENDON IS FINE.
WHOA...
BUT LET'S GO TO THE HOSPITAL JUST TO BE SAFE...
GO TELL HIS HOMEROOM TEACHER, PLEASE.
O--
OKAY.

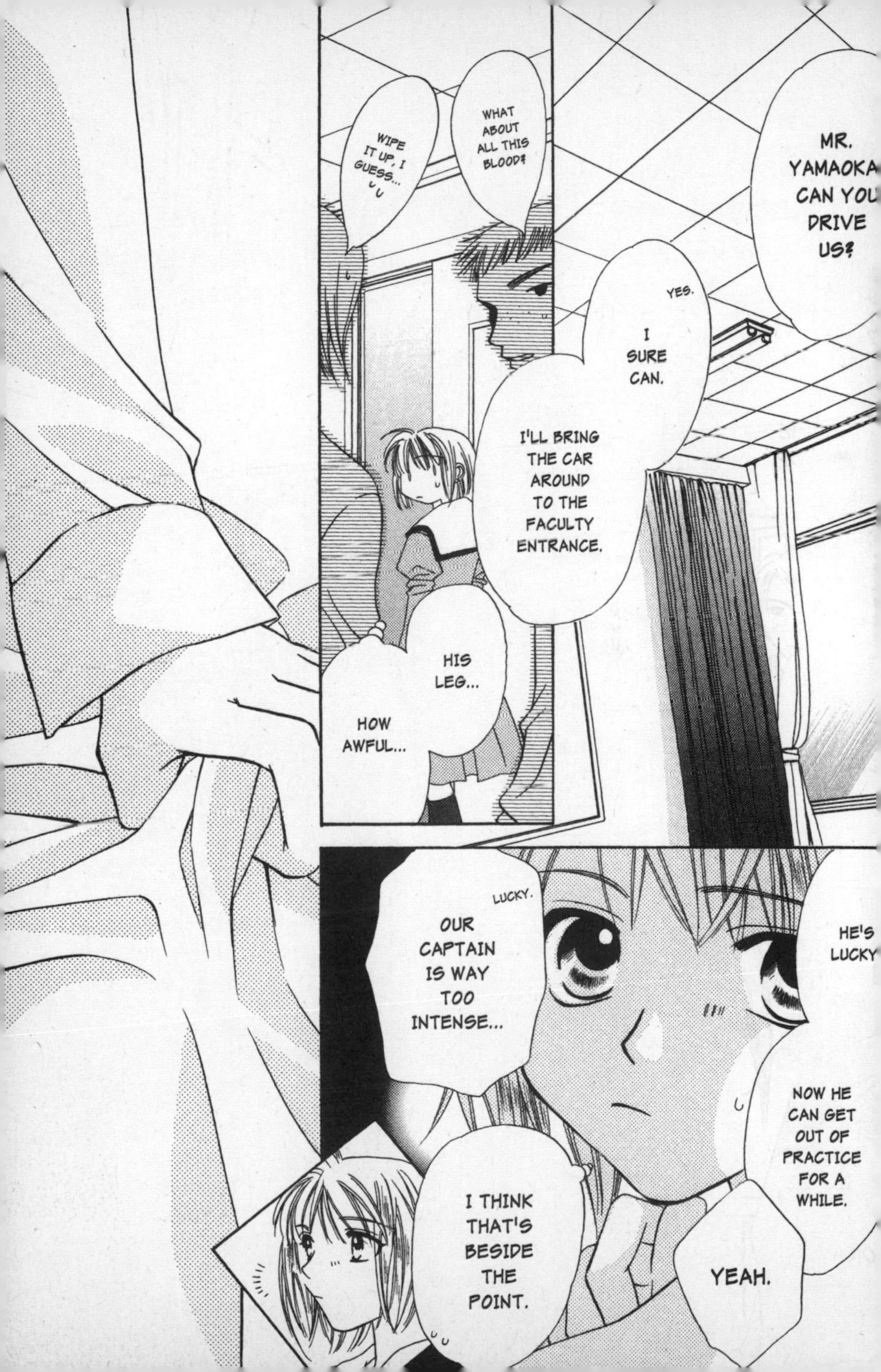
MR. YAMAOKA CAN YOU DRIVE US?
YES.
I SURE CAN.
I'LL BRING THE CAR AROUND TO THE FACULTY ENTRANCE.
WHAT ABOUT ALL THIS BLOOD?
WIPE IT UP, I GUESS...
HIS LEG...
HOW AWFUL...
HE'S LUCKY
NOW HE CAN GET OUT OF PRACTICE FOR A WHILE.
YEAH.
LUCKY.
OUR CAPTAIN IS WAY TOO INTENSE...
I THINK THAT'S BESIDE THE POINT.

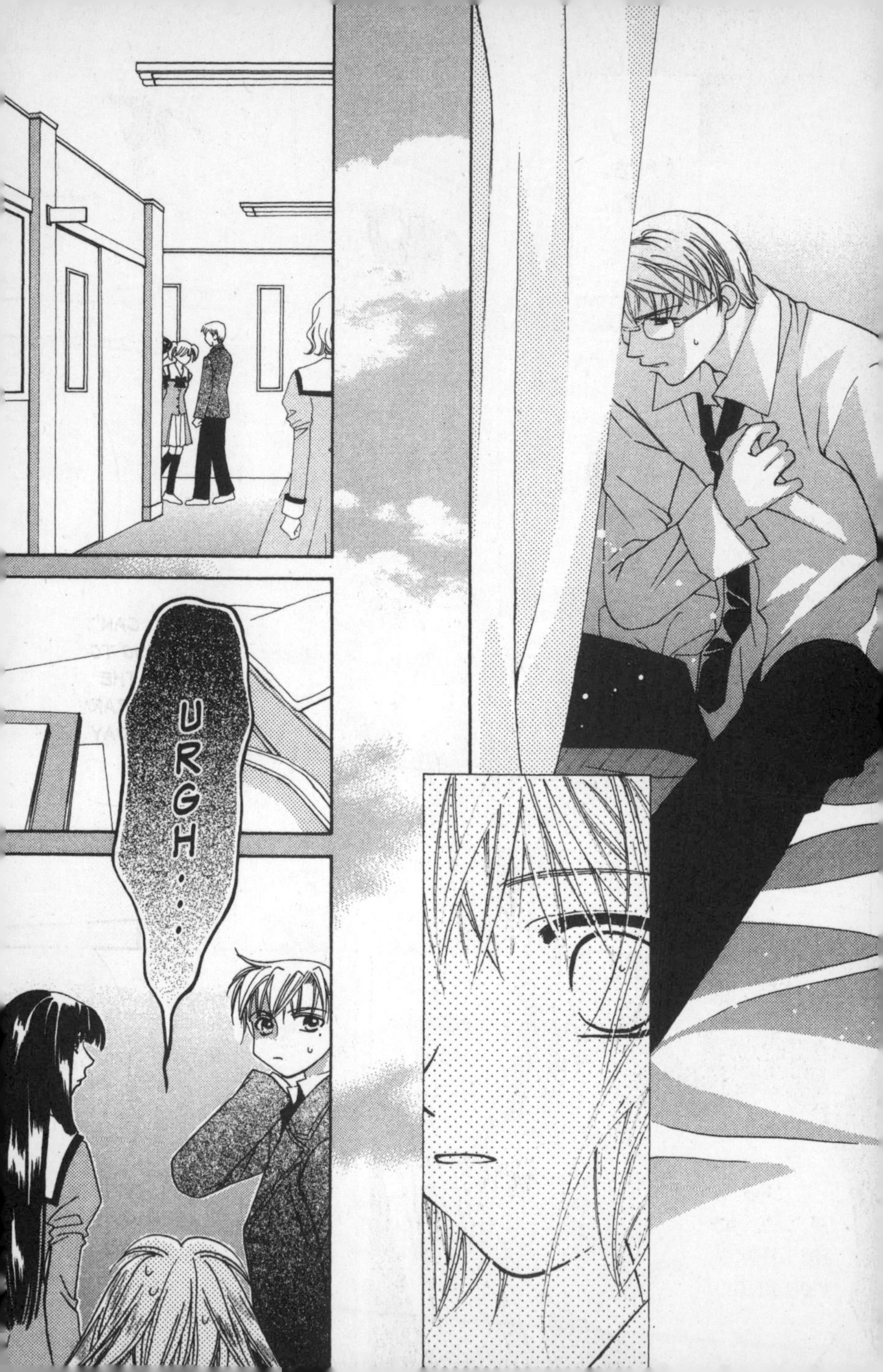
URGH...

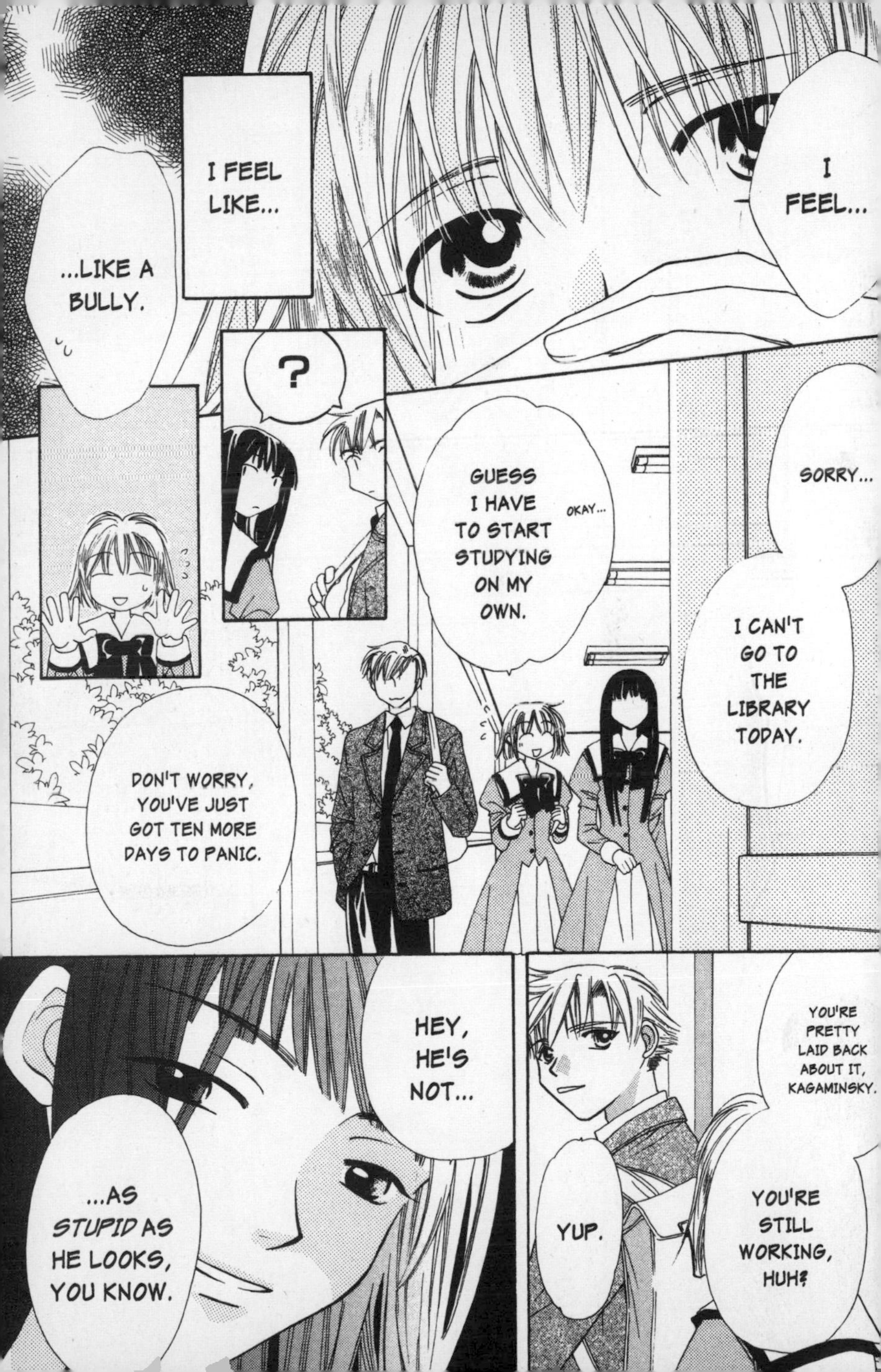
I FEEL...
I FEEL LIKE...
...LIKE A BULLY.
SORRY...
I CAN'T GO TO THE LIBRARY TODAY.
GUESS I HAVE TO START STUDYING ON MY OWN.
OKAY...
?
DON'T WORRY, YOU'VE JUST GOT TEN MORE DAYS TO PANIC.
YOU'RE PRETTY LAID BACK ABOUT IT, KAGAMINSKY.
YOU'RE STILL WORKING, HUH?
YUP.
HEY, HE'S NOT...
...AS *STUPID* AS HE LOOKS, YOU KNOW.

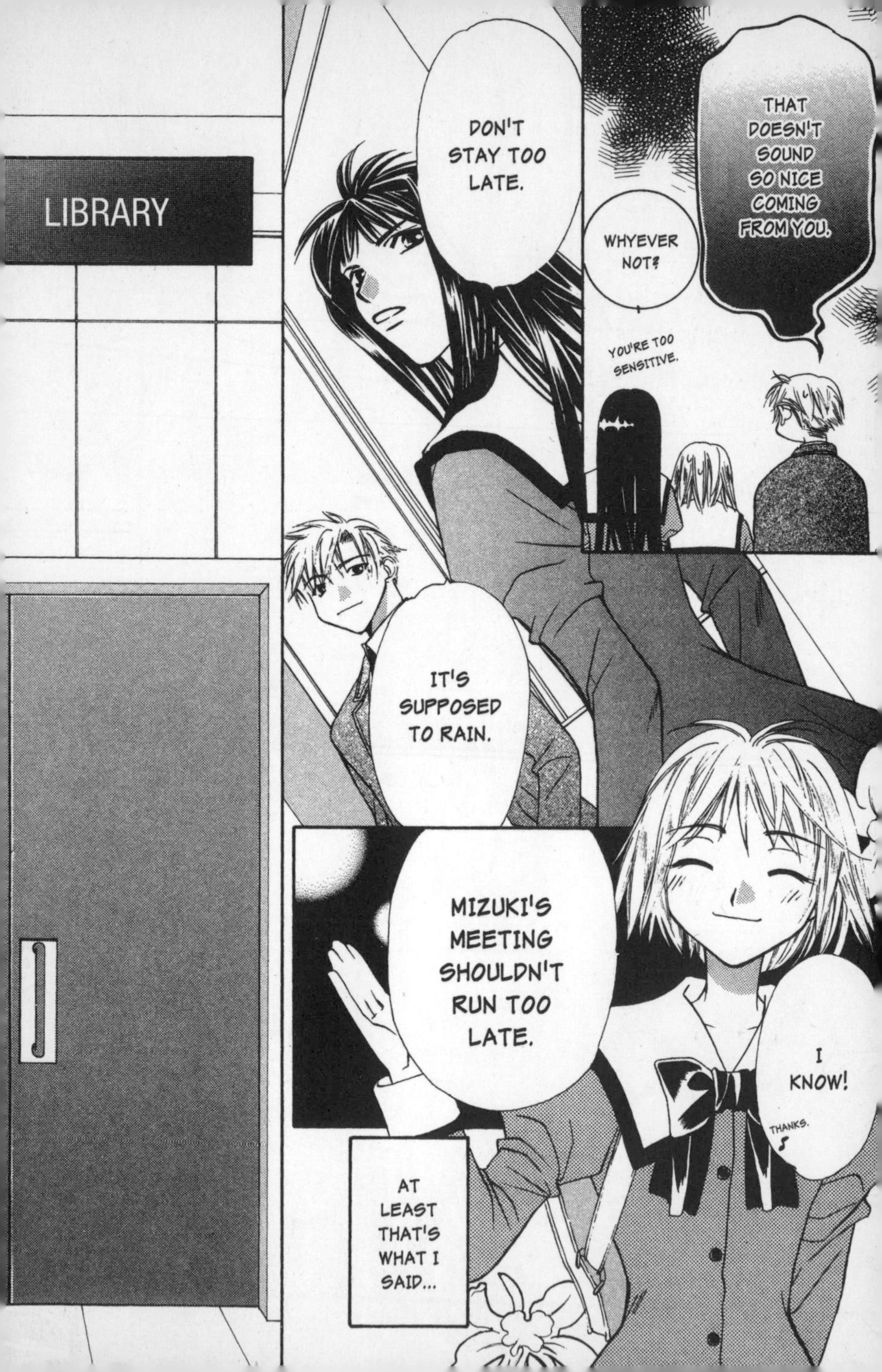
THAT DOESN'T SOUND SO NICE COMING FROM YOU.
WHYEVER NOT?
YOU'RE TOO SENSITIVE.
DON'T STAY TOO LATE.
IT'S SUPPOSED TO RAIN.
I KNOW!
THANKS.
MIZUKI'S MEETING SHOULDN'T RUN TOO LATE.
AT LEAST THAT'S WHAT I SAID...
LIBRARY

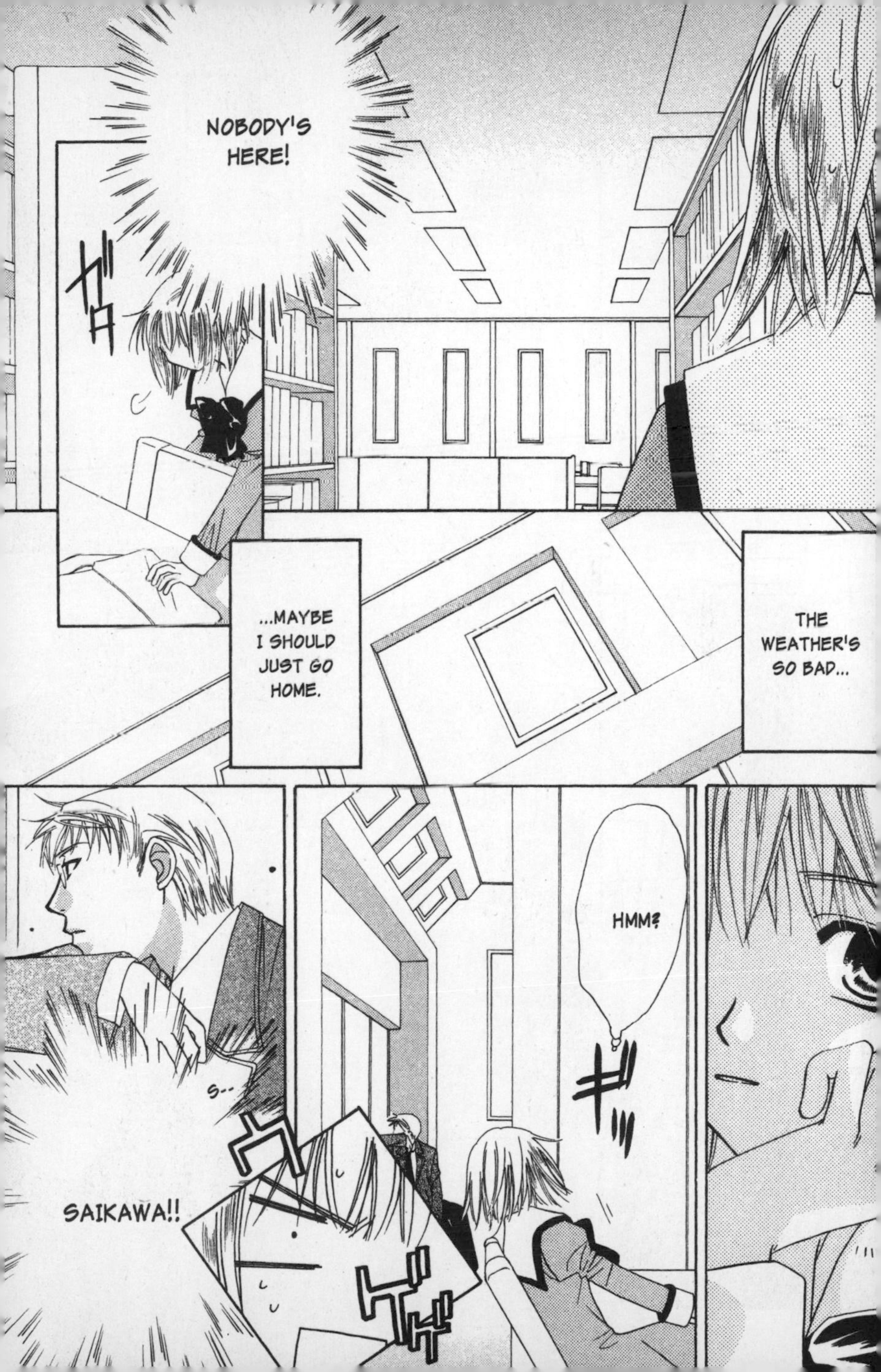
NOBODY'S HERE!
THE WEATHER'S SO BAD...
...MAYBE I SHOULD JUST GO HOME.
HMM?
S--
SAIKAWA!!

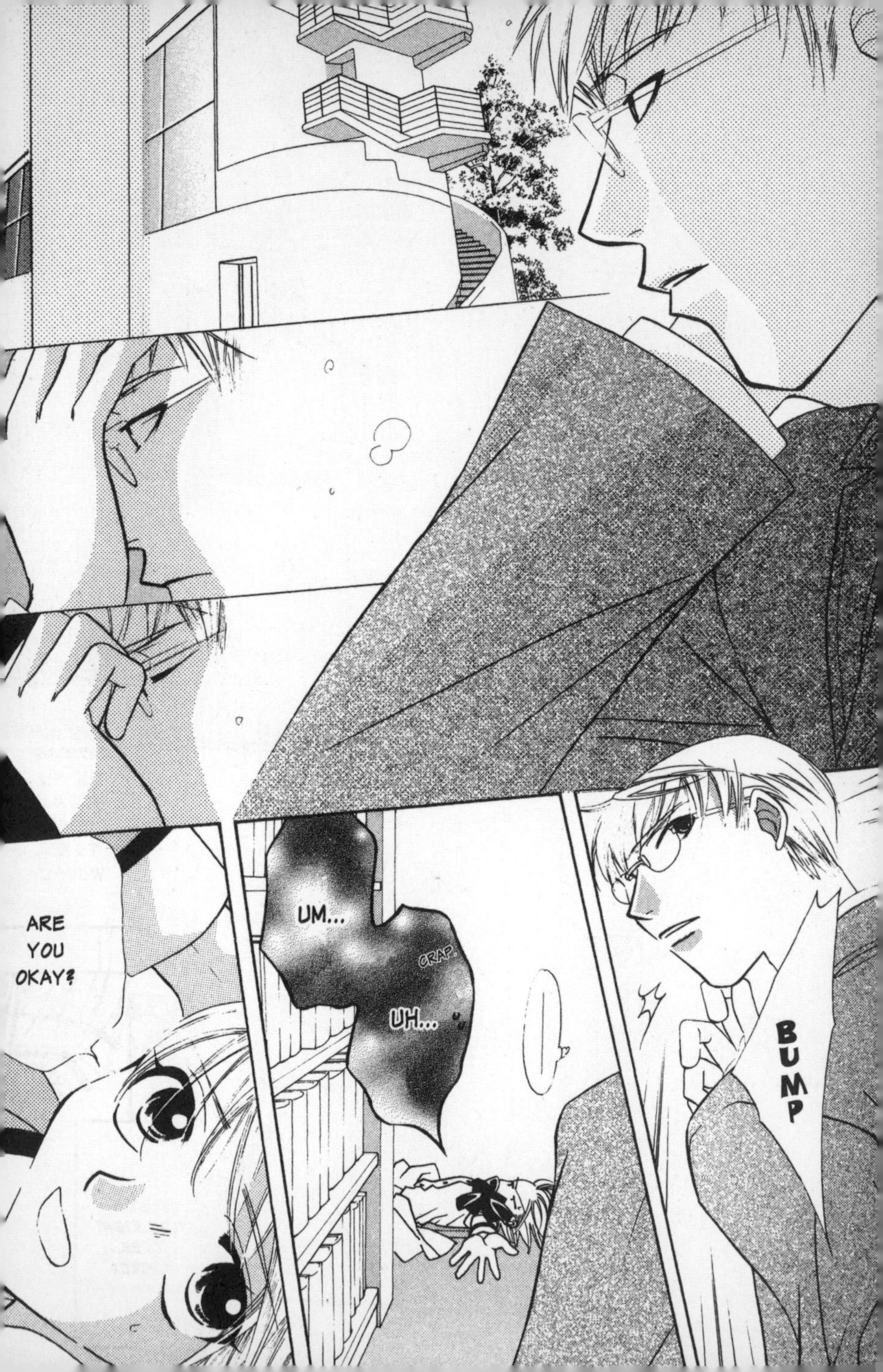
BUMP
UM...
CRAP
UH...
ARE YOU OKAY?

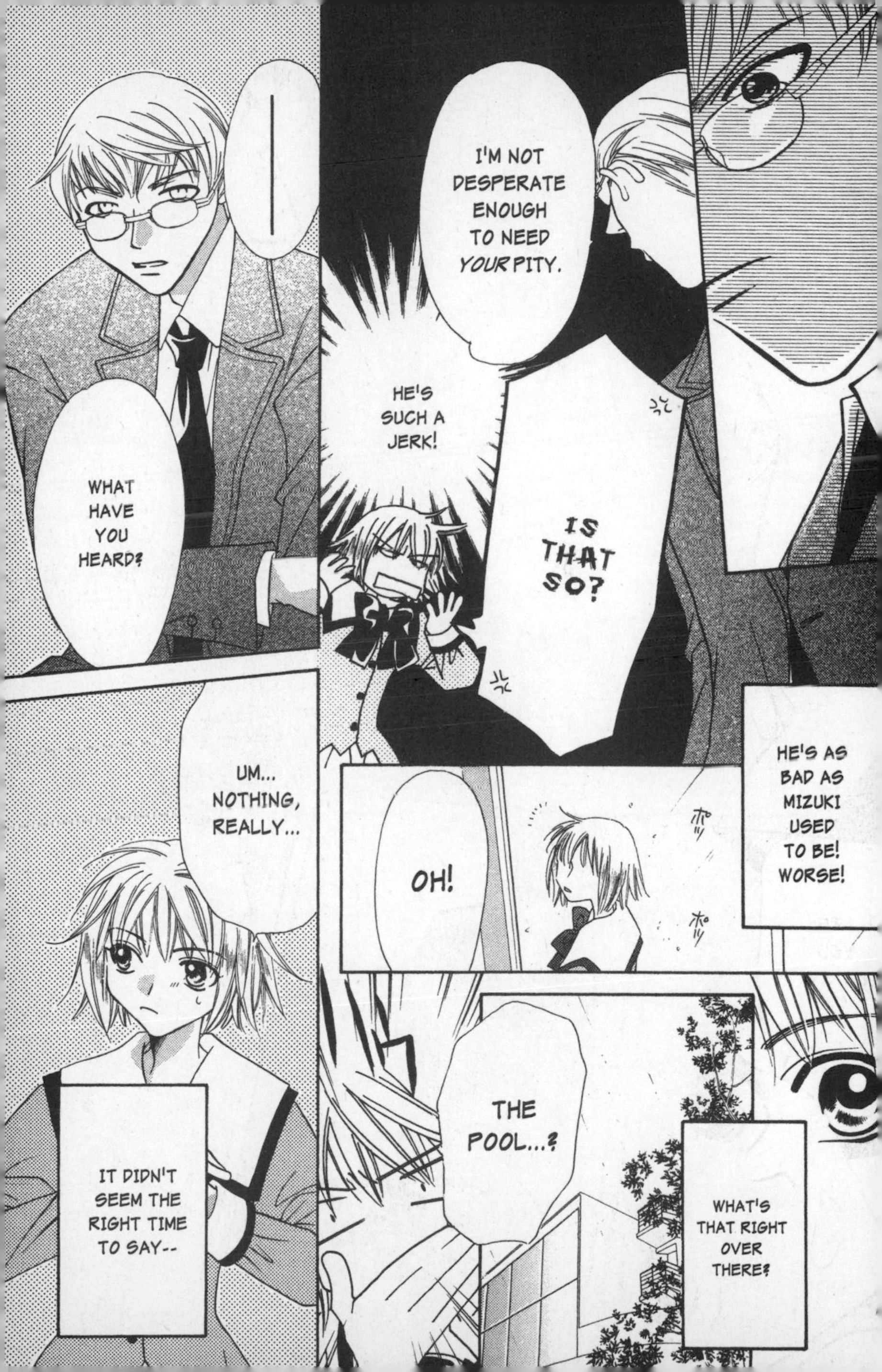
IS THAT SO?
I'M NOT DESPERATE ENOUGH TO NEED *YOUR* PITY.
HE'S SUCH A JERK!
WHAT HAVE YOU HEARD?
HE'S AS BAD AS MIZUKI USED TO BE! WORSE!
OH!
UM... NOTHING, REALLY...
IT DIDN'T SEEM THE RIGHT TIME TO SAY--
WHAT'S THAT RIGHT OVER THERE?
THE POOL...?

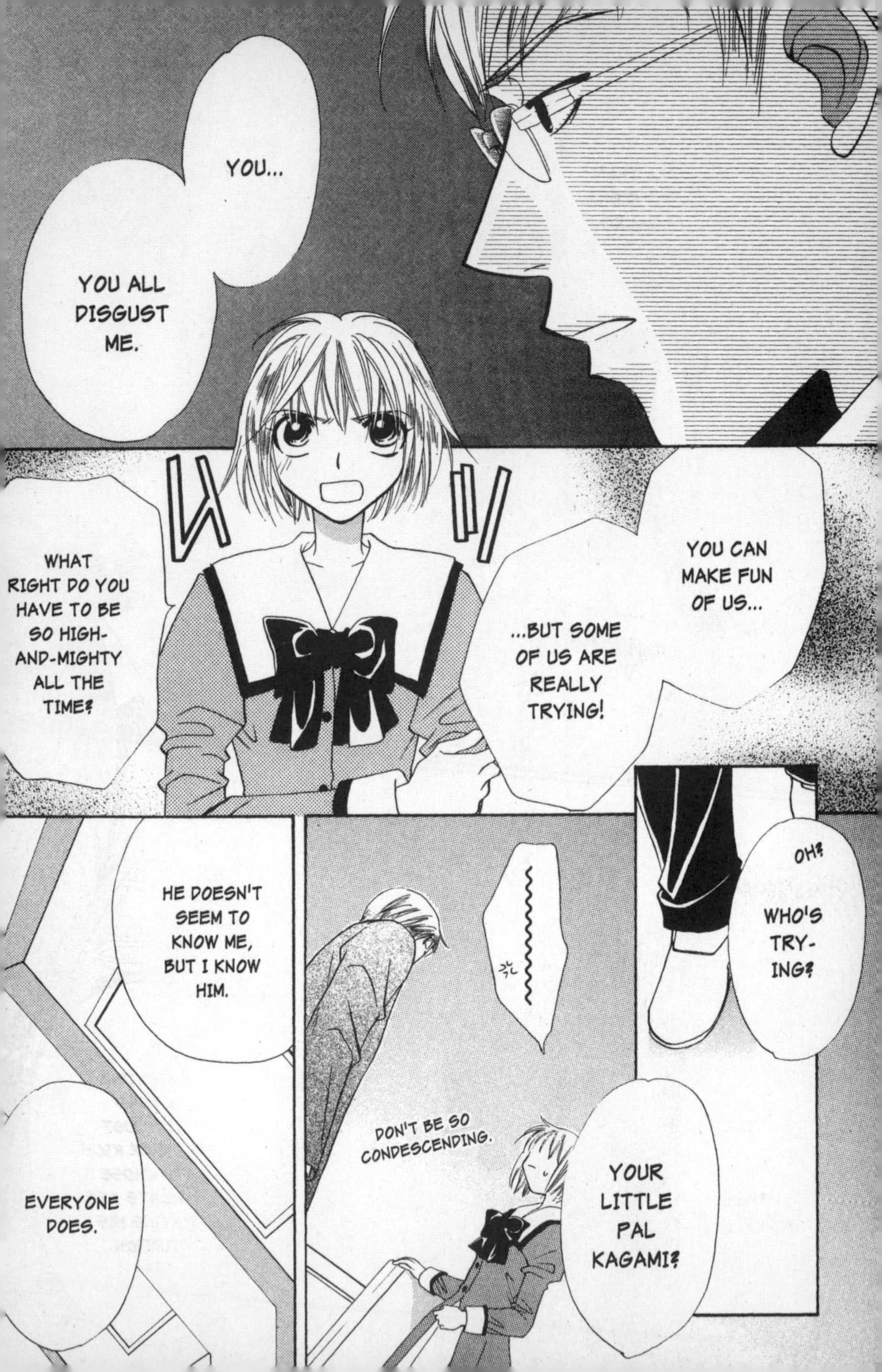
YOU...
YOU ALL DISGUST ME.
YOU CAN MAKE FUN OF US...
...BUT SOME OF US ARE REALLY TRYING!
WHAT RIGHT DO YOU HAVE TO BE SO HIGH-AND-MIGHTY ALL THE TIME?
OH?
WHO'S TRY-ING?
YOUR LITTLE PAL KAGAMI?
DON'T BE SO CONDESCENDING.
HE DOESN'T SEEM TO KNOW ME, BUT I KNOW HIM.
EVERYONE DOES.

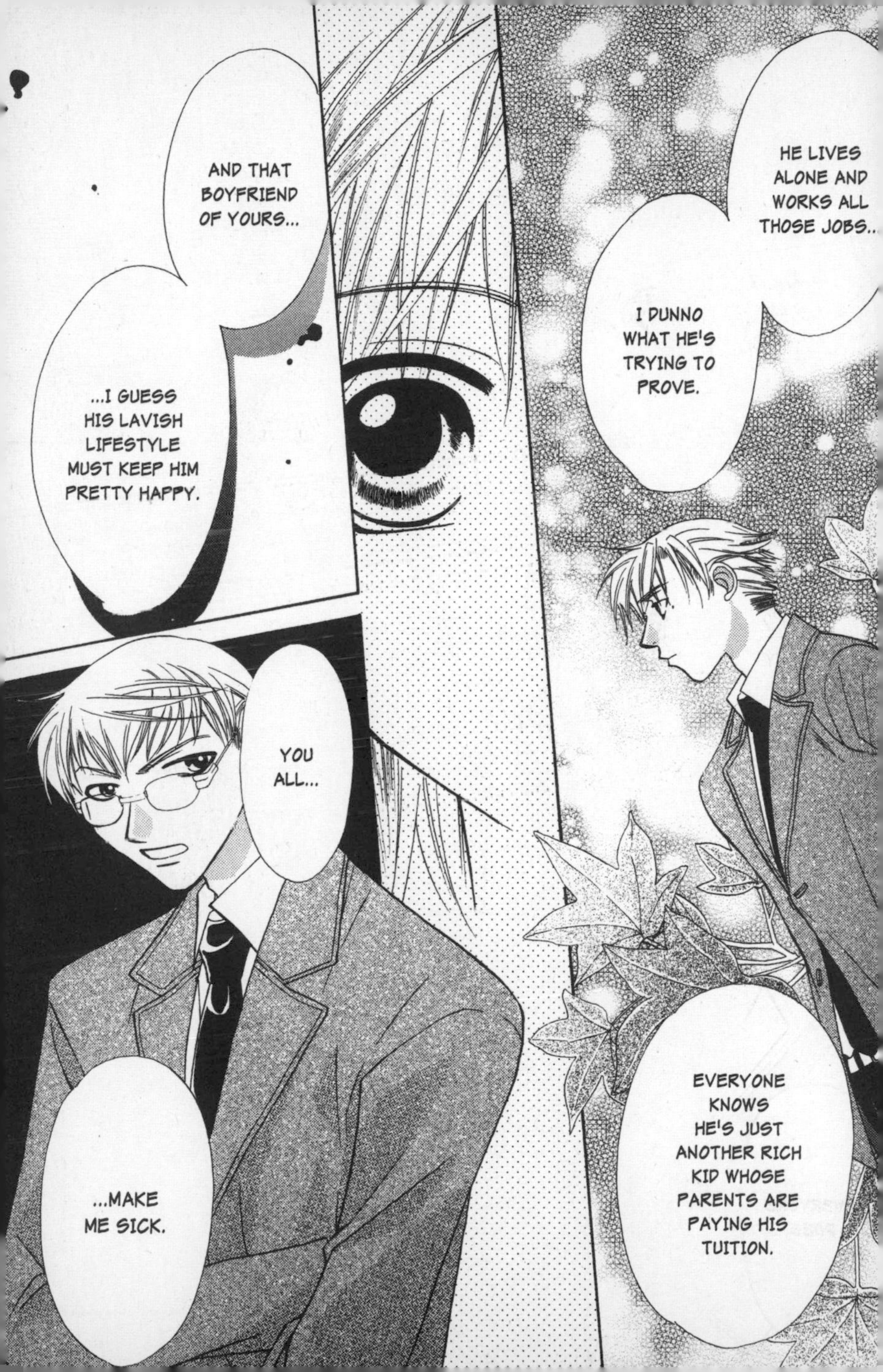
HE LIVES ALONE AND WORKS ALL THOSE JOBS...
I DUNNO WHAT HE'S TRYING TO PROVE.
EVERYONE KNOWS HE'S JUST ANOTHER RICH KID WHOSE PARENTS ARE PAYING HIS TUITION.
AND THAT BOYFRIEND OF YOURS...
...I GUESS HIS LAVISH LIFESTYLE MUST KEEP HIM PRETTY HAPPY.
YOU ALL...
...MAKE ME SICK.

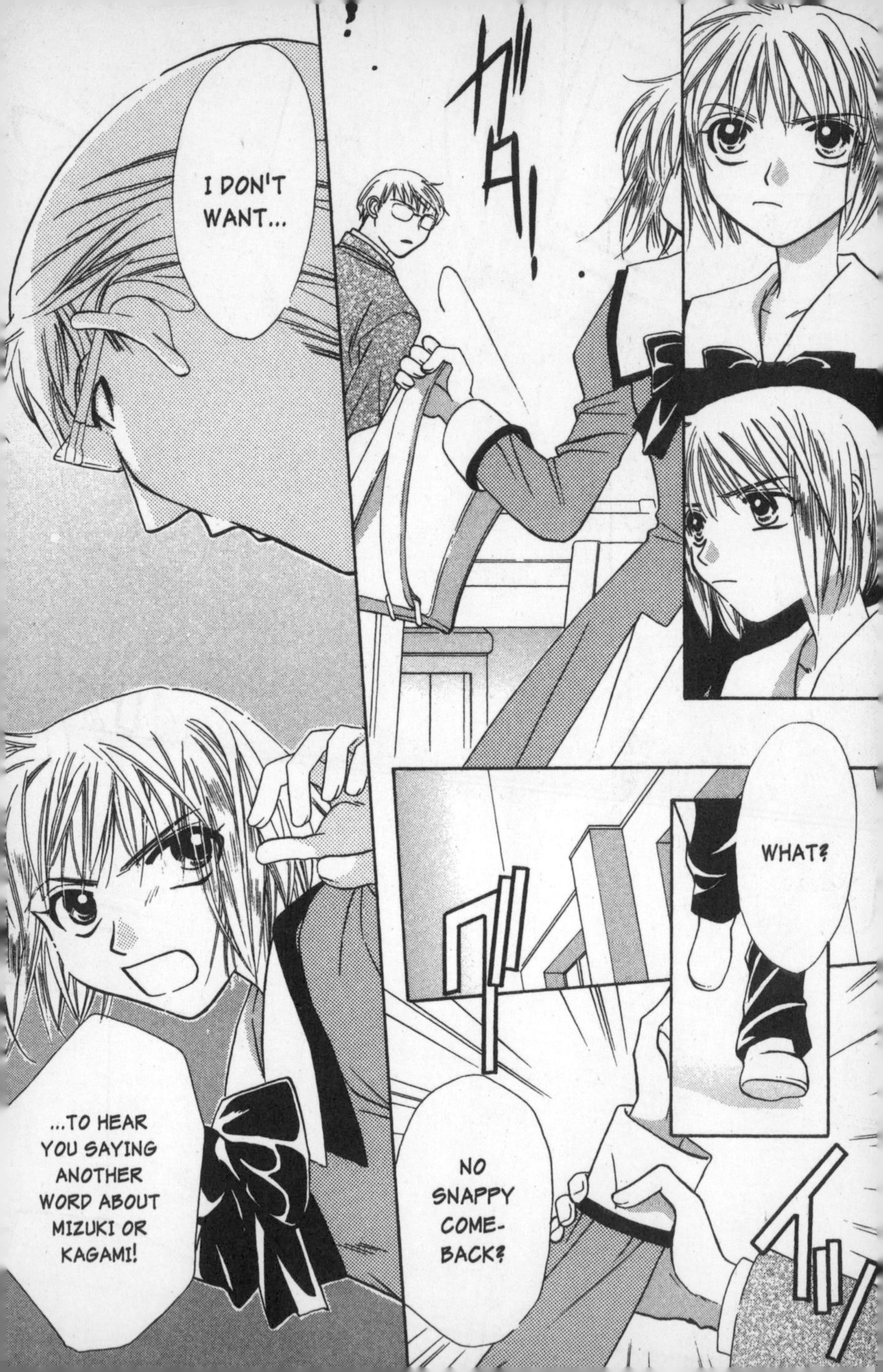
ガタ!
WHAT?
NO SNAPPY COME-BACK?
I DON'T WANT...
...TO HEAR YOU SAYING ANOTHER WORD ABOUT MIZUKI OR KAGAMI!

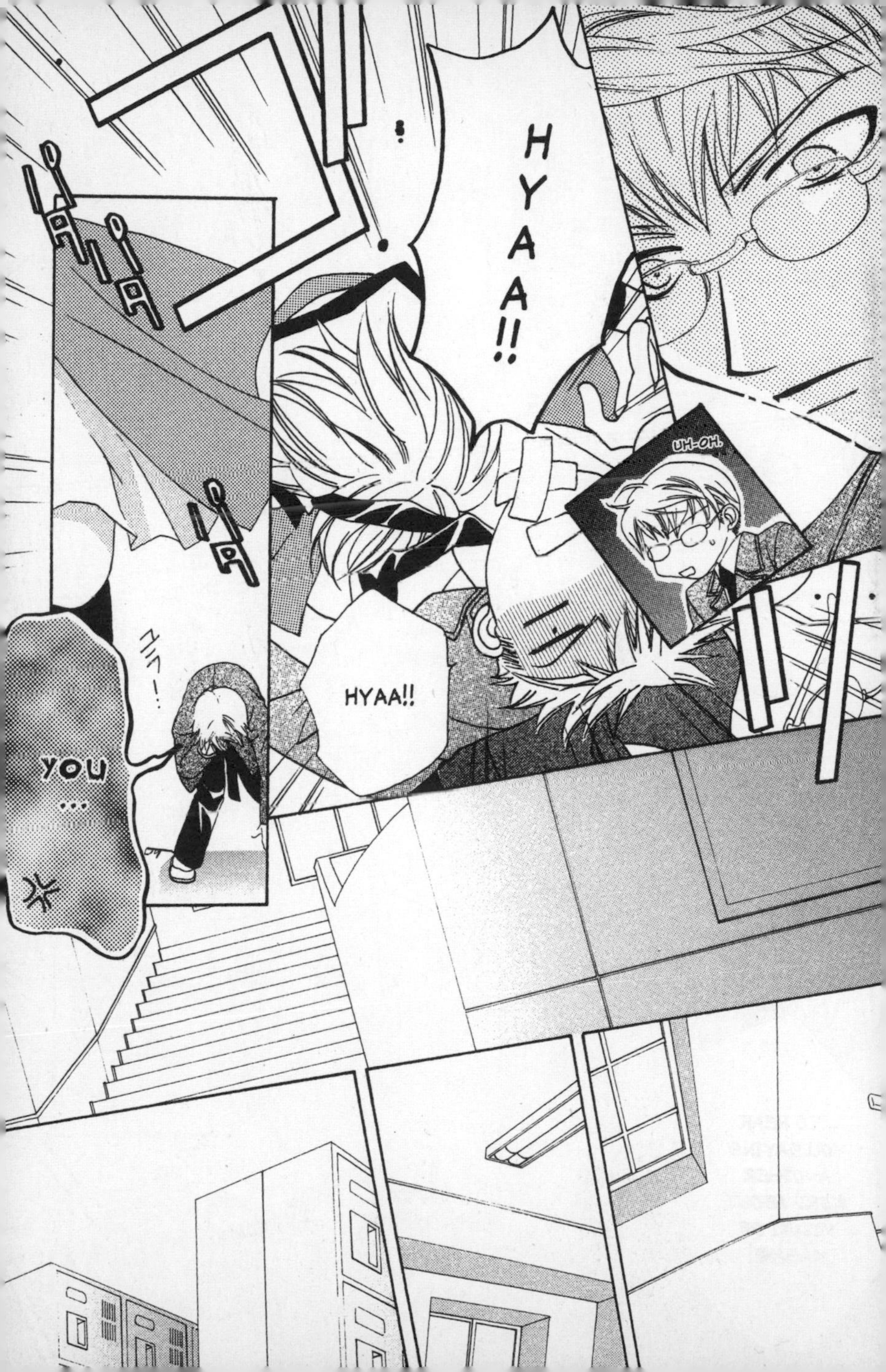
HYAA!!
UH-OH.
HYAA!!
YOU ...

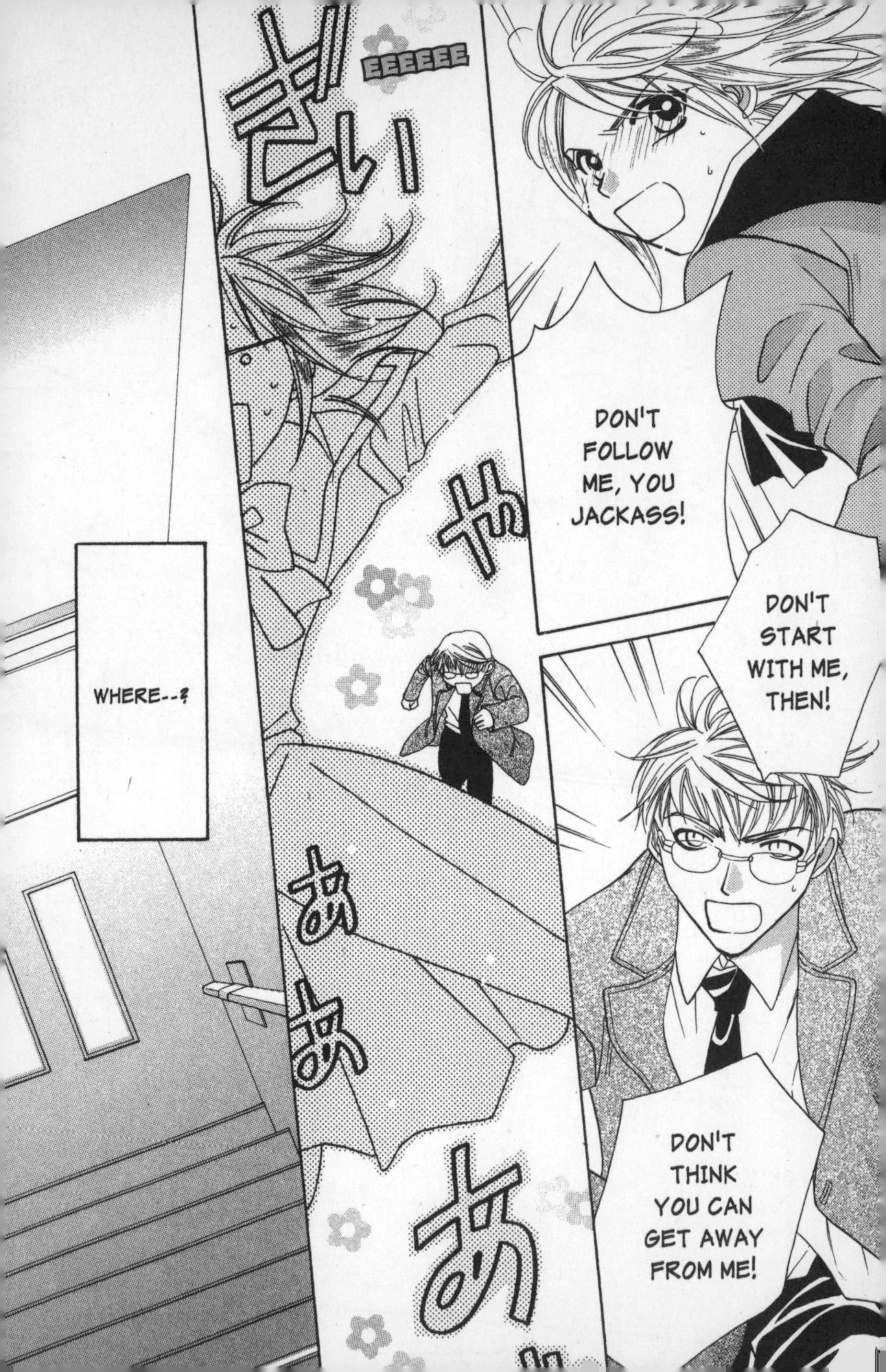
DON'T FOLLOW ME, YOU JACKASS!
DON'T START WITH ME, THEN!
DON'T THINK YOU CAN GET AWAY FROM ME!
EEEEEE
きいーやあああ
WHERE--?

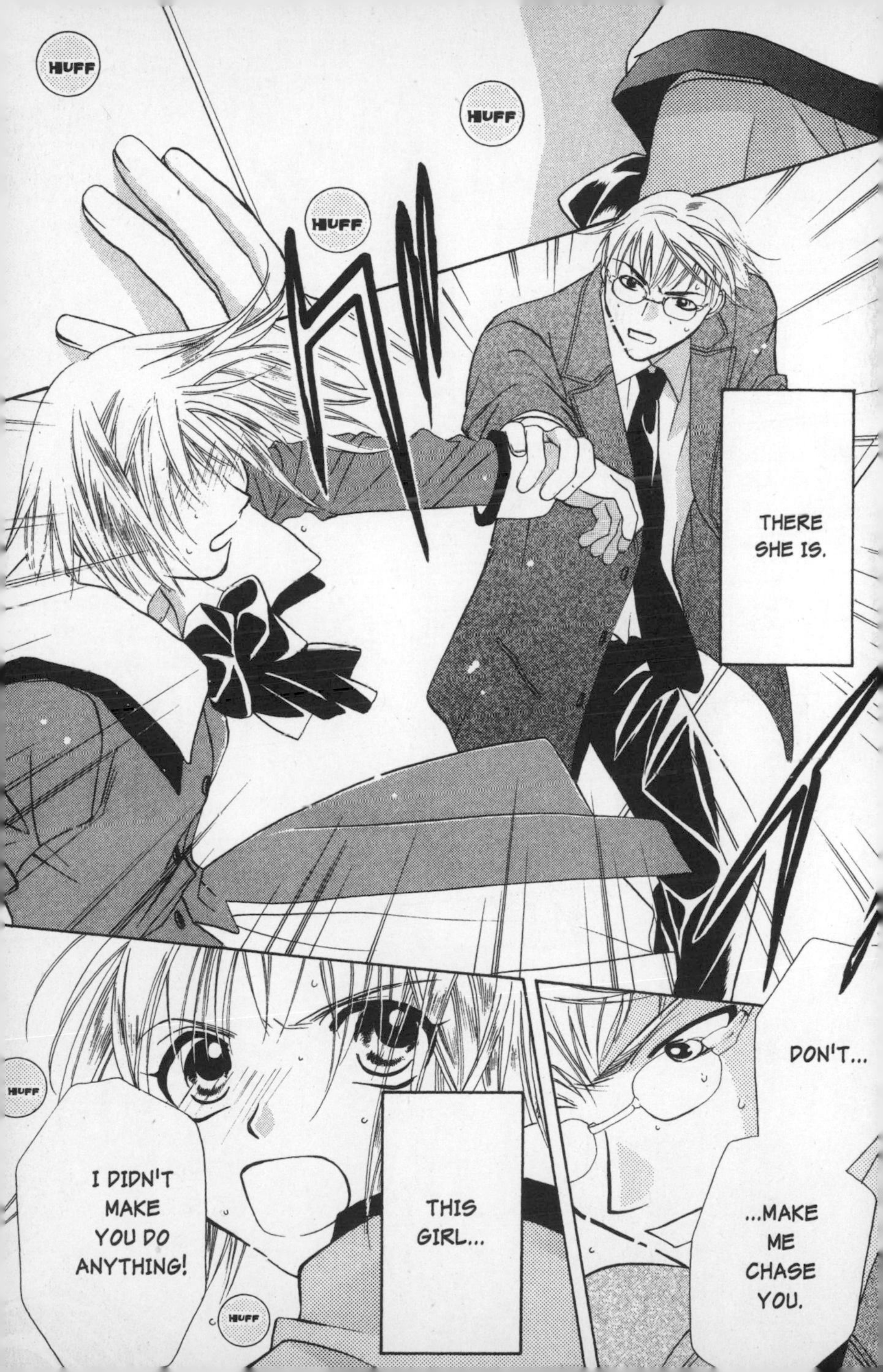
HUFF
HUFF
HUFF
THERE SHE IS.
DON'T...
...MAKE ME CHASE YOU.
THIS GIRL...
HUFF
I DIDN'T MAKE YOU DO ANYTHING!
HUFF

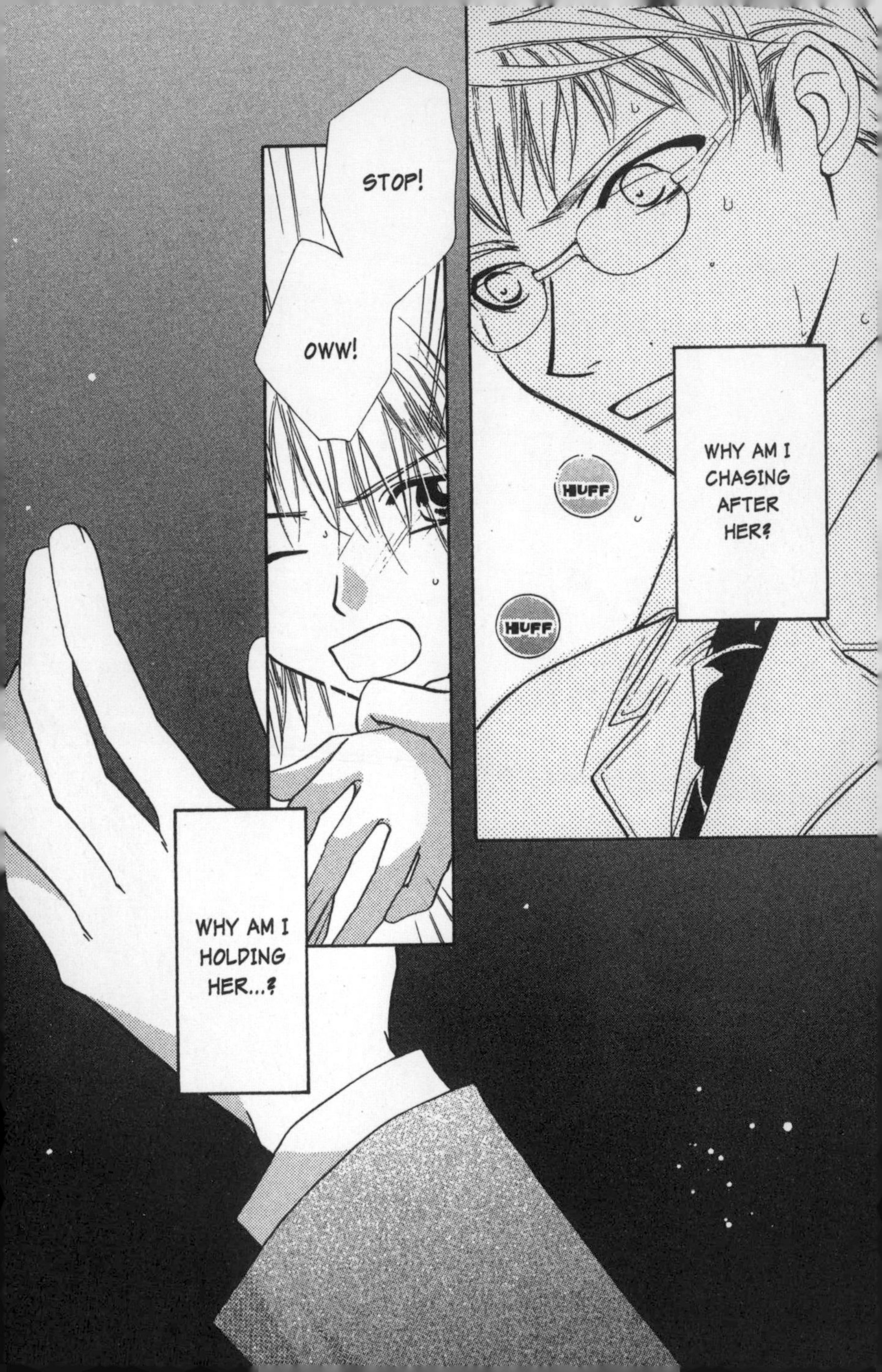
WHY AM I CHASING AFTER HER?
HUFF
HUFF
STOP!
OWW!
WHY AM I HOLDING HER...?

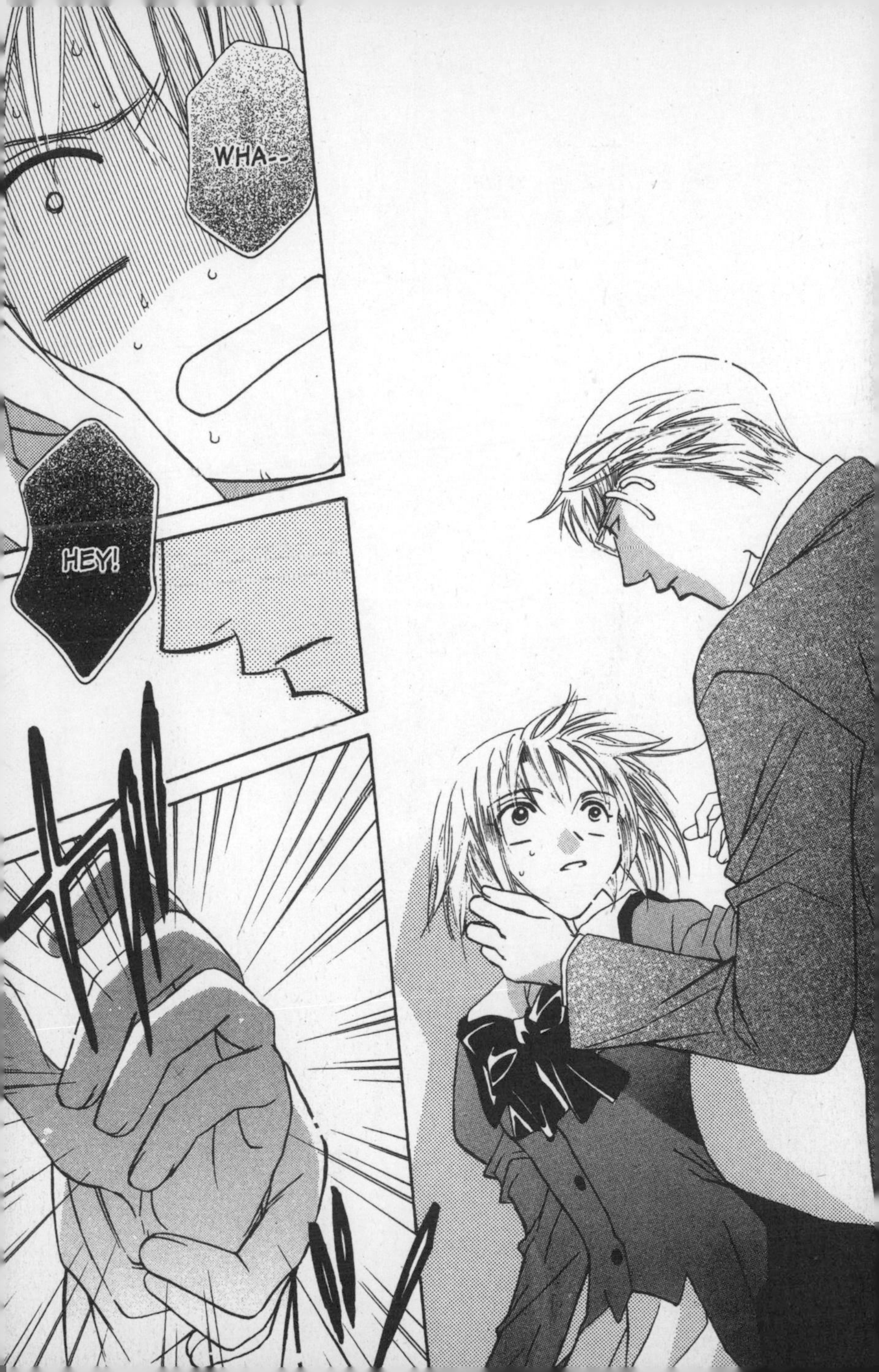
WHA--
HEY!

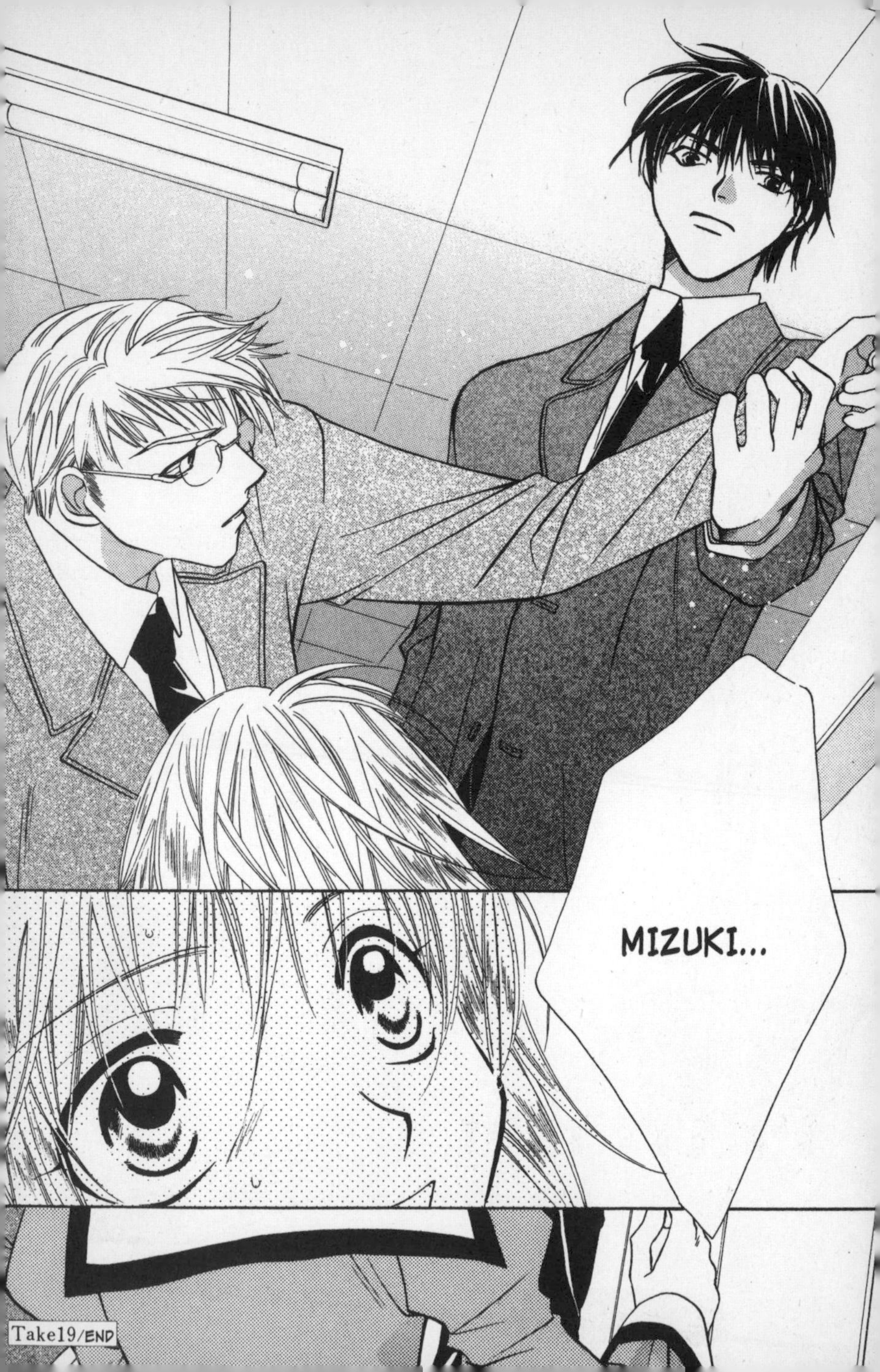
MIZUKI...
Take19/END

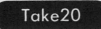

PLATINUM *garden*

Take20

FUJITA'S SUMMER, 2002

THANKS TO THE HOUSEPLANT TREND, THE NUMBER OF PLANTS IN MY ROOMS HAS INCREASED THIS YEAR...BUT IT'S HARD FOR A PERSON WITH A BLACK THUMB LIKE ME...

I'M SO SORRY...

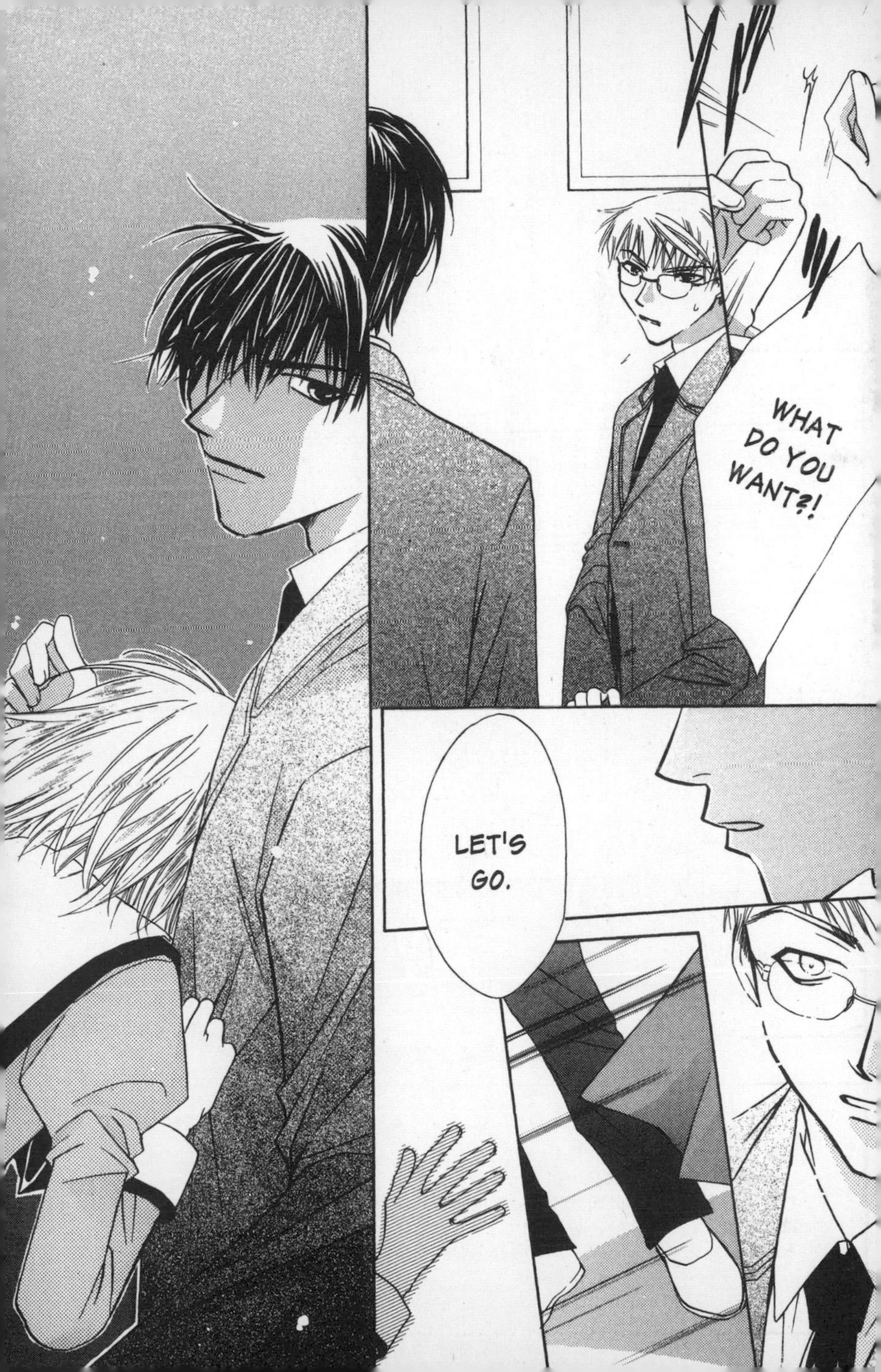
WHAT DO YOU WANT?!
LET'S GO.

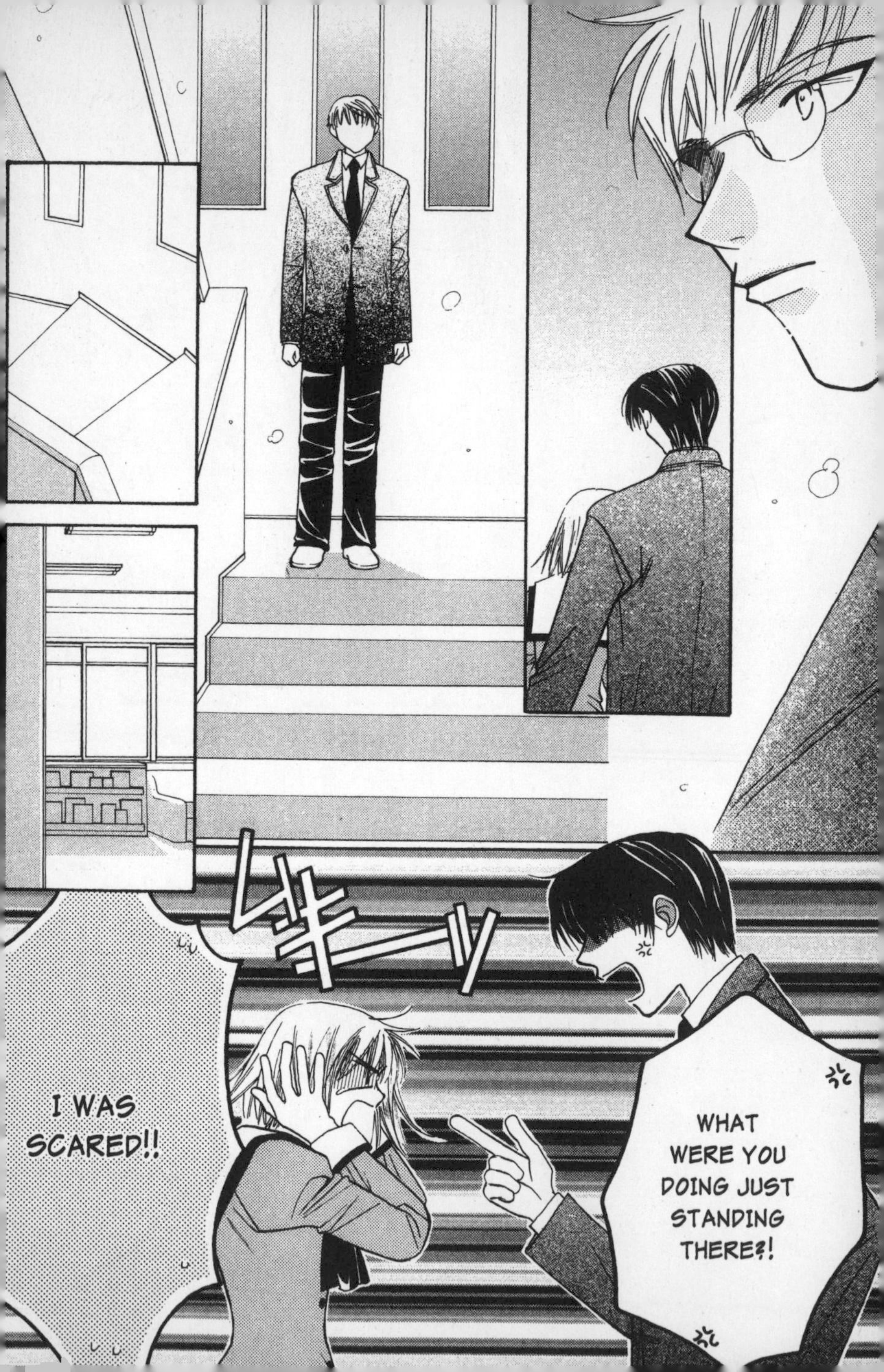
ムキーッ
WHAT WERE YOU DOING JUST STANDING THERE?!
I WAS SCARED!!

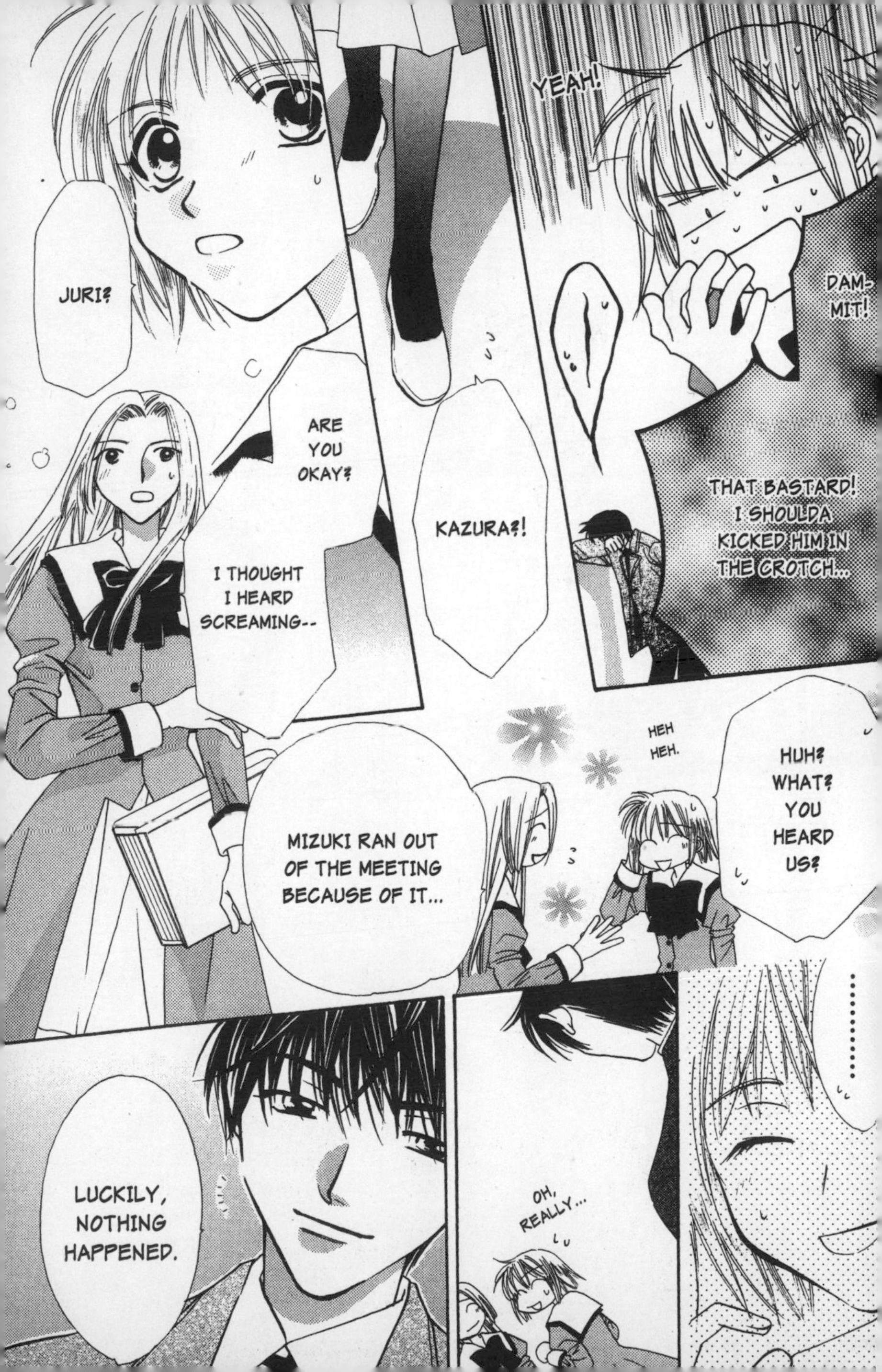

YEAH!
DAM-MIT!
THAT BASTARD! I SHOULDA KICKED HIM IN THE CROTCH...
KAZURA?!
JURI?
ARE YOU OKAY?
I THOUGHT I HEARD SCREAMING--
HUH? WHAT? YOU HEARD US?
HEH HEH.
MIZUKI RAN OUT OF THE MEETING BECAUSE OF IT...
....
OH, REALLY...
LUCKILY, NOTHING HAPPENED.

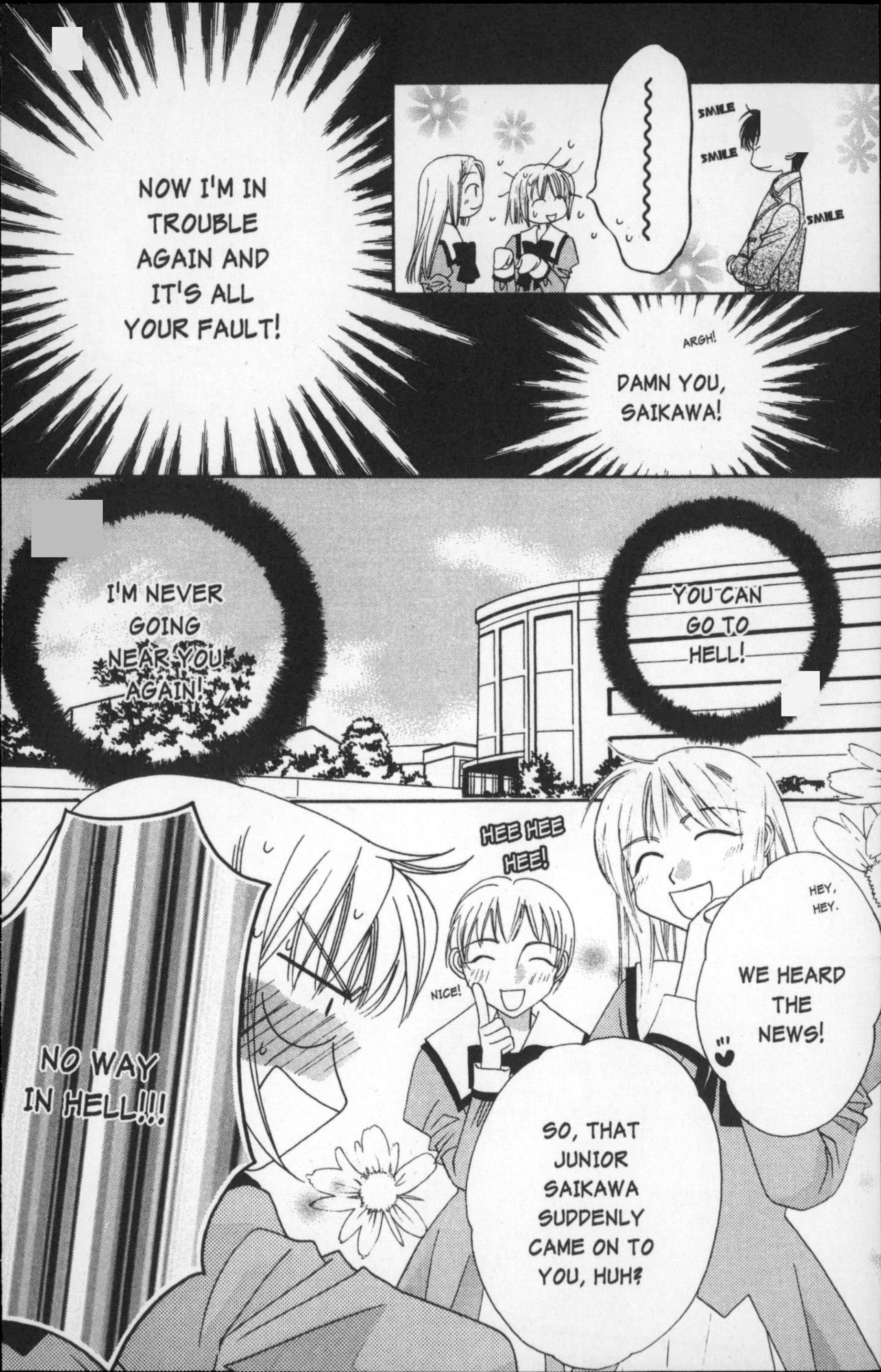

SMILE
SMILE
SMILE
ARGH!
DAMN YOU, SAIKAWA!
NOW I'M IN TROUBLE AGAIN AND IT'S ALL YOUR FAULT!
YOU CAN GO TO HELL!
I'M NEVER GOING NEAR YOU AGAIN!
HEY, HEY.
WE HEARD THE NEWS!
HEE HEE HEE!
NICE!
SO, THAT JUNIOR SAIKAWA SUDDENLY CAME ON TO YOU, HUH?
NO WAY IN HELL!!!

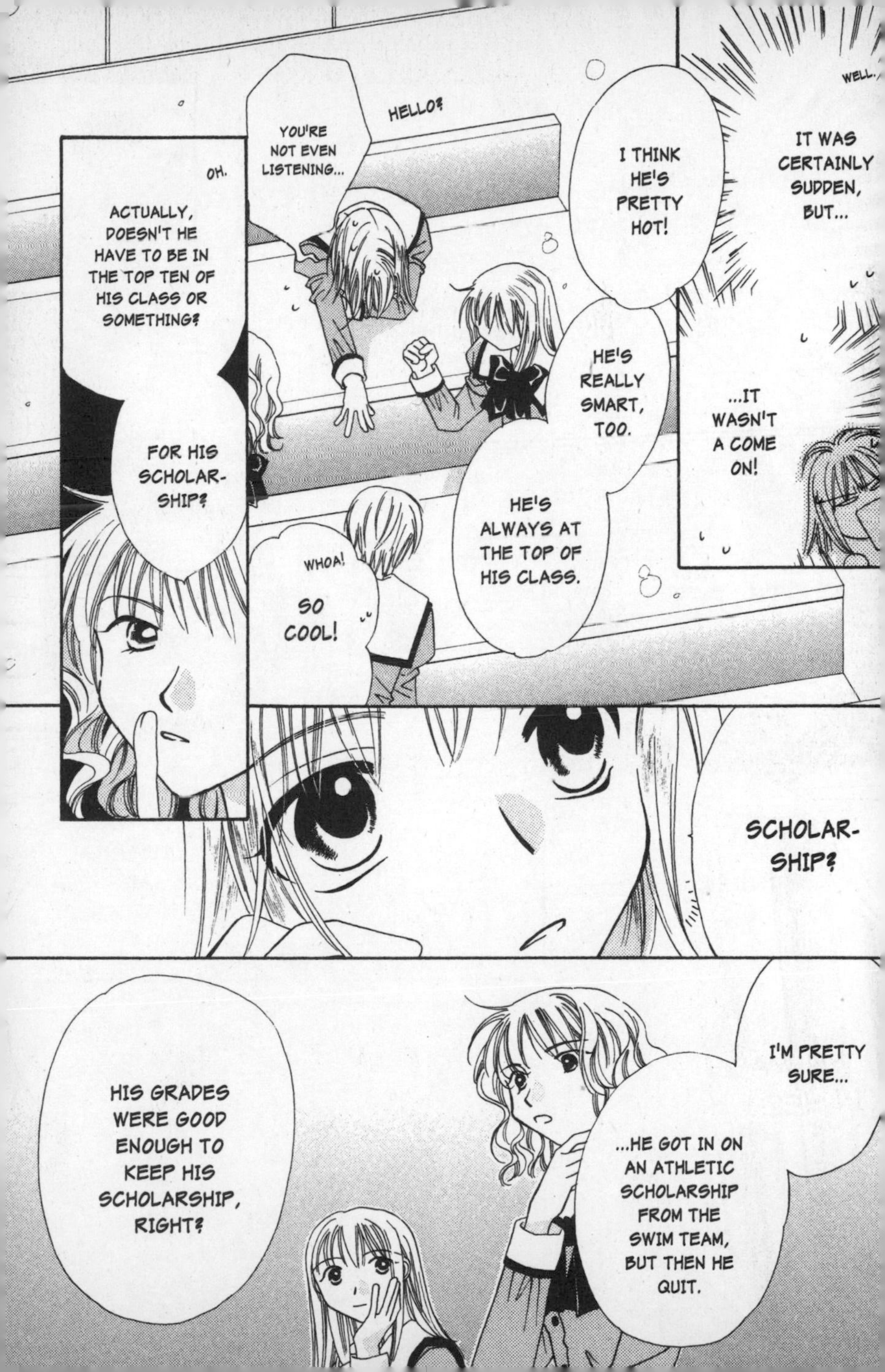
WELL.
IT WAS CERTAINLY SUDDEN, BUT...
...IT WASN'T A COME ON!
I THINK HE'S PRETTY HOT!
HELLO?
YOU'RE NOT EVEN LISTENING...
HE'S REALLY SMART, TOO.
HE'S ALWAYS AT THE TOP OF HIS CLASS.
WHOA!
SO COOL!
OH.
ACTUALLY, DOESN'T HE HAVE TO BE IN THE TOP TEN OF HIS CLASS OR SOMETHING?
FOR HIS SCHOLAR-SHIP?
SCHOLAR-SHIP?
I'M PRETTY SURE...
...HE GOT IN ON AN ATHLETIC SCHOLARSHIP FROM THE SWIM TEAM, BUT THEN HE QUIT.
HIS GRADES WERE GOOD ENOUGH TO KEEP HIS SCHOLARSHIP, RIGHT?

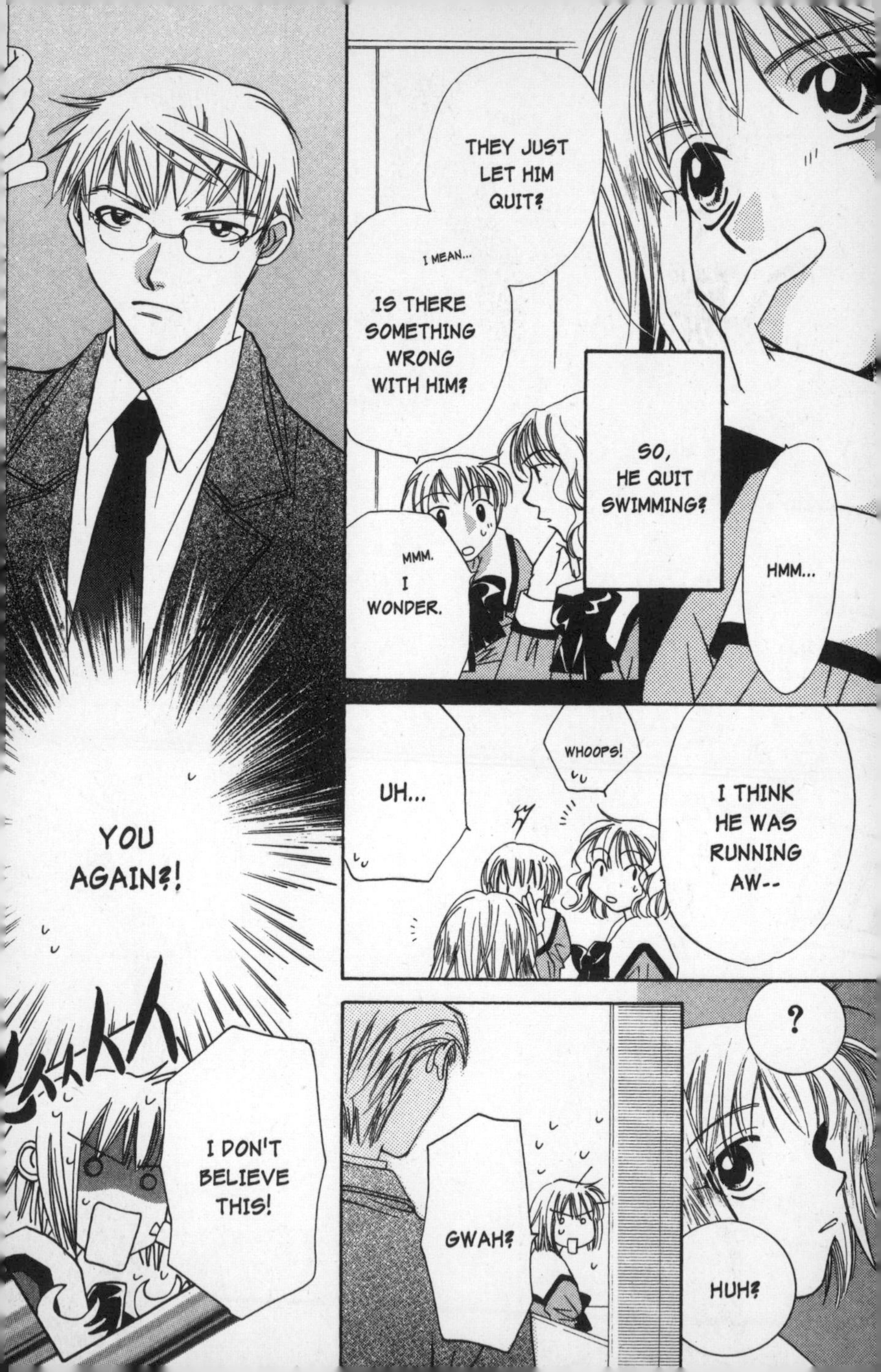
THEY JUST LET HIM QUIT?
I MEAN...
IS THERE SOMETHING WRONG WITH HIM?
SO, HE QUIT SWIMMING?
HMM...
MMM. I WONDER.
I THINK HE WAS RUNNING AW--
WHOOPS!
UH...
YOU AGAIN?!
?
HUH?
GWAH?
I DON'T BELIEVE THIS!

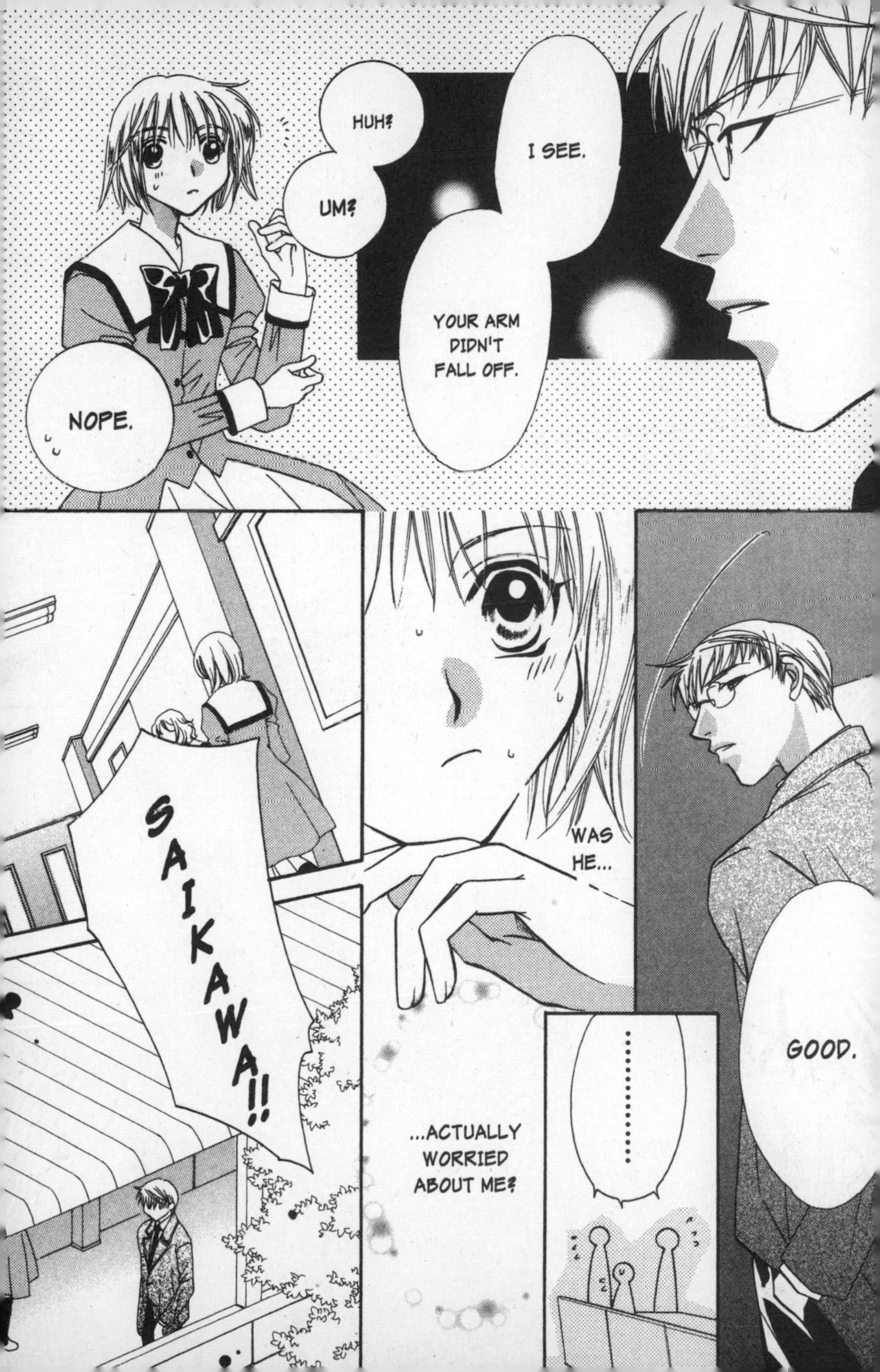
I SEE.
YOUR ARM DIDN'T FALL OFF.
HUH?
UM?
NOPE.
GOOD.
WAS HE...
......
...ACTUALLY WORRIED ABOUT ME?
SAIKAWA!!

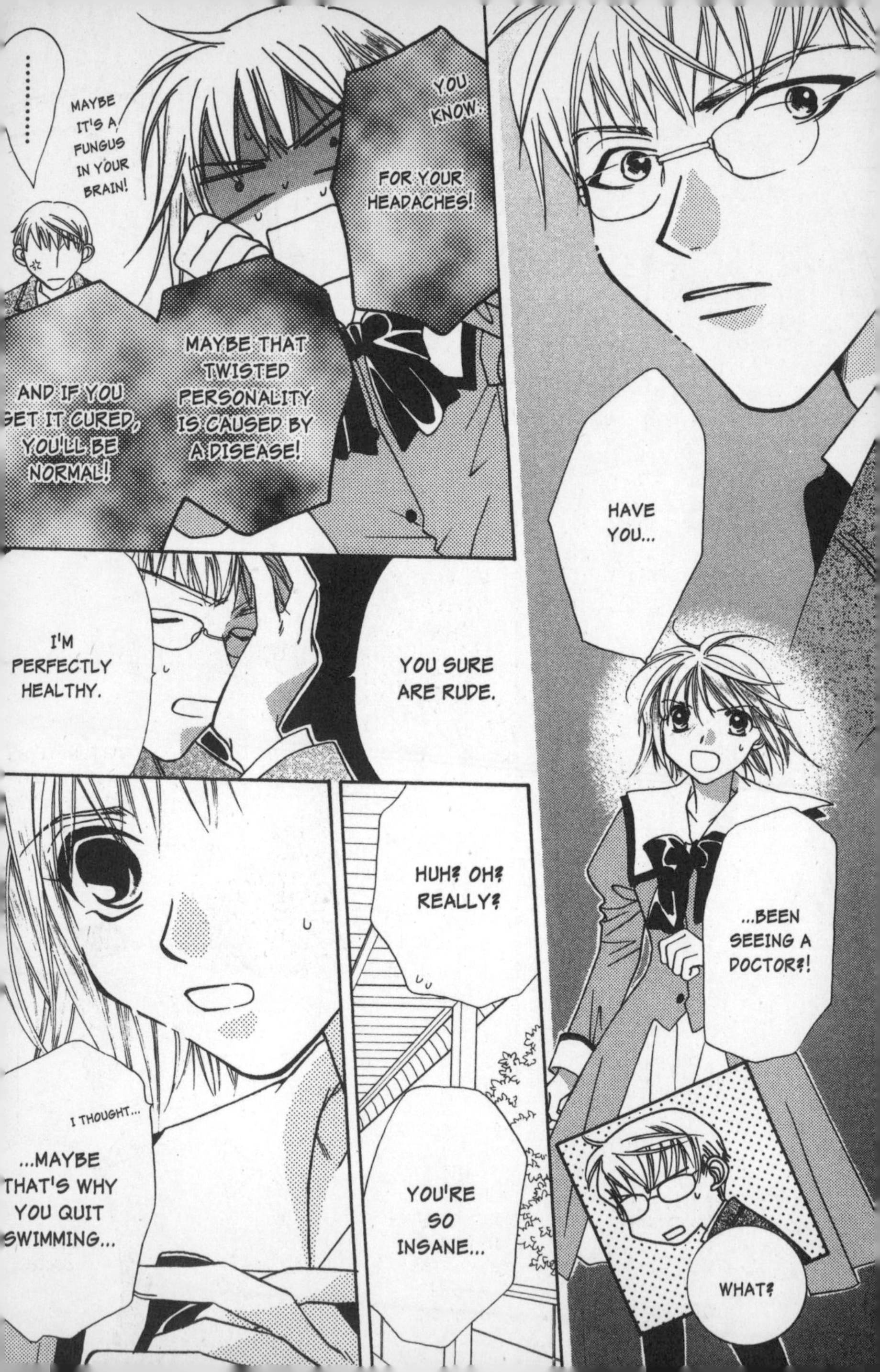
HAVE YOU...
...BEEN SEEING A DOCTOR?!
WHAT?
YOU KNOW.
FOR YOUR HEADACHES!
MAYBE THAT TWISTED PERSONALITY IS CAUSED BY A DISEASE!
AND IF YOU GET IT CURED, YOU'LL BE NORMAL!
MAYBE IT'S A FUNGUS IN YOUR BRAIN!
......
YOU SURE ARE RUDE.
I'M PERFECTLY HEALTHY.
HUH? OH? REALLY?
YOU'RE SO INSANE...
I THOUGHT...
...MAYBE THAT'S WHY YOU QUIT SWIMMING...

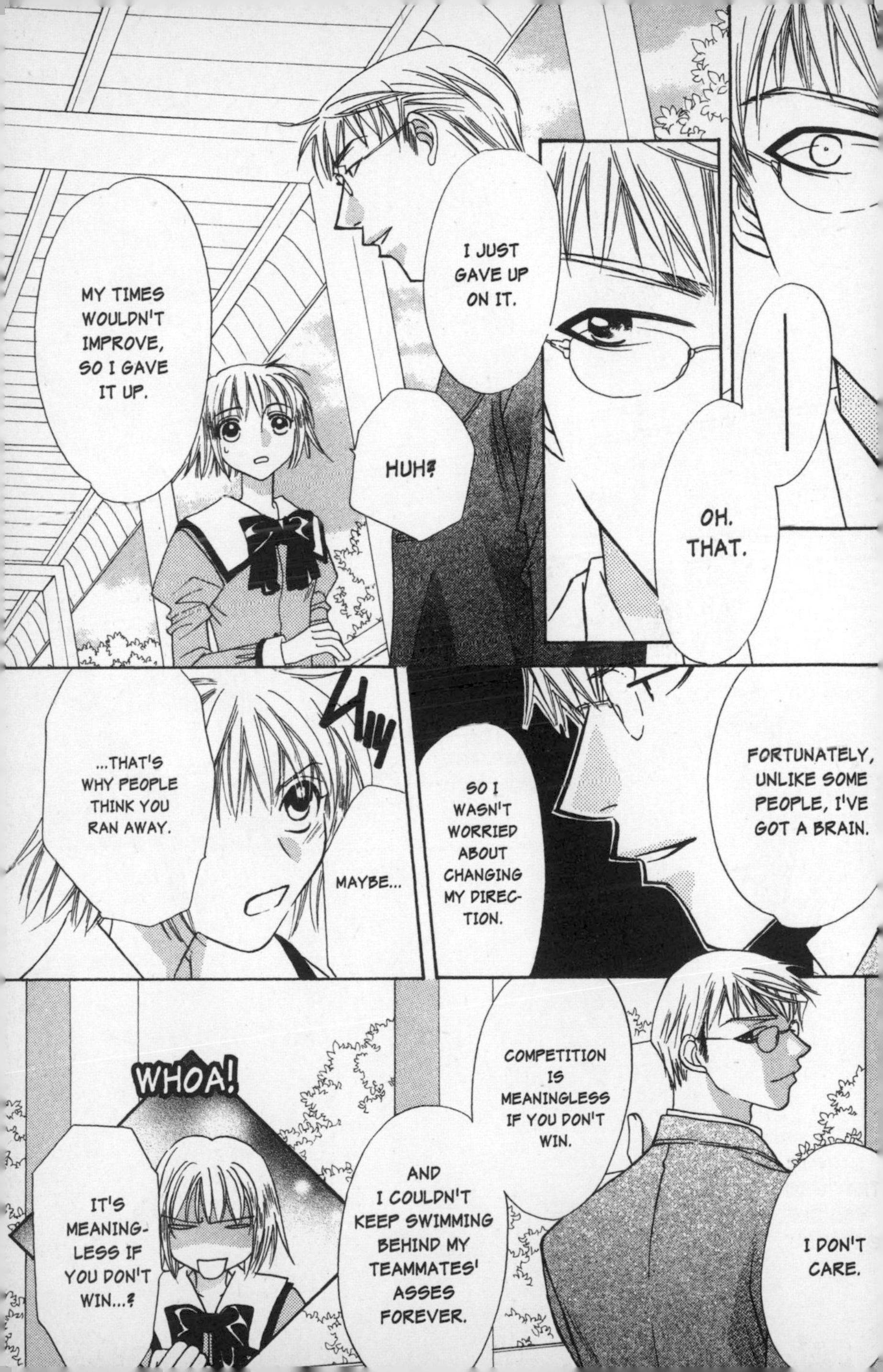
OH. THAT.
I JUST GAVE UP ON IT.
HUH?
MY TIMES WOULDN'T IMPROVE, SO I GAVE IT UP.
FORTUNATELY, UNLIKE SOME PEOPLE, I'VE GOT A BRAIN.
SO I WASN'T WORRIED ABOUT CHANGING MY DIREC-TION.
MAYBE...
...THAT'S WHY PEOPLE THINK YOU RAN AWAY.
I DON'T CARE.
COMPETITION IS MEANINGLESS IF YOU DON'T WIN.
AND I COULDN'T KEEP SWIMMING BEHIND MY TEAMMATES' ASSES FOREVER.
WHOA!
IT'S MEANING-LESS IF YOU DON'T WIN...?

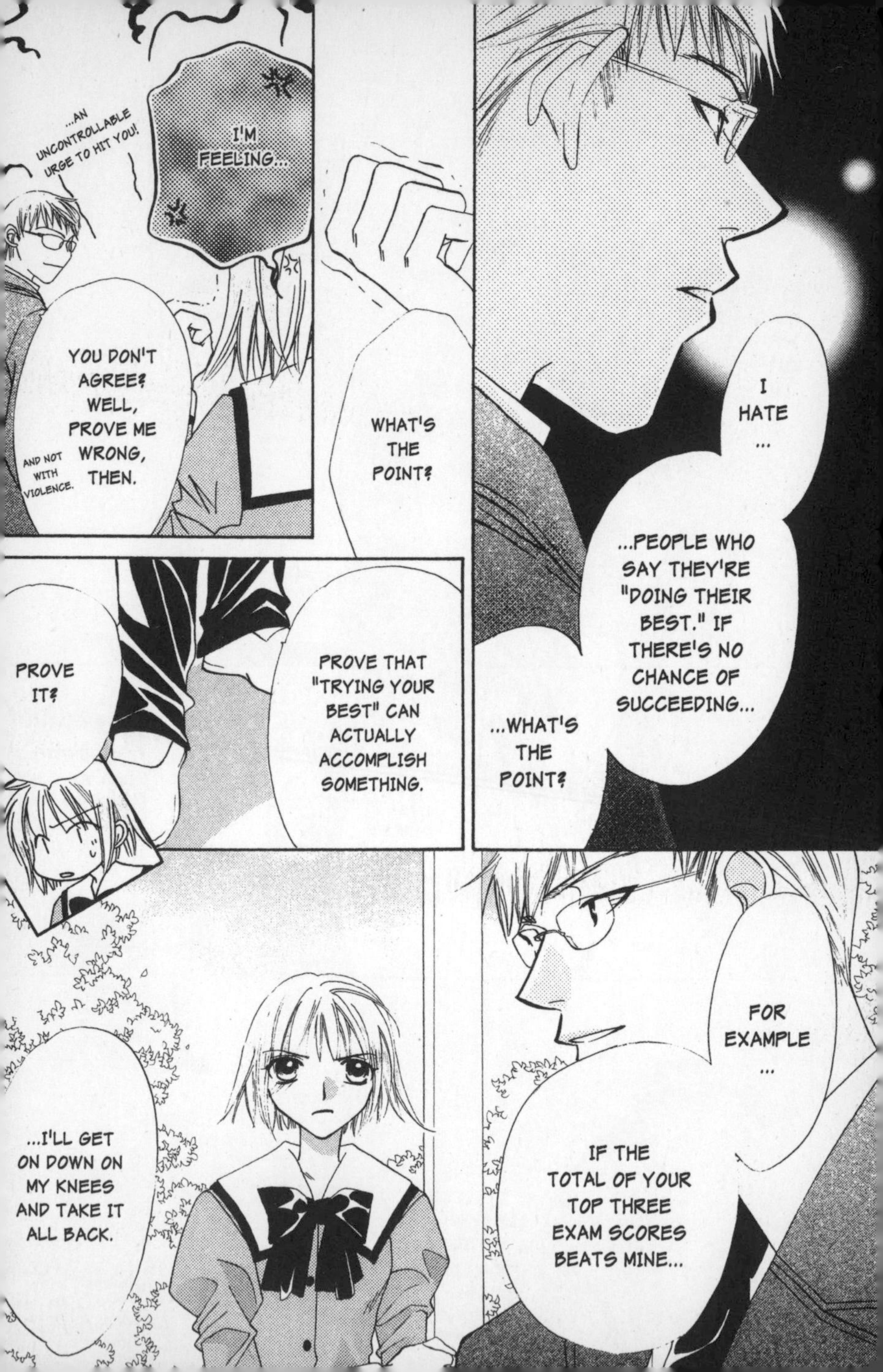
I HATE ...
...PEOPLE WHO SAY THEY'RE "DOING THEIR BEST." IF THERE'S NO CHANCE OF SUCCEEDING...
...WHAT'S THE POINT?
WHAT'S THE POINT?
I'M FEELING...
...AN UNCONTROLLABLE URGE TO HIT YOU!
YOU DON'T AGREE? WELL, PROVE ME WRONG, THEN.
AND NOT WITH VIOLENCE.
PROVE THAT "TRYING YOUR BEST" CAN ACTUALLY ACCOMPLISH SOMETHING.
PROVE IT?
FOR EXAMPLE ...
IF THE TOTAL OF YOUR TOP THREE EXAM SCORES BEATS MINE...
...I'LL GET ON DOWN ON MY KNEES AND TAKE IT ALL BACK.

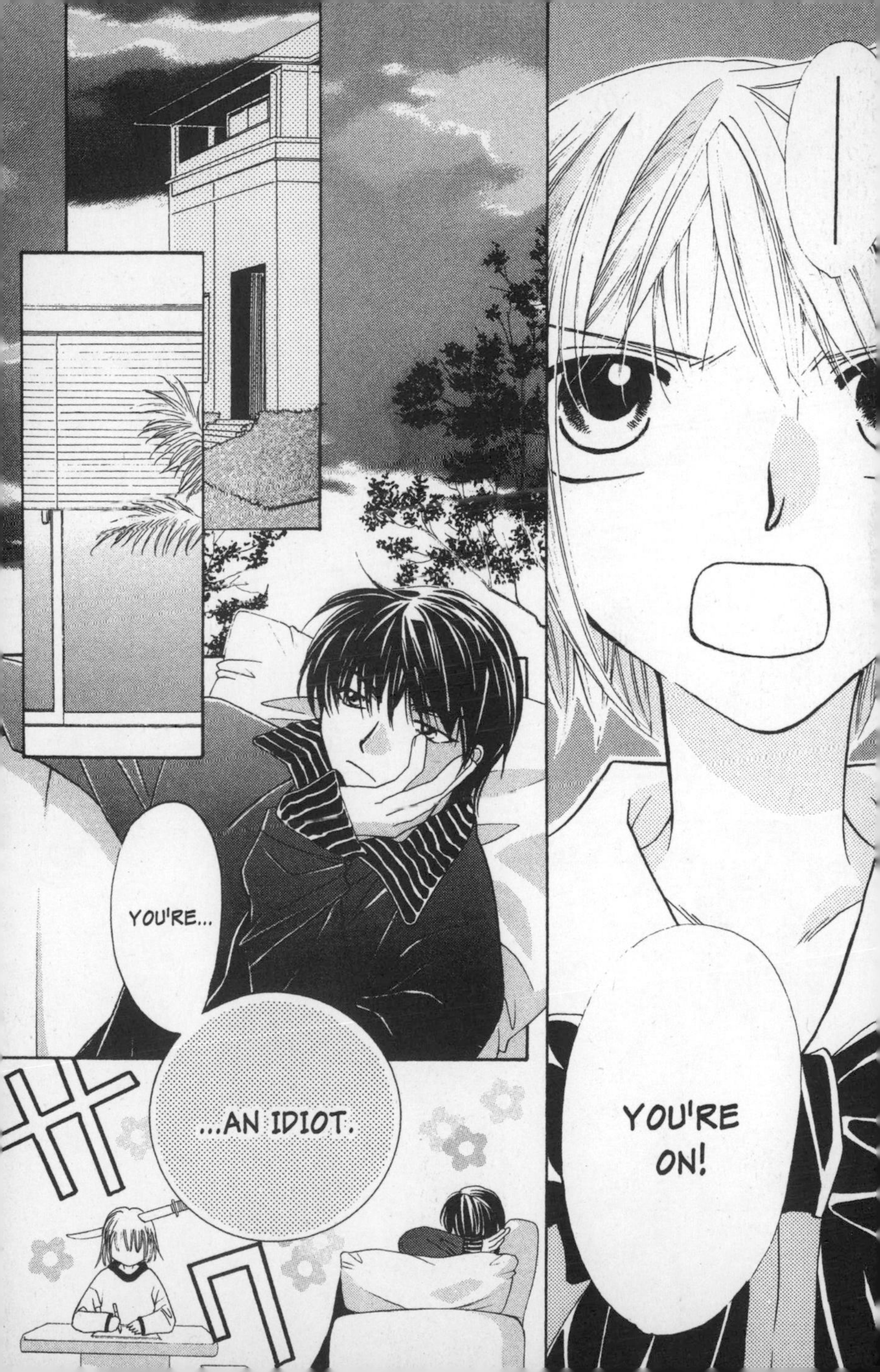
YOU'RE ON!
YOU'RE...
...AN IDIOT.

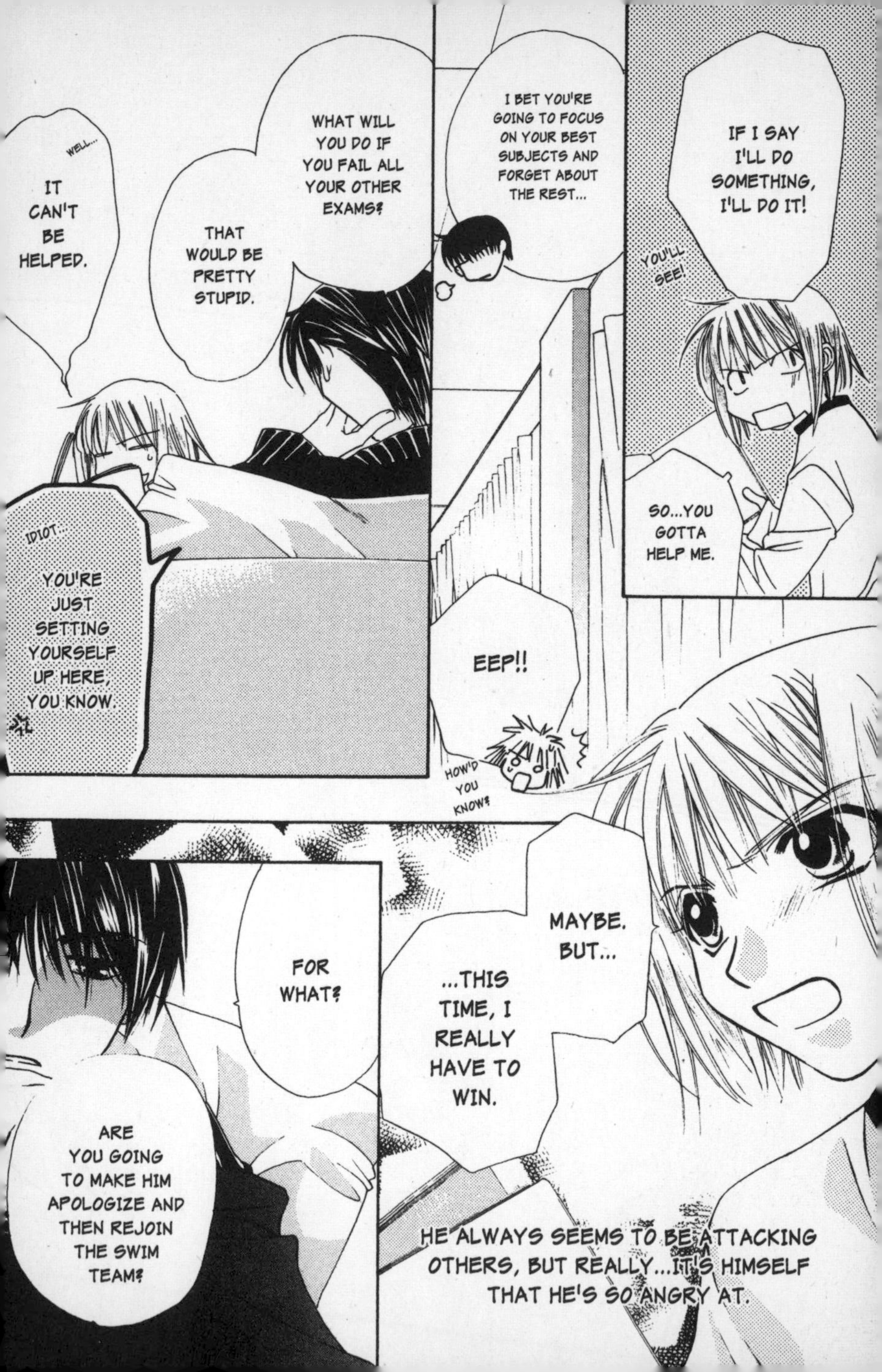
IF I SAY I'LL DO SOMETHING, I'LL DO IT!
YOU'LL SEE!
SO...YOU GOTTA HELP ME.
I BET YOU'RE GOING TO FOCUS ON YOUR BEST SUBJECTS AND FORGET ABOUT THE REST...
EEP!!
HOW'D YOU KNOW?
WHAT WILL YOU DO IF YOU FAIL ALL YOUR OTHER EXAMS?
WELL...
IT CAN'T BE HELPED.
THAT WOULD BE PRETTY STUPID.
IDIOT...
YOU'RE JUST SETTING YOURSELF UP HERE, YOU KNOW.
MAYBE. BUT...
...THIS TIME, I REALLY HAVE TO WIN.
FOR WHAT?
ARE YOU GOING TO MAKE HIM APOLOGIZE AND THEN REJOIN THE SWIM TEAM?
HE ALWAYS SEEMS TO BE ATTACKING OTHERS, BUT REALLY...IT'S HIMSELF THAT HE'S SO ANGRY AT.

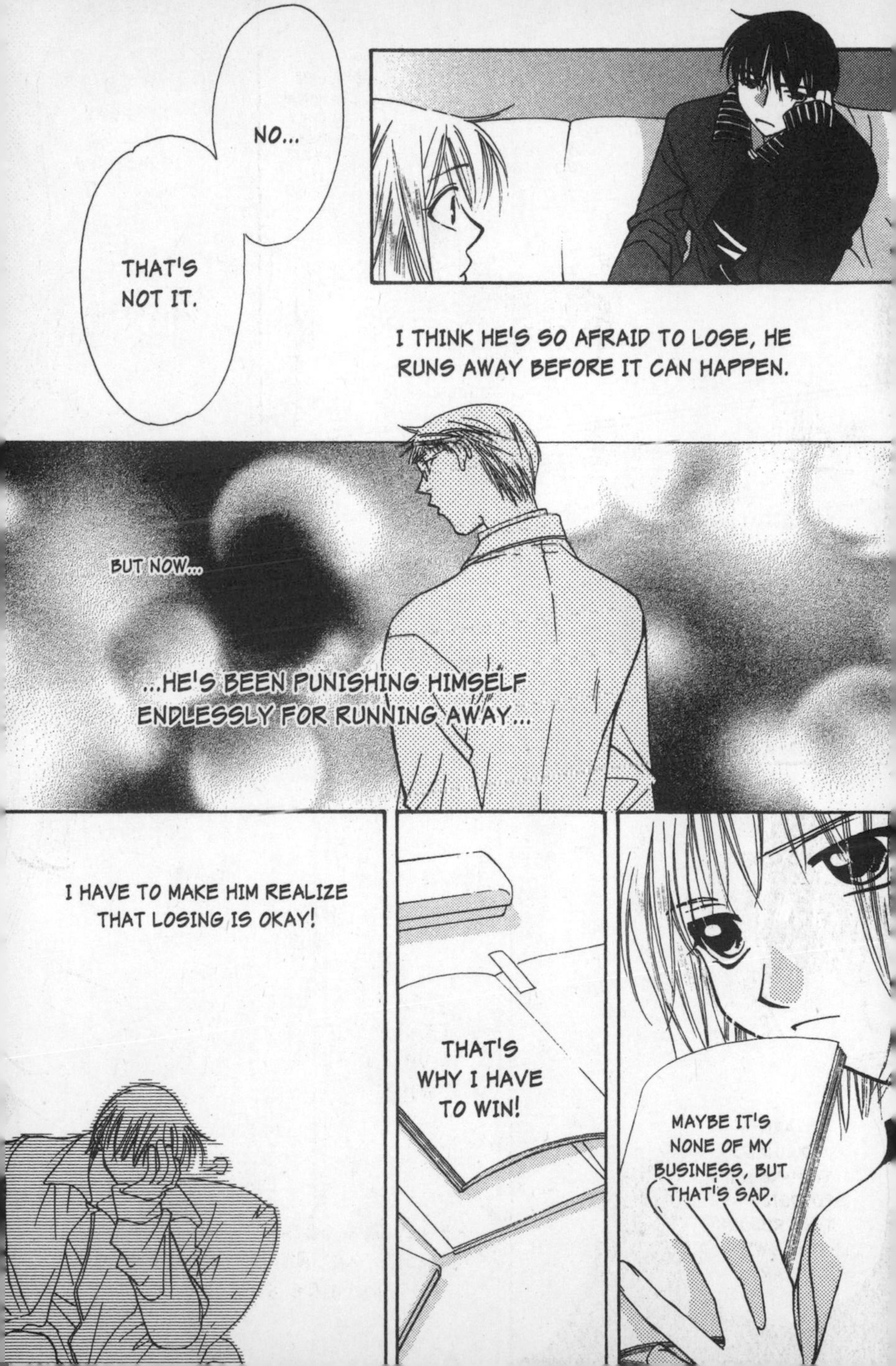
I THINK HE'S SO AFRAID TO LOSE, HE RUNS AWAY BEFORE IT CAN HAPPEN.
NO... THAT'S NOT IT.
BUT NOW...
...HE'S BEEN PUNISHING HIMSELF ENDLESSLY FOR RUNNING AWAY...
MAYBE IT'S NONE OF MY BUSINESS, BUT THAT'S SAD.
THAT'S WHY I HAVE TO WIN!
I HAVE TO MAKE HIM REALIZE THAT LOSING IS OKAY!

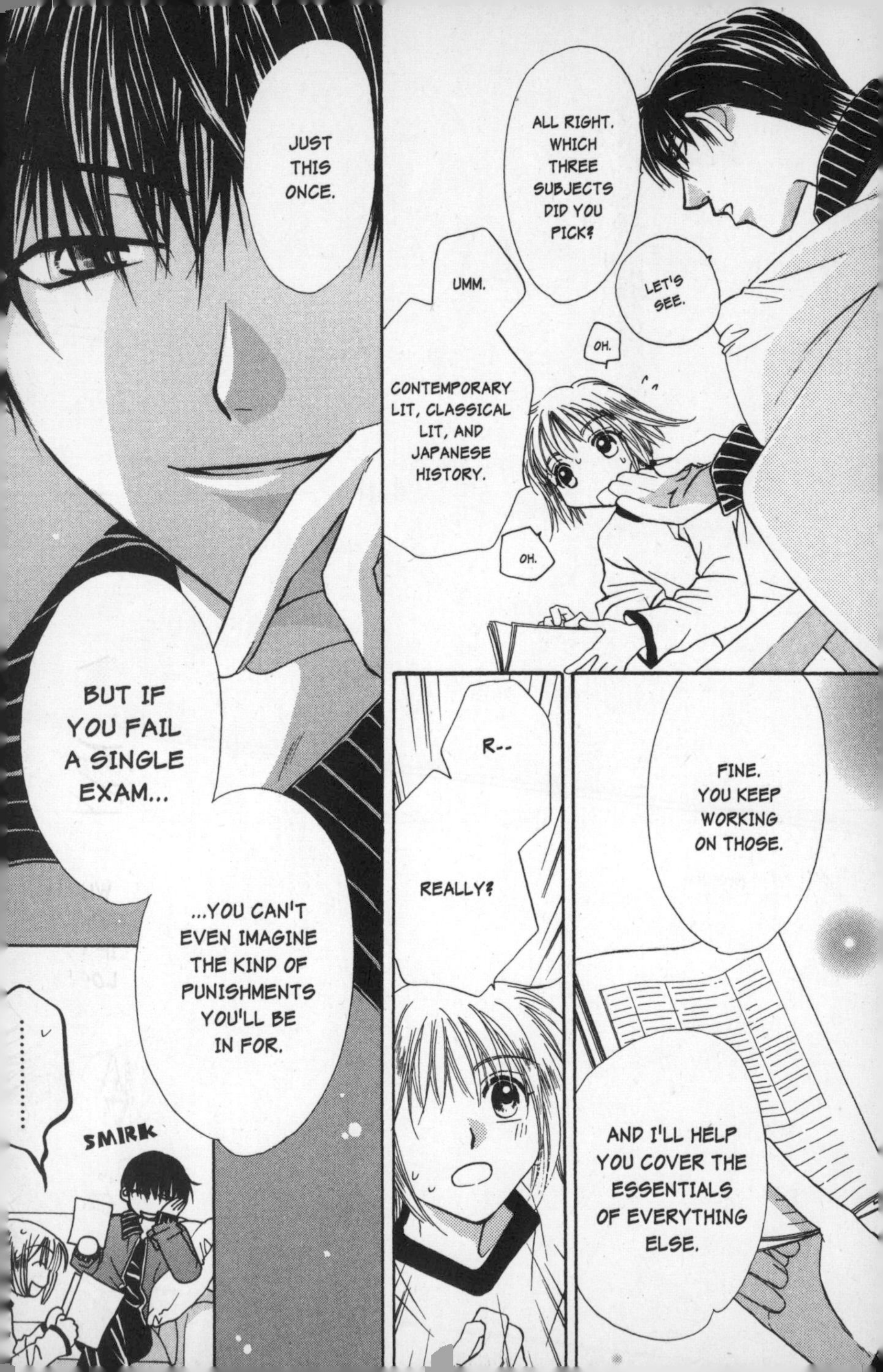

ALL RIGHT. WHICH THREE SUBJECTS DID YOU PICK?
LET'S SEE.
UMM.
OH.
CONTEMPORARY LIT, CLASSICAL LIT, AND JAPANESE HISTORY.
OH.
FINE. YOU KEEP WORKING ON THOSE.
AND I'LL HELP YOU COVER THE ESSENTIALS OF EVERYTHING ELSE.
R--
REALLY?
JUST THIS ONCE.
BUT IF YOU FAIL A SINGLE EXAM...
...YOU CAN'T EVEN IMAGINE THE KIND OF PUNISHMENTS YOU'LL BE IN FOR.
......
SMIRK

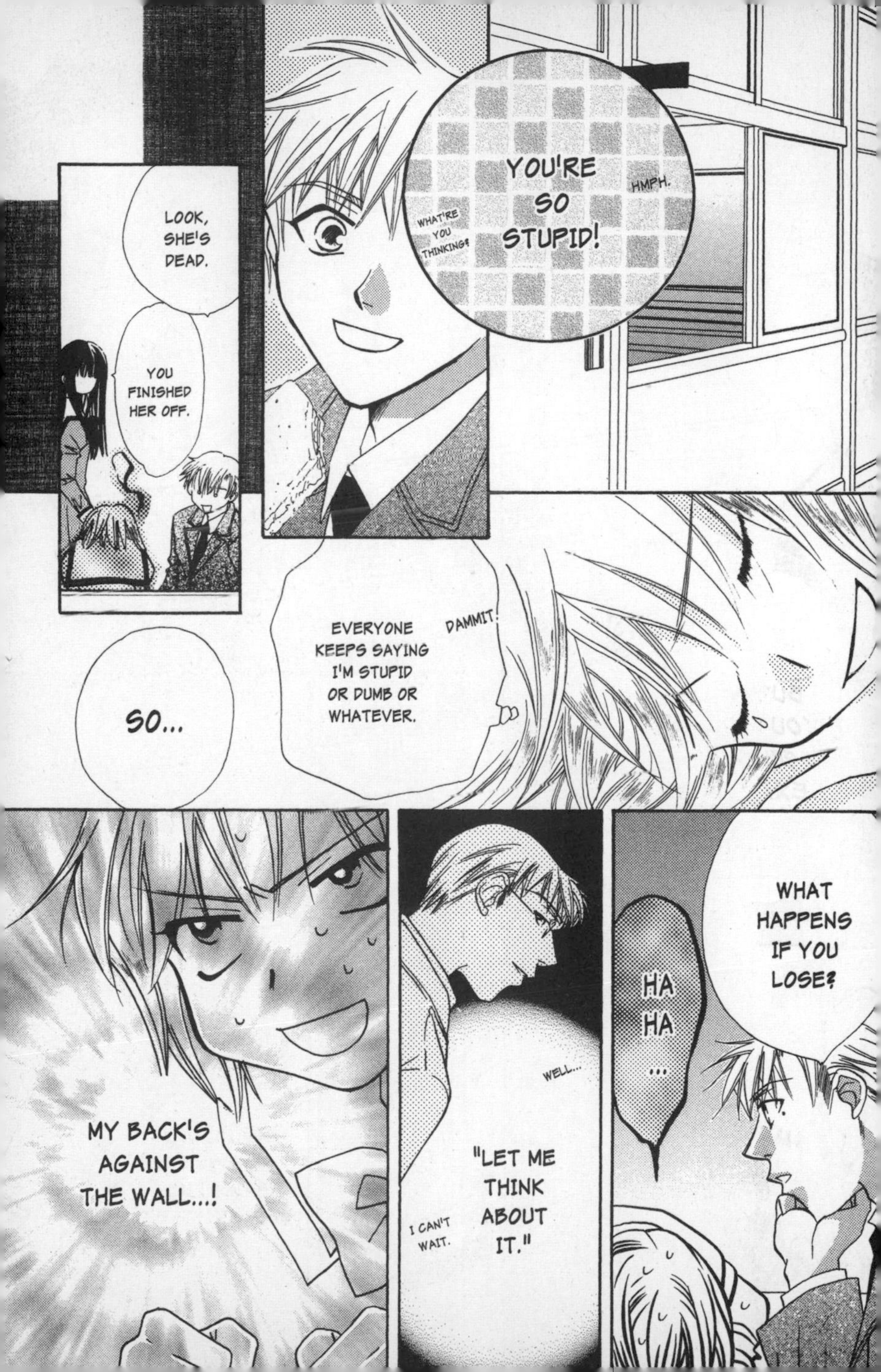
HMPH.
YOU'RE SO STUPID!
WHAT'RE YOU THINKING?
LOOK, SHE'S DEAD.
YOU FINISHED HER OFF.
DAMMIT.
EVERYONE KEEPS SAYING I'M STUPID OR DUMB OR WHATEVER.
SO...
WHAT HAPPENS IF YOU LOSE?
HA HA ...
WELL...
"LET ME THINK ABOUT IT."
I CAN'T WAIT.
MY BACK'S AGAINST THE WALL...!

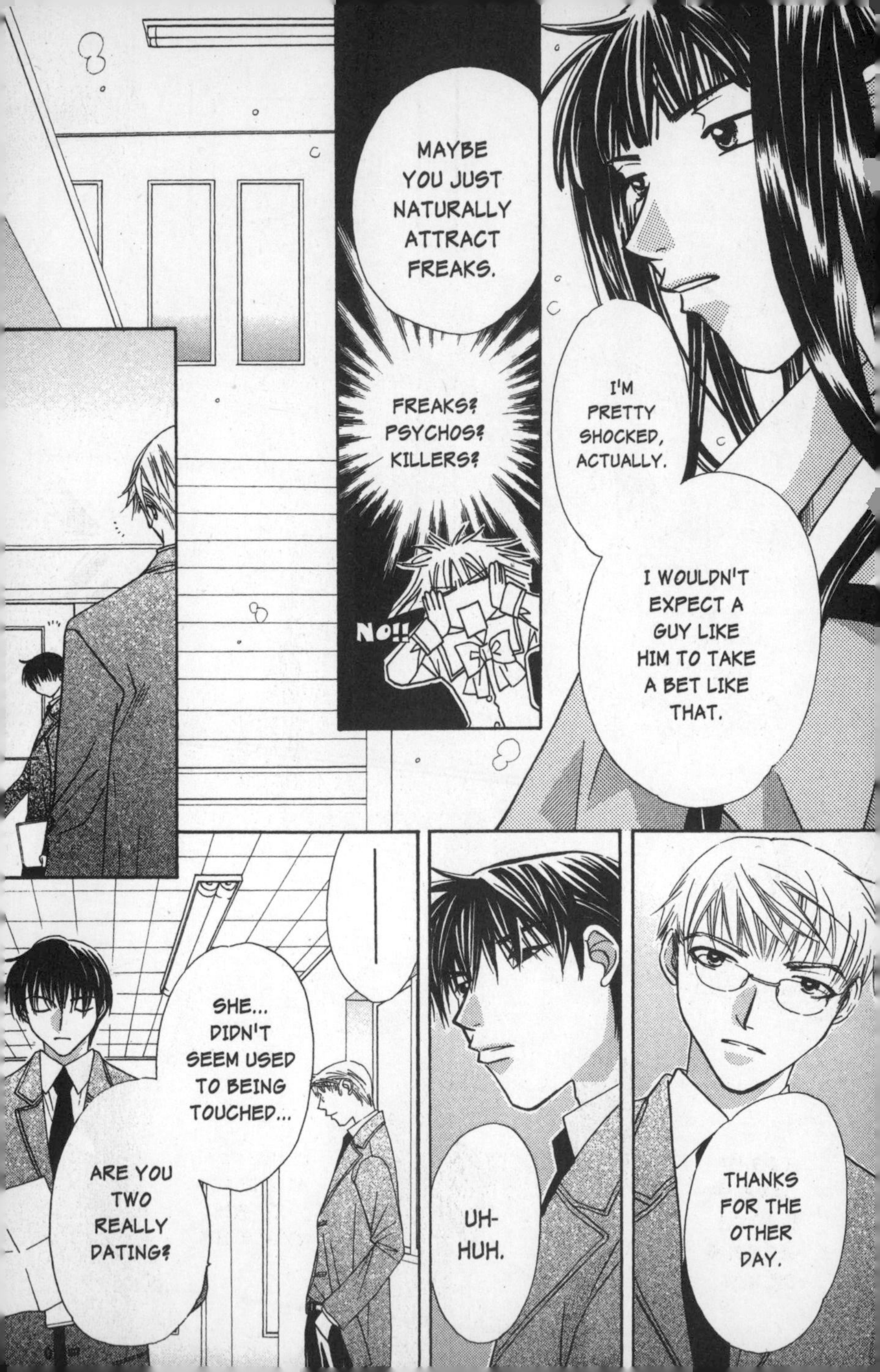
I'M PRETTY SHOCKED, ACTUALLY.
I WOULDN'T EXPECT A GUY LIKE HIM TO TAKE A BET LIKE THAT.
MAYBE YOU JUST NATURALLY ATTRACT FREAKS.
FREAKS? PSYCHOS? KILLERS?
NO!!
THANKS FOR THE OTHER DAY.
UH-HUH.
SHE... DIDN'T SEEM USED TO BEING TOUCHED...
ARE YOU TWO REALLY DATING?

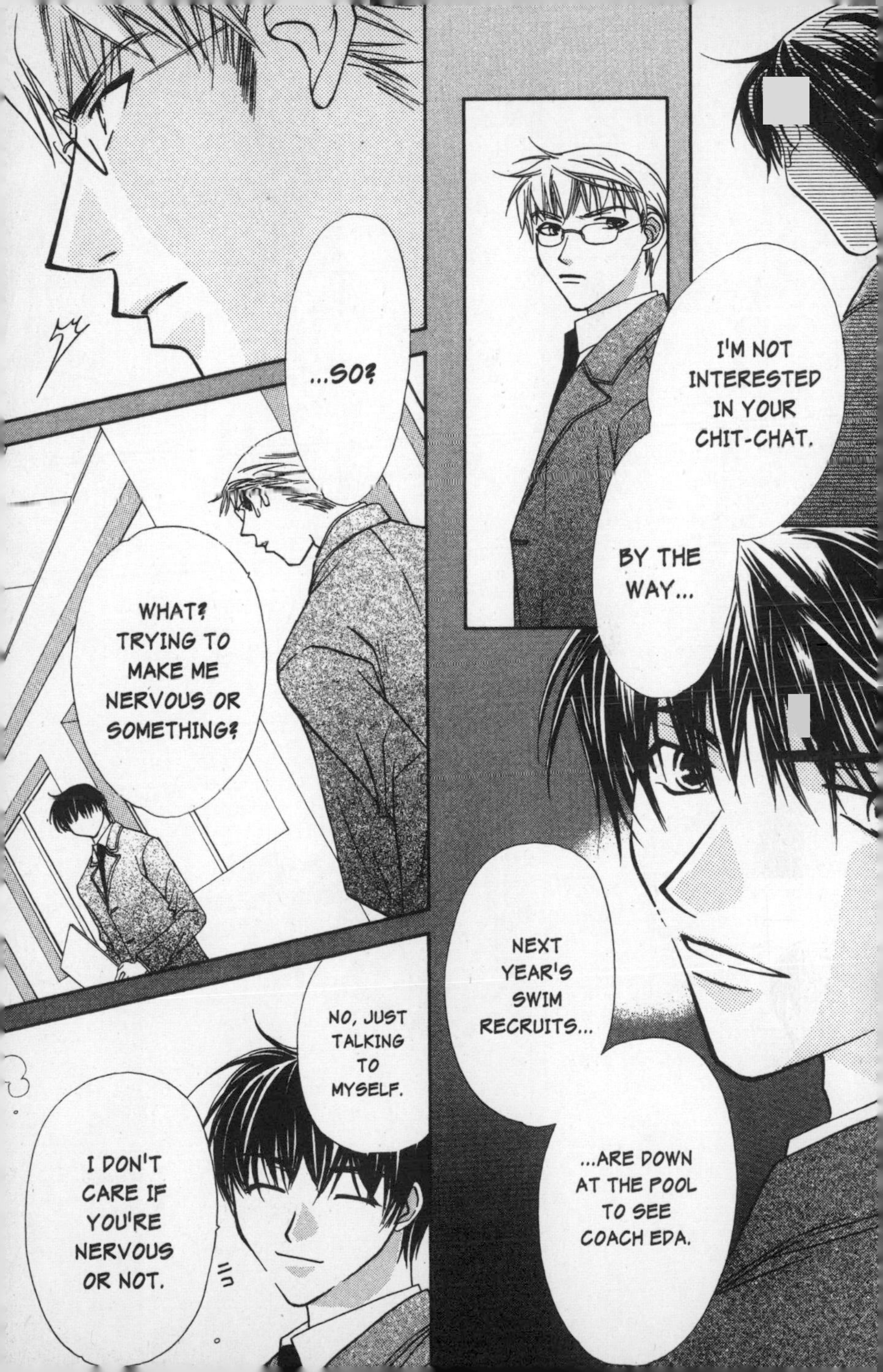
I'M NOT INTERESTED IN YOUR CHIT-CHAT.
BY THE WAY...
NEXT YEAR'S SWIM RECRUITS...
...ARE DOWN AT THE POOL TO SEE COACH EDA.
...SO?
WHAT? TRYING TO MAKE ME NERVOUS OR SOMETHING?
NO, JUST TALKING TO MYSELF.
I DON'T CARE IF YOU'RE NERVOUS OR NOT.

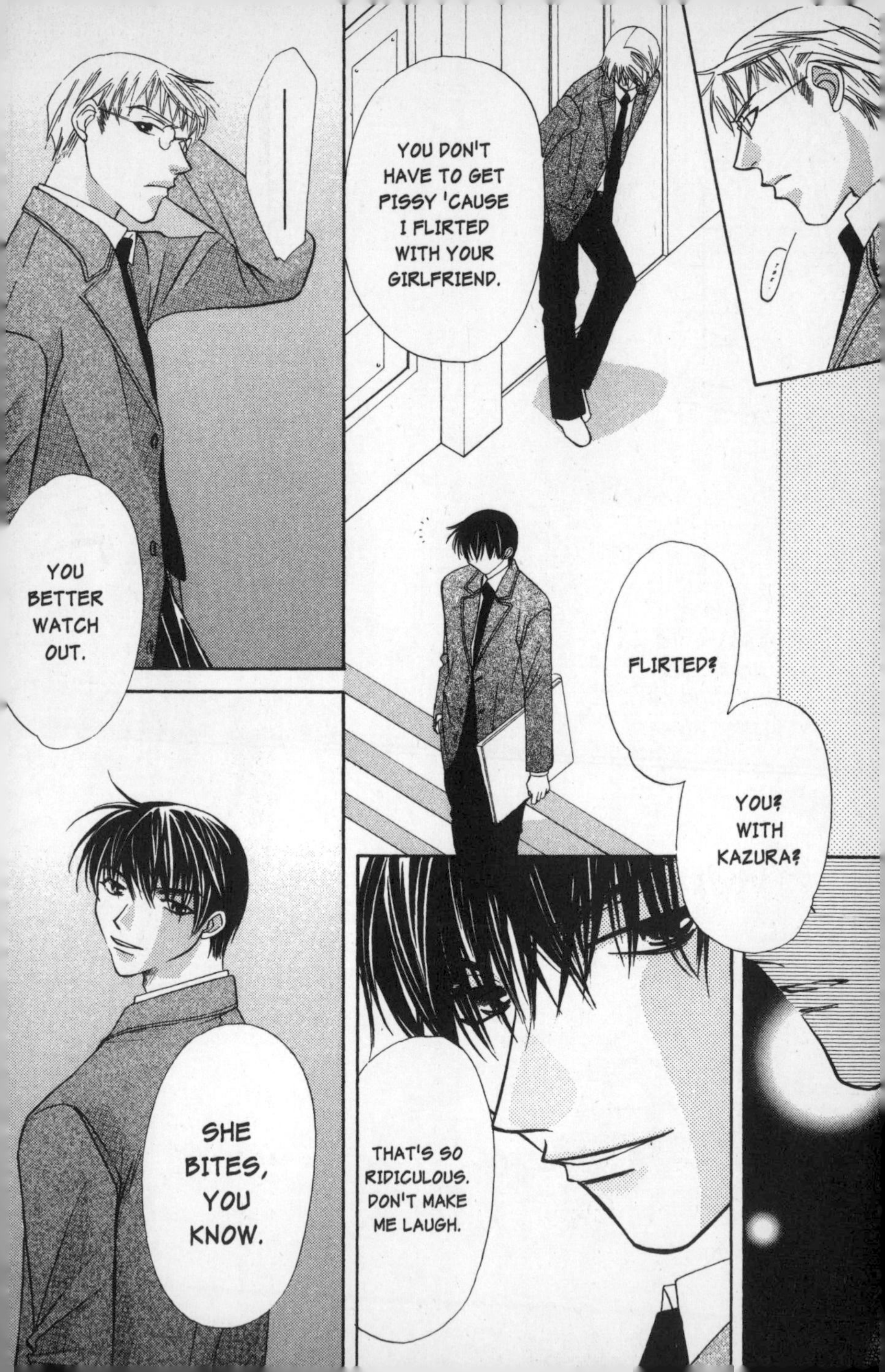
YOU DON'T HAVE TO GET PISSY 'CAUSE I FLIRTED WITH YOUR GIRLFRIEND.
FLIRTED?
YOU? WITH KAZURA?
THAT'S SO RIDICULOUS. DON'T MAKE ME LAUGH.
YOU BETTER WATCH OUT.
SHE BITES, YOU KNOW.

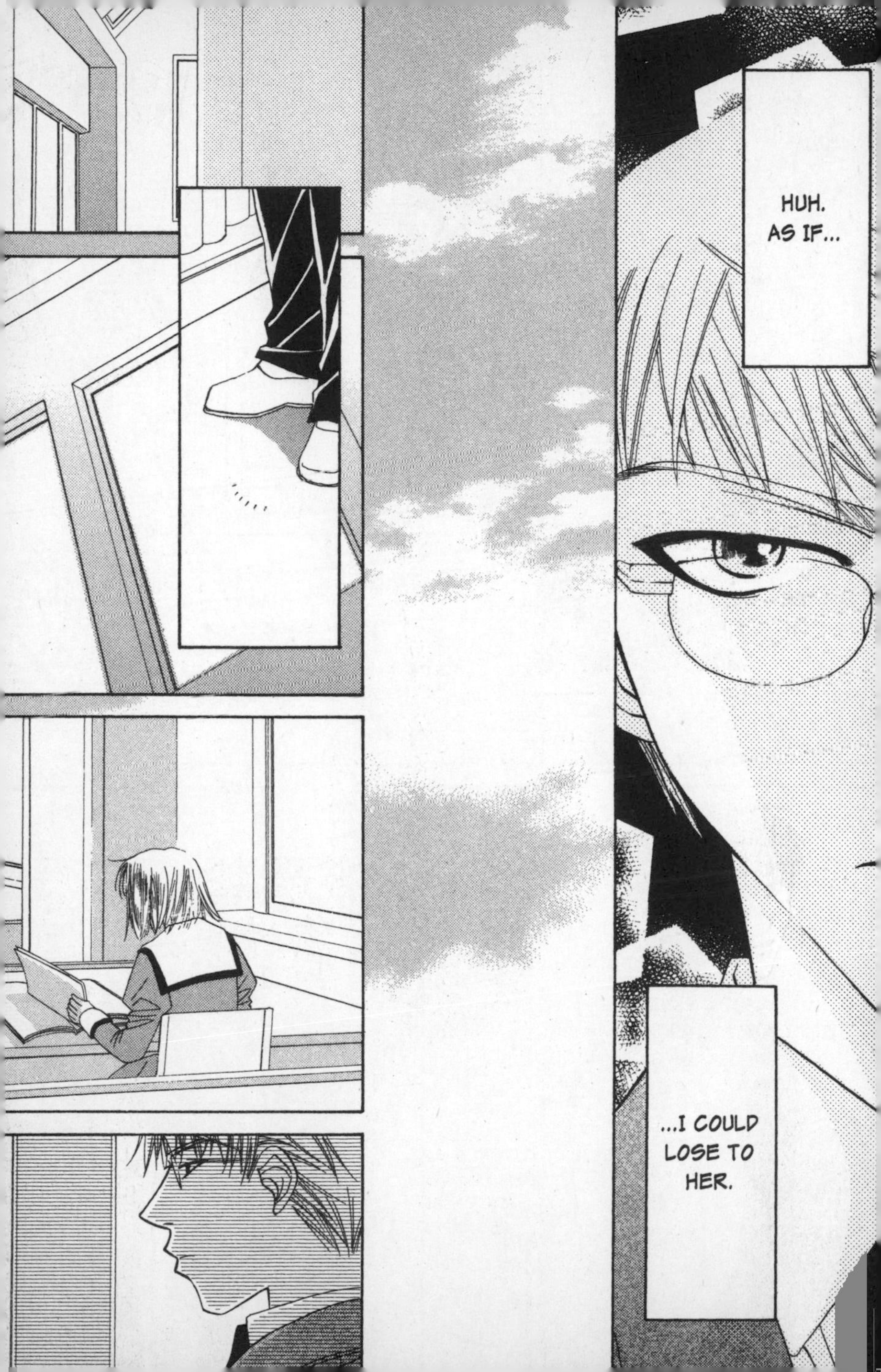
HUH. AS IF...
...I COULD LOSE TO HER.

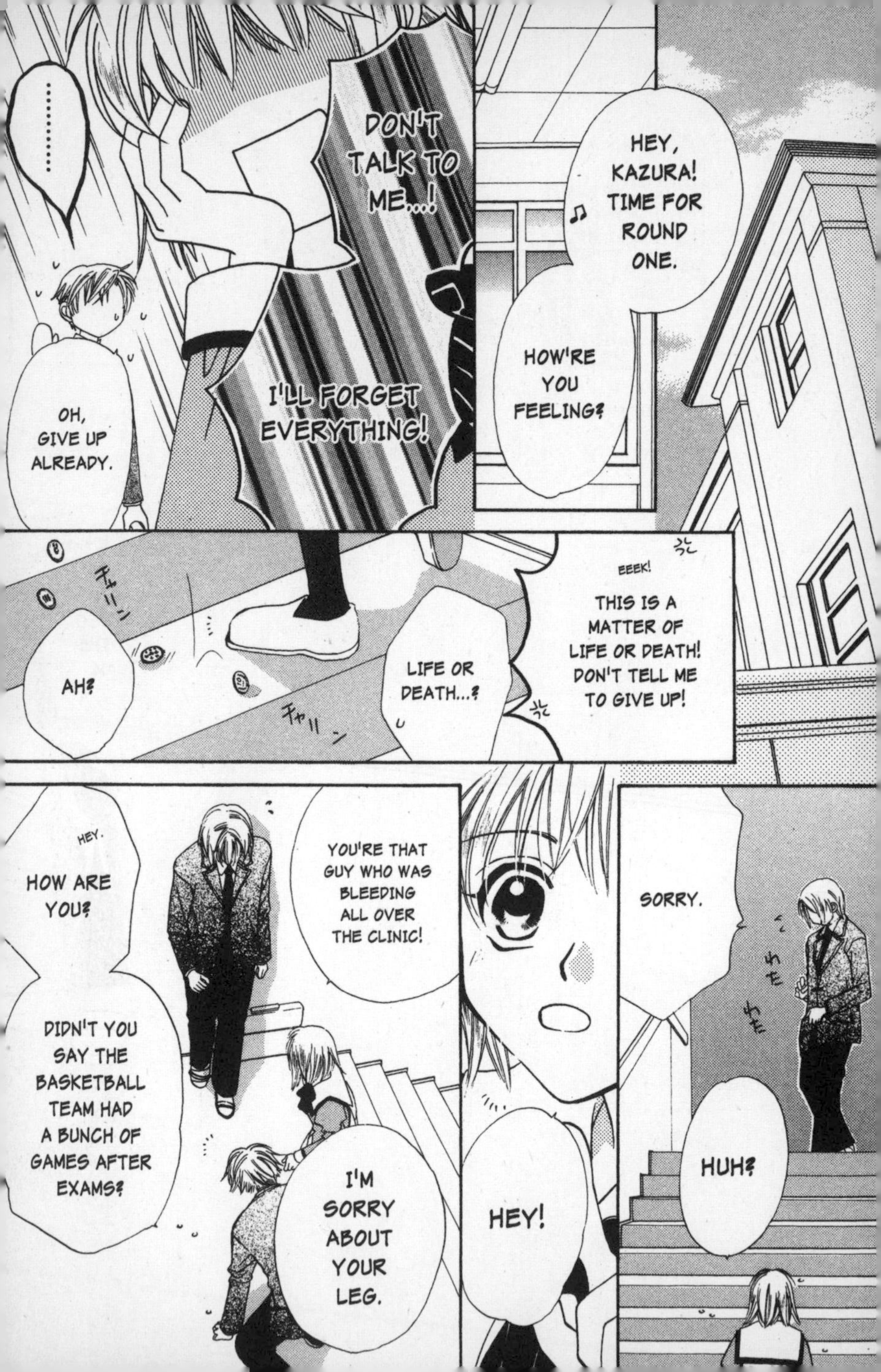
HEY, KAZURA! ♪ TIME FOR ROUND ONE.
HOW'RE YOU FEELING?
DON'T TALK TO ME...!
......
I'LL FORGET EVERYTHING!
OH, GIVE UP ALREADY.
EEEK!
THIS IS A MATTER OF LIFE OR DEATH! DON'T TELL ME TO GIVE UP!
LIFE OR DEATH...?
AH?
SORRY.
HUH?
HEY!
YOU'RE THAT GUY WHO WAS BLEEDING ALL OVER THE CLINIC!
HEY.
HOW ARE YOU?
DIDN'T YOU SAY THE BASKETBALL TEAM HAD A BUNCH OF GAMES AFTER EXAMS?
I'M SORRY ABOUT YOUR LEG.

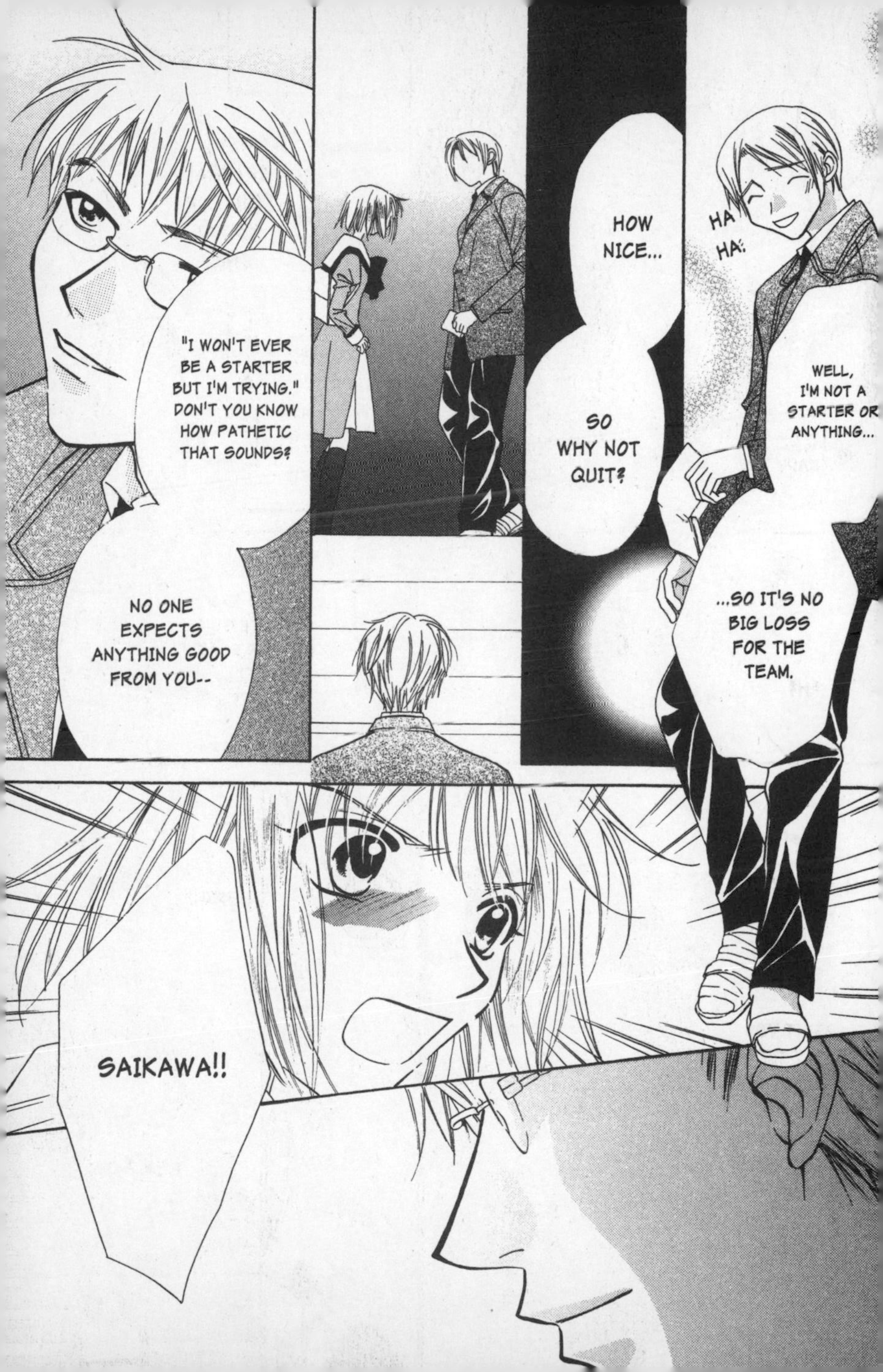
HA HA
WELL, I'M NOT A STARTER OR ANYTHING...
...SO IT'S NO BIG LOSS FOR THE TEAM.
HOW NICE...
SO WHY NOT QUIT?
"I WON'T EVER BE A STARTER BUT I'M TRYING." DON'T YOU KNOW HOW PATHETIC THAT SOUNDS?
NO ONE EXPECTS ANYTHING GOOD FROM YOU--
SAIKAWA!!

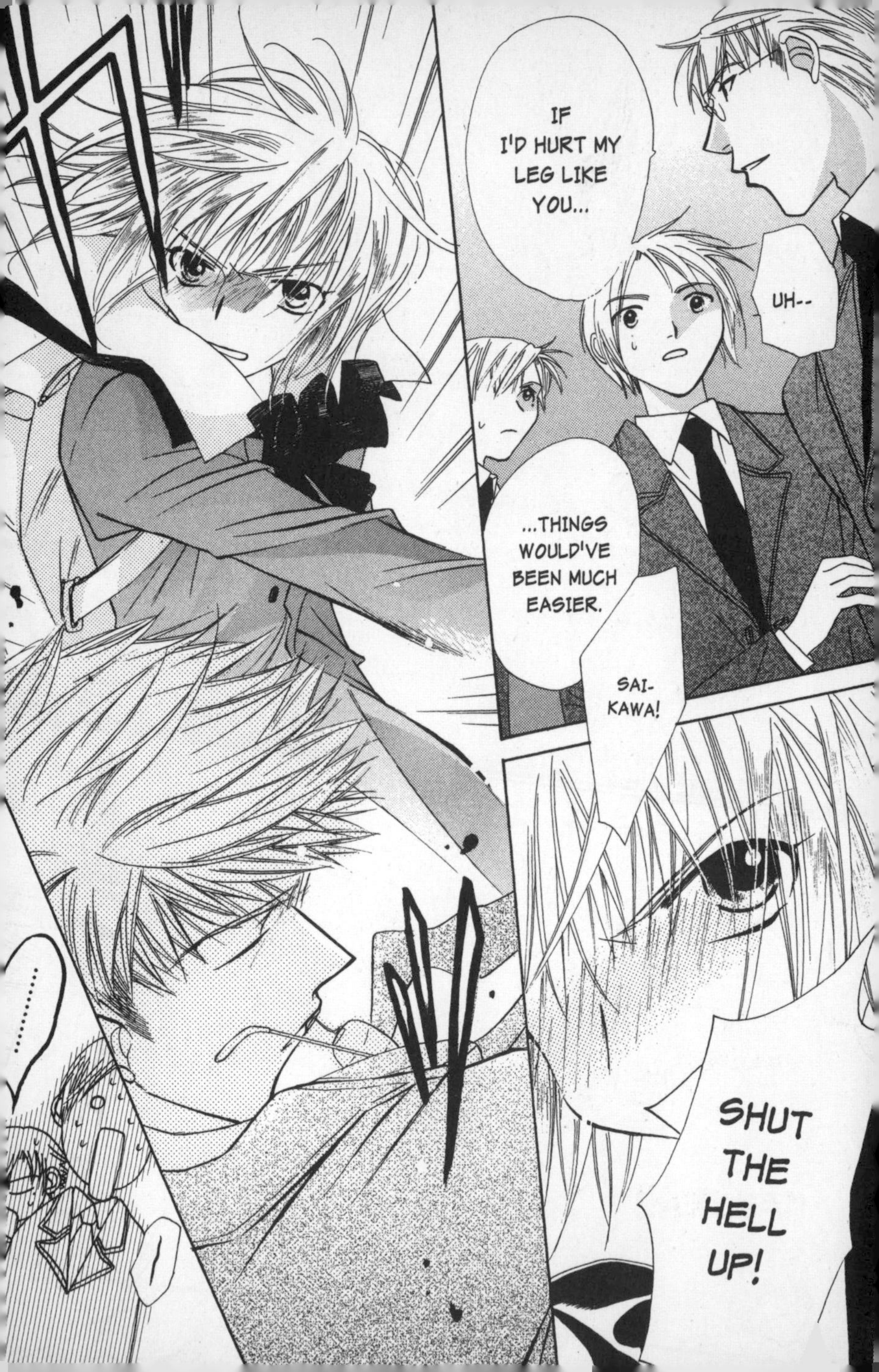
IF I'D HURT MY LEG LIKE YOU...
UH--
...THINGS WOULD'VE BEEN MUCH EASIER.
SAI-KAWA!
SHUT THE HELL UP!
......

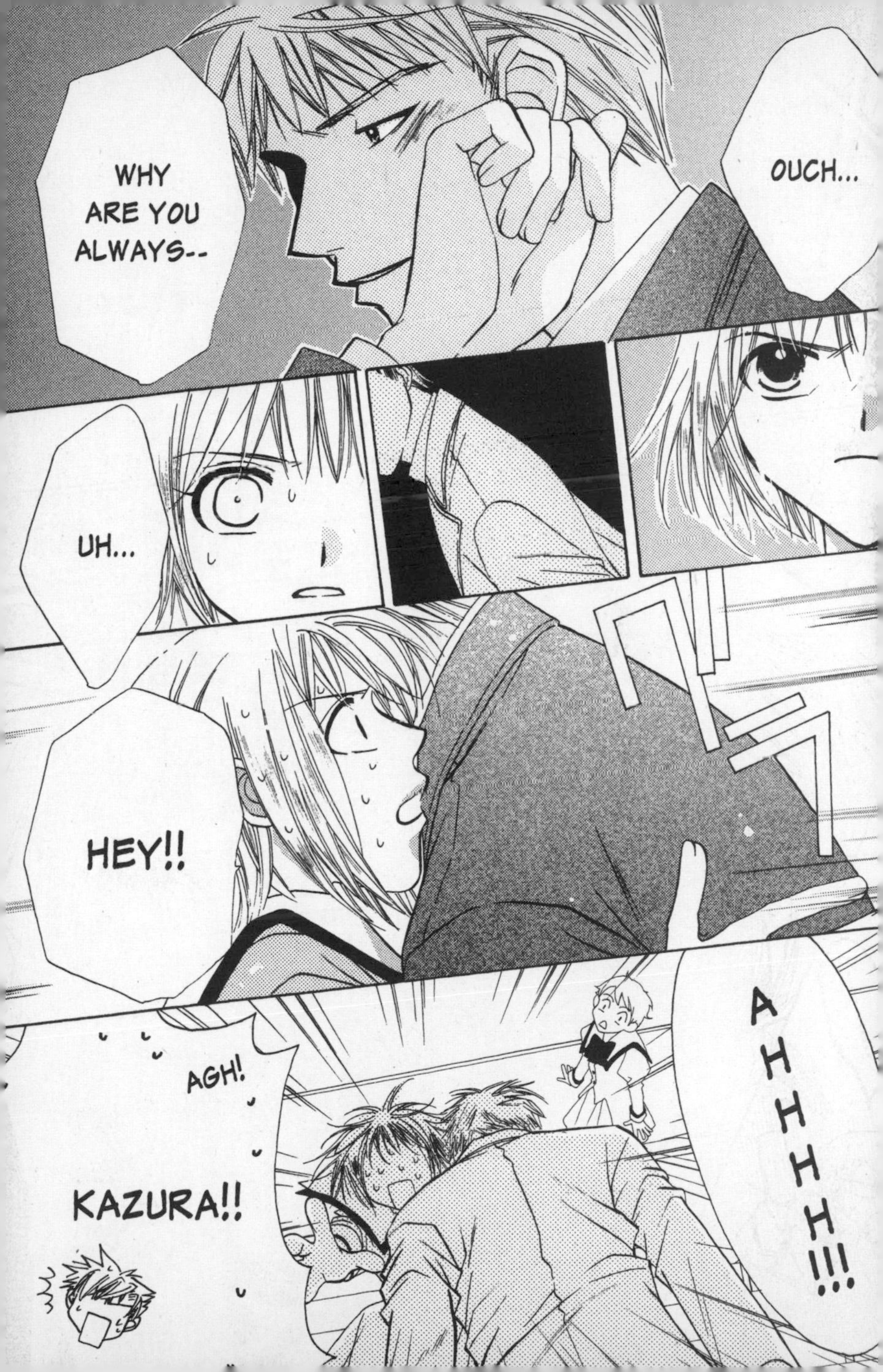
OUCH...
WHY ARE YOU ALWAYS--
UH...
HEY!!
AHHHH!!!
AGH!
KAZURA!!

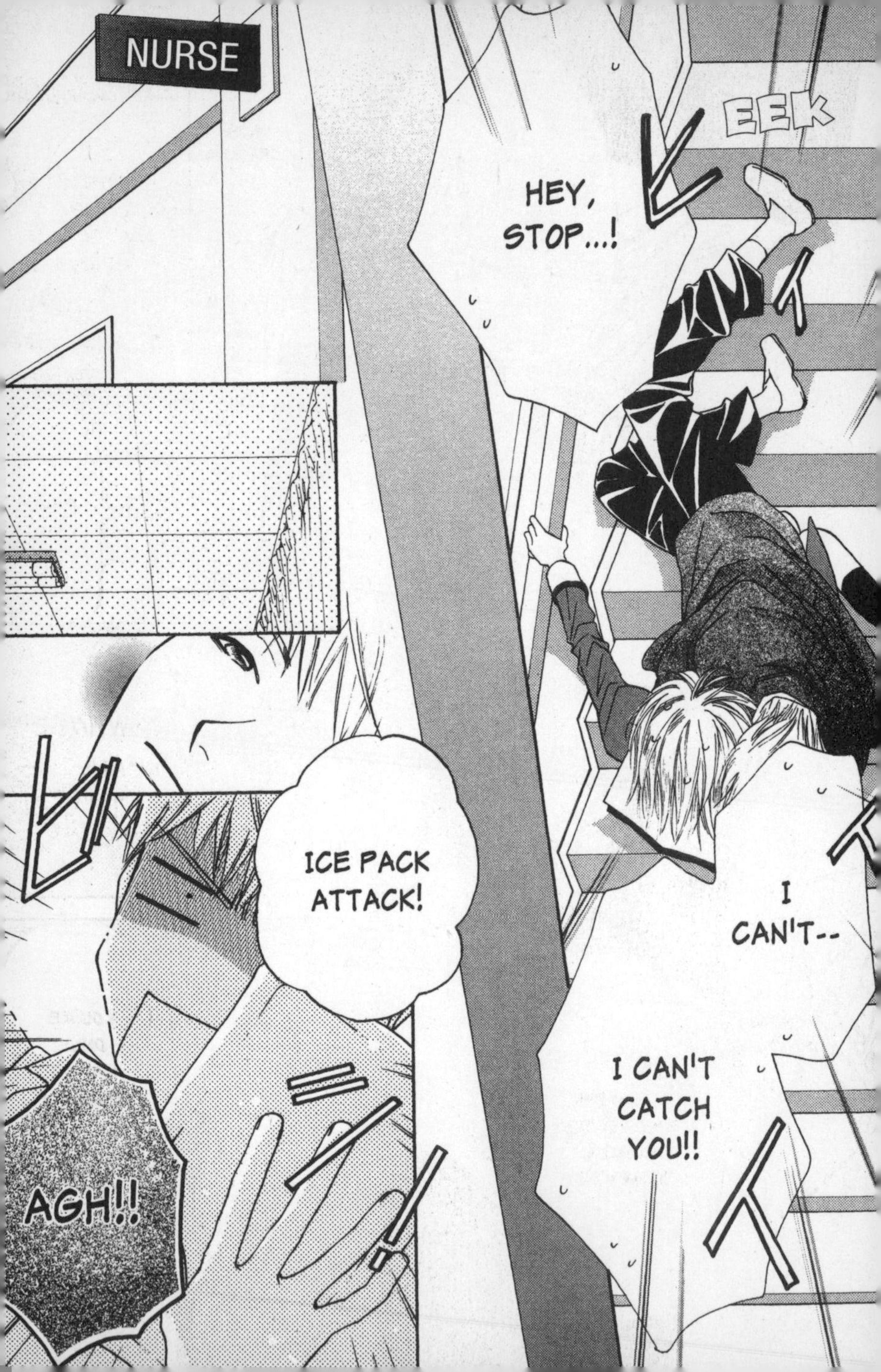
EEK
HEY, STOP...!
I CAN'T--
I CAN'T CATCH YOU!!
NURSE
ICE PACK ATTACK!
AGH!!

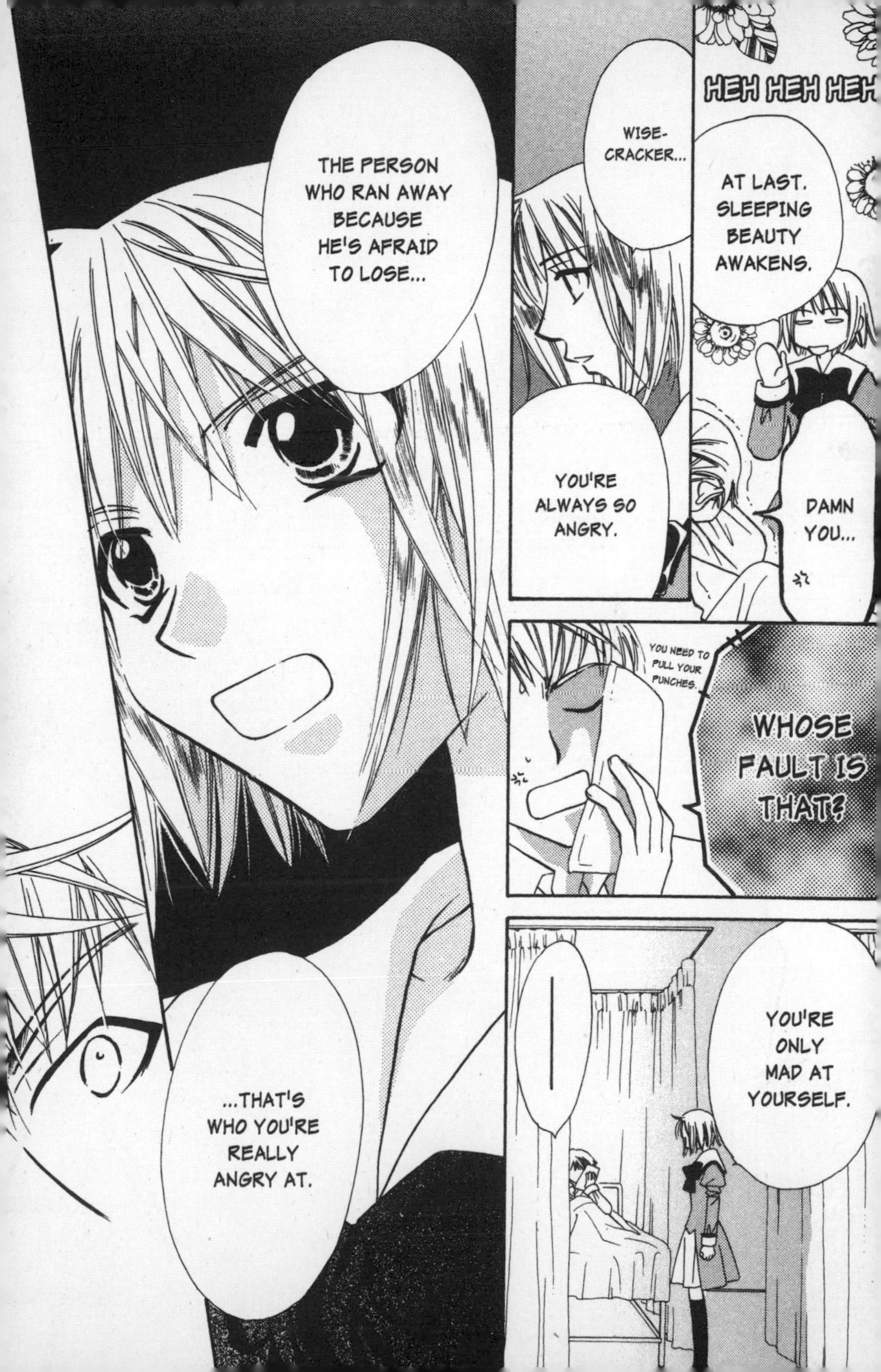
HEH HEH HEH
AT LAST. SLEEPING BEAUTY AWAKENS.
DAMN YOU...
WISE-CRACKER...
YOU'RE ALWAYS SO ANGRY.
WHOSE FAULT IS THAT?
YOU NEED TO PULL YOUR PUNCHES.
YOU'RE ONLY MAD AT YOURSELF.
THE PERSON WHO RAN AWAY BECAUSE HE'S AFRAID TO LOSE...
...THAT'S WHO YOU'RE REALLY ANGRY AT.

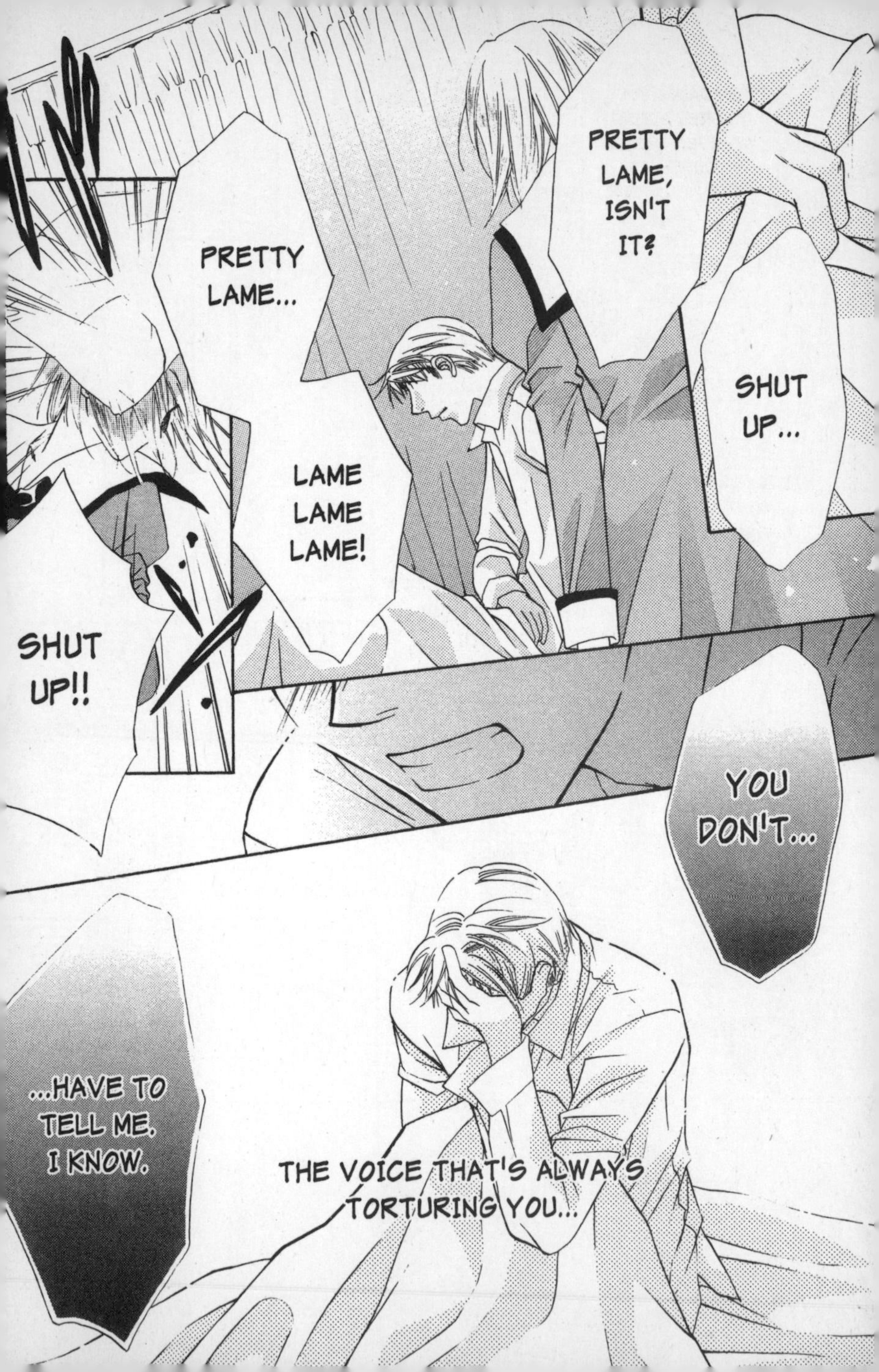
PRETTY LAME, ISN'T IT?
SHUT UP...
PRETTY LAME...
LAME LAME LAME!
SHUT UP!!
YOU DON'T...
...HAVE TO TELL ME. I KNOW.
THE VOICE THAT'S ALWAYS TORTURING YOU...

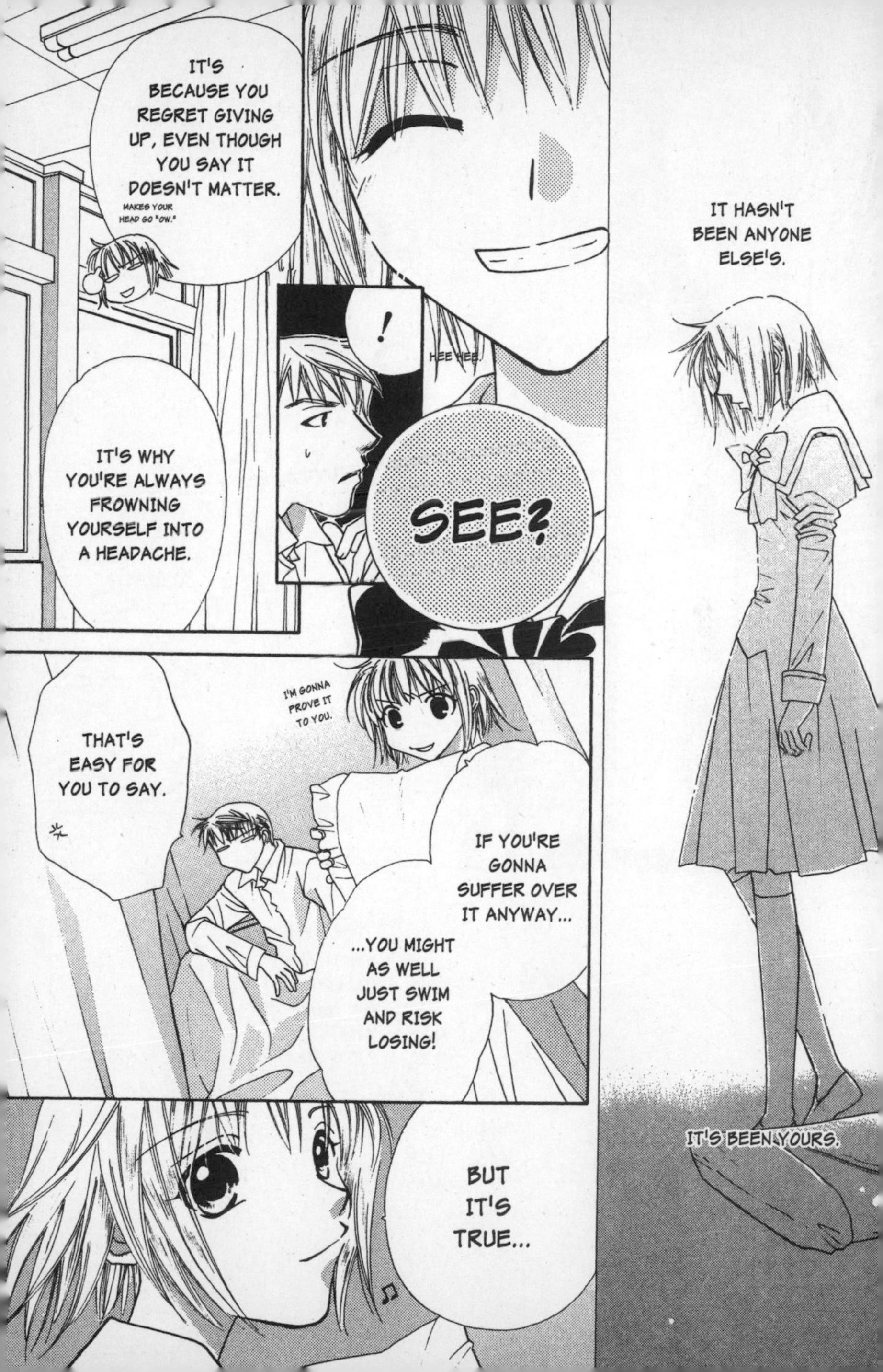
IT HASN'T BEEN ANYONE ELSE'S.
IT'S BEEN YOURS.
IT'S BECAUSE YOU REGRET GIVING UP, EVEN THOUGH YOU SAY IT DOESN'T MATTER.
MAKES YOUR HEAD GO "OW."
IT'S WHY YOU'RE ALWAYS FROWNING YOURSELF INTO A HEADACHE.
!
HEE HEE.
SEE?
THAT'S EASY FOR YOU TO SAY.
IF YOU'RE GONNA SUFFER OVER IT ANYWAY...
...YOU MIGHT AS WELL JUST SWIM AND RISK LOSING!
I'M GONNA PROVE IT TO YOU.
BUT IT'S TRUE...

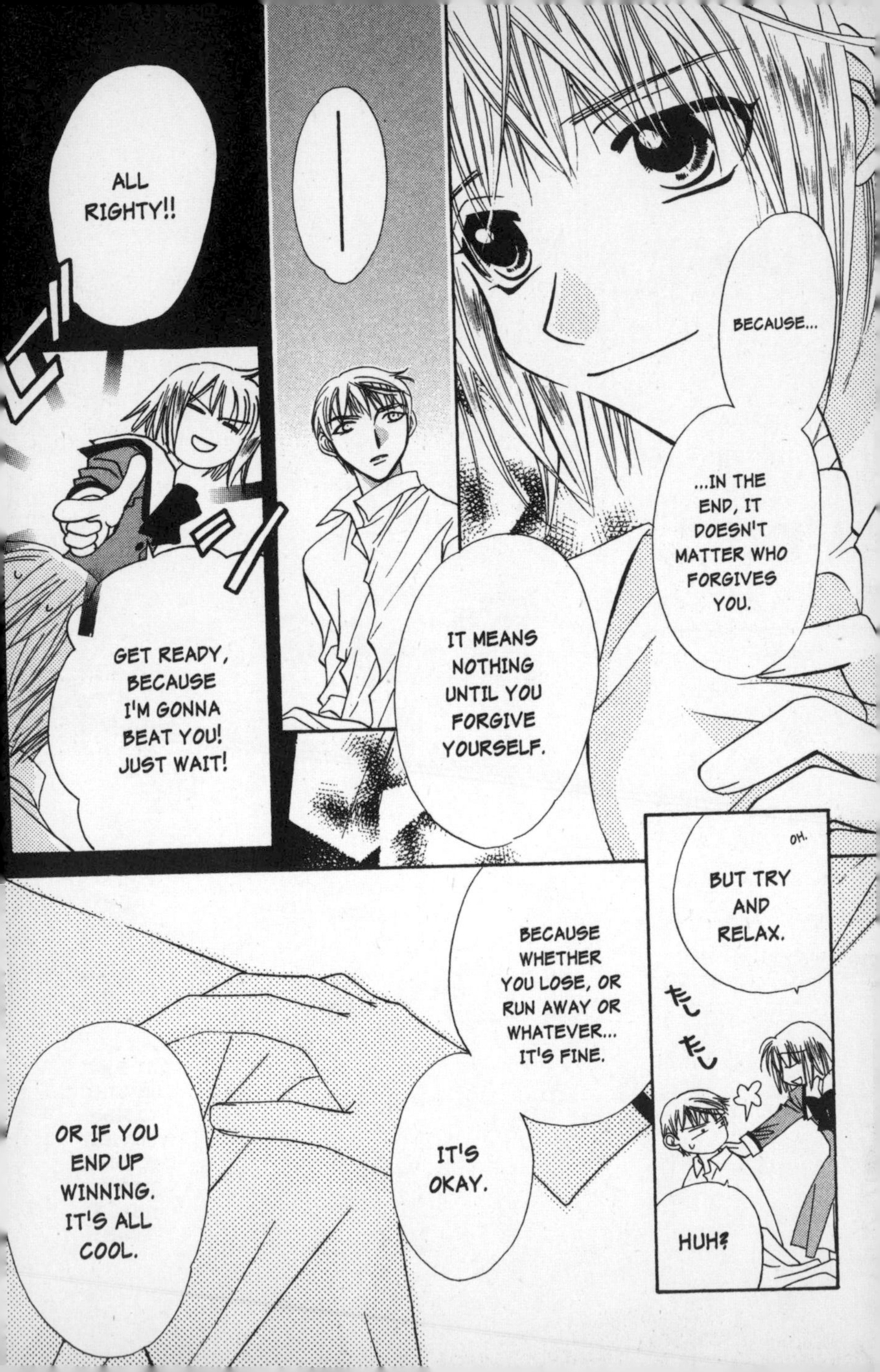
BECAUSE...
...IN THE END, IT DOESN'T MATTER WHO FORGIVES YOU.
IT MEANS NOTHING UNTIL YOU FORGIVE YOURSELF.
—
ALL RIGHTY!!
GET READY, BECAUSE I'M GONNA BEAT YOU! JUST WAIT!
OH.
BUT TRY AND RELAX.
たし たし
HUH?
BECAUSE WHETHER YOU LOSE, OR RUN AWAY OR WHATEVER... IT'S FINE.
IT'S OKAY.
OR IF YOU END UP WINNING. IT'S ALL COOL.

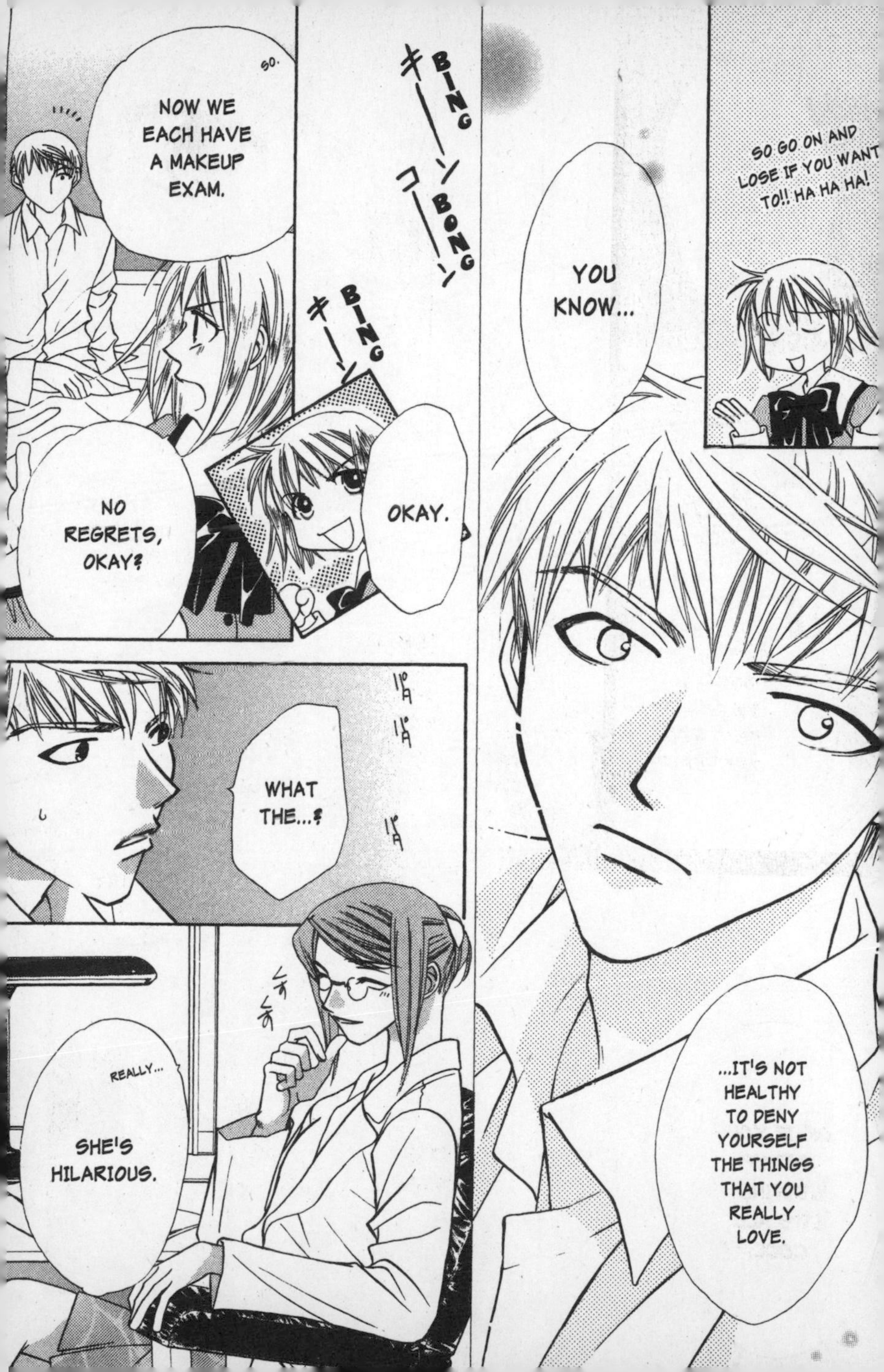
SO GO ON AND LOSE IF YOU WANT TO!! HA HA HA!
YOU KNOW...
...IT'S NOT HEALTHY TO DENY YOURSELF THE THINGS THAT YOU REALLY LOVE.
キーンコーン
BING BONG
キーン
BING
SO.
NOW WE EACH HAVE A MAKEUP EXAM.
NO REGRETS, OKAY?
OKAY.
ぱ ぱ ぱ
WHAT THE...?!
くす くす
REALLY...
SHE'S HILARIOUS.

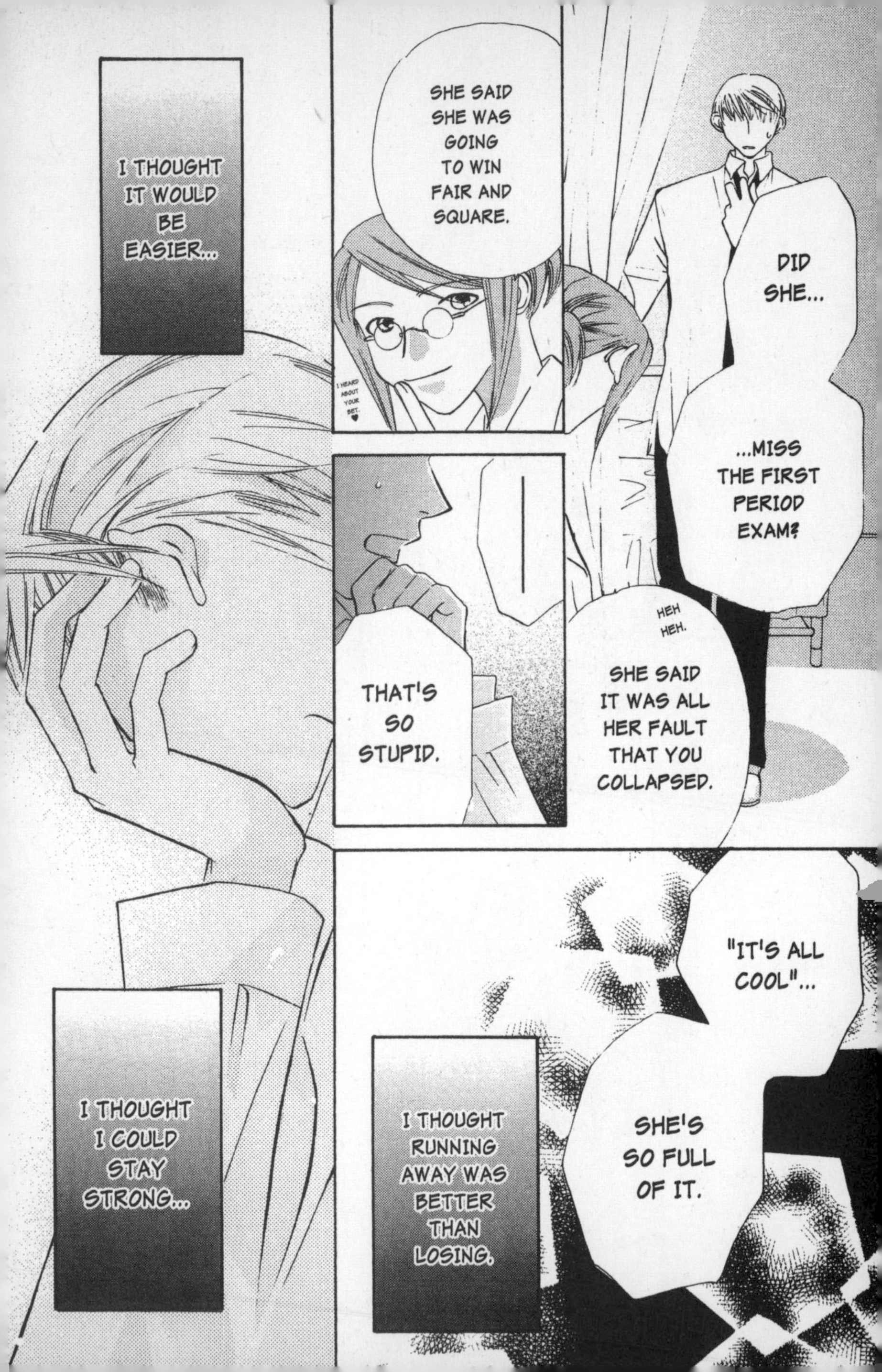
DID SHE...
...MISS THE FIRST PERIOD EXAM?
SHE SAID SHE WAS GOING TO WIN FAIR AND SQUARE.
I HEARD ABOUT YOUR BET. ♥
HEH HEH.
SHE SAID IT WAS ALL HER FAULT THAT YOU COLLAPSED.
THAT'S SO STUPID.
"IT'S ALL COOL"...
SHE'S SO FULL OF IT.
I THOUGHT RUNNING AWAY WAS BETTER THAN LOSING.
I THOUGHT IT WOULD BE EASIER...
I THOUGHT I COULD STAY STRONG...

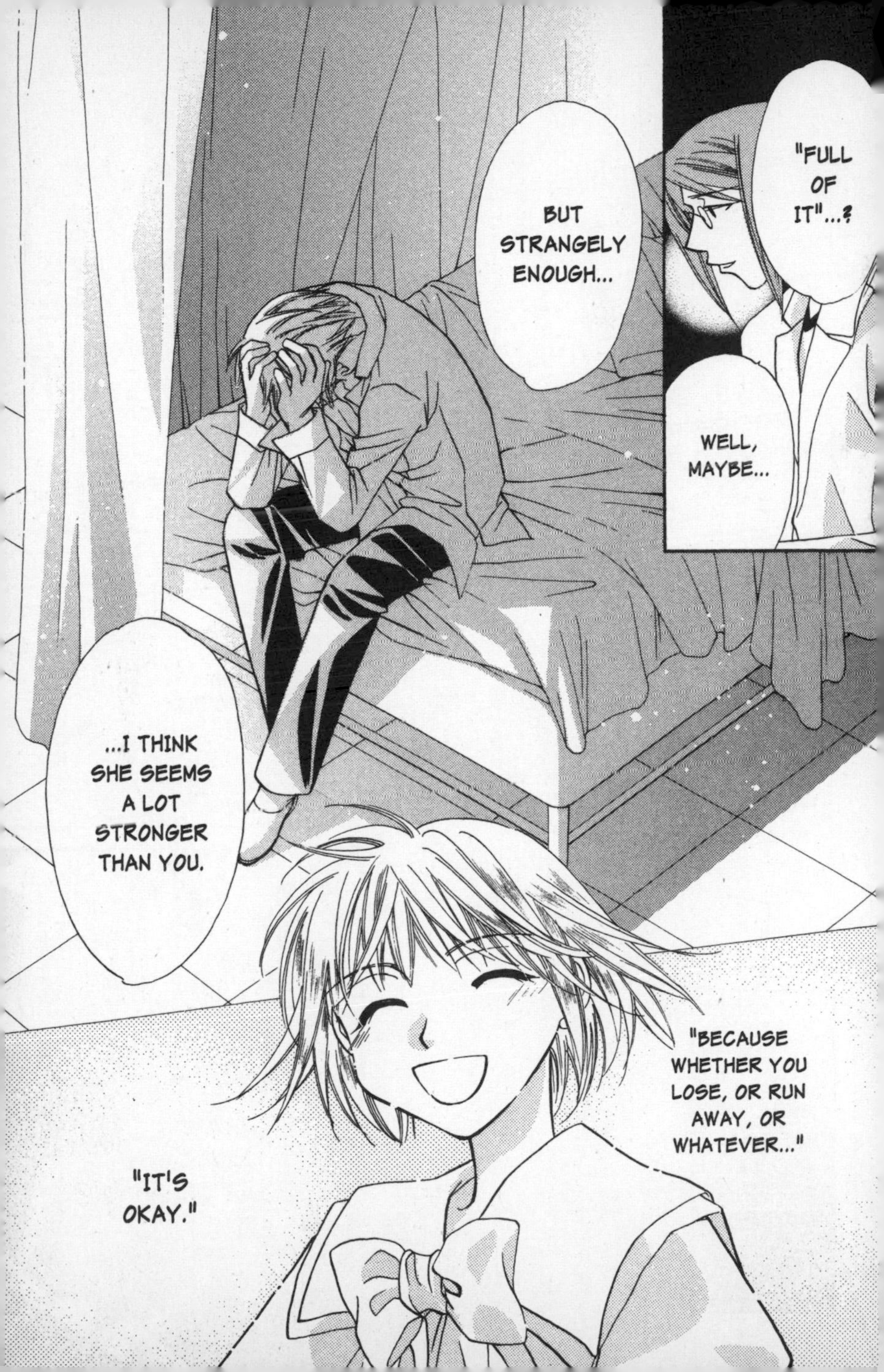
"FULL OF IT"...?
WELL, MAYBE...
BUT STRANGELY ENOUGH...
...I THINK SHE SEEMS A LOT STRONGER THAN YOU.
"BECAUSE WHETHER YOU LOSE, OR RUN AWAY, OR WHATEVER..."
"IT'S OKAY."

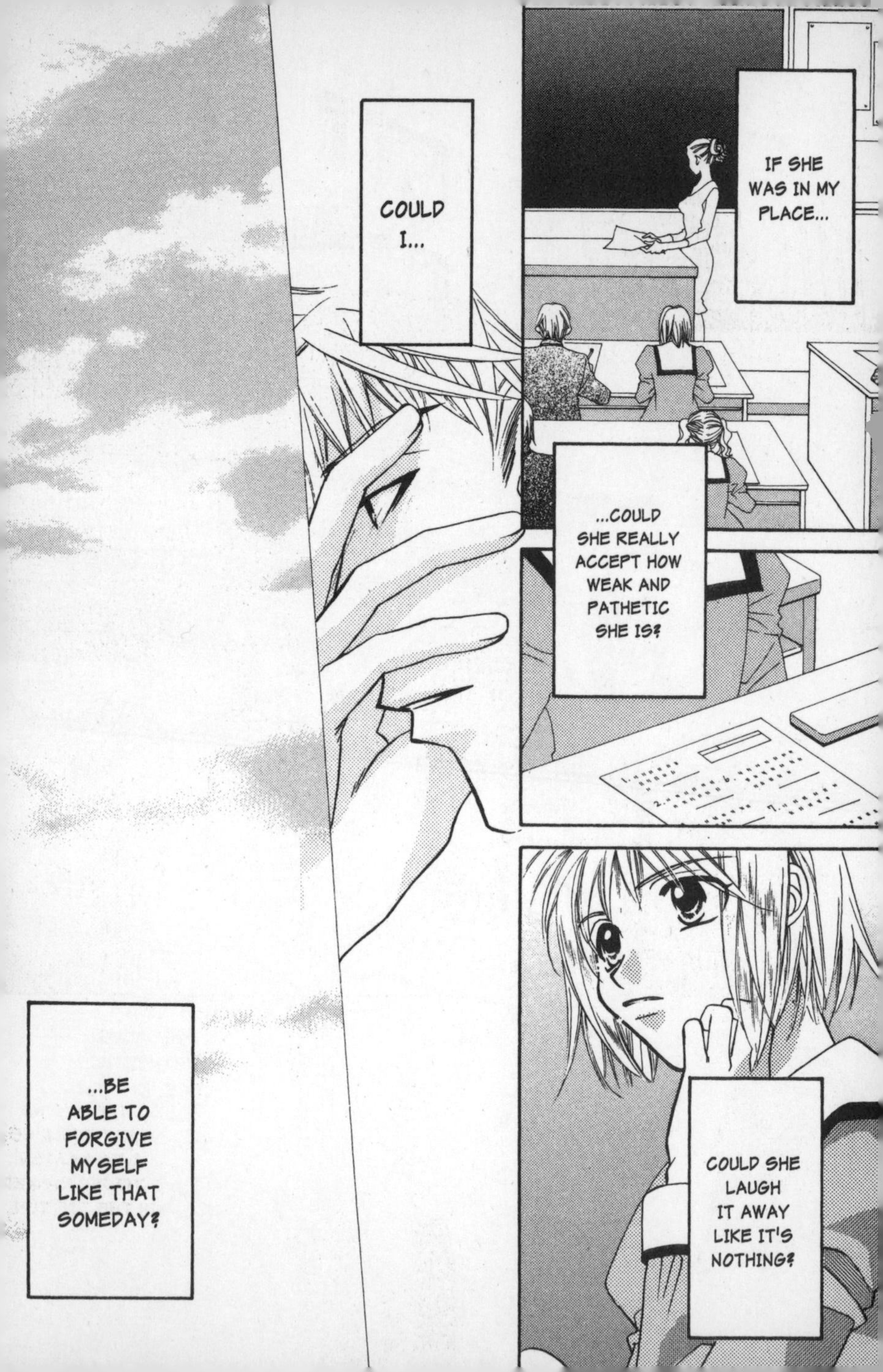
IF SHE WAS IN MY PLACE...
...COULD SHE REALLY ACCEPT HOW WEAK AND PATHETIC SHE IS?
COULD SHE LAUGH IT AWAY LIKE IT'S NOTHING?
COULD I...
...BE ABLE TO FORGIVE MYSELF LIKE THAT SOMEDAY?

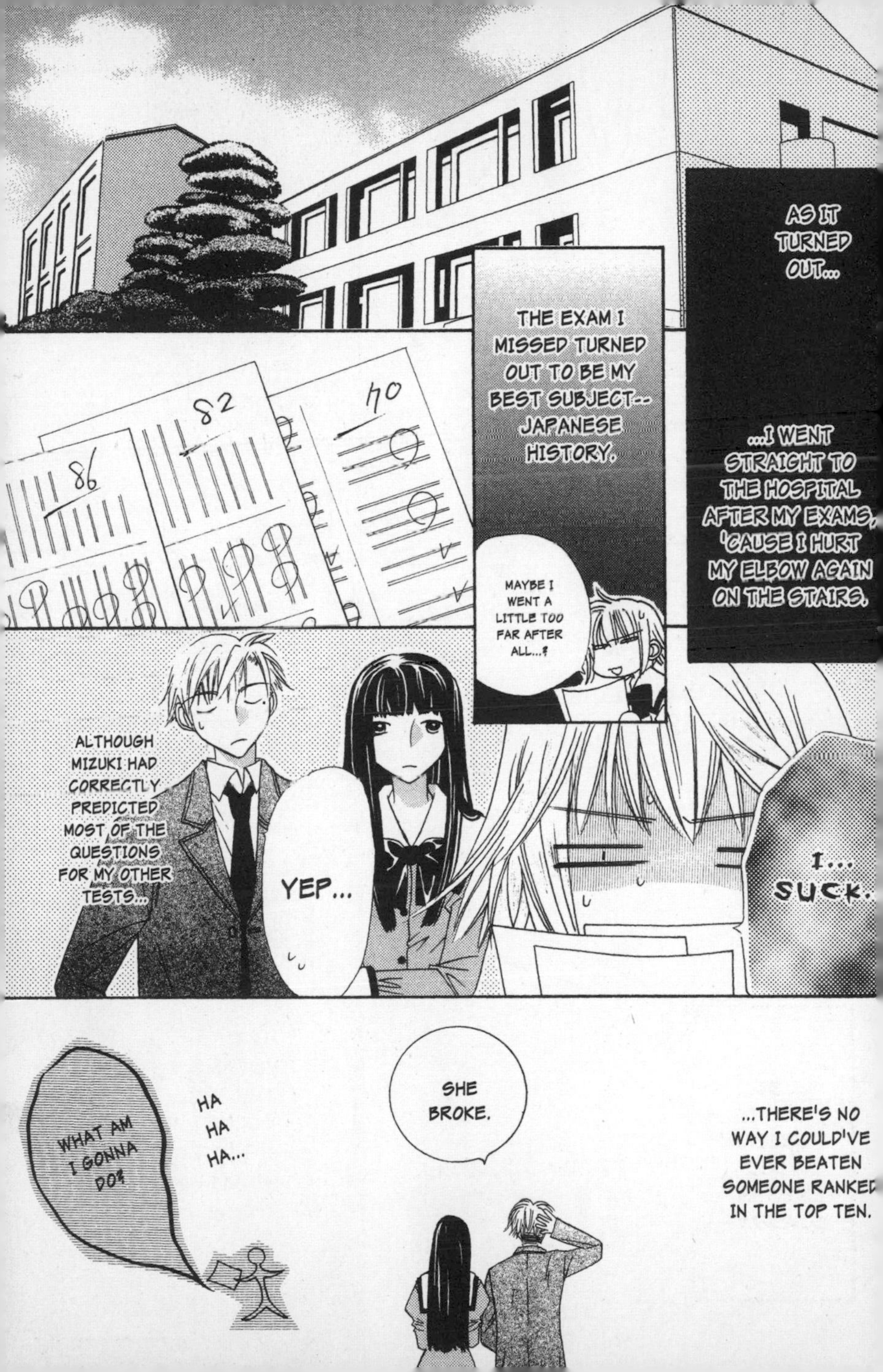

AS IT TURNED OUT...
...I WENT STRAIGHT TO THE HOSPITAL AFTER MY EXAMS, 'CAUSE I HURT MY ELBOW AGAIN ON THE STAIRS.
THE EXAM I MISSED TURNED OUT TO BE MY BEST SUBJECT--JAPANESE HISTORY.
MAYBE I WENT A LITTLE TOO FAR AFTER ALL...?
I... SUCK.
YEP...
ALTHOUGH MIZUKI HAD CORRECTLY PREDICTED MOST OF THE QUESTIONS FOR MY OTHER TESTS...
...THERE'S NO WAY I COULD'VE EVER BEATEN SOMEONE RANKED IN THE TOP TEN.
SHE BROKE.
HA HA HA...
WHAT AM I GONNA DO?

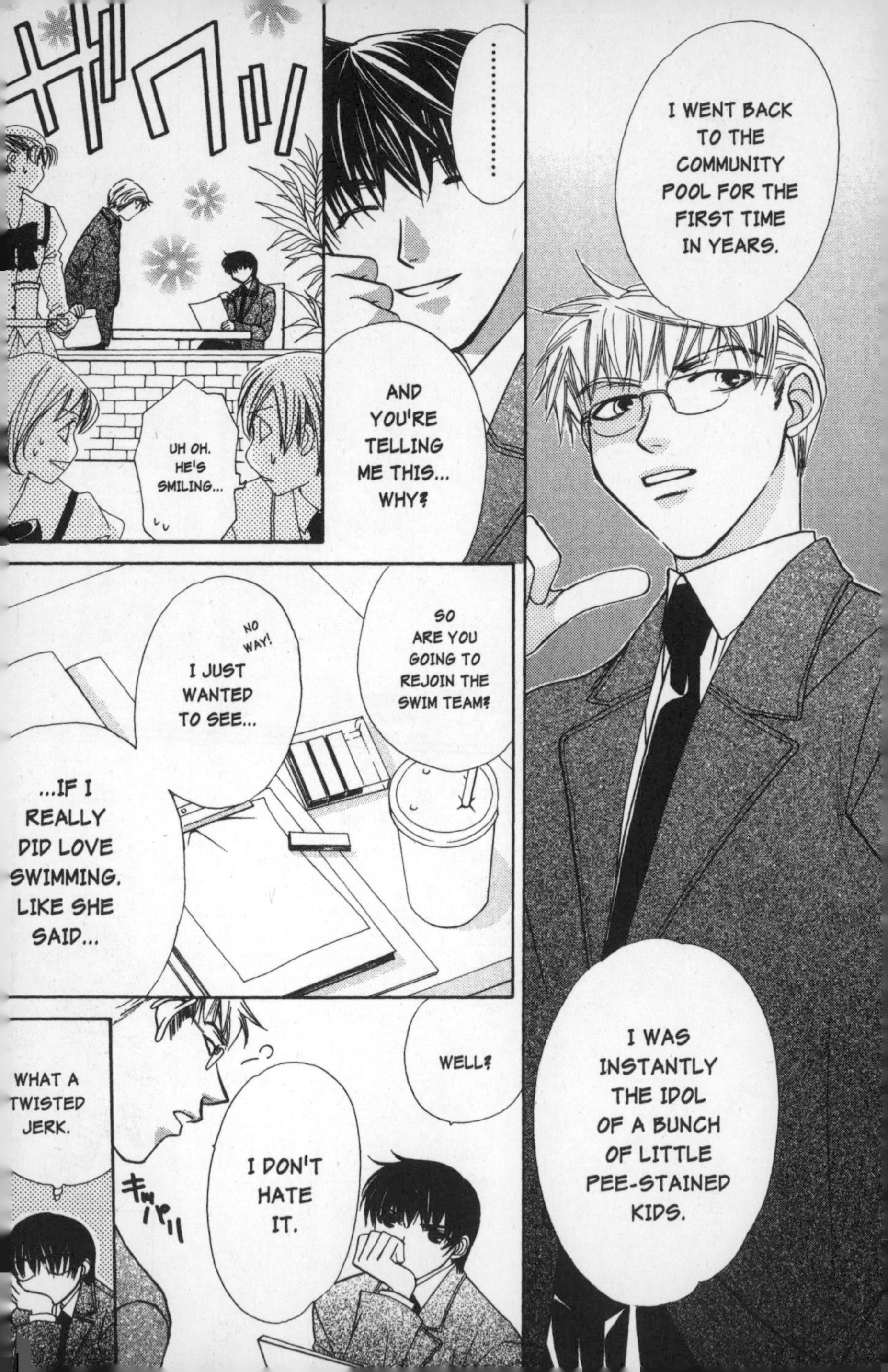
I WENT BACK TO THE COMMUNITY POOL FOR THE FIRST TIME IN YEARS.
I WAS INSTANTLY THE IDOL OF A BUNCH OF LITTLE PEE-STAINED KIDS.
....
AND YOU'RE TELLING ME THIS... WHY?
ザワッ
UH OH. HE'S SMILING...
SO ARE YOU GOING TO REJOIN THE SWIM TEAM?
NO WAY!
I JUST WANTED TO SEE...
...IF I REALLY DID LOVE SWIMMING. LIKE SHE SAID...
WELL?
I DON'T HATE IT.
キッパリ
WHAT A TWISTED JERK.

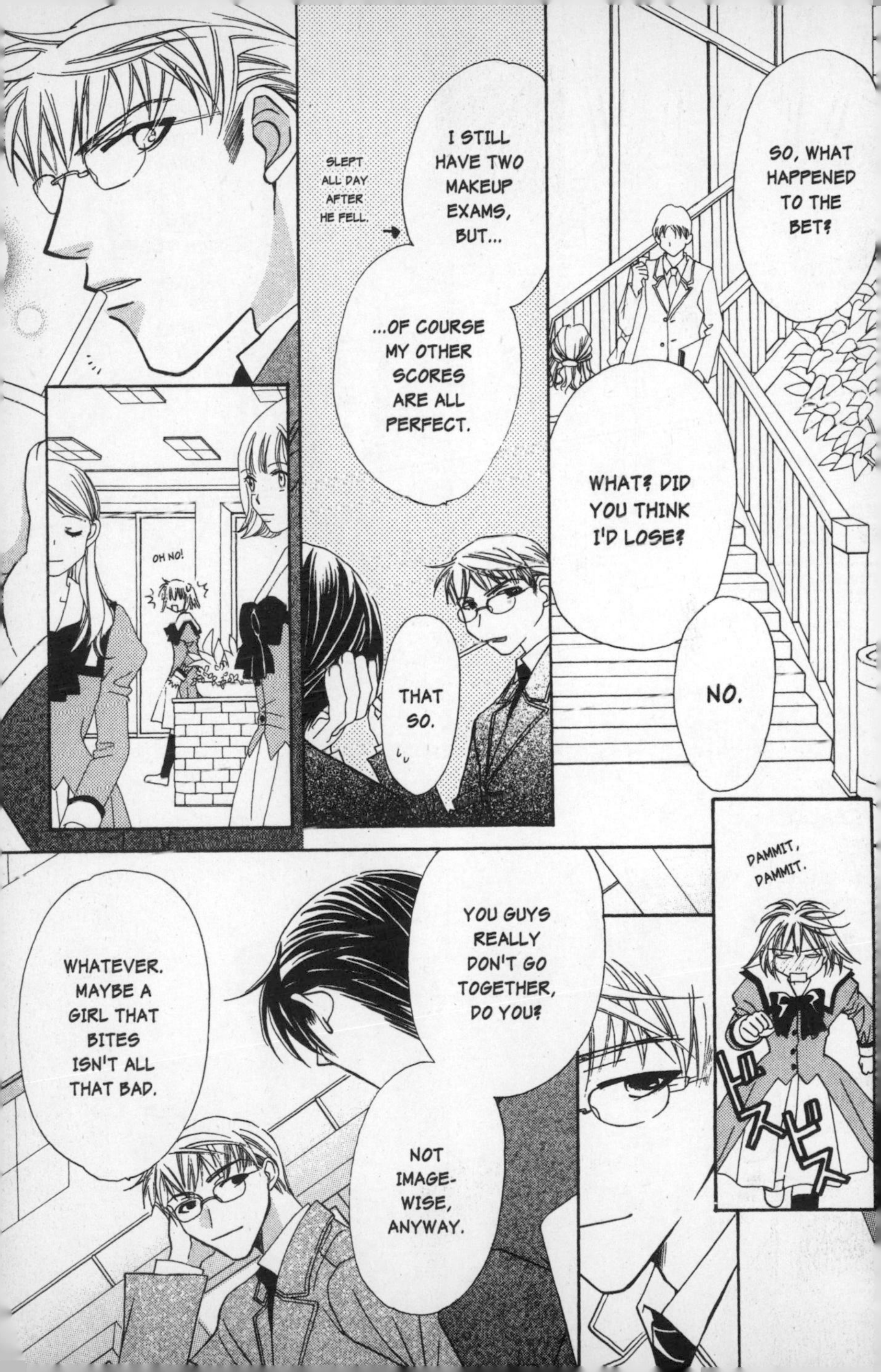
SO, WHAT HAPPENED TO THE BET?
WHAT? DID YOU THINK I'D LOSE?
NO.
I STILL HAVE TWO MAKEUP EXAMS, BUT...
SLEPT ALL DAY AFTER HE FELL.
...OF COURSE MY OTHER SCORES ARE ALL PERFECT.
THAT SO.
OH NO!
DAMMIT, DAMMIT.
YOU GUYS REALLY DON'T GO TOGETHER, DO YOU?
NOT IMAGE-WISE, ANYWAY.
WHATEVER. MAYBE A GIRL THAT BITES ISN'T ALL THAT BAD.

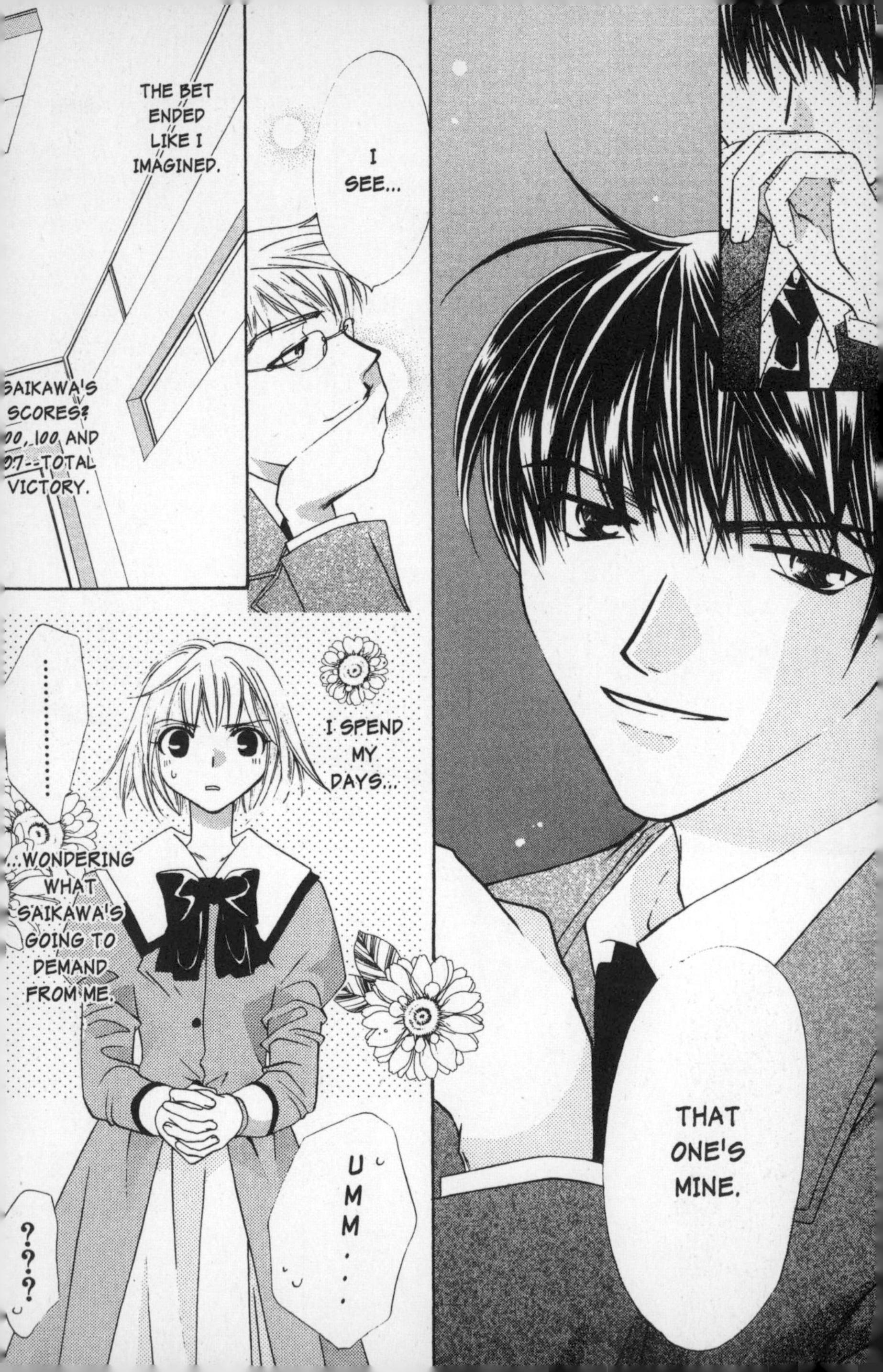
THAT ONE'S MINE.
I SEE...
THE BET ENDED LIKE I IMAGINED.
SAIKAWA'S SCORES? 00, 100 AND 07--TOTAL VICTORY.
I SPEND MY DAYS...
...WONDERING WHAT SAIKAWA'S GOING TO DEMAND FROM ME.
......
UMM...
???

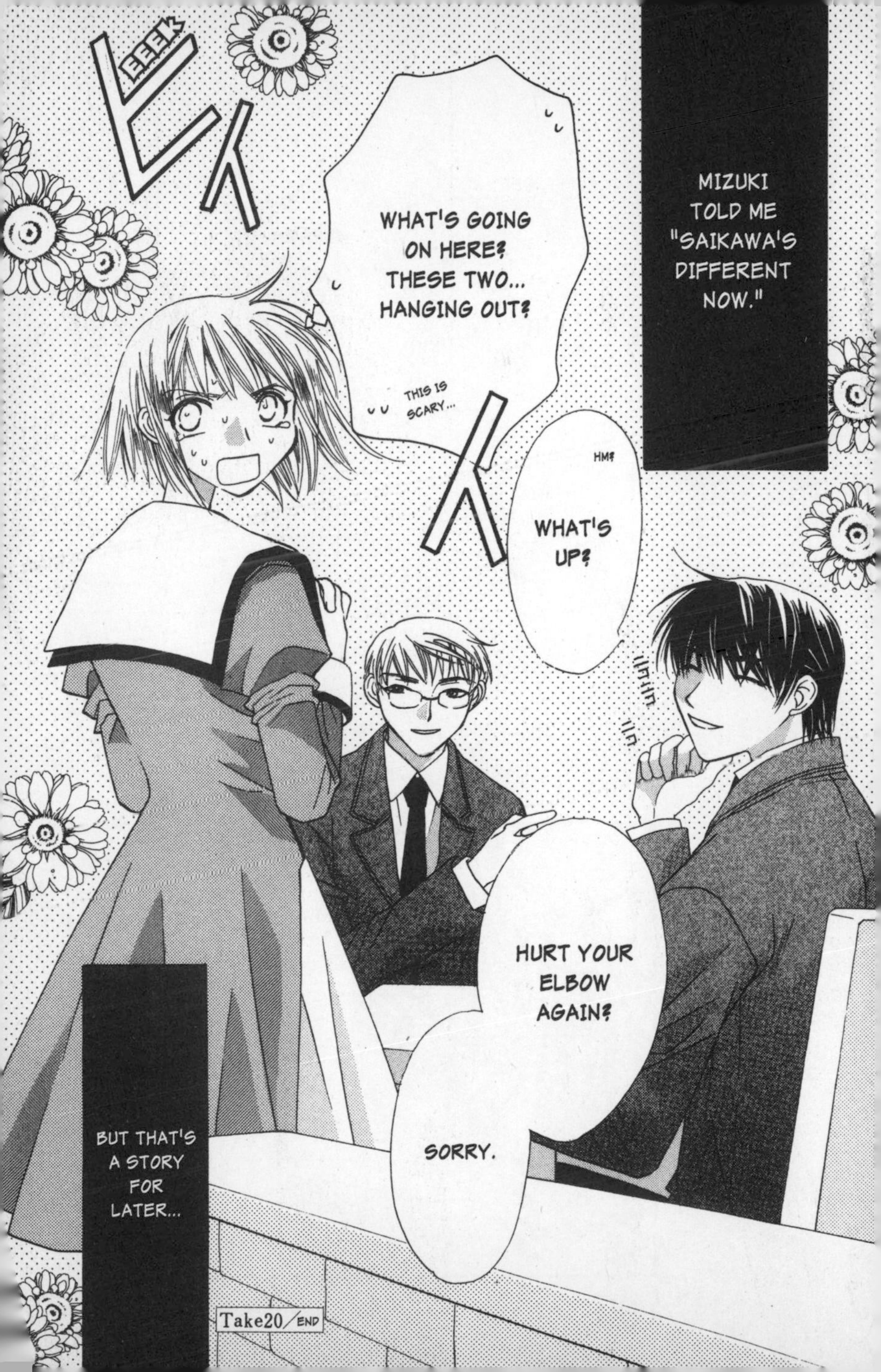
MIZUKI TOLD ME "SAIKAWA'S DIFFERENT NOW."
EEEK
WHAT'S GOING ON HERE? THESE TWO... HANGING OUT?
THIS IS SCARY...
HM? WHAT'S UP?
HURT YOUR ELBOW AGAIN?
SORRY.
BUT THAT'S A STORY FOR LATER...
Take20/END

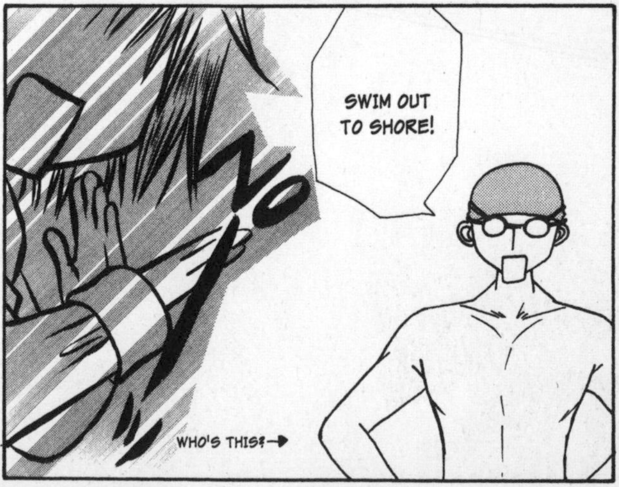
SWIM OUT
TO SHORE!
WHO'S THIS?

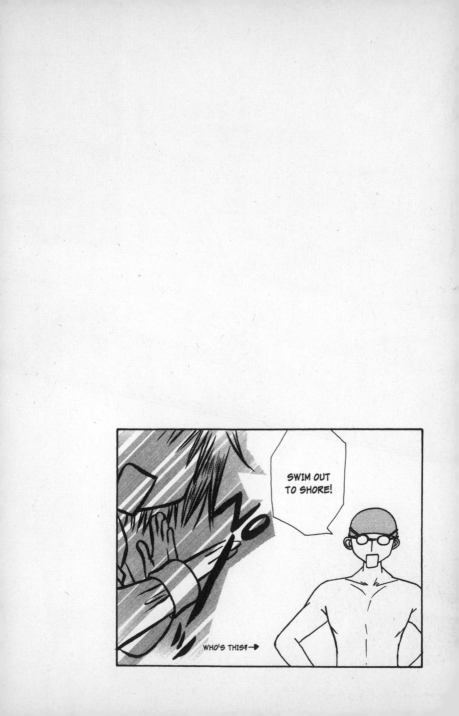

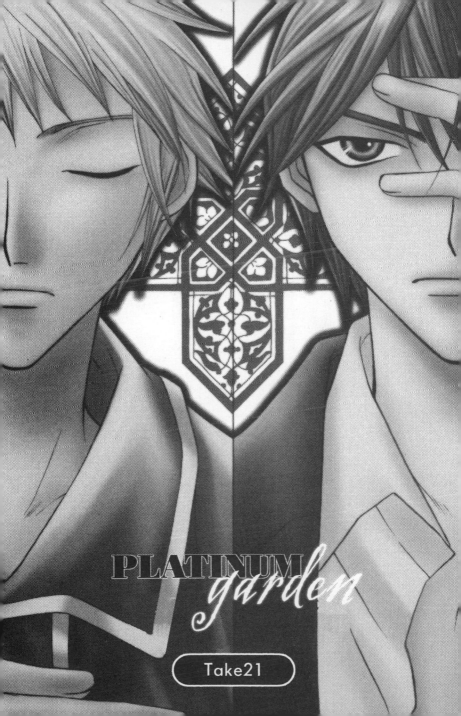

PLATINUM
garden

Take21

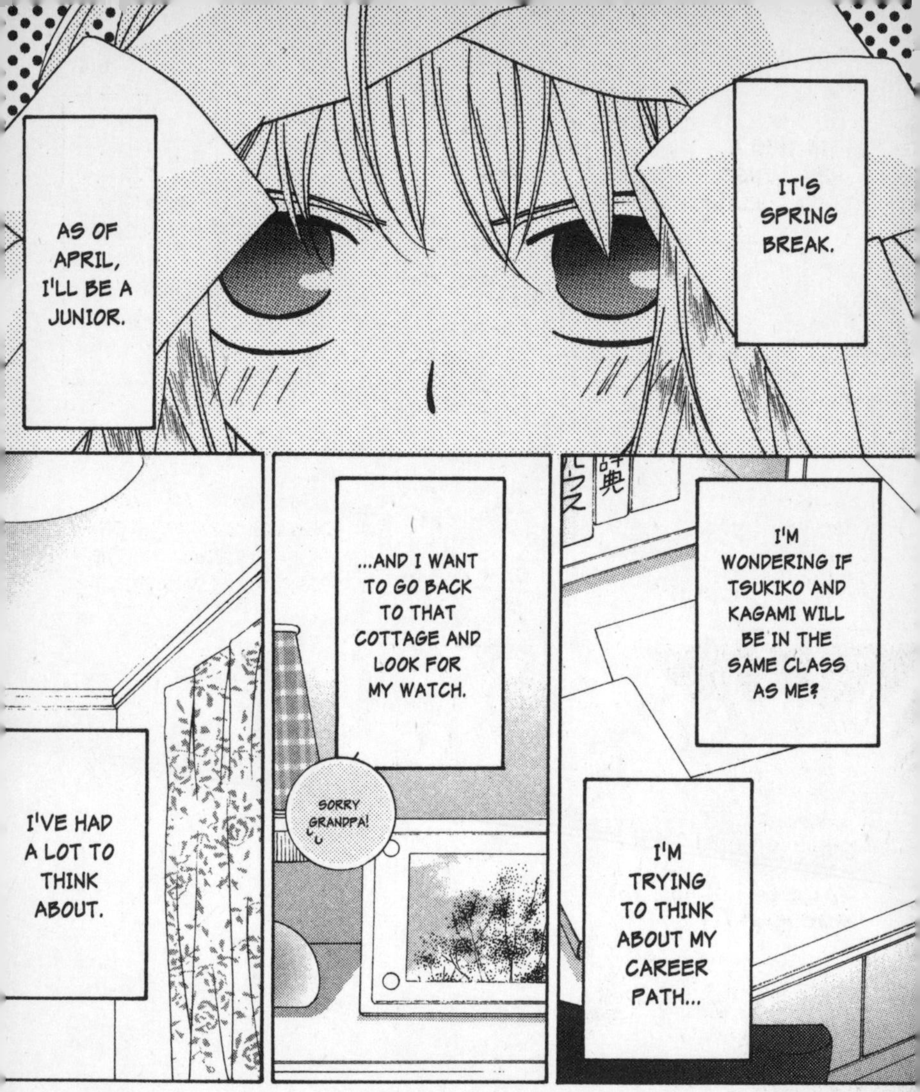
IT'S SPRING BREAK.
AS OF APRIL, I'LL BE A JUNIOR.
I'M WONDERING IF TSUKIKO AND KAGAMI WILL BE IN THE SAME CLASS AS ME?
I'M TRYING TO THINK ABOUT MY CAREER PATH...
...AND I WANT TO GO BACK TO THAT COTTAGE AND LOOK FOR MY WATCH.
SORRY GRANDPA!
I'VE HAD A LOT TO THINK ABOUT.

FUJITA'S SUMMER, 2002

I'M A BIG FAN OF HOME MAKEOVER SHOWS!
I WATCH THEM ALL THE TIME.
WHENEVER I SEE SOMETHING I LIKE,
I DECIDE TO GIVE IT A TRY, BUT...

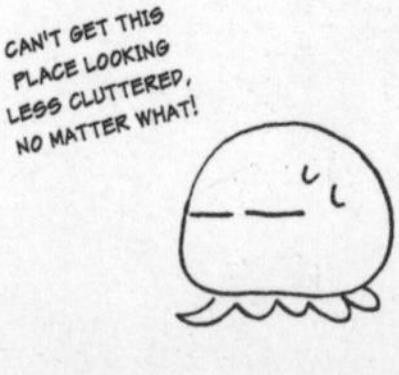
CAN'T GET THIS PLACE LOOKING LESS CLUTTERED, NO MATTER WHAT!

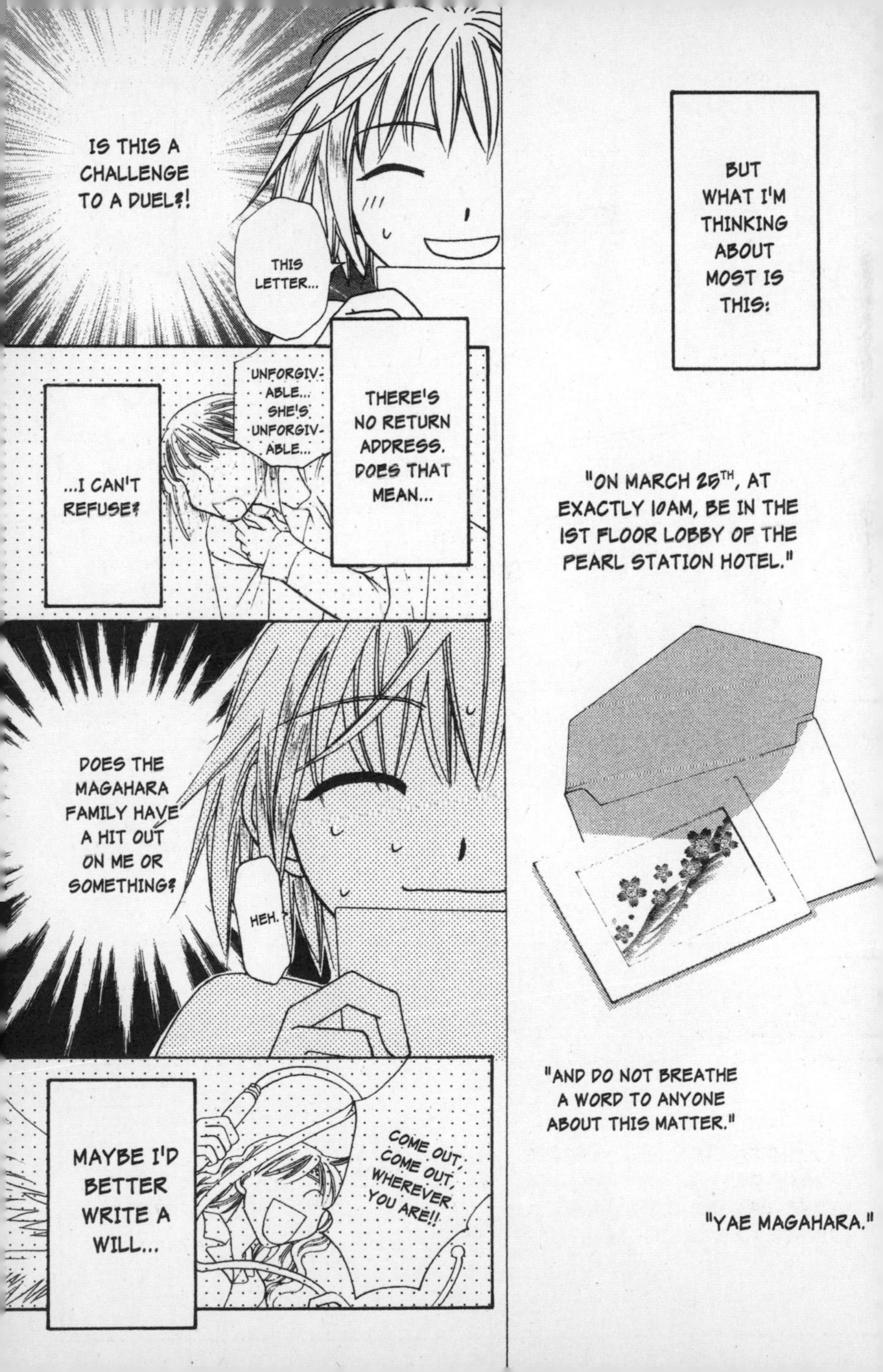
BUT WHAT I'M THINKING ABOUT MOST IS THIS:
"ON MARCH 25TH, AT EXACTLY 10AM, BE IN THE 1ST FLOOR LOBBY OF THE PEARL STATION HOTEL."
"AND DO NOT BREATHE A WORD TO ANYONE ABOUT THIS MATTER."
"YAE MAGAHARA."
THIS LETTER...
IS THIS A CHALLENGE TO A DUEL?!
THERE'S NO RETURN ADDRESS. DOES THAT MEAN...
UNFORGIV-ABLE... SHE'S UNFORGIV-ABLE...
...I CAN'T REFUSE?
HEH.
DOES THE MAGAHARA FAMILY HAVE A HIT OUT ON ME OR SOMETHING?
COME OUT, COME OUT, WHEREVER YOU ARE!!
MAYBE I'D BETTER WRITE A WILL...

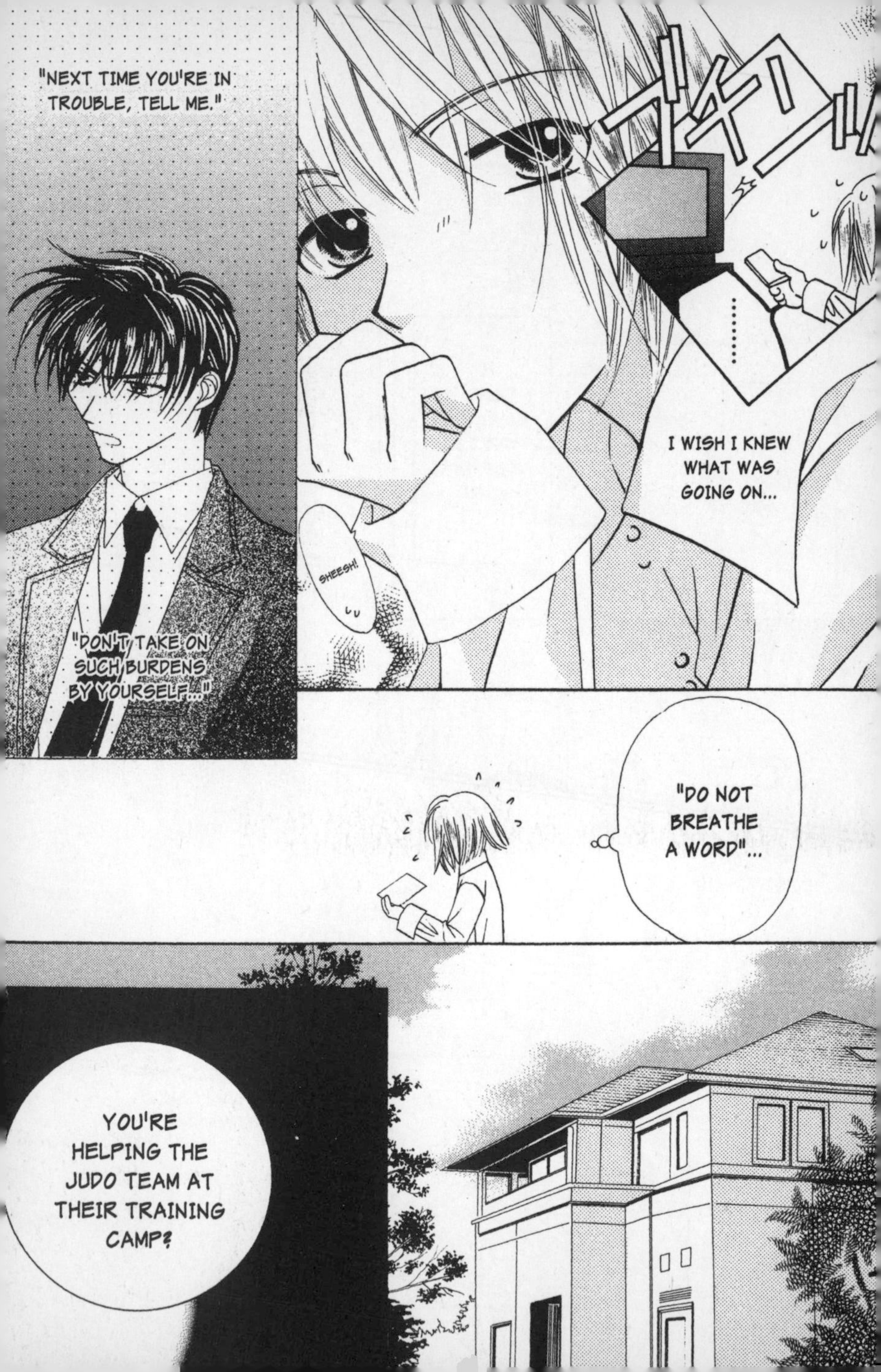
I WISH I KNEW WHAT WAS GOING ON...
SHEESH!
"NEXT TIME YOU'RE IN TROUBLE, TELL ME."
"DON'T TAKE ON SUCH BURDENS BY YOURSELF..."
"DO NOT BREATHE A WORD"...
YOU'RE HELPING THE JUDO TEAM AT THEIR TRAINING CAMP?

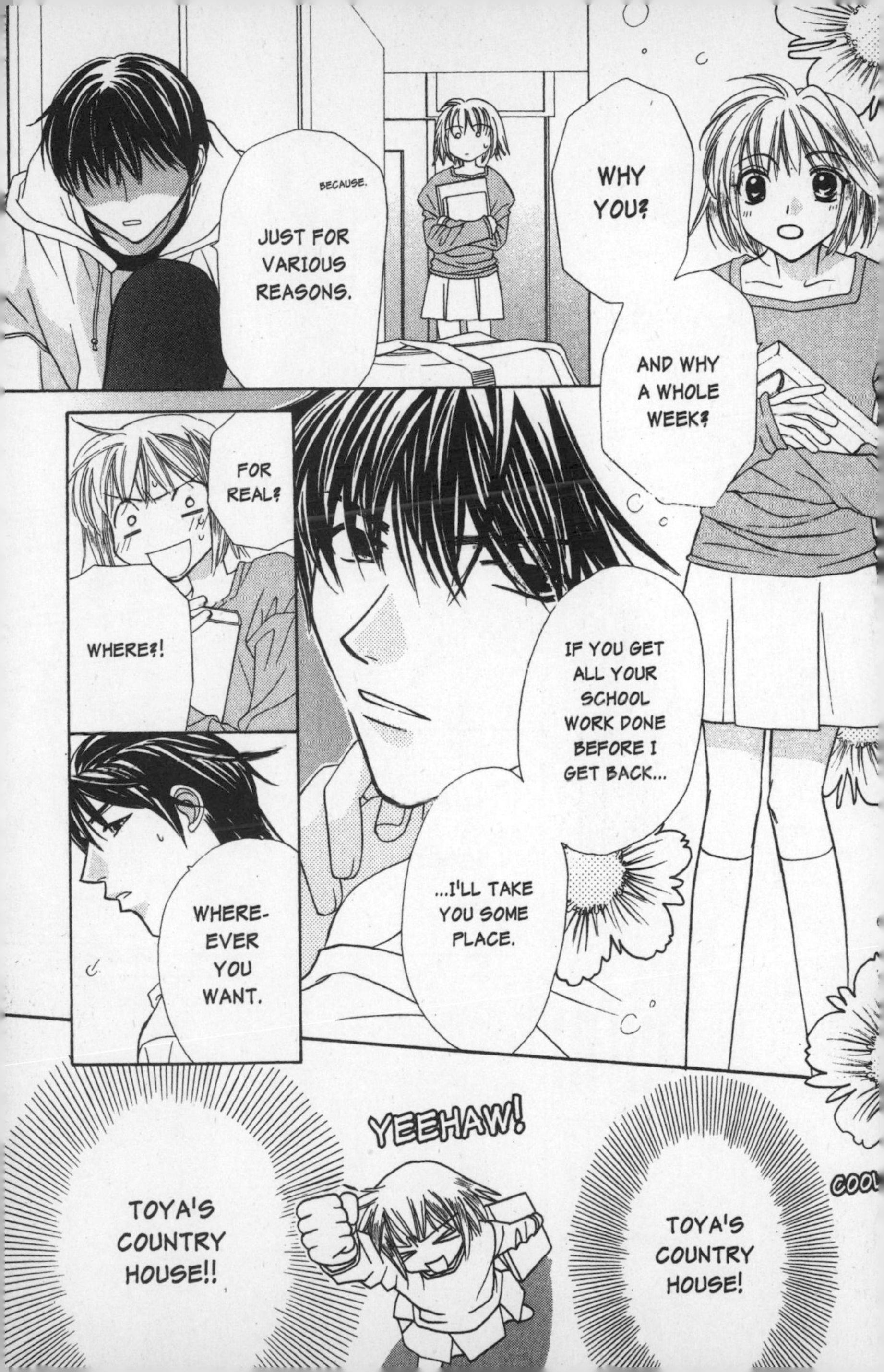
WHY YOU?
BECAUSE.
JUST FOR VARIOUS REASONS.
AND WHY A WHOLE WEEK?
IF YOU GET ALL YOUR SCHOOL WORK DONE BEFORE I GET BACK...
...I'LL TAKE YOU SOME PLACE.
FOR REAL?
WHERE?!
WHERE-EVER YOU WANT.
TOYA'S COUNTRY HOUSE!
COOL
YEEHAW!
TOYA'S COUNTRY HOUSE!!

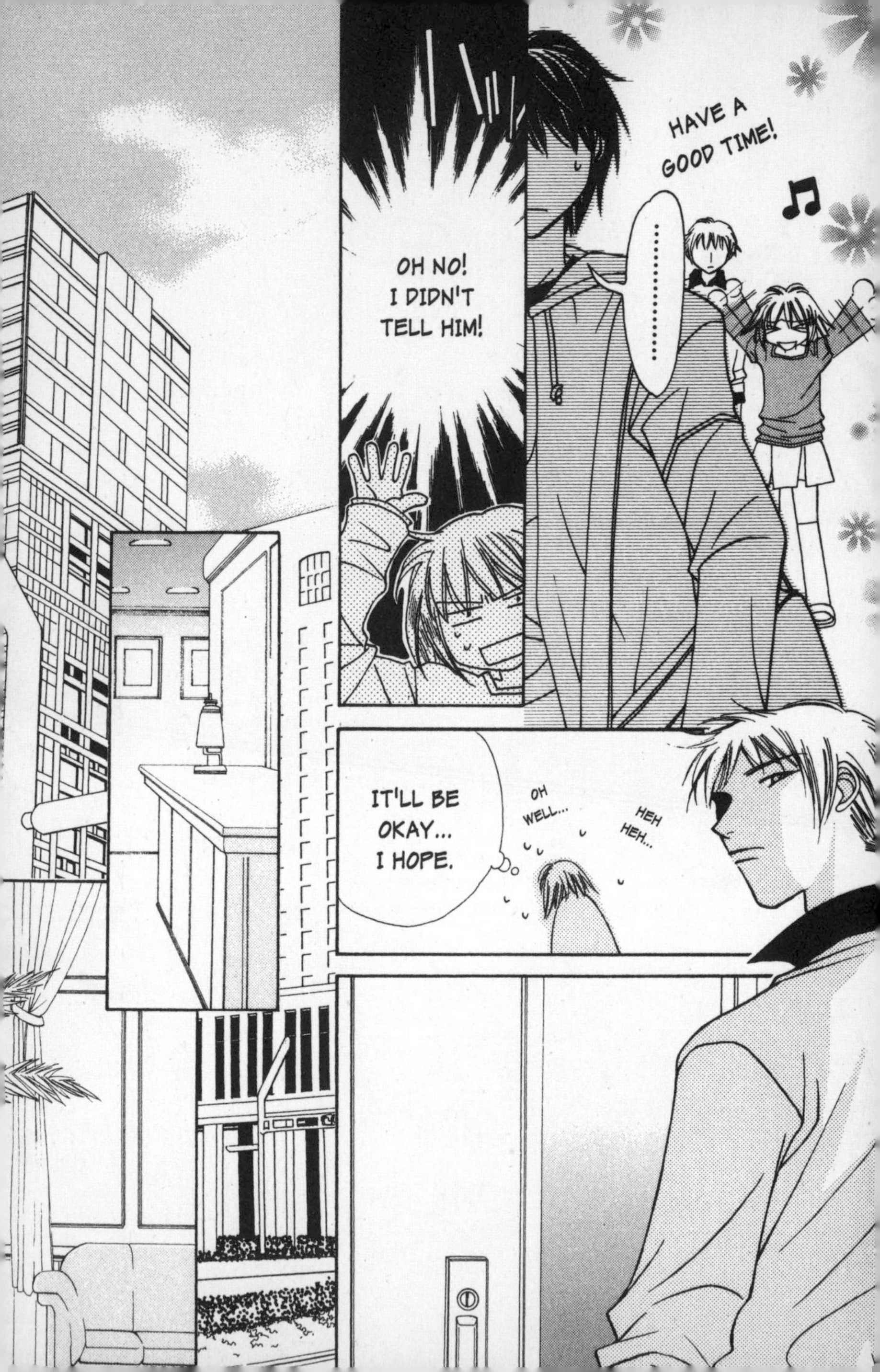
HAVE A GOOD TIME!
......
OH NO! I DIDN'T TELL HIM!
HEH HEH...
OH WELL...
IT'LL BE OKAY... I HOPE.

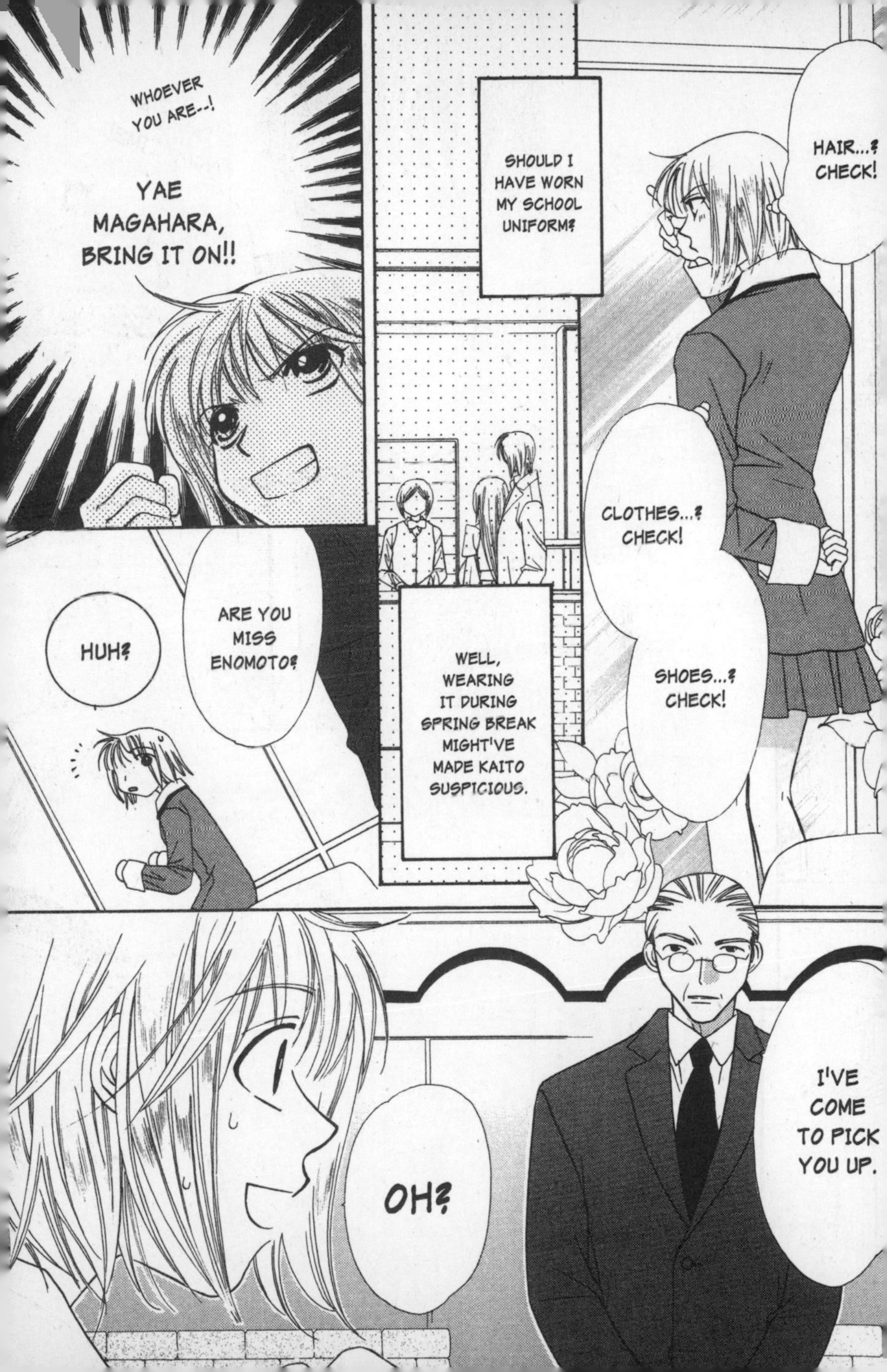
HAIR...? CHECK!
CLOTHES...? CHECK!
SHOES...? CHECK!
SHOULD I HAVE WORN MY SCHOOL UNIFORM?
WELL, WEARING IT DURING SPRING BREAK MIGHT'VE MADE KAITO SUSPICIOUS.
WHOEVER YOU ARE--!
YAE MAGAHARA, BRING IT ON!!
ARE YOU MISS ENOMOTO?
HUH?
I'VE COME TO PICK YOU UP.
OH?

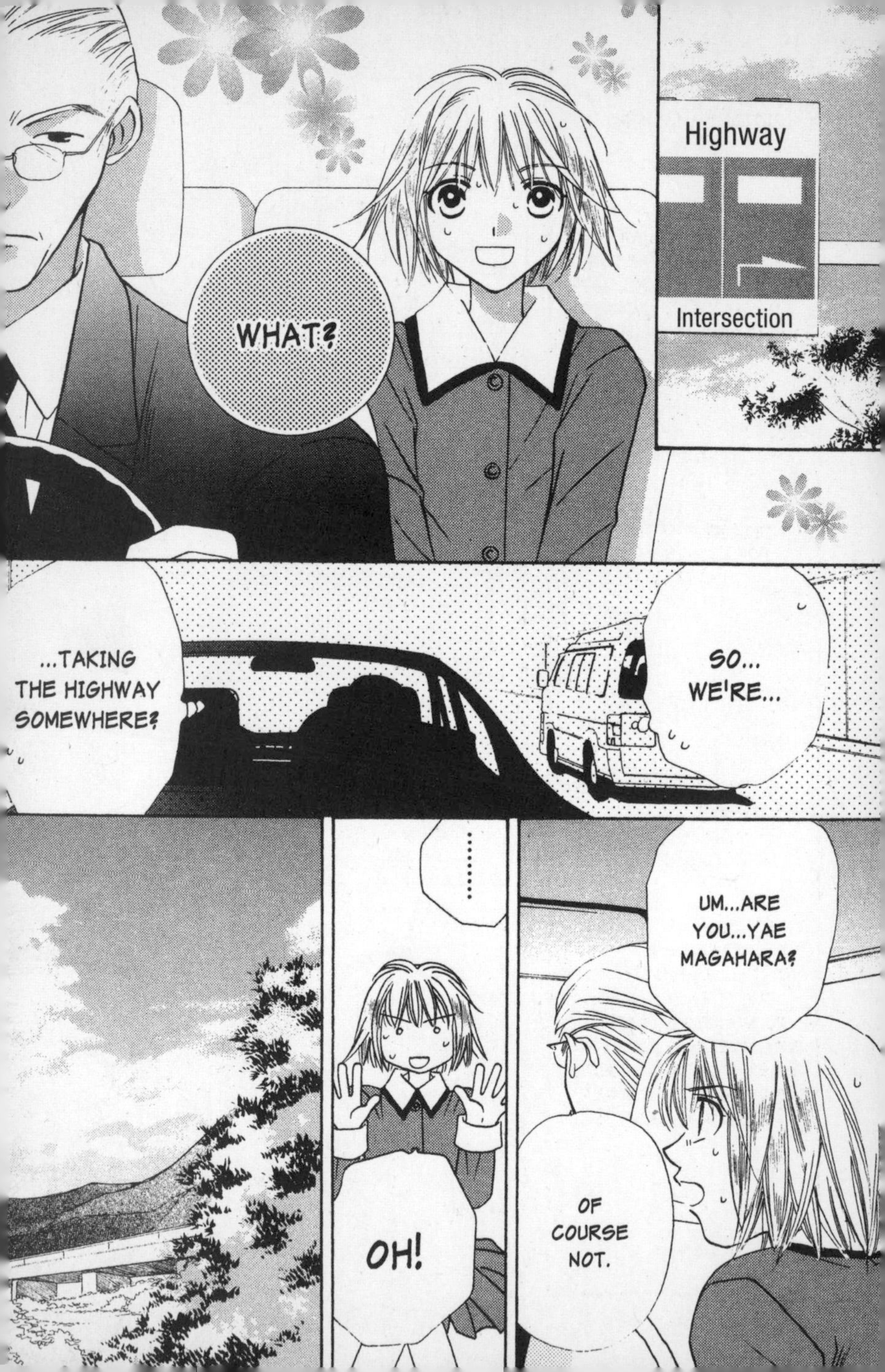
Highway
Intersection
WHAT?
SO... WE'RE...
...TAKING THE HIGHWAY SOMEWHERE?
UM...ARE YOU...YAE MAGAHARA?
OF COURSE NOT.
......
OH!

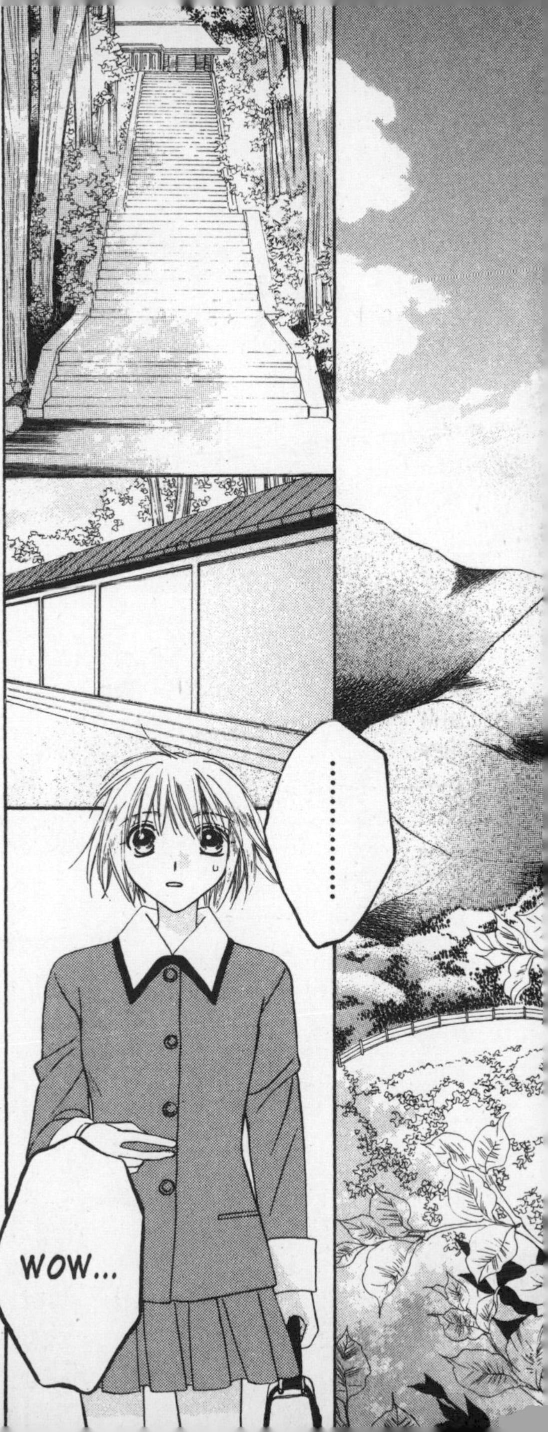
......
WOW...

IDIOTIC RAMBLINGS III

IN THE LAST TWO VOLUMES I DISCUSSED "THE DOG INCIDENT." THIS TIME, LET'S TALK ABOUT MY ENDLESS KIMONO RESEARCH. KIMONOS ARE SO BEAUTIFUL! I LOVE LOOKING AT THEM. BUT I'VE ONLY WORN A LONG-SLEEVED KIMONO ONCE (FOR MY BROTHER'S WEDDING) AND A YUKATA WHEN I WAS LITTLE. BUT I HAD TO BUY KIMONO MAGAZINES FOR THIS VOLUME...

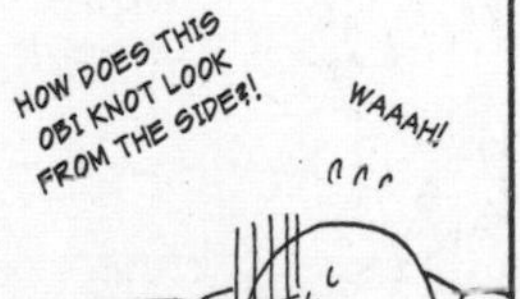
HOW DOES THIS OBI KNOT LOOK FROM THE SIDE?!
WAAAH!

I'M STRUGGLING TO LEARN... BUT I TRULY THINK KIMONOS ARE JUST EXQUISITE. RIGHT NOW, IT'S ALL I CAN DO TO ADMIRE FROM AFAR... BUT SOMEDAY, I HOPE I CAN LEARN TO WEAR A KIMONO PROPERLY. THAT WOULD MAKE ME SO HAPPY!

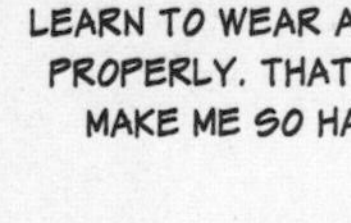
HOPE TO SEE YOU AGAIN IN VOLUME SIX! TAKE CARE!

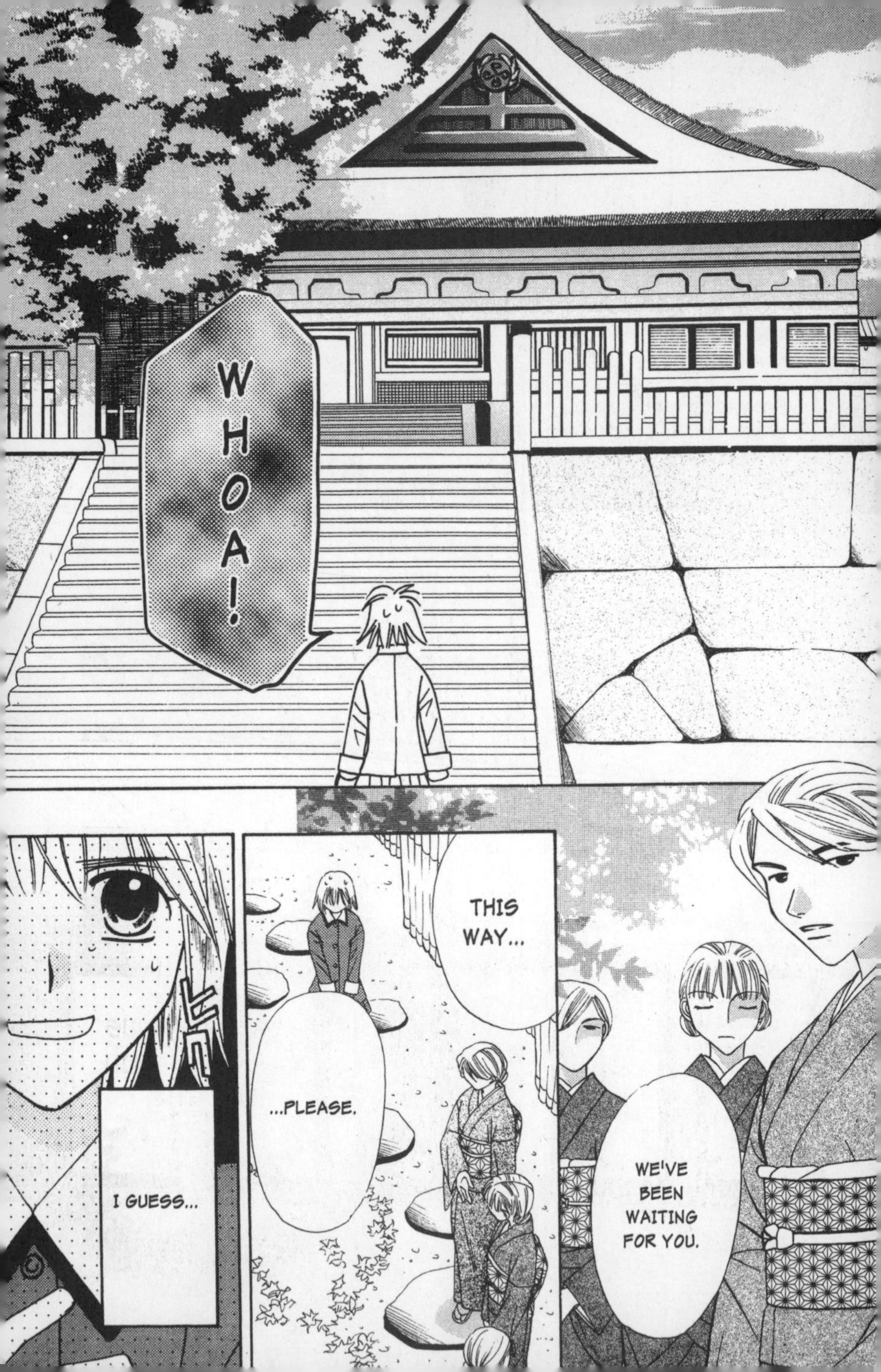
WHOA!
WE'VE BEEN WAITING FOR YOU.
THIS WAY...
...PLEASE.
I GUESS...

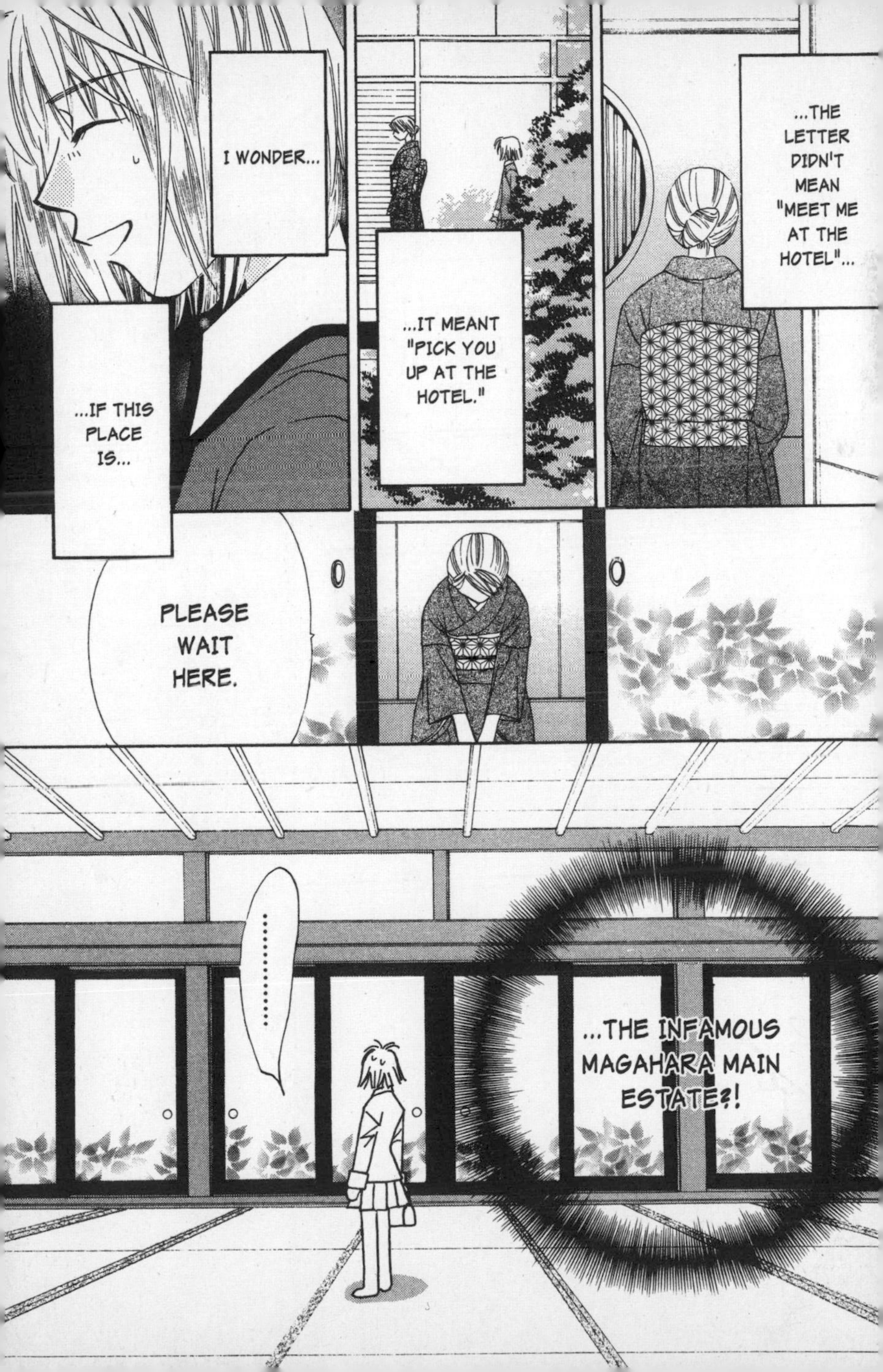
...THE LETTER DIDN'T MEAN "MEET ME AT THE HOTEL"...
...IT MEANT "PICK YOU UP AT THE HOTEL."
I WONDER...
...IF THIS PLACE IS...
PLEASE WAIT HERE.
...THE INFAMOUS MAGAHARA MAIN ESTATE?!
......

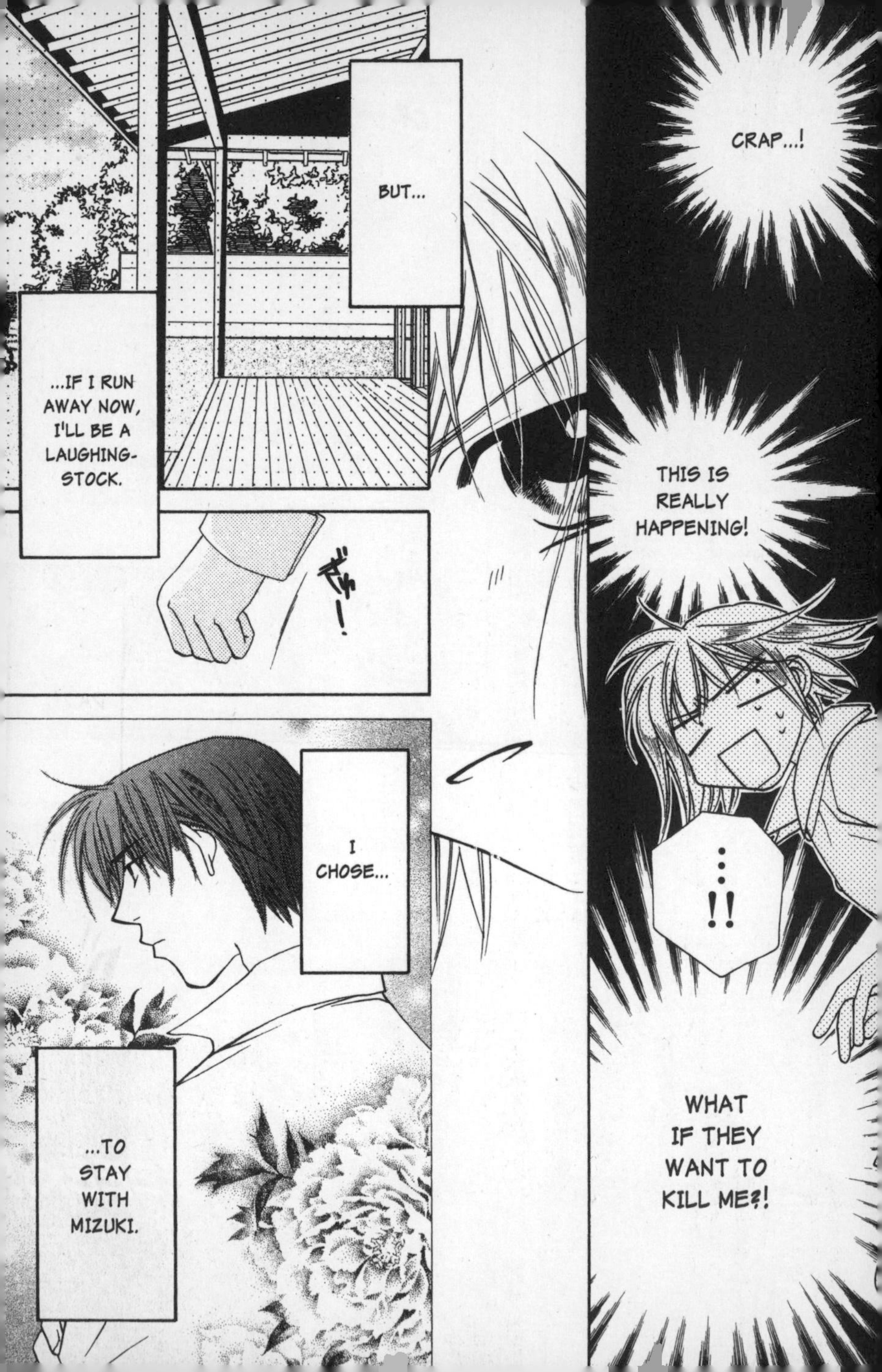
CRAP...!
THIS IS REALLY HAPPENING!
...!!
WHAT IF THEY WANT TO KILL ME?!
BUT...
...IF I RUN AWAY NOW, I'LL BE A LAUGHING-STOCK.
I CHOSE...
...TO STAY WITH MIZUKI.

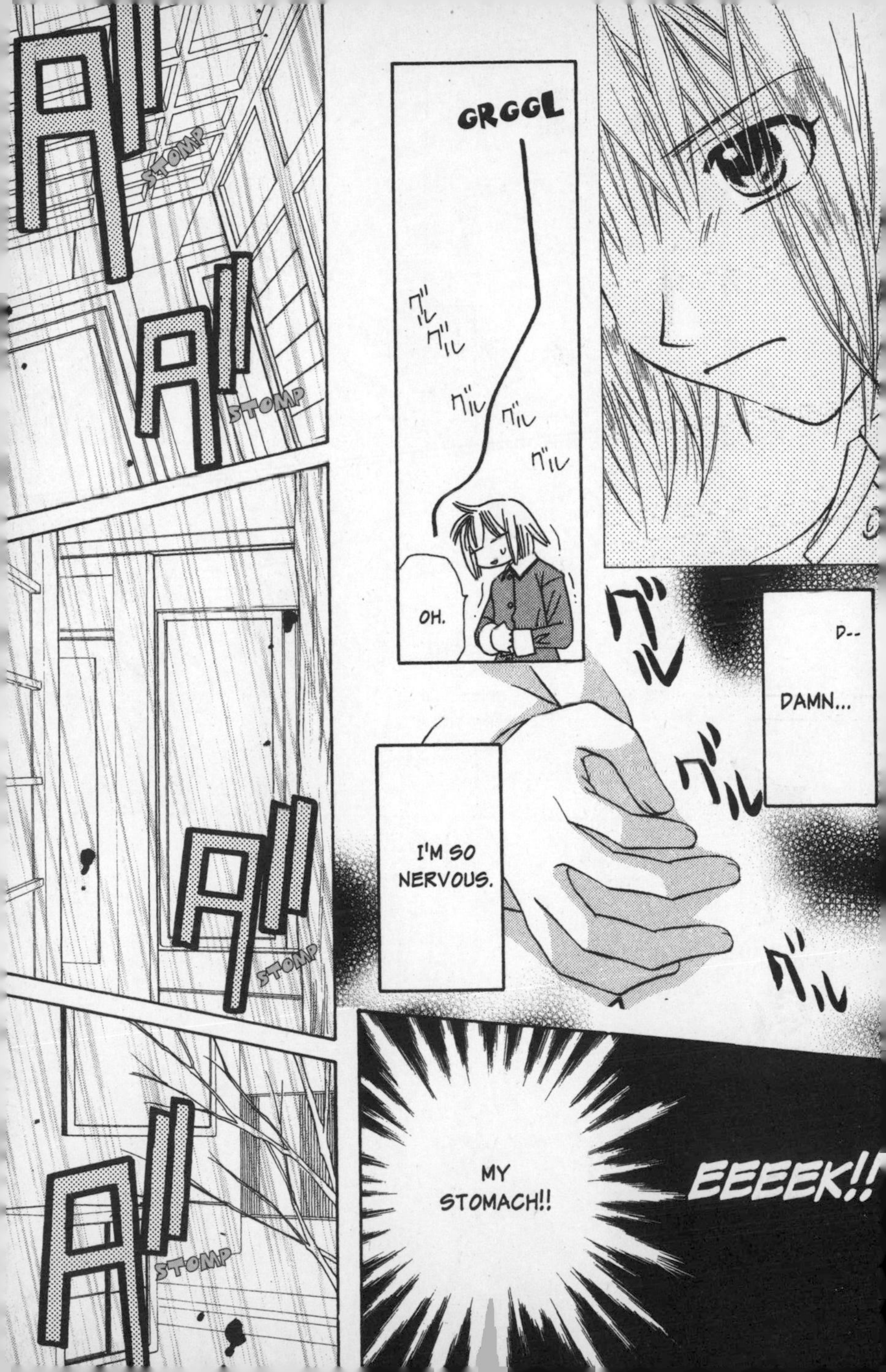
GRGGL
グル
グル
グル
グル
グル
OH.
グル
D--
DAMN...
グル
I'M SO NERVOUS.
グル
EEEEK!!
MY STOMACH!!
A!
STOMP
A!
STOMP
A!
STOMP
A!
STOMP

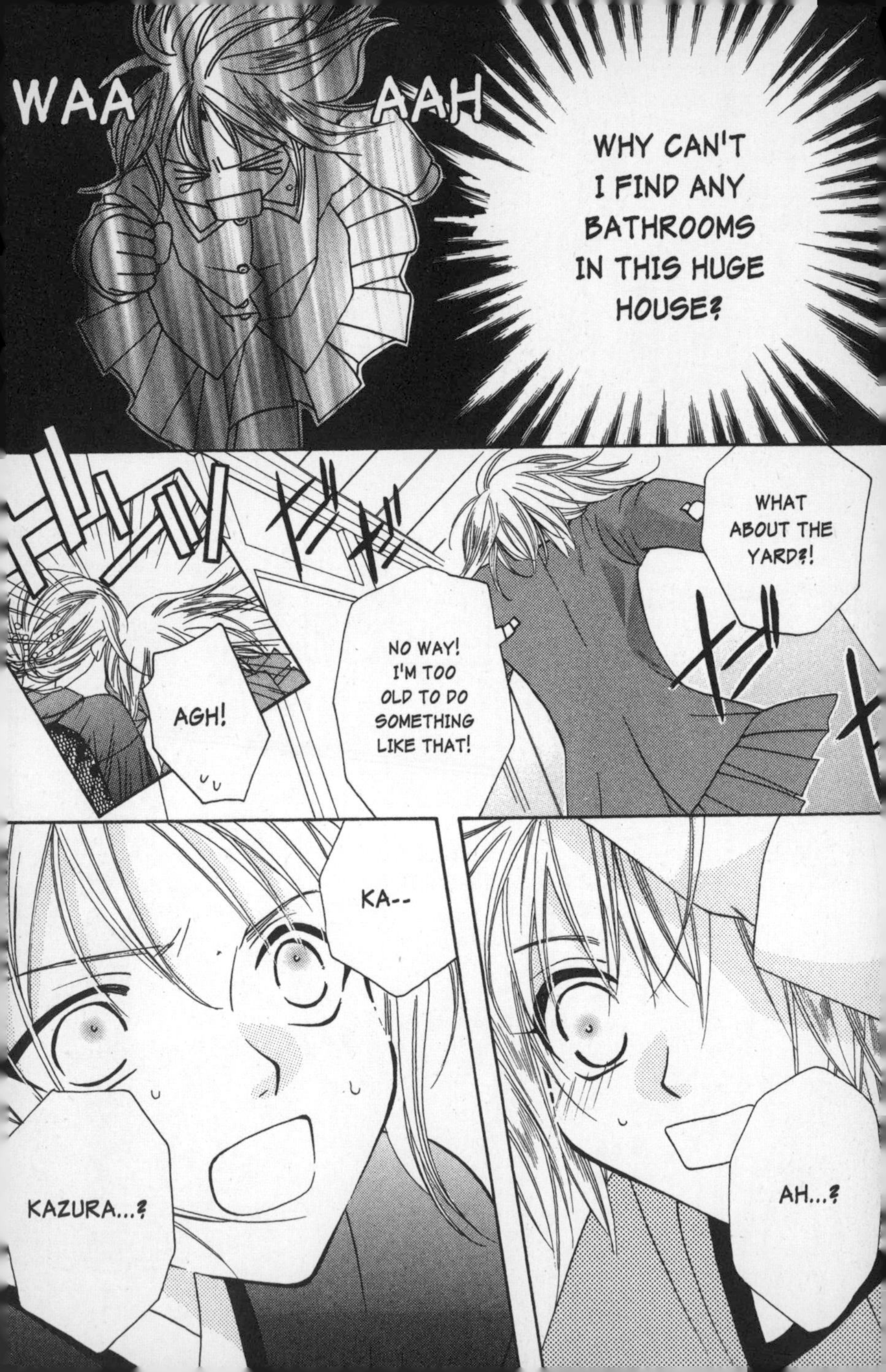
WAA AAH
WHY CAN'T I FIND ANY BATHROOMS IN THIS HUGE HOUSE?
WHAT ABOUT THE YARD?!
NO WAY! I'M TOO OLD TO DO SOMETHING LIKE THAT!
AGH!
AH...?
KA--
KAZURA...?

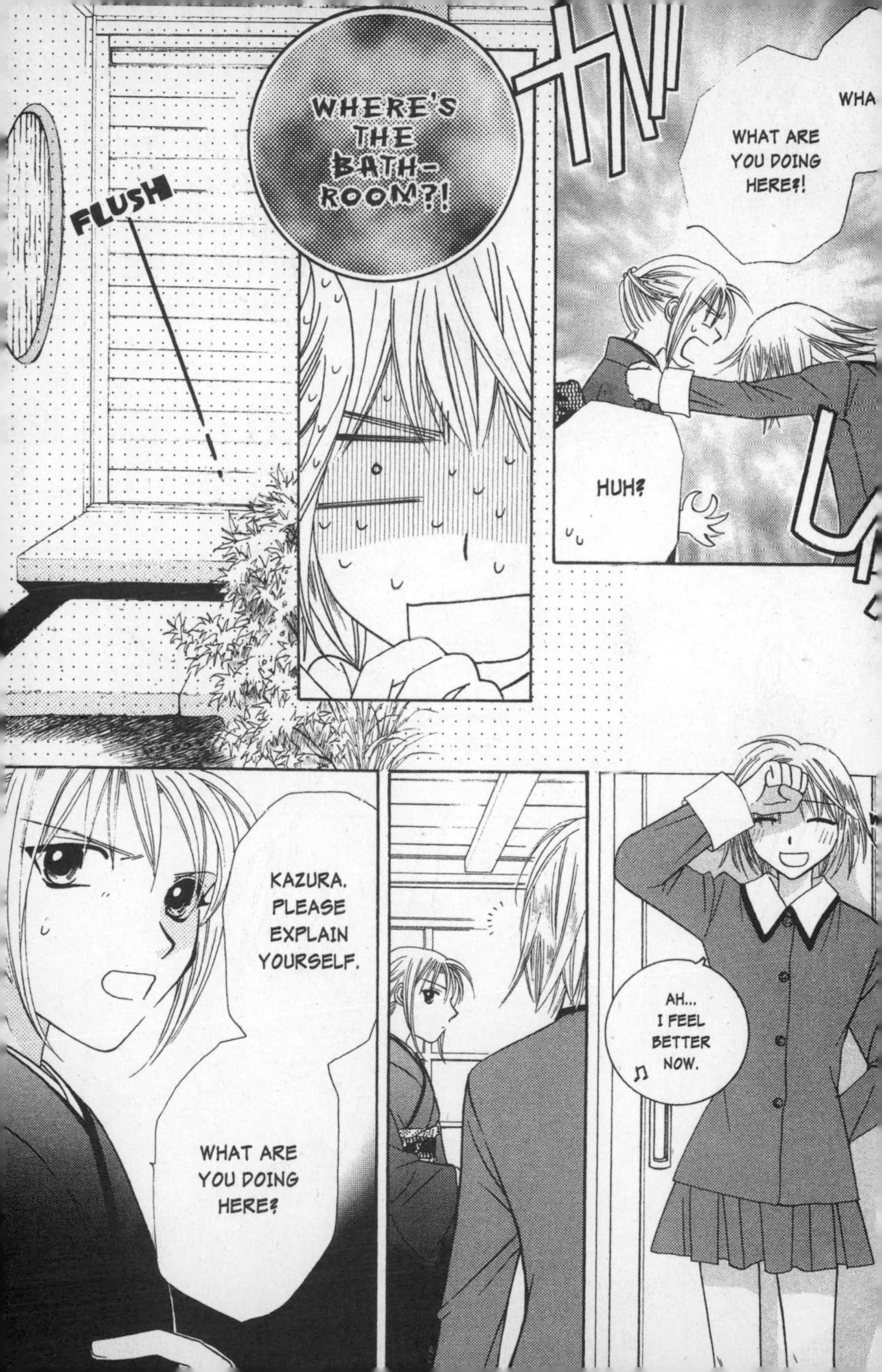
WHA
WHAT ARE YOU DOING HERE?!
HUH?
WHERE'S THE BATH-ROOM?!
FLUSH
AH... I FEEL BETTER NOW.
KAZURA. PLEASE EXPLAIN YOURSELF.
WHAT ARE YOU DOING HERE?

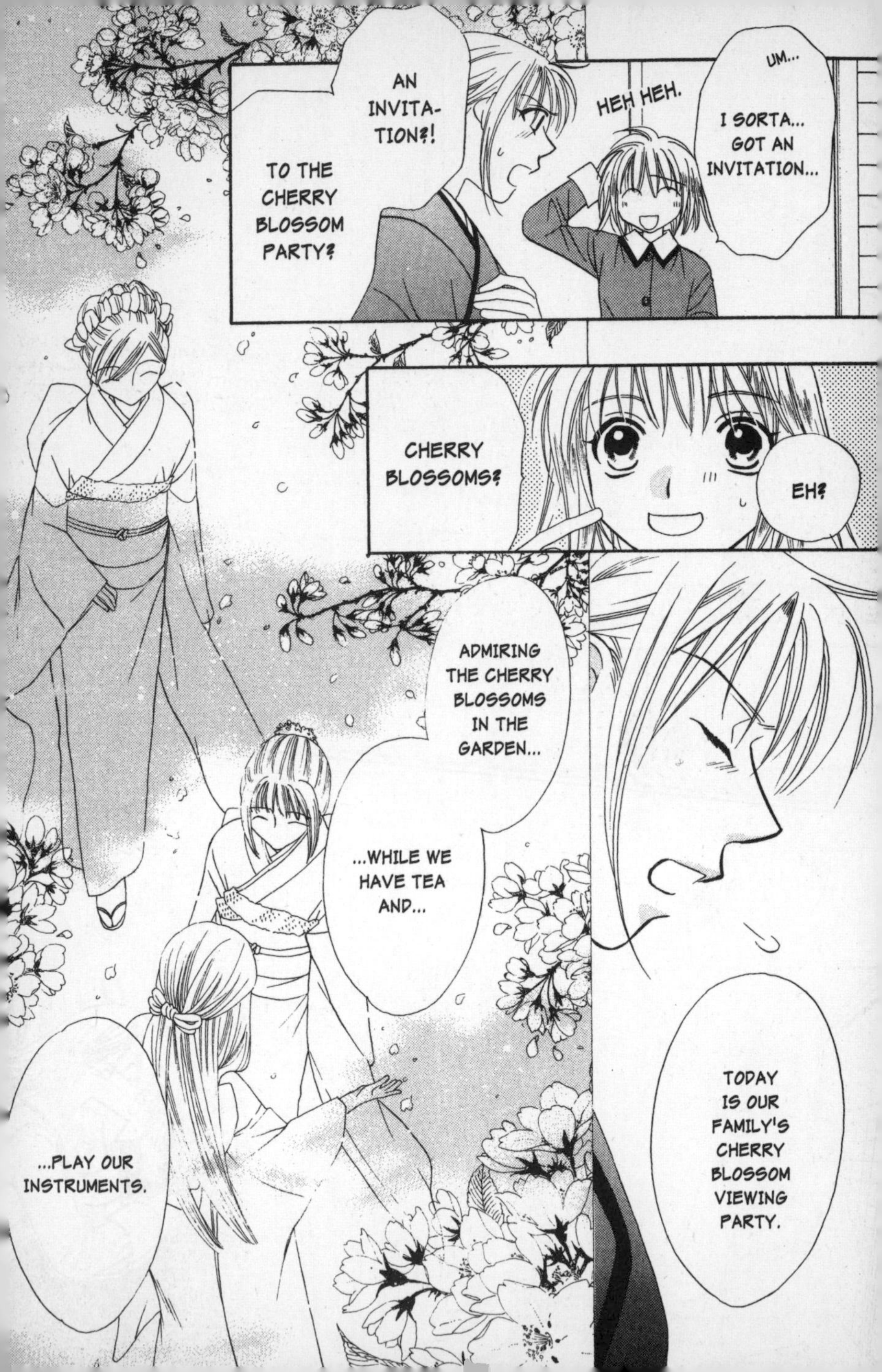
UM...
I SORTA... GOT AN INVITATION...
HEH HEH.
AN INVITATION?!
TO THE CHERRY BLOSSOM PARTY?
EH?
CHERRY BLOSSOMS?
TODAY IS OUR FAMILY'S CHERRY BLOSSOM VIEWING PARTY.
ADMIRING THE CHERRY BLOSSOMS IN THE GARDEN...
...WHILE WE HAVE TEA AND...
...PLAY OUR INSTRUMENTS.

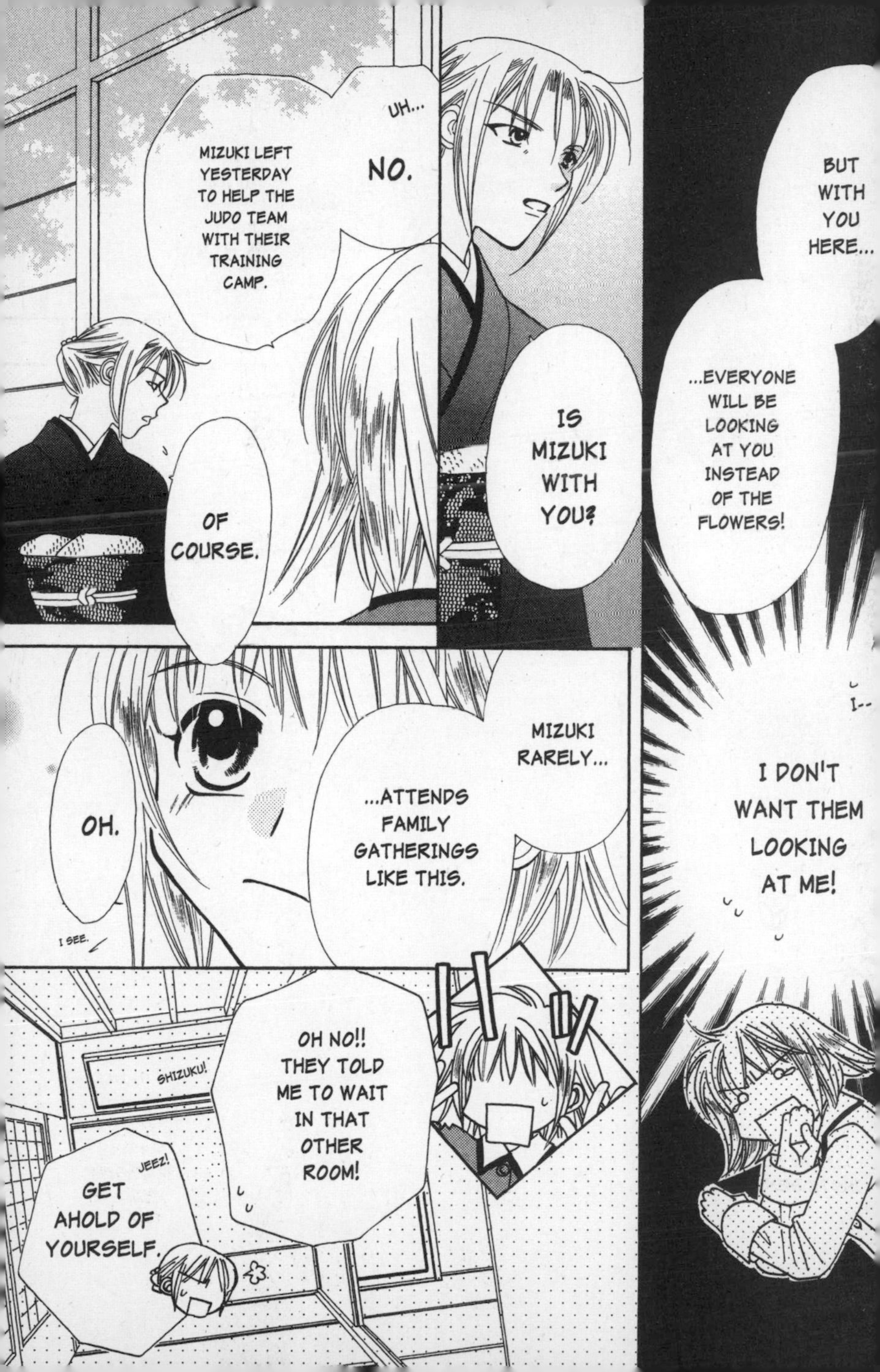
BUT WITH YOU HERE...
...EVERYONE WILL BE LOOKING AT YOU INSTEAD OF THE FLOWERS!
I--
I DON'T WANT THEM LOOKING AT ME!
IS MIZUKI WITH YOU?
UH...
NO.
MIZUKI LEFT YESTERDAY TO HELP THE JUDO TEAM WITH THEIR TRAINING CAMP.
OF COURSE.
MIZUKI RARELY...
...ATTENDS FAMILY GATHERINGS LIKE THIS.
OH.
I SEE.
OH NO!! THEY TOLD ME TO WAIT IN THAT OTHER ROOM!
SHIZUKU!
JEEZ!
GET AHOLD OF YOURSELF.

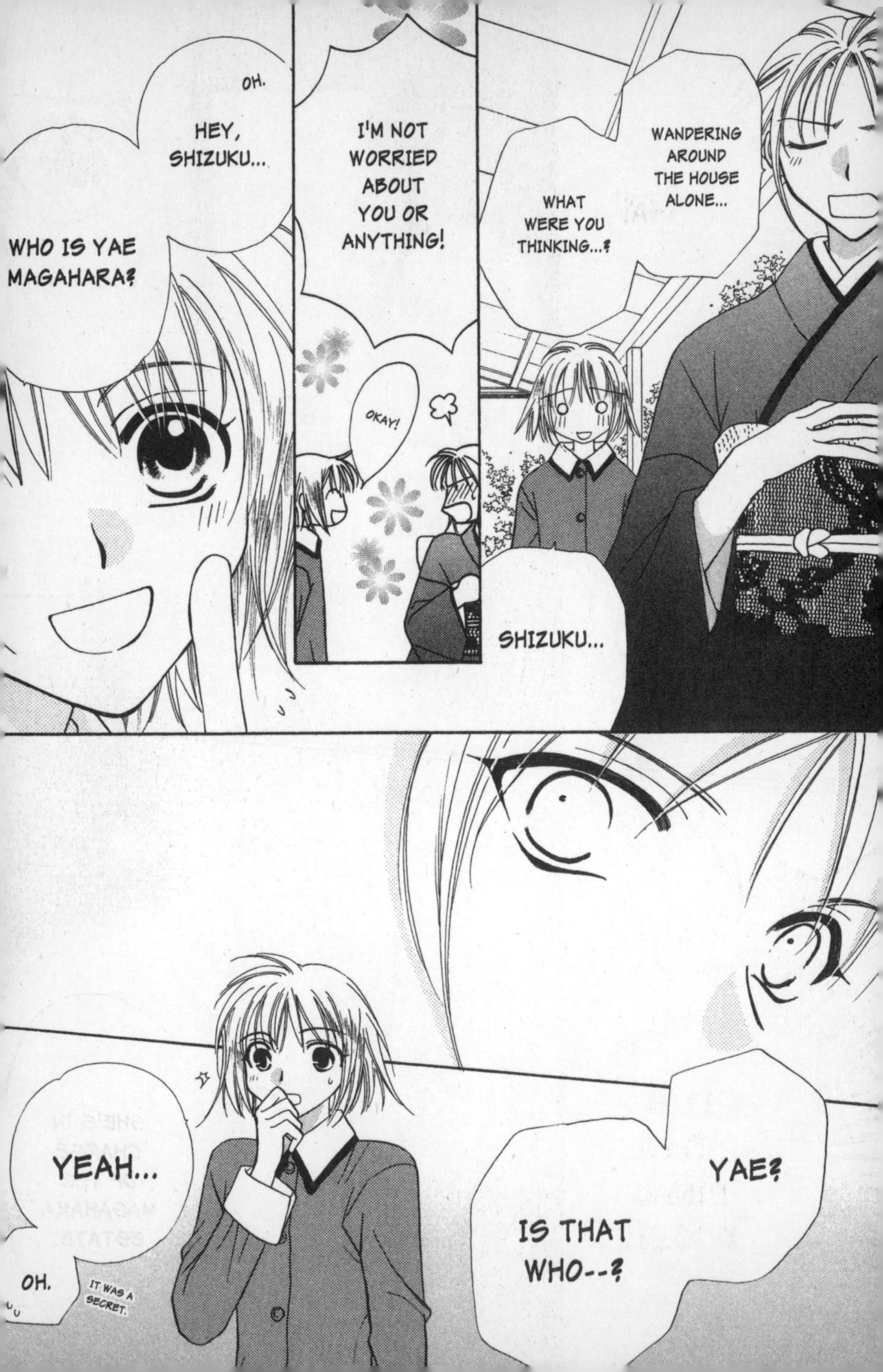
WANDERING AROUND THE HOUSE ALONE...
WHAT WERE YOU THINKING...?
SHIZUKU...
I'M NOT WORRIED ABOUT YOU OR ANYTHING!
OKAY!
OH.
HEY, SHIZUKU...
WHO IS YAE MAGAHARA?
YAE?
IS THAT WHO--?
YEAH...
OH.
IT WAS A SECRET.

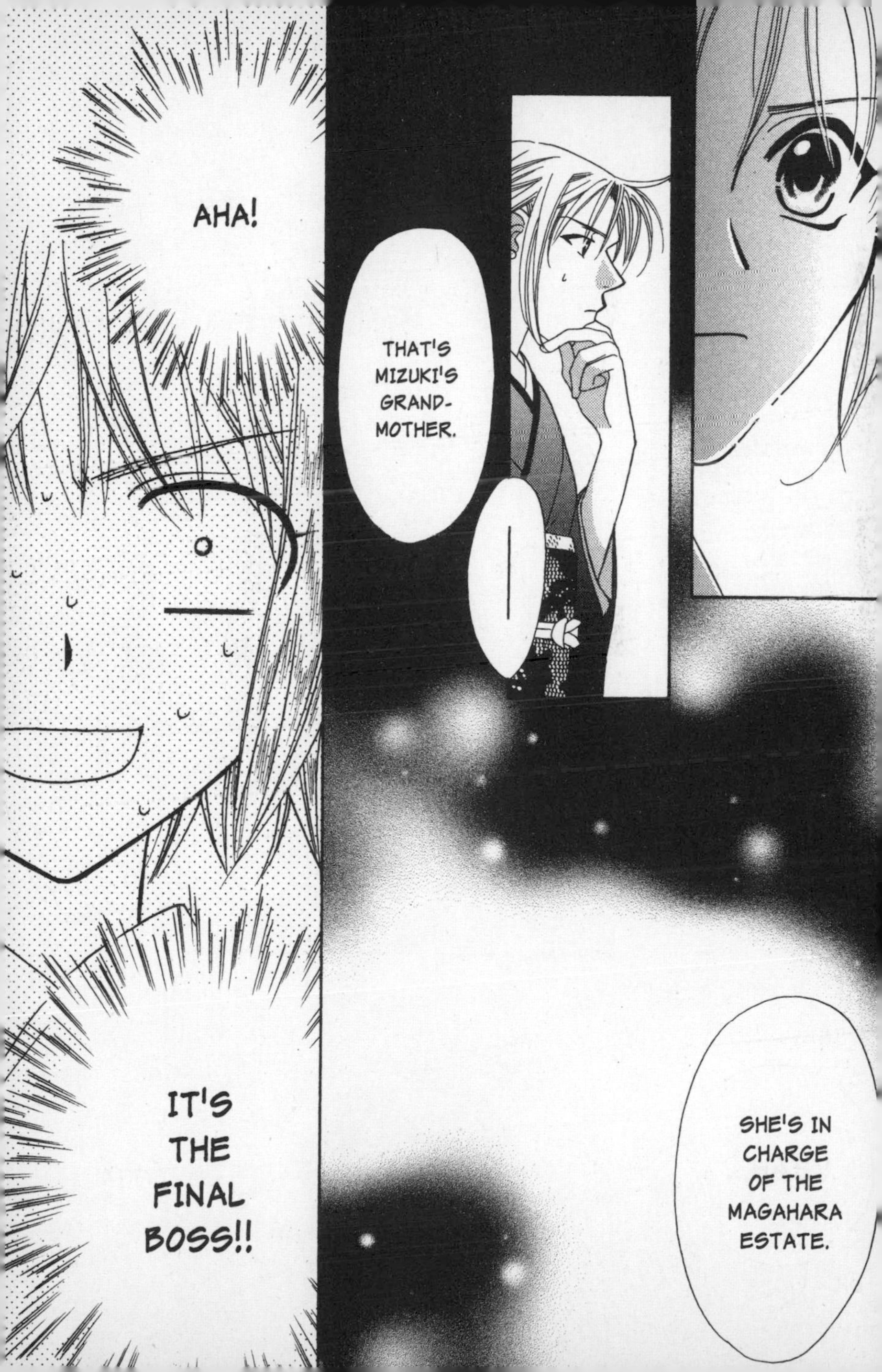

THAT'S MIZUKI'S GRAND-MOTHER.
—
SHE'S IN CHARGE OF THE MAGAHARA ESTATE.
AHA!
IT'S THE FINAL BOSS!!

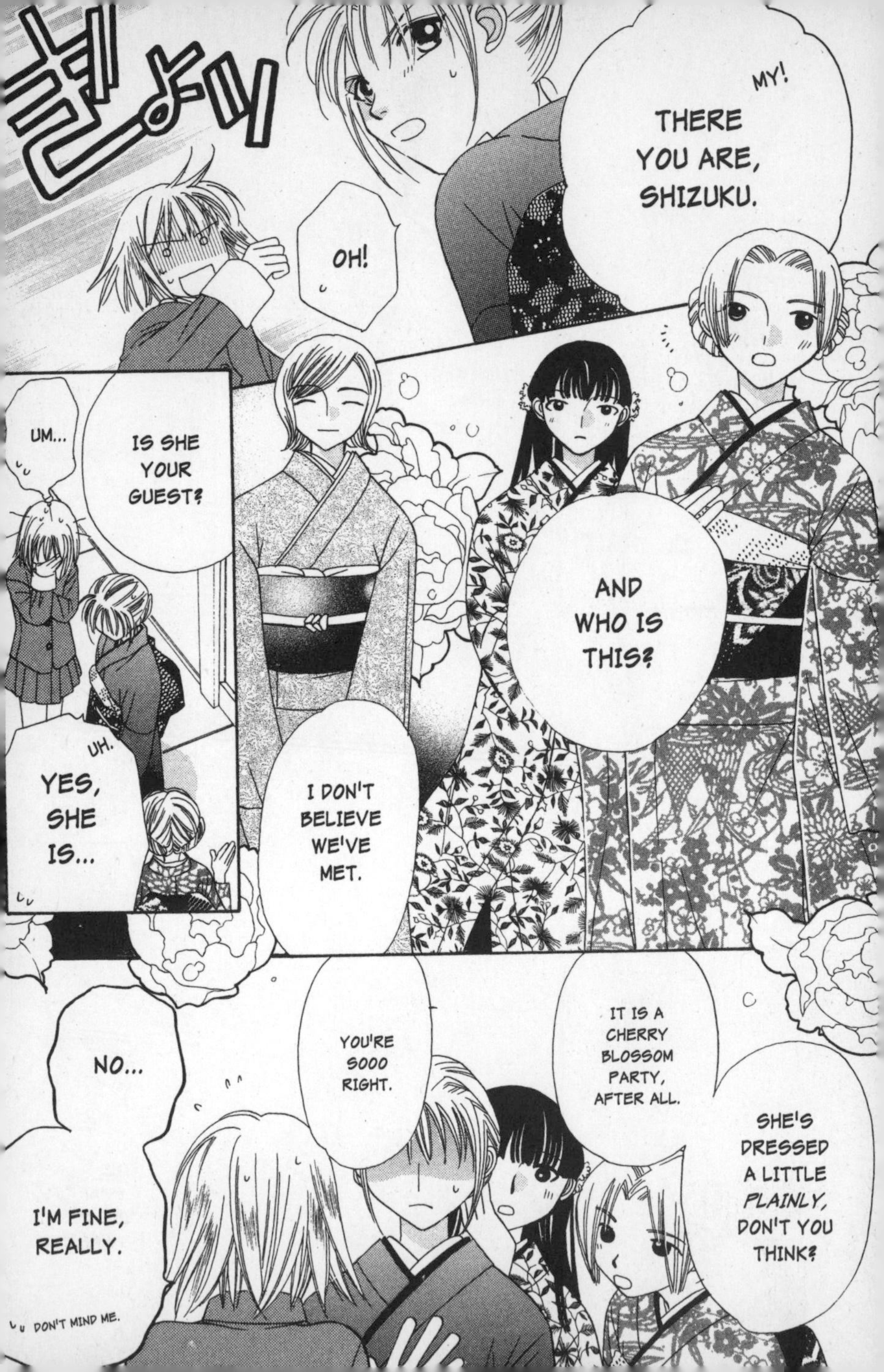
MY! THERE YOU ARE, SHIZUKU.
OH!
AND WHO IS THIS?
I DON'T BELIEVE WE'VE MET.
IS SHE YOUR GUEST?
UM...
UH. YES, SHE IS...
SHE'S DRESSED A LITTLE *PLAINLY*, DON'T YOU THINK?
IT IS A CHERRY BLOSSOM PARTY, AFTER ALL.
YOU'RE SOOO RIGHT.
NO...
I'M FINE, REALLY.
DON'T MIND ME.

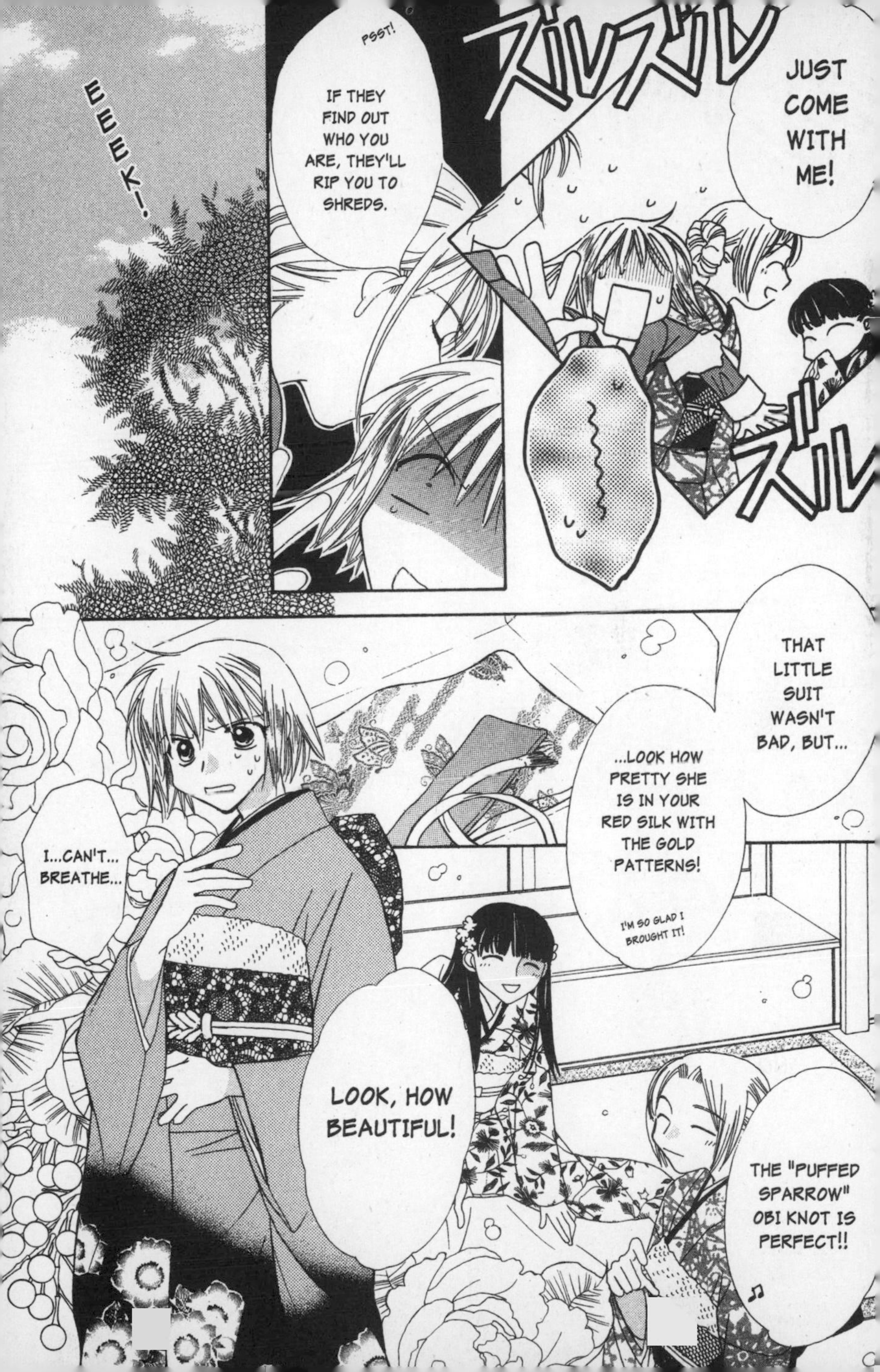
ズルズル
JUST COME WITH ME!
ズル
PSST!
IF THEY FIND OUT WHO YOU ARE, THEY'LL RIP YOU TO SHREDS.
EEEEK!
THAT LITTLE SUIT WASN'T BAD, BUT...
...LOOK HOW PRETTY SHE IS IN YOUR RED SILK WITH THE GOLD PATTERNS!
I'M SO GLAD I BROUGHT IT!
THE "PUFFED SPARROW" OBI KNOT IS PERFECT!! ♫
LOOK, HOW BEAUTIFUL!
I...CAN'T... BREATHE...

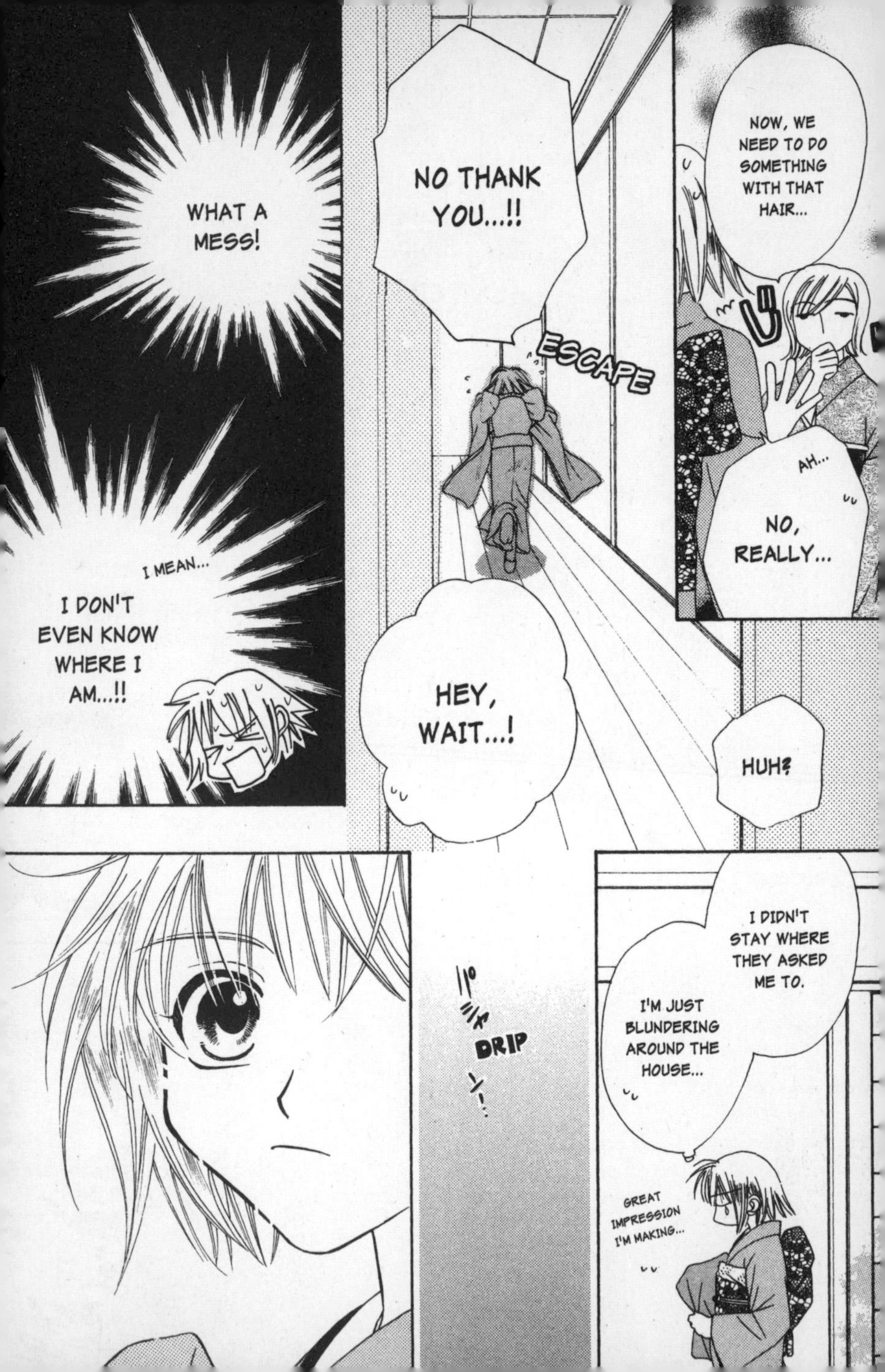
NOW, WE NEED TO DO SOMETHING WITH THAT HAIR...
AH...
NO, REALLY...
NO THANK YOU...!!
ESCAPE
HEY, WAIT...!
HUH?
WHAT A MESS!
I MEAN...
I DON'T EVEN KNOW WHERE I AM...!!
I DIDN'T STAY WHERE THEY ASKED ME TO.
I'M JUST BLUNDERING AROUND THE HOUSE...
GREAT IMPRESSION I'M MAKING...
DRIP

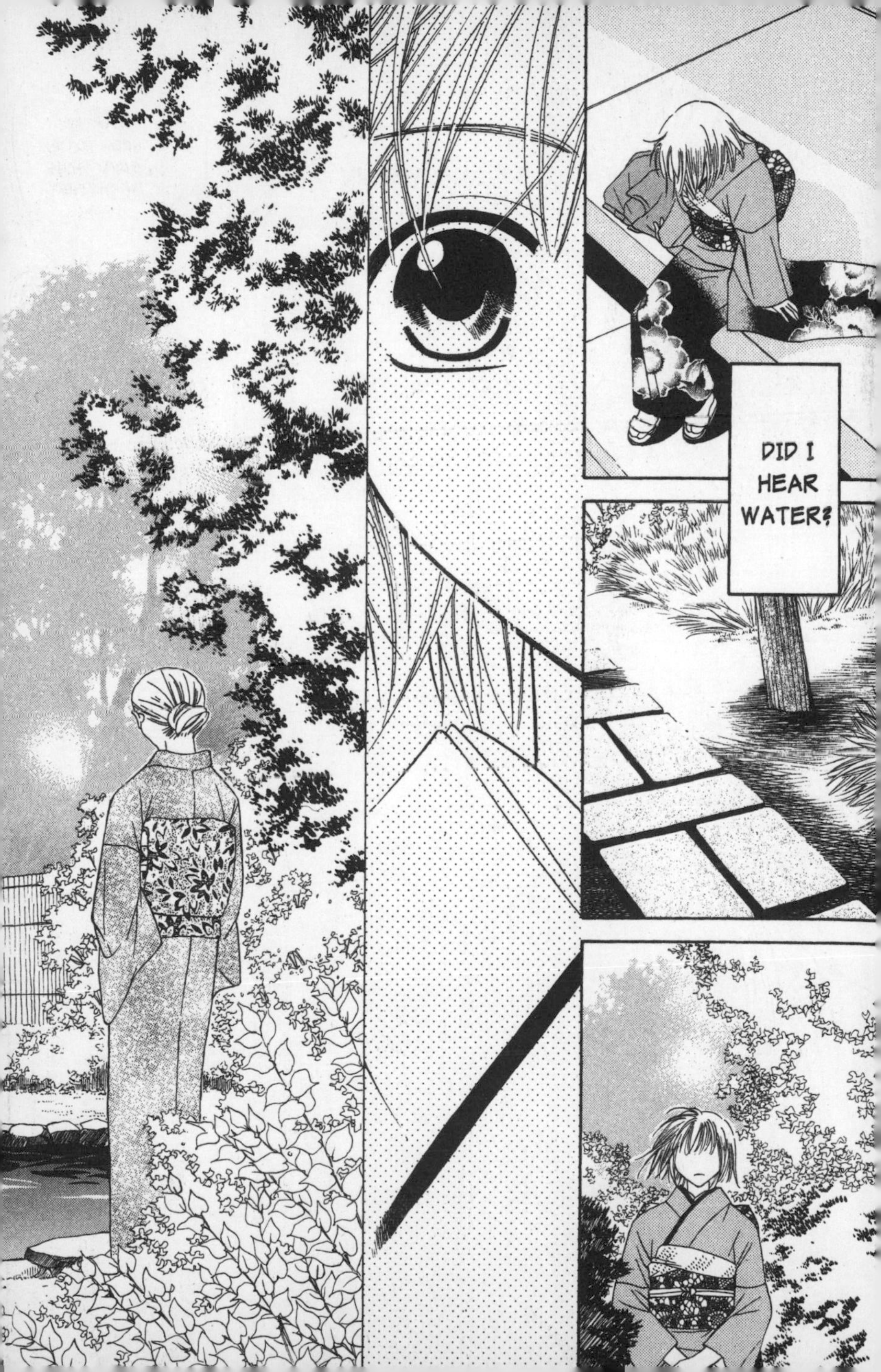
DID I HEAR WATER?

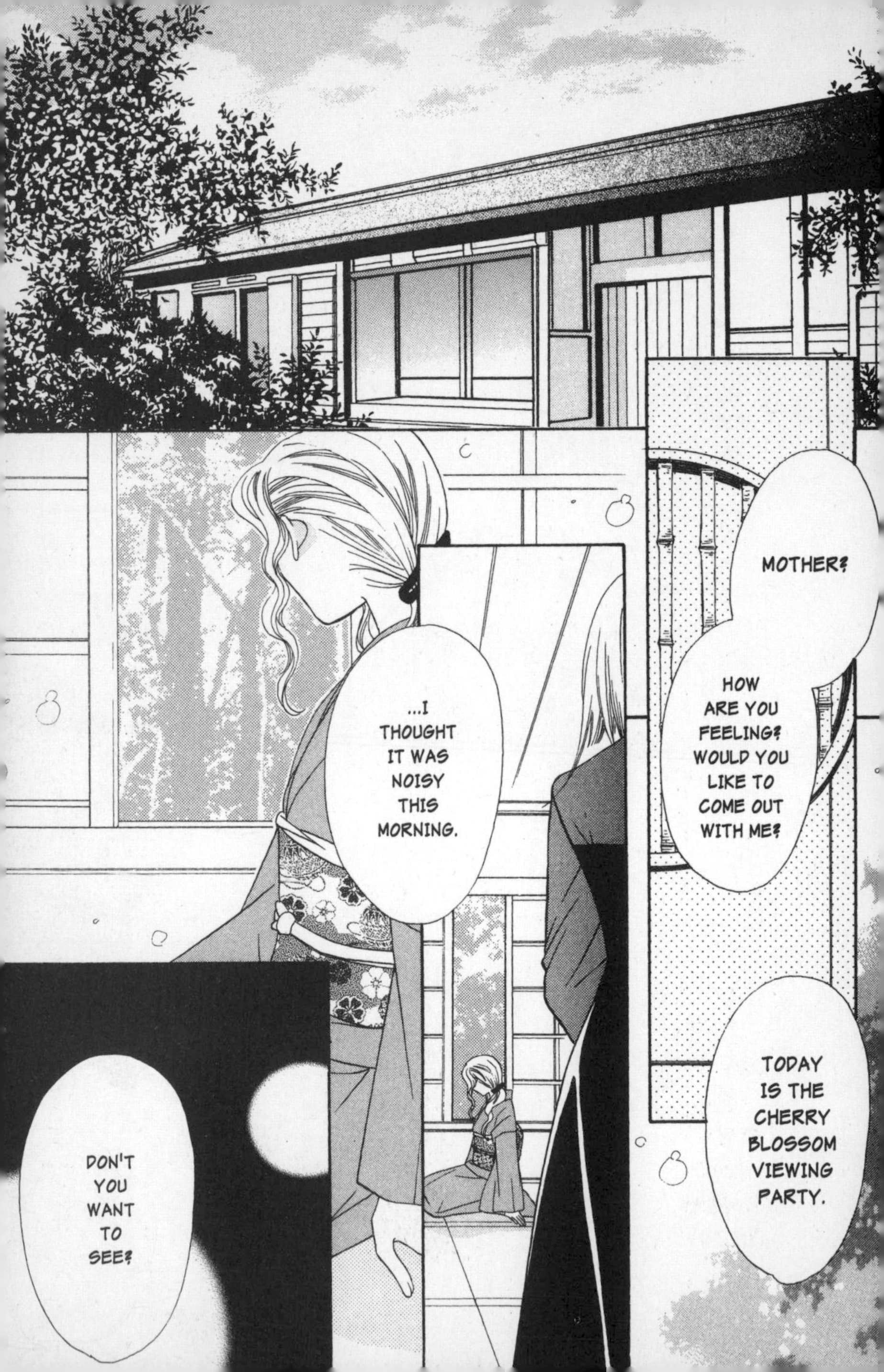
MOTHER?
HOW ARE YOU FEELING? WOULD YOU LIKE TO COME OUT WITH ME?
TODAY IS THE CHERRY BLOSSOM VIEWING PARTY.
...I THOUGHT IT WAS NOISY THIS MORNING.
DON'T YOU WANT TO SEE?

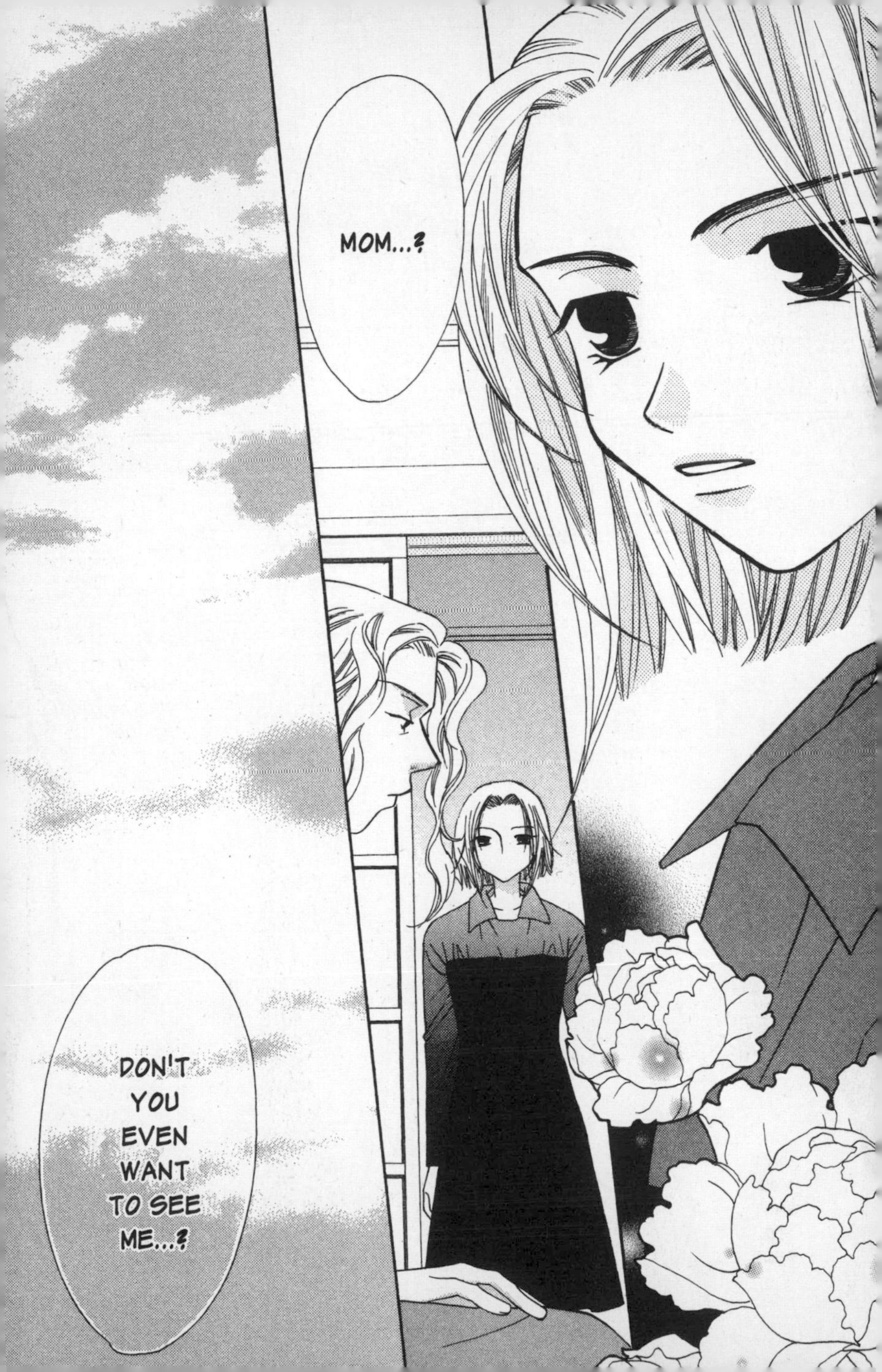
MOM...?
DON'T YOU EVEN WANT TO SEE ME...?

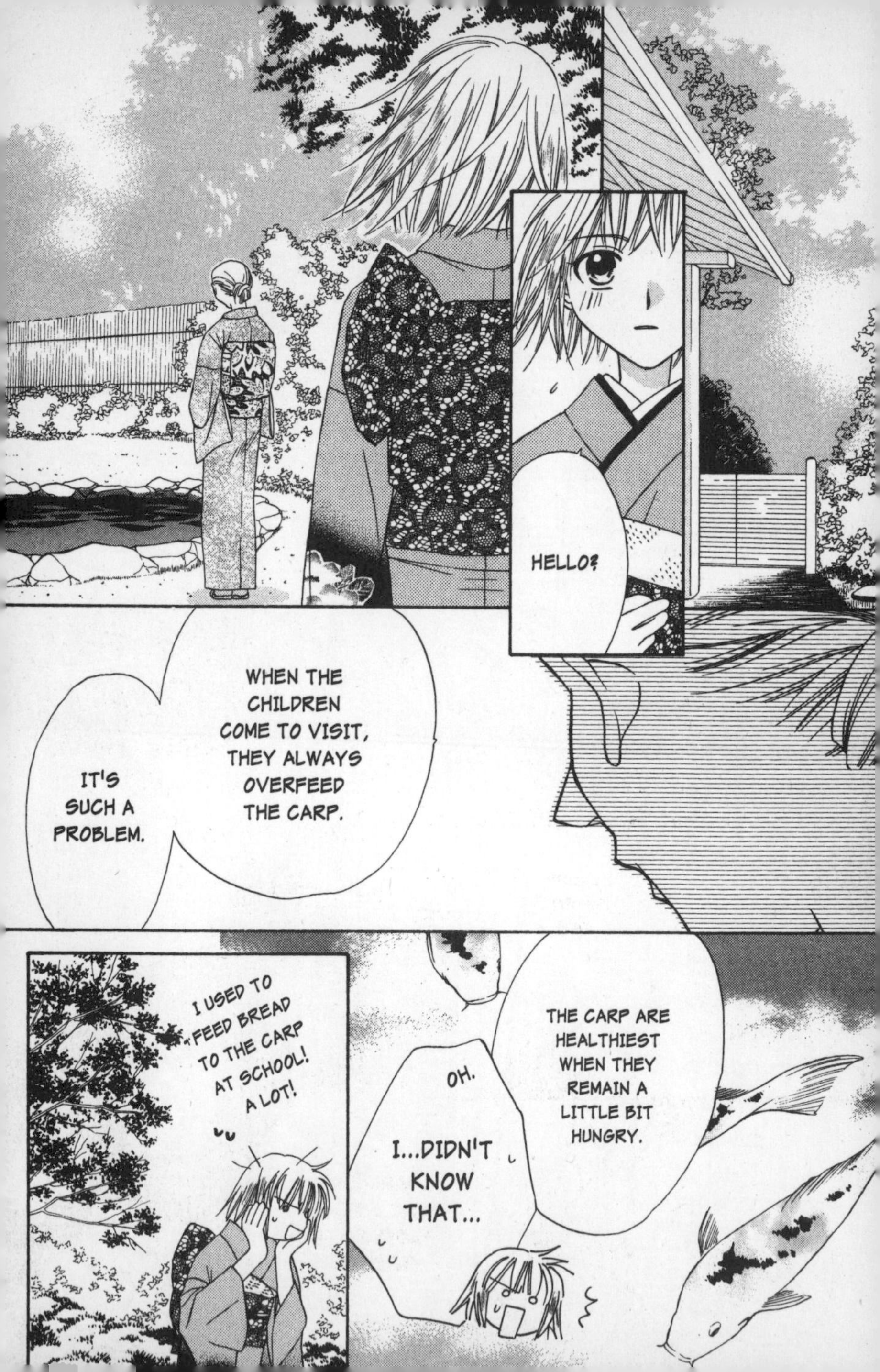
HELLO?
WHEN THE CHILDREN COME TO VISIT, THEY ALWAYS OVERFEED THE CARP.
IT'S SUCH A PROBLEM.
THE CARP ARE HEALTHIEST WHEN THEY REMAIN A LITTLE BIT HUNGRY.
OH.
I...DIDN'T KNOW THAT...
I USED TO FEED BREAD TO THE CARP AT SCHOOL! A LOT!

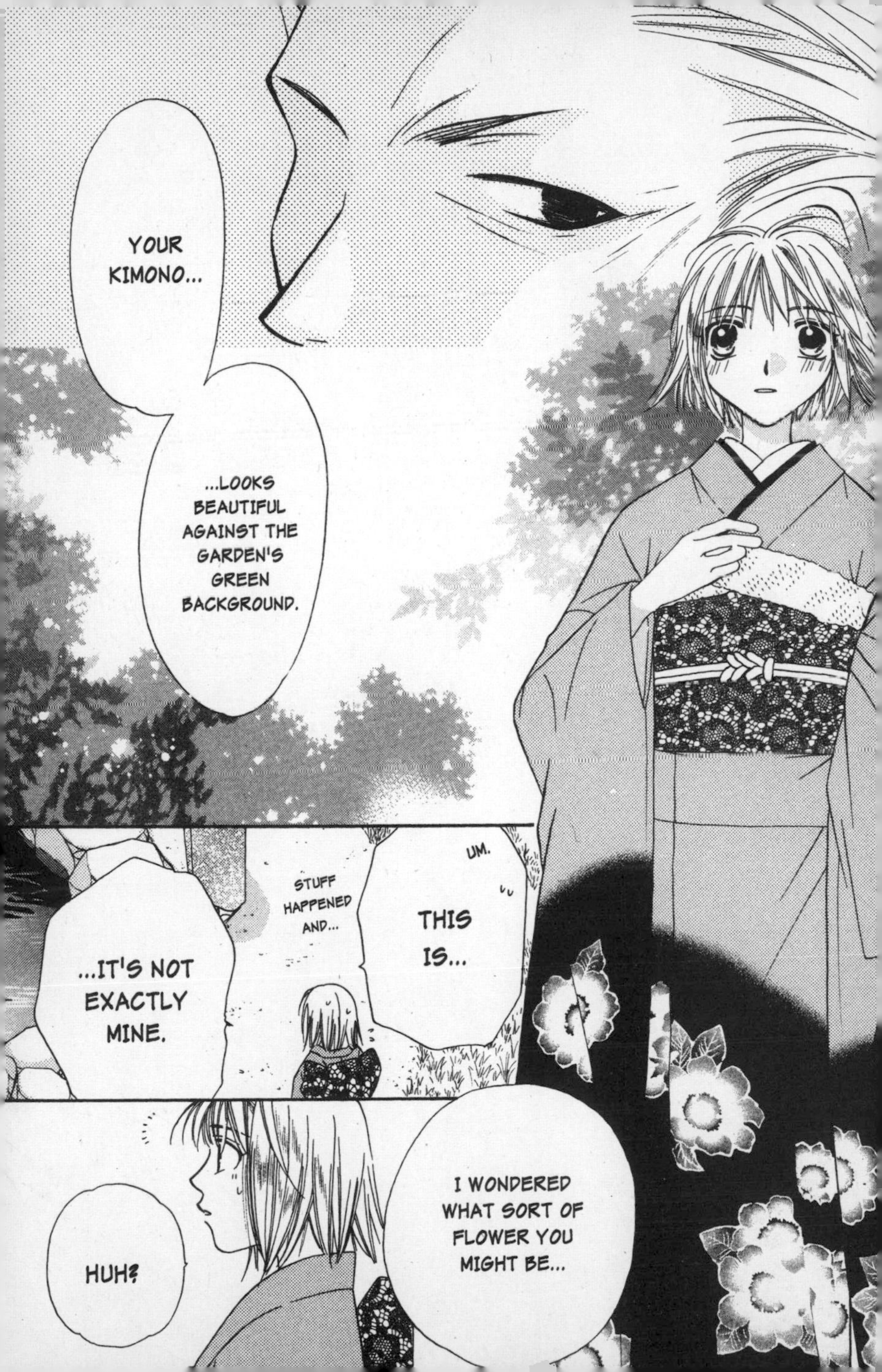
YOUR KIMONO...
...LOOKS BEAUTIFUL AGAINST THE GARDEN'S GREEN BACKGROUND.
UM.
THIS IS...
STUFF HAPPENED AND...
...IT'S NOT EXACTLY MINE.
I WONDERED WHAT SORT OF FLOWER YOU MIGHT BE...
HUH?

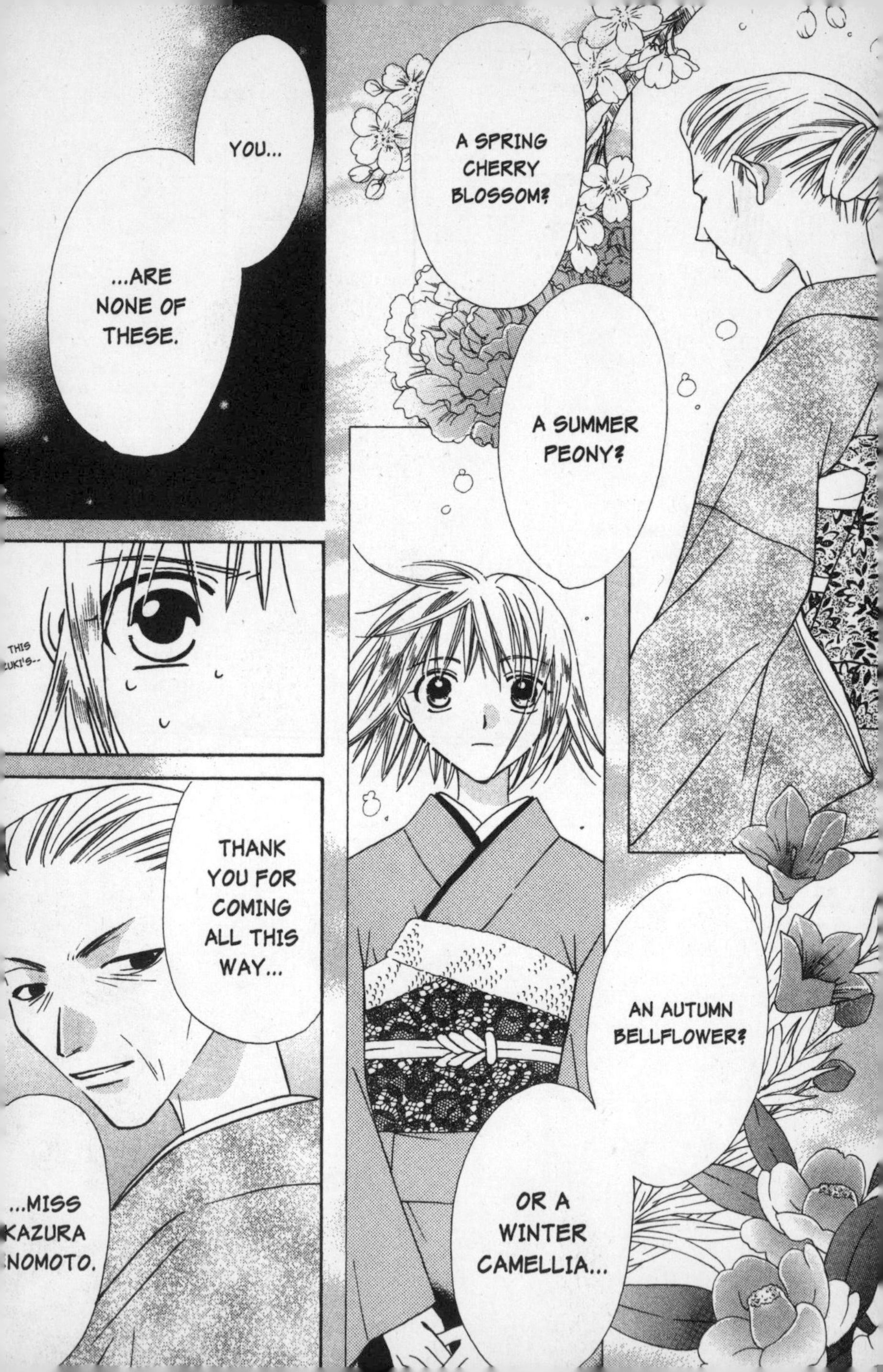
A SPRING CHERRY BLOSSOM?
A SUMMER PEONY?
AN AUTUMN BELLFLOWER?
OR A WINTER CAMELLIA...
YOU...
...ARE NONE OF THESE.
THIS ZUKI'S..
THANK YOU FOR COMING ALL THIS WAY...
...MISS KAZURA NOMOTO.

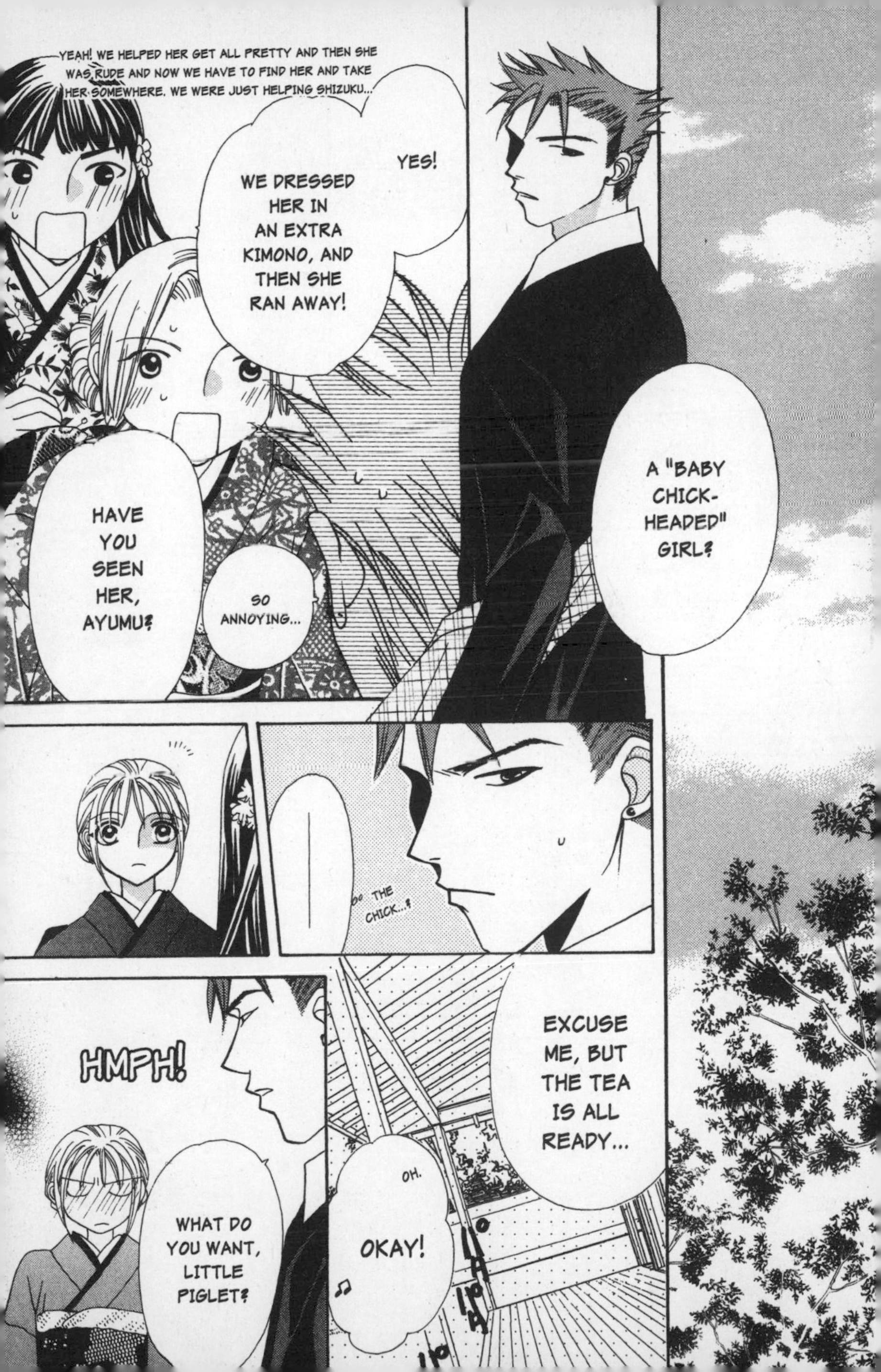
WE DRESSED HER IN AN EXTRA KIMONO, AND THEN SHE RAN AWAY!
YES!
YEAH! WE HELPED HER GET ALL PRETTY AND THEN SHE WAS RUDE AND NOW WE HAVE TO FIND HER AND TAKE HER SOMEWHERE. WE WERE JUST HELPING SHIZUKU...
HAVE YOU SEEN HER, AYUMU?
SO ANNOYING...
A "BABY CHICK-HEADED" GIRL?
...THE CHICK...?
EXCUSE ME, BUT THE TEA IS ALL READY...
OH.
OKAY!
HMPH!
WHAT DO YOU WANT, LITTLE PIGLET?

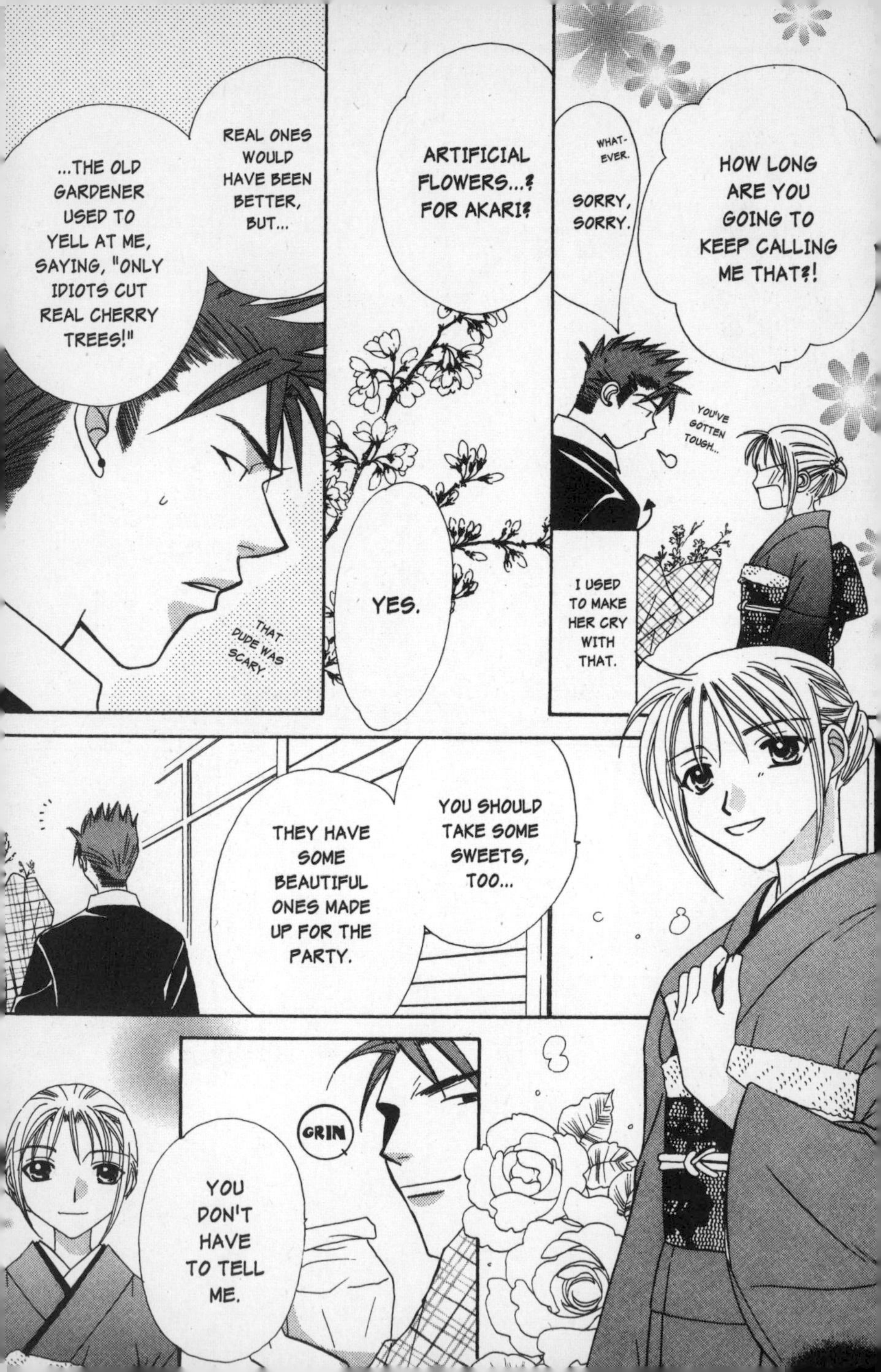
HOW LONG ARE YOU GOING TO KEEP CALLING ME THAT?!
WHAT-EVER.
SORRY, SORRY.
YOU'VE GOTTEN TOUGH...
I USED TO MAKE HER CRY WITH THAT.
ARTIFICIAL FLOWERS...? FOR AKARI?
YES.
REAL ONES WOULD HAVE BEEN BETTER, BUT...
...THE OLD GARDENER USED TO YELL AT ME, SAYING, "ONLY IDIOTS CUT REAL CHERRY TREES!"
THAT DUDE WAS SCARY.
YOU SHOULD TAKE SOME SWEETS, TOO...
THEY HAVE SOME BEAUTIFUL ONES MADE UP FOR THE PARTY.
GRIN
YOU DON'T HAVE TO TELL ME.

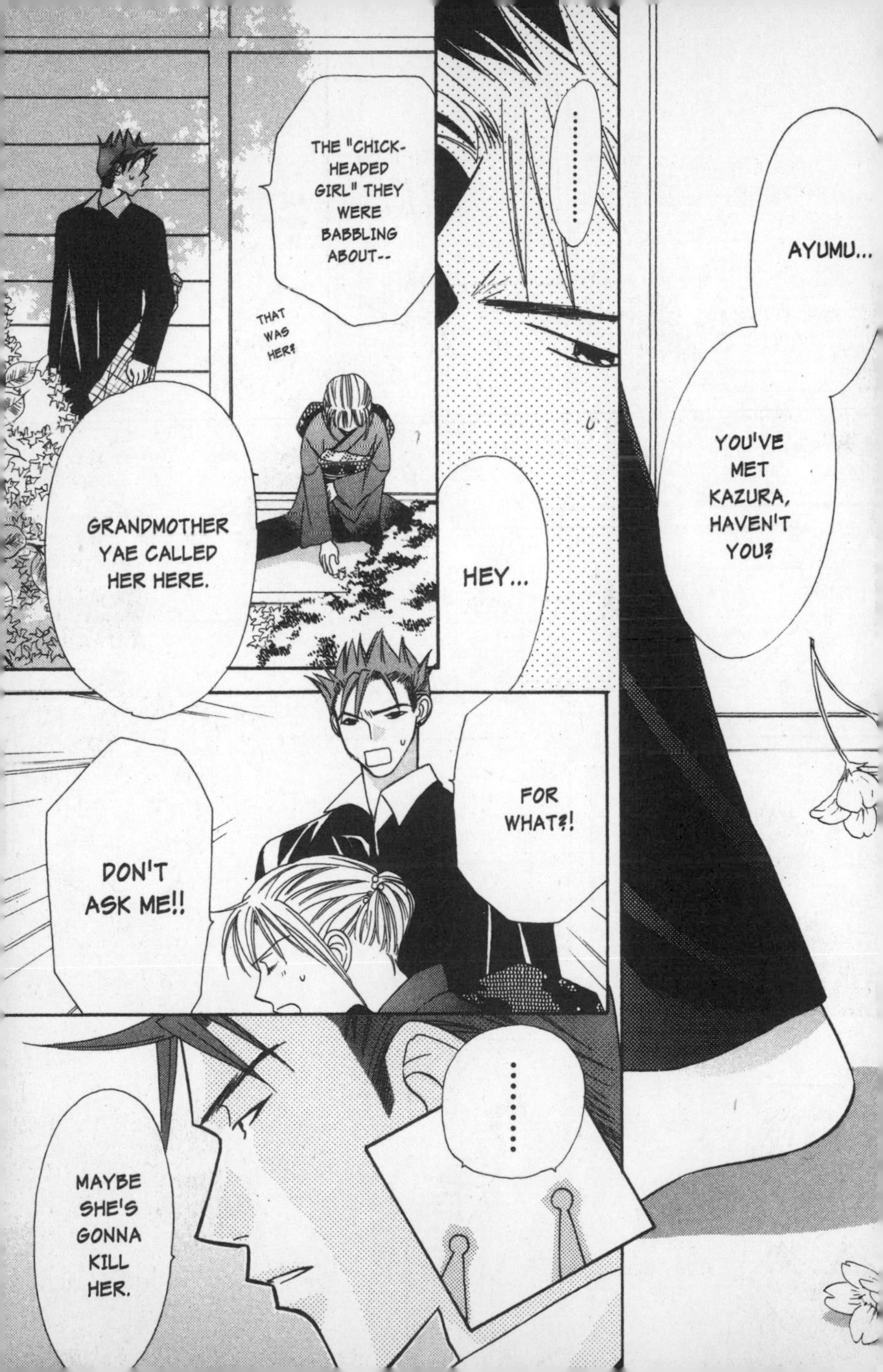
AYUMU...
YOU'VE MET KAZURA, HAVEN'T YOU?
......
HEY...
THE "CHICK-HEADED GIRL" THEY WERE BABBLING ABOUT--
THAT WAS HER?
GRANDMOTHER YAE CALLED HER HERE.
FOR WHAT?!
DON'T ASK ME!!
......
MAYBE SHE'S GONNA KILL HER.

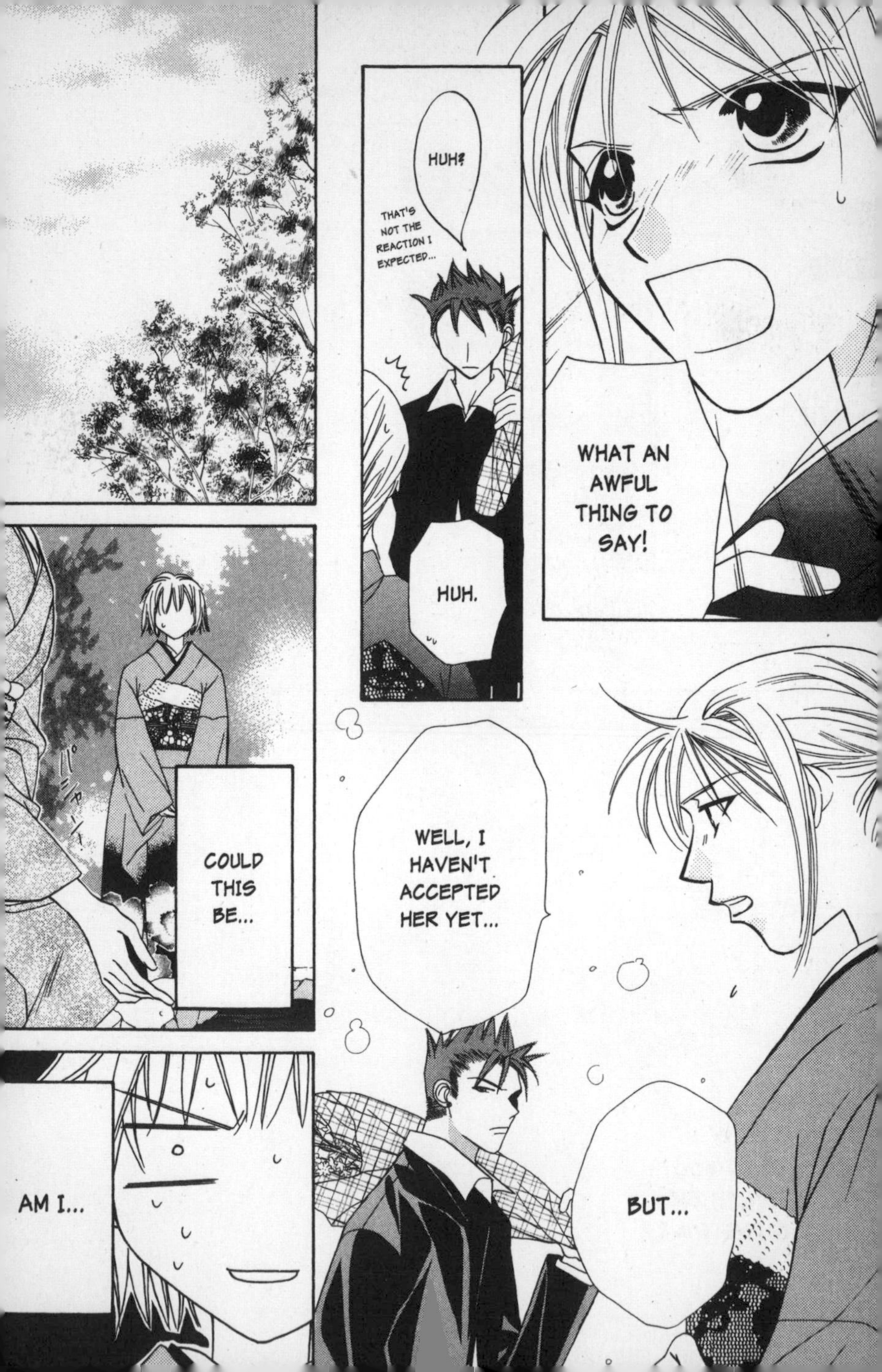
WHAT AN AWFUL THING TO SAY!
HUH?
THAT'S NOT THE REACTION I EXPECTED...
HUH.
WELL, I HAVEN'T ACCEPTED HER YET...
BUT...
COULD THIS BE...
AM I...